MOUNTAINEERING IN SCOTLAND

and

UNDISCOVERED SCOTLAND

by W.H.MURRAY

THE AUTHOR'S TWO SCOTTISH MOUNTAINEERING CLASSICS COMBINED INTO ONE VOLUME

with twenty maps and diagrams by

ROBERT ANDERSON

D1344169

Bâton Wicks Publications

Mountaineering in Scotland was first published by J.M.Dent and Sons Ltd. London
© by W.H.Murray, 1947

Undiscovered Scotland was first published by J.M.Dent and Sons Ltd., London
© W.H. Murray, 1951.

This compilation volume is a photoreprint of the two original books, published in 1979
by Diadem Books Limited., London
Reprinted 1980
Reprinted 1982
Reprinted 1986
Reprinted as a tradepaperback in 1992

This edition (tradepaperback) published by Bâton Wicks, London 1997.
© by Anne Murray, 1997
ISBN 1-898573-23-9
A CIP catalogue record for this title is available from the British Library.

All rights reserved. No part of this publication may be reproduced, stored in a retrieval system in any form or by any means, without prior permission of the publisher, nor be otherwise circulated in any form of binding or cover other than that in which it is published and without a similar condition being imposed on the subsequent purchaser.

Printed and bound in Great Britain by Hartnolls Ltd., London and Bodmin.

Bâton Wicks Publications, London
all trade enquiries to:
Cordee, 3a DeMontfort Street, Leicester LE1 7HD

W. H. MURRAY

MOUNTAINEERING IN SCOTLAND

Bill Murray, two years before his capture in WWII. (Photo: courtesy Baton Wicks).

THERE is a region of heart's desire
   free for the hand that wills;
land of the shadow and haunted spire,
land of the silvery glacier fire,
land of the cloud and the starry choir,
   magical land of hills;
loud with the crying of winds and streams,
thronged with the fancies and fears of dreams.

There are perils of knightly zest
   fit for the warrior's craft;
pitiless giants with rock-bound crest,
mystical wells for the midnight rest,
ice-crowned castles and halls, to test
   steel with the ashen shaft;
realms to be won by the well-swung blow,
rest to be earned from the yielding foe.

Frosted cities of timeless sleep
   wait for the errant knight;
kingly forest and frowning steep,
spirits of mist and of fathomless deep,
snow-winged dragons of fear that keep
   watch o'er each virgin height;
treasure of dawn and a crown of stars
his who can shatter the frozen bars.

All that the wanderer's heart can crave,
   life lived thrice for its lending,
hermit's vigil in dreamlit cave,
gleams of the vision that Merlin gave,
comrades till death, and a wind-swept grave,
   joy of the journey's ending:—
Ye who have climbed to the great white veil,
heard ye the chant? Saw ye the Grail?

(From the Collected Poems of Geoffrey Winthrop Young.)

Contents

Photographs

between pages 136 and 137

Maps and Diagrams

1 *Twenty-four Hours on the Cuillin*

IT WAS TEN O'CLOCK at night, in Glen Brittle. The June sun had left our little cluster of tents, which nestled behind a screen of golden broom between the Atlantic and the Cuillin. Eastward, the peaks were written along the sky in a high, stiff hand. High above us, the brown precipice of Sron na Ciche, which reacts, chameleon-like, to every subtle change of atmosphere, was dyed a bright blood-red in the setting sun.

I watched the lights fade from the rocks and white evening mist begin to creep round the hills, then I thought of having supper and retiring with a pipe to my sleeping-bag. But in this hope I had reckoned without my friend, B. H. Humble; his head, adorned by a dilapidated panama, emerged of a sudden from the door of a nearby tent. The lighted eye, the mouth upturned at the corners, the warm colour—they all bore witness to a recent brain-storm. Humble had given birth to an idea. I regarded him with profound suspicion.

'It would be a fine night for a climb,' said Humble, tentatively.

'Well,' I hastily replied, 'there 's going to be no moon, no stars—it will be dark, cold, cloudy, and every cliff in mist. Granted that, it 's heresy to deny that all weather 's climbing weather.'

But Humble was paying no attention to me.

'We 'd start right now,' said he; 'go up Coire Banachdich, rest on the main ridge, then north along the tops.'

'And what then?'

'Leave it to me. . . .' And he looked away very mysteriously.

'On this very spot,' I protested, 'is to be had a hot meal, a quiet pipe, and an eiderdown sleeping-bag.' But I was merely according the flesh its privilege of free speech. The spirit was already aloft, I was pulling on my boots. . . .

I had faith in Humble. He is one of those men who brim with an incalculable alliance of ingenuity and energy. A rock-climb in his company has all the fascination of a mystery tour; one is likely to end, not on some nearby peak, but miles from anywhere in a rarely visited mountain stronghold. And if port be not made until all hours of the day or night, at least one returns buoyed by novelties and ballasted by exhaustion. Of one thing I felt certain: there was more in his taciturnity than met the eye. I knew him. What that 'more' might be I should have to wait for time to disclose. I packed a rucksack, picked up a rope, and we bade farewell to Maitland and Higgins, the two remaining members of our party.

A June gloaming in Skye is so long-drawn-out that one may usually climb on moderate rocks until eleven o'clock. But the mist had been brewing for an hour in the corries and now overflowed round every peak, complicating the problem of route-selection through the wilderness of screes and boulders that carpet Coire Banachdich. Up the wall that backs the corrie a winding route gives easy access to the main ridge. To find that route in mist at late twilight was another matter. Indeed it proved to be impossible.

We climbed the face by guess and by God a considerable height toward the crest, until an unavoidable traverse brought us to a square rock platform, like a balcony. The situation had a dramatic aspect that appealed to us. Below, the rocks plunged into blackness; above, they rose sheer into the mysteries of the mist. We resolved to bivouac until there was sufficient light for safe climbing.

There was just enough room on the ledge to accommodate us in comfort. Like difficulty, comfort on mountains is a term relative to the individual climber. We could stretch out at full length, heads pillowed on rope or rucksack. The hard rock made an indifferent mattress and night cloud a somewhat chill blanket, but luckily I have the capacity to sleep at will, any time and anywhere, and

> Weariness
> Can snore upon the flint, when resty sloth
> Finds the down pillow hard.

Humble wakened me at two a.m. The darkness was appreciably less but mist still enveloped us. We could now see to move, and in ten minutes arrived on the rim of the main ridge, at about three thousand feet. We turned northward and scrambled over the three tops of Sgurr na Banachdich. Immediately beyond Banachdich the ridge takes a big swing north-east, the first curve of the horse-shoe that encloses Coruisk. The route at this juncture was by no means easy to find; four ridges branch downward-bound, and it is only too easy to follow the wrong line. The compass, moreover, is untrustworthy, for magnetic rocks on Banachdich attract the needle.

After reconnaissance we saw close by the spike of Sgurr Thormaid, projecting like a dragon's fang through streamers of twisting cloud. We swarmed up one side and down the other, secure in the knowledge that our route was now correct. A traverse of the Cuillin ridge in mist is a stirring experience. The jagged edge, picturesque enough when clear, then astounds the eye with a succession of distorted towers. They impend suddenly through the clouds, grim, as wild in outline as any creation of nightmare.

At three a.m. we reached Sgurr a' Ghreadaidh. The dawn was well under way and sunrise might shortly be expected. Nothing was visible save mist, so we halted to cheer ourselves with a bite of food. I confess that I again fell asleep, curled up on a slab that gently tilted over the southern cliff. In a short while Humble roused me. He was justifiably in a state of high excitement. On every hand the mist was sinking, and slowly, one by one, each peak of the Cuillin reared a black tip through snow-white vapour.

Never again in summer have I seen a sight so magnificent. The clouds had now fallen to a uniform level at two thousand five hundred feet; just sufficient to hide the linking ridges and to isolate each pinnacle of the six-mile horse-shoe. From the mainland to far beyond the Outer Hebrides this cloud-mass formed an unbroken sea. Immediately beneath our feet the surface surged and spun as though impelled by inner vortices, rising and falling like the rollers of a mid-Atlantic swell. Over the submerged cols between each mountain the ocean poured and seethed in a never-ending flow.

The grey sky was steadily changing to cornflower blue and black rock to ashen. To obtain a still finer vantage point we moved east to Sgurr a' Mhadaidh. No sooner did we reach the top than the sun rose. Down in the basin of Coruisk, the cloud-surface at once flashed into flame, as though a stupendous crucible were filled with burning silver. The twenty turrets of the Cuillin, like islands lapped by fire-foam, flushed faintly pink. The shade crimsoned. Within a space of minutes, the rocks had run the gamut of autumn leafage, 'yellow, and black, and pale, and hectic red.'

Beyond such bare words one may say little. The mind fails one how miserably and painfully before great beauty. It cannot understand. Yet it would contain more. Mercifully, it is by this very process of not understanding that one is allowed to understand much: for each one has within him 'the divine reason that sits at the helm of the soul,' of which the head knows nothing. Find beauty; be still; and that faculty grows more surely than grain sown in season. However, I must be content to observe that here, for the first time, broke upon me the unmistakable intimation of a last reality underlying mountain beauty; and here, for the first time, it awakened within me a faculty of comprehension that had never before been exercised.

Humble indeed had not failed me. He had hoped for a noble panorama. But in the bleak hours around midnight not even he had dreamed that we should be led by cloud and fire to the land of promise. Since then I have always believed and repeatedly proved that the mountains reserve their fairest prize for the man who turns aside from common-sense routine. One might say that hills repay trust with generosity. In Glen Brittle, our companions when they awoke saw nothing but a steel-grey layer of low clouds, and not imagining that the peaks were in sunlight, commiserated us on such an unprofitable end to our waywardness.

Several of the best hours of our otherwise misspent lives thus passed away on Sgurr a' Mhadaidh. Towards nine o'clock the cloud-bank broke up and gradually dissolved. We scrambled down to the high col under Bidein Druim nan Ramh, and thence turned downward toward Coruisk by the Corrie of Solitude. Overhead, hardly a wisp of cloud remained; below, Loch Coruisk was a royal blue rippled with silver.

After winning clear of the screes in the corrie we walked the best part of two miles south, to the junction of the main burn and the loch. And here I add my voice to Humble's in exploding the myth of 'gloomy Coruisk.' The face of Scotland has so often been falsified by writers in search of melodrama that there is now difficulty in convincing people of the evidence of their own eyes. Far from being shadowed and overhung by beetling crags, Loch Coruisk has a fairly open situation, inasmuch as the Cuillin main ridge lies a couple of miles back. In spring and summer it is flooded by sunlight for the best part of the day. I have heard it further alleged that here grows no tuft of vegetation; yet when I stood beside the loch with Humble the very banks were alive with wild flowers, their hues offset by cool green shrubs and long grasses. We might have imagined ourselves transported to the land of Xanadu, where

> . . . . twice five miles of fertile ground
> With walls and towers were girdled round,
> And there were gardens, bright with sinuous rills.

A few of these flowers were rare, and Humble, who is an accomplished botanist, was highly gratified by some carnivorous specimens.

As I am ill content to rejoice in mountains yet not climb them, so I am compelled not only to admire lochs and rivers but to plunge in and swim. In either act knowledge of their charm is extended. Every condition for the ideal swim had here been satisfied, for the sun had more than warmed us on the four-mile tramp. There was no need to propose a bathe—of one accord we stripped and plunged. I have never known anything like it. The swim was unique in my own experience because all five senses were feasted to the full.

The sharp sting of that first dive cleared at one stroke the fogs of lethargy from the mind—at one stroke the world stood vivid. The corrie was full of sun and the song of the burn, gay with the flash of many colours and the dance of light on the loch, fresh with the scents of blossom and an aromatic tang of plants in morning air. I drank from the burn and the taste was sweet and lively to the palate. And these good reports, being gathered together in the mind, suddenly fused in image of the beauty we had seen during the supreme hour on Sgurr a' Mhadaidh: so that I knew, what until then I had not known, that the one Beauty pervades all things according to their nature, they having beauty by virtue of participation in it; and that in the degree of realizing its presence within us, so is life lived in fullness. The ecstasy of that morning is bright after eight years.

When at last we emerged dripping from the water we let our bodies dry in the hot sun while we ate our too little food. Our departure from camp had been just a thought casual. There is no appetite on earth to surpass a Skye appetite; one is permanently hungry. But now we were ravenous. However, shortage of food for a day is of no consequence; much more serious was Humble's plight. I was almost sorry for him. He is an ardent and expert photographer and he had brought a camera but no spools.

Our intention was to go down to the sea—one might almost say up to the sea, for parts of Coruisk are said to be below sea-level—and then go north up the far side of the loch to Sgurr Dubh, by the ascent of which we should return to the Glen Brittle side of the main ridge. Reviewing this project in my mind while we walked along the east bank of the loch, I began to regard the absence of spools as an unmixed blessing. On a fine day in the Cuillin there is no more insatiable devourer of the fleeting hours than a camera with Humble behind it. As it was, the surprising variety of plant life all along the two-mile bank of the loch caused many a halt and much botanical dawdling. I think we spent two hours over these two miles, for it was after noon when we arrived at Loch Scavaig.

All this while I had been promising myself another bathe. As befits a small sea-loch, Scavaig is green, deep and clear—a perfect swimming-pool in one of the most lonely and remote corners of Britain. What was our astonishment, then, when we arrived on the brink, to see a MacBrayne Line steamer sweep into the loch and drop anchor! Within fifteen minutes several boat-loads of tourists landed. They had arrived from Oban to see that world-famous view: Coruisk and the Black Cuillin.

At another time Humble and I might have selfishly resented this landing as a rude shattering of our solitude. Instead, we looked at each other with gleaming eyes. The same thought had simultaneously occurred to us both—food!

We negotiated swiftly with the officer in charge. In a few minutes we had been taken out to the ship in a motor-boat and were climbing on board. The first man I met on deck knew me, and to put the finishing touch to our luck he was officially in charge of the cruise. We explained our urgent need of a good meal. He introduced us to the captain and we found ourselves conducted as honoured guests to the first-class dining saloon. I must explain that my beard was a fortnight strong, that I was in shirt-sleeves and braces, bore a large coil of rope round my shoulders, and that my breeches were in tatters. Humble, I am glad to report, looked distinctly less disreputable, but any good effect was destroyed by his antique and sorely battered hat.

Having run the gauntlet of clean, cool, spruce, and inquisitive tourists on deck, we were mightily relieved to find the dining saloon empty. The stewards had never before entertained two starving climbers. They watched round-eyed while we polished off two helpings of every course throughout a lengthy menu.

Then followed a quart of cool beer. Ever since that day I have harboured tender feelings for the English tourist, and I raise my hat to the name of MacBrayne.

At three o'clock we went ashore and were introduced to a number of young ladies, who suspected that Humble and I were local colour engaged by Messrs. MacBrayne for their entertainment. The consensus of opinion regarding the view spread before us was this: that to set foot on the Cuillin either in mist or clear weather was certain death; and that Loch Coruisk was the deepest lake in Europe—otherwise, why had they been brought to see it?

The ladies were charming, and after a prolonged bout of photography we parted from them with regret. The time was now five o'clock and we should be hard pressed to reach Glen Brittle before dark. Our proposed route of ascent, by the east ridge of Sgurr Dubh, was over three thousand feet high, and one of the two longest rock-climbs in Britain. I would recommend that ridge as a paradise for a rock-climbing beginner. Apart from the initial trouble in climbing on to the ridge, one may thereafter proceed unroped up broad acres of boiler-plate slabs, whose rock is the roughest gabbro in all the Cuillin. In other words, it is so rough and reliable that only the grossest negligence could bring a man to harm. Here, too, one may learn balance and rhythm—the secrets of successful rock-work.

Humble and I kept our pace as slow as we could, consistent with continuous upward movement. The steamer slowly shrank to the size of a skiff and human figures became too small to be distinguished. White gulls wheeled and flashed across the green sparkle of Loch Scavaig. Meanwhile we sweltered under a grilling sun and were roasted by waves of heat reflected upward from the brown rock. The temperature must have been at least ninety degrees, and a raging thirst possessed our desiccated bodies. Beyond the summit, we threaded an involved descending route amongst huge crags, where we were obliged to rope down an overhang of twenty feet—our first use of a rope all day. At nine o'clock we stood on the rim of Coire a' Ghrunnda.

We were anxious to reach camp as soon as possible; our friends knew us too well to bother about a twenty-four hours' absence, but might feel less at ease thereafter. We decided, therefore, not to traverse sgurr Alasdair and instead went straight down to Coire a' Ghrunnda. Here, if you like, lies a genuinely gloomy loch—a black and glassy sheet of water framed by a chaos of screes as desolate as one may find in all Scotland. In the stream that flows from it we at last quenched our agonizing thirst. Then we set off downhill, skirting those terrific slabs in the corrie-bed, convex slabs that pour seaward, scored and burnished by ancient glaciers.

At ten-thirty p.m. we strolled into camp, exactly twenty-four hours after departure. Maitland and Higgins had proved friends indeed and a hot meal was waiting for us. This time, no earthly power, not even another Humble mystery tour, could have wooed me from supper, a quiet pipe, and that eiderdown sleeping-bag.

2 *The Cioch and Crack of Doom*

PROLONGED DROUGHT and blazing sun have almost invariably blessed my climbing days in Skye. I go in June. But in June 1937, when camping with J. K. W. Dunn in Glen Brittle, my luck suffered the inevitable relapse. We were half-way up the south-west buttress of Sgurr na h-Uamha when a full gale sprang from the south and spread-eagled us on the central slabs. It was the last big unclimbed buttress in the Cuillin. Therefore we battled our way to the top, fled before the wind to Sligachan, and not an hour too soon retired west to Glen Brittle. Heralded by the gale, rain stormed over the mountains and found us much inclined to rest on our laurels and keep dry. There was at first an indisputable pleasure to be wrung from lying warm and dry in one's sleeping-bag, listening to the vain beat of rain upon the tent-canvas, and thinking 'God help the sailors on a night like this!' After several hours the sound became monotonous; after three days we realized that there were worse things than a wet skin.

I amused myself by reminding Dunn of the less creditable episodes of his climbing career. He is one of the most hopelessly casual and yet friendly of men. To cite but one incident, typical of his way of life, he once sent me a telegram from the wilds of Kintyre, commanding me to climb with him on Nevis next day—but omitting to state time or place of meeting. I set off by car from Glasgow, staking all upon a chance encounter somewhere in Lochaber. Half-way there I happened to stop at Inverarnan hotel in Glen Falloch—to find Dunn, large and fair-haired, sprawling before the fire and wolfing hot scones and tea. I advanced to unleash my thunder, when 'Good man!' cried Dunn, 'I knew it was two to one you'd stop at Inverarnan.'

You cannot damn and blast a man whose eye is sparkling with delight at meeting you. I tried; but it was no use.

Thus it was in our storm-bound tent that wrath at his carefree habit kept me lively and was yet stayed by his infectious smile and naïve geniality. Against these I have no defence. My own more irritating behaviour he regarded with the phlegmatic calm of a noble but lazy mastiff. Despite such accord in idleness, three days of stored-up energy brewed a restlessness that drove us to action. We resolved that regardless of weather we should go on the fourth day to the best rock-climb in the Cuillin. To my own mind this was the Cioch direct and the Crack of Doom, which lie one above the other to form a thousand-foot route up the precipice of Sron na Ciche. To climb the first half by the Cioch pinnacle was practicable; but whether in rain we could cope with the Crack of Doom—by repute the hardest climb in Skye—was a question that I was unqualified to decide. We had not been there before.

The following day dawned with a rain-squall. We wakened, listened—and hastily shut our eyes again. But after a midday breakfast our resolution triumphed. As we made our preparations the weather relented. The rain went off and we set out in weak sunshine for Coire na Ciche, where the wet flanks of the circling sgurrs gleamed as though sheathed in tinfoil.

We spent an hour climbing up Coire Lagain and following a stony track under the mile-long cliffs of Sron na Ciche. Rooted four hundred feet above our heads, in the centre of the cliff, the pinnacle projected squat and gigantic, yet hardly distinguishable from below against the background of the main face. Its very presence there went long unsuspected until Professor Norman Collie, observing its shadow cast upon the cliff behind, deduced the existence of what has become one of the most famous rock-spires in Scotland. We proposed to climb by the direct route made in 1907 by Harland and Abraham.

After a few minutes' rest we roped up on a hundred feet of line. The rocks were still very wet, but the weather was fast turning to the lively breeze and sun that housewives call 'a good drying day.' Moreover, the cliff was gabbro, the roughest of mountain rock, to which wetness spells added difficulty only where the rock is water-worn or interlarded with basalt, or by chilling the fingers. The latter has caused several accidents heareabouts, but is not a trouble to which I am readily susceptible.

I started up a slab at the base of a long shallow chimney. There was more water in this natural drain-pipe than I liked, so at the earliest opportunity I climbed over the left wall on to the open face of the cliff, perhaps fifty feet above the screes. I found myself in a splendidly free situation, with the gabbro unrolling before me like a red ceremonial carpet. Dunn joined me and for a hundred feet we continued parallel to the chimney until the slabs converged on a little corner beneath a vertical nose. To the right and left, bulging rocks prevented an avoiding traverse.

I had been previously counselled that combined tactics—a 'shoulder' from the second man—had best be employed to vanquish this severe pitch. But the holds are definite, if small, and for a tall man like myself no aid is required. The high angle threw me out of balance, so that determined arm-pulling and quick climbing to avoid numbed fingers were the key to success. There followed a hard corner and rib; we zigzagged from one to the other and slowly advanced up to a bulwark of overbending crags.

The immense bastion of the rock above was unscalable, and to turn it we had to ford a river of slabs that fairly poured from the bulge on our left, two hundred feet down to the corrie. I launched out on a horizontal line of stepping-stones close beneath the overhang, and half-way across happened to look straight down to the screes, where I saw a large cairn that marked the landing-place of an unfortunate climber who had once fallen from my present position. The abominable practice of erecting cairns at such spots can hardly be condemned in strong enough terms. At the same instant there came a loud rushing sound like the noise of a high approaching wind. For one hopeless second I believed that a line-squall was coming at me. I clung to the rock like a limpet, and breathed a thankful prayer that Dunn weighed fourteen stone and myself but ten, that the rope was new and Dunn one of the best second men in Scotland.

The rush of wind changed to a long-drawn-out roar, lasting a full minute, and punctuated by terrific crashes from close below me. I then had good reason to recognize that alarming noise. A week before, when traversing the main ridge with J. Banford, I had left Sgurr Dearg in dense mist. After descending steep rock, we had embarked on a hand-traverse on the upper ledge of an overhang, at which the mist cleared, revealing not the main ridge a few feet below, but a chasm eight hundred feet deep. Aided by the sketchiest foothold, we were gaily swinging by our hands over the north-eastern precipice. We hastily retired and were no sooner clear of the ledge than the overhang, ledge and all, silently heeled over into the void in blocks like cottages, then dropped with that rushing noise that I heard now; with just that same roar when thousands of tons of rock crashed on the corrie.

I stood fascinated on the slabs until the avalanche ended, waiting until the last hoarse rattle of the small shot had fallen still. A breathless hush pervaded the mountain. Then I called to Dunn to let out the rope and continued the traverse with exaggerated caution, finding problems in foot-placing where five minutes ago I should have romped freely. This delicacy of nerve was promptly restored to more robust condition by the sudden uprise of the crux.

The traverse ended at a wet and slabby wall of twenty feet lying at right angles to the bastion. The middle of the wall was worn smooth and white, both by water and my predecessors' boot-nails. There was no place here for sensitivity to noise or memorial stones; such rock had to be dealt with in a mood of businesslike determination. Dunn, unfortunately, was still on the far side of the traverse and I had already run out seventy feet of rope, the weight of which was growing noticeable, and would by now have been a serious drag but for his skill in keeping it dry. However, his stance was good, those close at hand bad, so I left with him orders to be ready for an instant move should my rope give out, and then turned to the wall.

The principal difficulty was the glossiness of the rock, which after the coarse gabbro below lent a feeling of insecurity to each movement, not only of the feet but also of the hands, which, chilled by running water, found the tiny holes inadequate. Upon reaching the white patch half-way up I was therefore delighted to find two vertical cracks, wide enough to admit my finger-tips. With these for assistance, the doubtful downscrape of boots on the polished stone was much less dreadful than it had looked from below. This vital move accomplished, I clambered to the top. Before my rope quite ran out I reached a good ledge, from which I brought up Dunn.

Thus far the climbing had been of the most physically satisfying kind, making big demands on muscle and energy. The golden rule of rock-work—use the feet as much as possible, the arms as little as possible—must on the Cioch be often honoured in the breach. One must fight out one's way. For an untrained man I can think of no route more heart-breaking; and for a fit man, none more exhilarating.

We had now outflanked the girdle of the overhang and climbed a further long stretch of slabs, on which we were soon able to move together and which led us to the terrace under the Cioch pinnacle. The terrace sloped unevenly from the eastern gully on our left to the base of the pinnacle on our right. Directly in front arched that hugest sweep of gabbro known throughout the climbing world as 'The Cioch Slab,' from whose western edge sprang the Cioch, leaning towards us like the head of a lizard.

The day was growing ever more sunny as blue rents in the cloud-woof grew more frequent. After that most glorious of Cuillin climbs this unanticipated sun came like a liqueur at the close of a banquet, a final touch that raised our spirits to unprecedented heights. The ordinary route up the Cioch by the Slab and nape seemed too tame a conclusion, so we traversed westward to the direct finish on the nose. After scrambling up broken rocks to the right of the overhang, we climbed the left wall of a corner, wriggled up a steep, rough slab with few holds, and cautiously eased ourselves on to an awkward mantel-shelf. Immediately above, on the very tip of the nose, were a series of three knife-edges. Looked down upon from the top, these short blades, set one below the other like the teeth of a saw, wear a spectacular aspect; their situation is an airy one. But in the climbing of them resides no difficulty. Indeed, we found ourselves deliberately lingering over them—and savouring to the full that joyous sense of freedom they yield, that feel of hovering over space as though the climber were a bird on spread wings.

We pulled ourselves on to the broad roof and relaxed. Dunn lit up his pipe,

> A trophy which survived a hundred fights,
> A beacon which has cheered ten thousand nights,

and lay on his back, happily gazing into vacuity, while I rolled over on my stomach, head over the edge, and surveyed the cliffs below. Throughout the precipice of Sron na Ciche, in particular the area around the Cioch, there is a peculiar atmosphere, clean and spacious, which I have never observed so markedly on any other mountain. It arises perhaps from the free lift of the pale brown slabs and the unique bareness of them; for no vestige of vegetation is nourished in their crystalline rock. One's heart goes out to them, for the cliff has the same virginal purity as snow-peaks in a burst of sun, or green seas breaking white on a skerry.

Half an hour passed in delicious ease. And here indeed is the fine art of idling anywhere: there should be a mountain of work accomplished in the near past or instantly impending in the future. Where these twin conditions are both satisfied, as now, one may experience a double dose of bliss. At the close of our half-hour I proposed that we try the Crack of Doom. Dunn was enthusiastic, for I had kept this part of the programme to myself until I knew our day's form. We could then contain ourselves no longer and climbed down the nape of the pinnacle to the cliff.

A sharp descent and right-hand traverse along a shattered ledge brought us to the start of our route. It began as a deep groove, gradually growing shallow as it curved for a hundred and fifty feet up rough and tumbled slabs. On this first section, advancing by easy stages and husbanding energy for whatever might lie ahead, we encountered no difficulty. On the last thirty feet the groove became harder; then the cliff shot abruptly up, the groove swung hard to the left, and came to a sudden end at a right-angled corner. We stood on a sloping slab, on either side of which the corner walls rose sheer for fifty feet. The right-hand wall was split from top to bottom by a hanging chimney, set slightly at a tilt from right to left. We had arrived at the Crack of Doom.

While Dunn secured himself in the corner I scrutinized the crack to discover the worst. The tilt was clearly awkward, but twenty feet up a jammed stone augured a brief resting-place. Below that stone the crack was wide enough to admit one's right leg and arm. Above the stone I could see no holds at all and the crack narrowed. Although the outside walls were dry, trickling water filmed the interior.

Whenever Dunn declared himself ready I set to work. Facing sideways toward the corner I wedged my right arm in the crack as a balance-preserver and climbed by foothold only to the chock-stone. Those twenty feet were hard but not severe. Nevertheless, I had no doubts of what must follow, and there being no need to hurry, I stopped on the chock-stone for some two minutes until I felt completely rested. On the slab below me Dunn looked up with that smile of unbounded optimism that has cheered me up many an ice-clad pitch in winter. No matter how grim the prospect or precarious his own situation, he has the remarkable capacity of appearing unshakably safe and solid. Indeed, he inspires a leader with the sense of mutual confidence, which means much to the success of a climbing team.

I began to climb again. With every foot now gained the crack narrowed and the difficulties increased. At intervals on the outside edge were microscopic incut holds, too wide apart to provide continuous footing. In between these havens I retained position and mounted higher by slipping a foot inside the crack and turning the ankle to jam the boot. I had also to fight against the tilt of the crack, which tended to thrust my body outward; and since an arm might no longer be wedged, I was obliged to force a hand into the crack and make pressure-holds by clenching the fist. I imagine that a shorter man might find less trouble with the tilt than myself. With jammed foot and fist I thus pulled up my body from one sparse hold to another.

Unfortunately I had done almost sixty thousand feet of climbing on the Cuillin in sixteen days and my boot-nails were in a sad state of decrepitude, being not only worn to shreds but loose into the bargain. There was one edge-nail, on the inner side of my left boot, which tinkled as merrily as a dinner bell whenever my foot was shaken. This nail had repeatedly to be used on the miniature holds on the outside of the crack. One placed it carefully and applied the strain gently, in constant preparedness for its breaking off. Like a true friend it did not fail me in emergency.

Meanwhile I had progressed to the top of the crack, where a tongue of stone jutted overhead as though to mock my weariness. I again jammed myself, and for a few seconds halted to gather in strength for the final tussle. I put out my hand and grasped the top of the stone. With a last strenuous heave I pulled myself out of the crack, dangled for a second, then swarmed up, drawing myself into a flat-bottomed corner.

I frankly confess that although by no means exhausted, I was muscularly very tired indeed. In comparison with this crack, the Cioch direct, everywhere recognized as a standard 'severe,' seemed child's play. Yet the crack is eminently practicable; it calls for no feat of esoteric gymnastic.

While my breath was returning I looked over the edge to give Dunn a signal of success. My eye flashed a thousand feet past his head, down a cascade of slabs to the corrie. So absorbing had been the climb that till now I had felt little or no sense of height. My eye wandered further, down to the green fields of Glen Brittle, where black cloud-shadows were driven in herds by following sun-shafts. Beyond was the Atlantic, its wrinkled expanse scored by a dozen golden furrows, as though the outer islands, like low Viking ships, had ploughed those gleaming wakes when they stood out to the west.

Intense power was given to this simple vista by the frame of crags to my left, and once again I was struck by the truth of those words of Mummery, when he declared that the best route up a mountain is a difficult one. Only there, rather than upon the screes of an easy route, may one find a foreground of bold rock whose noble outline does no less than justice to the distant view; and only there, rather than upon the plod up a uniform slope, which dulls the mind, is one's whole being glowingly alive and keyed to full receptiveness. After one is up, there can be no doubt that ridge-walking is the finest occupation.

Being fully recovered, I gave Dunn a shout to come on. Like me, he went well to the chock-stone. Thenceforward, and despite his exceptional strength, his much greater weight placed him at a disadvantage; for my own body, being relatively light, has a high power-to-weight ratio. But Dunn was too skilful a mountaineer to climb anyhow but gracefully, and the only signs of difficulty were some hard breathing, and when he glanced up, his fair hair tumbled over his eyes, an expression of acute anguish that almost choked me with laughter. His expression immediately changed to a broad grin, his more explosive mirth being held, perforce, behind glistening eyes—a triumph of mind over matter which those who know the Crack of Doom will appreciate. He came on slowly but surely, and in due course was prostrated by my side.

We sat together for a while, coiling up the rope and congratulating each other on the best climb we had had in Skye. Then we went up to a *glacis* or broad slabby ledge, which ran leftward like a corridor on to the crest of Sron na Ciche. Where we emerged on the *glacis* a short final crag rose above us. I understand that this gives a very hard finish to the climb; to me it looked more suitable to rubbers on dry rock than to loose boot-nails on wet rock. We therefore turned to the corridor and walked on to the top of the mountain. We made there the brief halt that proper respect for such a hill demands, then pursued our way along the ridge to Sgurr Alasdair, descending thence to Coire Lagain, a thousand feet in five minutes by the rapids of the Stone Shoot—the longest scree-run in Scotland. On passing below the cliff of Sron na Ciche we threaded our way through hundreds of tons of new avalanche debris, and saw a fresh scar on the face a few hundred feet above the track. Gabbro holds may be the most reliable in the world, but in the mass, I fear, even gabbro is little more immune from decay than other rocks.

We returned to Glen Brittle, and that night I examined my boots. To an attentive ear the note they sounded had become unmistakably one of warning. Until I was new-shod there must be no more rock-climbing. Moreover, the very skin of my finger-tips was worn to a fragile tenuity. Next day we struck camp and departed for Glasgow.

3 Slav Route—Ben Nevis

FLANKED BY a cheerful fire, Dunn, W. M. Mackenzi e A. M. MacAlpine, and I sat round the breakfast table in the Scottish Mountaineering Club's hut on Ben Nevis. It was mid October 1937. I was entertaining myself with the hut's climbing register and speculating what was the full tale behind some of these cryptic entries: 'Observatory buttress—three hours rain and sleet,' or 'South Trident direct—half-gale.' They were succint enough in all conscience, but too tantalizing. They stimulated yet did not satisfy imagination. What tense moments, high on the mountain-wall, were hidden there? How many hard fights by a leader, silently witnessed by only a couple of friends on windswept ledges—and never again mentioned? I closed the book with a bang. 'What *are* we going to climb?' I asked.

'When the weather is foul,' said Mackenzie—and here he paused so that his audience could hear the wind soughing round the corners of the hut—'and the rain is coming down in sheets' —at which he looked pointedly out of the small window— 'there is only one thing to do——'

'Get back to bed,' I murmured.

Mackenzie's blue eyes flashed with indignation and the nostrils of his hawk-nose distended. He looked a perfect specimen of the intolerant man of action. 'The only thing to do,' he sternly continued, 'is to climb the hardest route on the mountain.'

'Why?' asked MacAlpine briskly.

'Why!' exploded Mackenzie. 'In rain you get miserable on an easy climb. But go to a hard climb and you forget the weather—all your interest goes to the rock.'

We could not deny there was an element of truth there.

A mild route would be dreary in the thick mist that choked this upper corrie of the Allt a' Mhuilinn: not a glimpse of the Spean valley two thousand feet below or of the cliffs rising two thousand feet above was vouchsafed us. We were housed like unwilling gods among the clouds. But there were limits to Mackenzie's theory; we were not like gods, immune from destruction.

'The hardest climb is Rubicon Wall,' I remarked, 'and that won't go in rain. You must have something else in mind.'

'Slav route,' said Mackenzie, sitting up very straight. But with these two words he had won me over. Like a magic charm they broke the spell of lethargy, for Slav route was then reputed to be the finest summer route on the mountain. The name Slav derives from two Czechoslovakian mountaineers with whom E. A. M. Wedderburn made the first ascent in 1934. So far as I knew, however, all ascents to date had been made either in rubbers or rope-soled shoes. And rubbers cannot be used on wet slabs.

'We'll try it in boots,' concluded Mackenzie. 'It's a full sixteen hundred feet—takes about four hours.' Then, brusquely, 'Nothing to it! Can't be more than very severe!' And his whole face lit up with infectious enthusiasm.

MacAlpine and I burst out laughing. Mackenzie is that happy companion, an unconscious humorist. There is a Confucian dictum that love of daring without understanding casts the shadow named rashness. If Mackenzie loved daring more than most virtues his understanding was commensurate, so that boldness of planning was balanced by prudence in execution, which in combine made him a first-class mountaineer. A party of four, however, was too large for so long a climb in wild weather. Dunn and MacAlpine therefore decided to go to Observatory ridge.

At eleven a.m. Mackenzie and I set out in a cold spit of rain toward the North-east buttress, the most tremendous cliff on the mountain. It marks the eastern limit of the two miles of precipice that ring the north face of Nevis. Its west flank and the east flank of Observatory ridge confront each other like opposing pages of a half-open book, in the angle of which is the unclimbed Zero gully. Slav route runs closely parallel with the gully on the rocks of the North-east buttress. To-day this grandeur of rock scenery was invisible to us, 'wrapt in dense cloud from base to cope,' but we were not ill content. We had the clean damp smell of mist in our nostrils, and in our eyes the thrust of a sudden tower through the veil, the looming and fading of vague buttresses, the hurried flitting through thinning wisps of unsuspected pinnacles, each gleaming with wet.

When we arrived in the great angle beneath Zero gully we found a small snow-field left over from the previous winter. As we went across, boot-nails crunching on the rough surface, I noticed that the snow was peppered here and there with stones discharged down the conduit of the gully, and an instant later the whirr and whine of a fragment was heard overhead. It went wide, like a warning shot across our bows. In another minute we were in neutral waters under the dripping protection of the North-east buttress.

We roped up on a hundred feet of line, with Mackenzie as leader. The exact line of Slav route was unknown to us and Mackenzie made a false start up pouring wet slabs, which grew ever more smooth and precipitous until eighty feet up his hardy optimism began to flag. It became plain that he was tilting at a watermill and he came down, chastened by the truth that Nevis rocks and routes are not only as God made them, but generally worse. There could now be no doubt that the start of Slav route was a prominent rib hard against Zero gully. It projected through drizzling mist with a hostile aspect that sapped much of our booted confidence, and I found myself counting the hours of daylight to calculate the limits of attack.

Mackenzie's false start was in the end a psychological gain, for after wandering half an hour on rocks that no mortal was ever intended to climb, he found those that were so intended unusually yielding. Wiry and lean as a courtyard cat, he went as though on midnight tiles, with a vigorous rhythm, up the front of the rib. I thought the rock bulged awkwardly at me when I followed. Mackenzie was standing on a niche, which he vacated as my hand groped over its edge, and, since the rocks directly above overhung, disappeared round a corner to the left. I took his place, hitched myself to a rock-spike, and quickly paid out the rope over my shoulder, for he had clearly struck top form and was travelling with speed on rocks that were not easy. There came a long halt. Not a movement for several minutes.

I became aware why Mackenzie had been so very prompt in departing—a rivulet was pouring from the eave on to the back of my neck. And there was no room on the cramped ledge to avoid it. I could turn and twist, I could bend and stretch as I liked, but that stream found a joint in my clothing. Like Wordsworth's cataract, it haunted me like a passion. It passes my understanding how it is possible for October rain water on Nevis to be so cold and remain liquid.

After I was completely saturated I heard my call from above. I went round the corner and traversed narrow ledges on the gable of the rib. They brought me to a piton driven into a crack at the top edge of the wall. The piton was presumably a relic of the first ascent and Mackenzie was using it as a rope belay.

'He was no fool who nailed this place,' announced Mackenzie, eyeing the sloping roof which swept overhead parallel to our traverse. 'Take a look and tell me what you make of it.'

I peered over the top and saw a bare, yellowish slab spread with a film of water. Its lower half sharply dipped to the eave overlooking our last stance; the top half curled steeply upward to some unknown destination. At such a sight I could imagine a bishop turning apostate and cleaving to materialist philosophy. An air of stark reality clung to that slab.

'Slavs must climb very well,' I suggested. 'Still, it 's not so bad but what it might be worse.' Although it is needless to encourage a leader like Mackenzie, it is a second man's duty not to discourage him.

We said no more, for Mackenzie climbed up to the slab and

waited while I tied myself to the piton. Then he crept out sideways, using one-nail footholds on a thin split in the rock. From the middle he began to move slowly up, carefully placing each foot, gently transferring his weight to it, and so balancing up by nail-friction aided by a minimum of hand-hold. As he arrived at the final upcurl I watched with breathless interest. He took one long look and climbed down a step or two. Then I saw what I had not seen before: a second piton in the rock immediately under the crux.

'A karabiner!' demanded Mackenzie, like Richard III calling for a horse at Bosworth, that he might 'enact more wonders.' I rummaged in my rucksack for the required article, a steel ring with a spring-clip, which I passed up to him. He clipped the ring on to both the piton and the rope, the latter freely running through the centre. Thus doubly protected against a fall, he advanced once more to the crux. The footholds were minute, but not too small to take the thin edge of a side-nail, or at least enough of it to support the body. The real difficulty, and the most trying, was the lack of adequate holds for numbed fingers. The wind, too, had chosen to swirl round Observatory ridge and drive the rain still more icily. It is usually thus; mountain nature is not chivalrous and wields the sword of cold most fiercely when the plight of the climber is sorest. At length he disappeared, and like a curtain drawn to close his performance a wreath of cloud floated over the top of the slab.

In a few minutes there came through the mist a muffled 'Phew!'—a short silence, then, 'I 'm up!'—followed by a joyful laugh and later a few piercing whistles, which echoed weirdly against the neighbouring cliffs.

At last he shouted to me to come on. I obeyed with alacrity, and ten minutes later we had reunited on a spacious platform. I removed the karabiner *en route* but left the pitons behind. I generally hold that pitons should be taken out after use and the rocks left clean. But we had been thankful to find them there and thought that others might be thankful too. I have since twice led the pitch in boots in dry weather and thought pitons unnecessary; in rain and wind, when the slab is very severe, at least one is essential. There is no other belay.

The question before our meeting was whether the last pitch was merely a sample of the fourteen hundred feet above. It was a horrid possibility. If so, the best thing we could do would be to climb down it again. The last thought, and the fact that it was now my turn to lead, contributed to my illogical conviction that the worst was over. The route appeared to continue up an open corner to the left, where a grey column rose seventy feet between broken walls. I found the column technically hard. The holds were particularly small and ran with water, which poured up my sleeve to the chest whenever I was so misguided as to take a high handhold. With numbed fingers I felt the upper part of the column to be rather exposed. After we had relished its clean-cut intricacy and taken refuge behind a square block crowning its top, our thoughts became dominated by the threat of immense slabs ahead. They seemed to bend up and over in vast red sheets, streaming with water, and the only visible route ran by an eighty-foot chute to an overhung corner.

We reconnoitred along an easy traverse which led us to the very verge of Zero gully. On our left was the chute, on our right the gully, water-slides both, and repulsive enough to induce a shudder in examining climbers. They were impossible. Between them reared a high right-angled step which, were it climbable, must allow us to outflank either impasse. I made the attempt, floating up like a ballet-dancer, accompanied by the bubble and tinkle of water-music; my choir, a thousand treble voices. I was soon able to put the issue beyond doubt. After a hard climb I went up a low vertical wall to the crest of a rib overlooking Zero gully. Mackenzie then led through and vanished over a square-cut crest.

While these proceedings were in hand I was fascinated by the sanguinary appearance of the water that trickled over the red rocks to my left. It reminded me of that gruesome line of Tennyson's, 'The red-ribb'd ledges drip with a silent horror of blood'—a line that rejoiced the bloodthirsty heart of my boyhood, disgusted my more tender adolescence, and which my manhood now recognized with grim amusement as no extravagance. My poetic reflections, however, were disturbed by a tug on the rope and some expletives from above, whose tenor was more akin to the subject of my thoughts than Mackenzie knew. I had, it seemed, been called more than once. Perpendicular rock with good hold is a rare pleasure to the climber, and the party forgathered above the step in high spirits.

From now onward the difficulties abated. Yet the route selection remained all-engrossing and at one place we had to use combined tactics. For a thousand feet the climb continued up a series of vertical walls, which progressively became shorter, the average angle of the cliff being lessened by a myriad ledges, broad and narrow. Throughout this upper part of the route we moved together, which provided me, as second man, with much brisk work in managing a rope stiff and heavy with water. From such rope management I always derive the greatest delight—striving for a perfection that is, alas, never to be realized.

When the cloud locally thickened we appeared at times like the most insubstantial of wraiths, drifting through the shifting mists like the wolves in a Russian melodrama. Climbing thus through cloud we could not see what height we were gaining, and the route gradually took to itself a sort of epic quality. It rolled on and on, magnificently and unendingly, until one thought that since it had continued so long it must go on for ever. On subsequent visits I have observed the same quality. It is the sure sign of a great rock-climb, of mountaineering as distinct from crag-climbing.

After four hours' ascent there became noticeable that strange freedom of atmosphere, a lightening and movement of air, that indicates nearness to a summit. At four o'clock we arrived on the boulder-fields of the plateau and went in search of the cairn. Suddenly I noticed the rain. Shafts of wind drew attention to my clothes. I was soaked to the skin as though I had newly swum in the Allt a' Mhuilinn.

'You were right,' I said to Mackenzie, 'about forgetting bad weather on a good climb. But we knew it was raining at that slab!'

My honest tribute was suspect. Mackenzie was alert. He would make no damaging admissions that might be used in evidence against him.

'Raining!' he exclaimed. 'Not a drop—dry all day till now!'

And on that contention he took his stand, nor would he yield an inch. But later that evening, when we sat before a glowing fire in the hut, I observed him record the ascent in the official Climbs Book, and surreptitiously glancing over his shoulder, read this laconic narrative: 'Slav route—wet.'

4 *On the Rannoch Wall in Winter*

The Cliff and the Moor

OF ALL LOWLAND SCENES that which most compels my admiration is the stateliness of tall trees on a broad lawn. It is a harmony of the vertical and horizontal, simple, serene; its effect on the mind a perfect calm: ideas that in Greek architecture culminate in the Parthenon. Among Scottish mountains, and there alone, have I seen its most noble demonstration in the cliffs of the Buachaille Etive Mor, towering over the vast flatness of the moor of Rannoch. But the shape of the peak itself is happily not classic. From ten miles over the moor it reminds me of a neolithic arrow-head; from the road near Kingshouse Inn, of a Gothic cathedral, raised to a height of 3,345 feet, based in proportion, and spired.

Thus in the cliff and moor we see the classic calm; in the peak and sky the Gothic aspiration; opposed ideas, here reconciled in bewitching harmony. For the Gothic spire is an outward, visible expression of the inward, invisible soaring of man's spirit toward union with the beautiful. Therefore it is a form profoundly satisfying to the eye; for it fires the mind with thought of the eternal, and we call that fire the love of beauty, and the emotion it arouses the awe of God.

When there is created within our minds this state so difficult for mere intellect to understand—a blend in one of an inward movement of mind and a flawless calm—or when an artist is given grace to project it in outer forms, there emerges the highest beauty, peace. For in true peace there are ever present and reconciled two logically irreconcilable elements—stillness and motion, rest and love, silence and song. Wherever there is a union of the pairs of opposites so perfect that Reason confounded cries: 'Two distincts, division none!' there too is an exceeding and eternal weight of beauty.

From the porphyry of Buachaille the chisel of God has carved that for us in symbol. And if it be courteous to say, until we are aware in the midst of our climbing that mountains are but the sign of things higher, we may be climbers but we have not begun to understand mountains, or mountaineers.

In consequence of this demonstration I admit (what is true of few hills) that the best of Buachaille may be experienced from the roadway. It is a humbling thought for a keen rock-climber. On the other hand, the paradoxical harmony in contrast of the eastern cliffs with the moor is nowhere so well appreciated as from the Buachaille itself, either from the summit, or better still from the most perpendicular rocks—the Rannoch Wall of the Crowberry ridge. In a lecture to the Scottish Mountaineering Club in 1939, I showed a slide of Agag's groove on Rannoch Wall, which depicted the mountaineer as a fly crawling on the face of a skyscraper, and with the words, 'This climb commands a magnificent prospect over the moor of Rannoch,' raised no little laughter. The reader may have similar doubts. Therefore I propose to show him the climb, not under too good conditions, so that he may know how photographs, by revealing only part of the truth, distort the whole.

Agag's Groove

From a tower close under the summit of Buachaille, the Crowberry ridge drops nine hundred feet north-east. Its sheer eastern flank remained unclimbed until 1934, intimidating climbers so long as more obvious routes remained unexplored. In that year G. C. Williams opened up the cliff by a good but relatively short route, whose name, Rannoch Wall, has since been applied to the whole face. In August 1936 the tallest part of Rannoch Wall fell to J. F. Hamilton, who used a groove, barely visible from below, to climb the three hundred and sixty feet from the lowest corner to the top centre. From the delicate tread of Agag was derived the name of his new route. I had the good luck to witness his first ascent. No photograph can convey its sensational aspect as watched from below: on no short summer climb have I seen a bolder lead. But the 'fly-on-a-wall' appearance is misleading and constitutes a libel on a splendid route.

One morning in December 1937 I arrived at the Glencoe-Glen Etive cross-roads with Dunn, MacAlpine, and Mackenzie. We had made no definite plans, for new snow had come on the hills and a black frost held the earth spellbound. The air was still as death, so that sounds from a long distance came sharp to the ear, and our footfalls rang hollow on the roadway.

With nipped ears and much stamping of feet, we stood at the cross-roads in brief debate. It occurred to us then that a winter ascent of the Rannoch Wall would provide high interest, and we surveyed the Buachaille to see what opportunity offered. The colours of the rock showed unnaturally clear—dove-grey, brown, and palest red, projecting through a snow-sprinkle that sparkled like salt. Here and there a smaller crag, softly black as though smoke-stained, was girdled by the white ribbon of ledge and gully. Rannoch Wall stared down at us, more free of frost than any other part of the mountain. Its angle and a day or two of sun had kept it clean, but within the groove we feared that deadly combination, ice-glaze and loose powder-snow.

We resolved to inspect the conditions more closely from the foot of Curved ridge, so turned south to Coupal Bridge in Glen Etive and thence tramped the moor for an hour and scrambled among the lower rocks to the water-slide below the ridge. There was one little mountain ash close by, miraculously springing from a ledge of solid stone. Its twigs were exquisitely beaded with ice and it looked like a crystal chandelier. I have passed beside it well over a hundred times and regard it as an old friend of heroic fortitude—how *does* it contrive to wring life from its chosen block of porphyry, winter after bitter winter? One may only marvel in vain—and pass humbly on. The water-slide was frozen and step-cutting was required. Under the swing of my axe, an icicle on the left wall, twice the size of an elephant's tusk, cracked like a rifle shot; and left a sudden silence, which for a moment seemed to brood over us like a hovering of wings, then as suddenly to vanish.

Ten minutes later our boot-nails were grating on Curved ridge and we drew up parallel to the Rannoch Wall. From all over the wall came a hard metallic glitter, emanating from invisible frost cressets. As a whole, the wall displayed a gratifying freedom from the snow that dusted the remainder of the mountain. Agag's groove looked most inviting.

'The sun has certainly been getting at it,' said Dunn with a delighted grin. 'But what about the groove? We 'll probably find it lined with green ice.'

'There may be black ice at the crux,' said Mackenzie, in a tone that implied that such would be a point in its favour.

'But there 's no snow,' I pointed out. 'Only the leader need carry an axe. We can always come down if it won't go.'

'At thirty-two feet per second per second!' added MacAlpine.

We honoured him with the half-laughing snort due to one's jesting friends; for in fact one may rope down the groove from any of its stances, which have first-class belays. Without more ado we crossed C gully to the cairn at the foot of the climb. We put on balaclava helmets and all available scarves and sweaters until we bulged like polar bears, then roped up with Mackenzie as leader, myself second, followed by Dunn. MacAlpine, who was suffering from a strained muscle, spent the day on Curved ridge. We all retained our rucksacks, but left two axes beside the cairn. Mackenzie carried the third slung at his waist.

The lowest end of the groove was eighty feet overhead, separated from us by a wall, which Mackenzie took in two pitches by bringing me up to a small half-way stance. That first eighty feet was not specially difficult; better than that, it was delightful. The rock lies indeed at a high angle, coarse, clean-cut, and well provided with little square holds—ideal both for boots and gloved fingers.

On joining Mackenzie in the start of the groove I at once looked around for ice, but save for straggling filaments, spreading vein-like on the main wall, there was none. No more than moderately difficult, the groove rose long, wide, and arching to the crux. At close quarters it is not so much a groove as a curving ledge, one hundred and eighty feet in length and about three feet broad, sometimes less and rarely more. As we climbed slowly upward we had a knowledge of complete safety that seemed at odd variance with our progress up the most vertical cliff in central Scotland. The feeling induced was pure elation—height and distance were a sparkling wine poured to the mind from a rock decanter. And to this blend of height and distance my attention was inevitably and repeatedly drawn as I waited on comfortable stances while the man above or below was climbing.

Near the top of the groove I came upon one especially well-upholstered couch—a hollow cushioned with crowberries, which in summer ripeness affords the climber both bed and board, but whose hoary counterpane gave me a chill welcome in frost. I sat there and first paid out Mackenzie's rope and then drew in Dunn's. I felt, perhaps, something of the pleasure of that raven, which as long as man can remember has nested on the neighbouring crags of Raven's gully—I looked straight out from the rock-wall, snugly conscious of the unseen drop below, as a man may nestle more happily in his bed when he hears the rainstorm beat upon his window. My gaze met nothing till it met the moor, lightly whitened as though veiled by frail lace, through which the brown heath glowed like an inner warmth. Along the farthest fringe, behind Schichallion and beyond Loch Rannoch, ran between sky and earth a broad belt of brume, the colour of the Cuillin after rain on a still evening.

Meanwhile, Mackenzie had climbed twenty-five feet to find that our protecting groove had petered out in a nest of bulging rocks. He was still a hundred feet beneath the crest of Crowberry ridge, and by a traverse to the left must now embark upon the open face. Immediately above him was the crux of the climb, twenty feet of almost vertical rock, the last fifteen of which, jutting like a squat nose, were split by a crack whence a climber may look between his legs to the screes. In this crack we anticipated ice.

'Look out for squalls,' Mackenzie said casually. 'If there's no ice then the frost has probably loosened some of the holds.' And with these parting words he stepped from the groove on to a ledge on the open wall. He climbed to the nose, where for a moment I saw him outlined against blue sky. He had stopped to strip off his gloves. Then he vanished like the boy in the Indian rope-trick.

I waited for the ominous sound of his axe, but five minutes passed without even the faintest noise from above. If there were loose holds I could trust Mackenzie not to use them; or to use them correctly. He was apt to leave loose holds rather than throw them down, arguing that loose holds are not of necessity bad holds. I was startled by a whirr, and a black shape dashed towards Curved ridge. It was my other old friend—the raven. He had watched many a climb of mine on Buachaille. He wheeled round the base of Crowberry ridge and led my eyes down to the moor. The Glencoe road ran like a grey thread to the Blackmount. It was absurd to say that this new road spoiled the scenery. As well might one say that a scratch could spoil the facade of Chartres Cathedral. The road was dominated by the scenery—lost in it. Perhaps, by comparison, it helped to lend some meaning to an immense scale of things otherwise beyond comprehension. A shout came from above. Mackenzie was up.

Dunn arrived and anchored himself in my former berth. I moved on to the face. The change from security to extreme exposure at once quickened up my pulse—a physiological advantage that assists one to climb well on the crux. I paused for a second to familiarize myself with the sweep of the rock, then climbed to a sloping ledge below the nose. So far as I could see there was not a vestige of ice in the crack, which errs on the shallow side: ''Tis not so deep as a well, nor so wide as a church door; but 'tis enough.' Like Mackenzie, I thought it well to remove my gloves. Foothold was available, not within the crack, but on either side. I thought the holds very small for boots, and the angle made it awkward to take them properly without leaning out on the finger-tips—which I wished to avoid as my fingers were numb. As I went up I tested each hand-hold before putting weight on it. It is good policy to regard a cracked bulge with suspicion, however secure it may seem; like Byron's column, this particular specimen has seen better days:

> By a lone wall a lonelier column rears
> A grey and grief-worn aspect of old days;
> 'Tis the last remnant of the wreck of years—

and as such one of the holds in the crack came away in my hand. I tossed it into space and looked down sideways to watch it crash into C gully. I could also see that my rope hung well clear of the rock and that our two axes seemed directly underneath my heels. All sensation was now beginning to leave my hands and I lost no more time in reaching the top.

A noteworthy fact of that last twenty feet is that whenever one begins to climb, all sense of undue exposure vanishes before the great technical interest of the rock—unless one deliberately chooses to stop and look down. One forgets one's environment as one forgets it while reading a good book.

Mackenzie was sitting on a small platform on top of the nose. He looked cold, but refused to admit to any severe chill in the air, although his own breath was a visible witness against him. There still remained eighty feet of hard climbing, and since gloves could not be worn Mackenzie decided to take it in one run-out of rope, and by thus saving time, to temper the frost to the bare finger.

He went to the left on another ledge of traverse, carefully stepping over a large loose boulder *en route*, and once again I was alone. The sun was low down in the south and the shadow of Buachaille, which in summer is cast in a perfect cone over the flat face of Rannoch moor, fell now to the more hilly north. Kingshouse Inn, the merest white speck, was engulfed within the edge of the shadow. The Buachaille must rob that inn of a great deal of sunshine although the two lie two and a half miles apart. Great depth and immeasurable distance commingled in that subtle harmony of which I spoke, but which must be seen and felt before it can be understood in words.

Fully twenty minutes passed, and then with Dunn's arrival I was free to follow Mackenzie. I felt the exposure here much more than at the crux, and the reason is not hard to discover: the climbing being less difficult one has more leisure to think of one's position. The rock must lie at an angle of about eighty degrees; in other words, to the climber it seems practically perpendicular. Although the face is basically sound, great caution was required in dealing with detached stones, and on the last six feet, the steepest of all, another hold broke in my hand. I was prepared for it and no damage was done. It is none the less worth noting, for the benefit of others, that it looked absolutely secure. Snow on the ridge and frost on the face are melted by the sun and trickle into the cracks, where the water in again freezing must inevitably prise loose some of the holds. Therefore in hard frost on Rannoch Wall every hold on the last hundred feet must be tested, even though its summer staunchness be known. I am anxious not to convey the impression that Agag's groove is unsound. On the contrary it is excellent; as good porphyry as any on the mountain. It ranks equal to most gabbro.

I emerged on the crest of Crowberry ridge on the gently sloping rocks above 'the slabs.' Mackenzie, who was now fully gloved, took in Dunn's rope for me while I sat on the edge and tried to thaw my paralysed fingers. Even to one much accustomed to rock-work, a man climbing those last eighty feet of Rannoch Wall made a startling sight. The depth and sheerness seemed to suck both eye and breath into the gully, and Dunn's presence on the wall, as he climbed with studied ease above remote scree, appeared an incredible flouting of natural laws. I know of no other rock-climb that strikes me in that way.

When the whole party had assembled we coiled up the ropes and advanced over the frost-hoared rocks of Crowberry tower to the summit. The biting cold did not dispose us to linger and the sun was setting in a smother of frothy cloud. There would be more snow on the morrow. We retired down Curved ridge, and retrieving our axes, returned with all dispatch to a bright fire and hot dinner at Kingshouse Inn.

5 *The Deep-cut Chimney of Stob Coire nam Beith*

ONCE EVERY WEEK, Dunn, Mackenzie, and used to forgather for supper at MacAlpine's house in Glasgow. There we met on Thursdays to exchange yarns and hatch mountaineering plots. It may be deduced from a reading of Herodotus that the ancient Persians owed much success in war to the habit of planning their strategy at nightly carousals and revising it in the morning when they were sober. Imagination thus illumined method. On the same principle many a new route was first made in MacAlpine's sitting-room, where we never failed to find the cheering stimuli of a blazing fire, deep arm-chairs, and tankards of beer. If these schemes could afterwards pass the severe test of dawn-hour on the day of action, one could safely say they were practicable. These nights of merriment and discussion were something we looked forward to only less than the climb itself, and this was the only climbing-combination I knew that over a period of years consistently planned in advance. There was a peculiar appeal in such long-distance planning—a keen satisfaction in seeing deliberated efforts draw to fruition in face of many a setback.

One of our hardest campaigns was the struggle with the Deep-cut chimney of Stob Coire nam Beith in Glencoe—the north-westerly peak of Bidean nam Bian. Underneath these two summits sprawls a northern corrie, whose west wall is the great east cliff of Stob Coire nam Beith, rising twelve hundred feet, broken by weather into a chaos of ridge and buttress. At the centre of the mass the biggest buttress is split to its base by a narrow gully named Deep-cut chimney; to the left and right of which are No. 3 buttress and No. 4. The chimney ends four hundred feet above the screes in a small amphitheatre from which eight hundred feet of open rock rise to the summit. In 1936 there was still no record of any ascent of this chimney.

The first skirmish was undertaken in spring of that year by Mackenzie and Dunn, who were preceded on the climb by J. A. Brown and T. D. Mackinnon. They failed, being turned away by an ugly overhang at the second pitch, where Dunn was obliged to stand for half an hour under a waterfall, whose volume increases with the years. But with such men as these failure can generally be made to show profits. Not only did Dunn subsequently lead the ascent of a rib to the right of the chimney, but Mackenzie by careful study acquired an exact knowledge of the chimney's features. That same day Mackinnon and Brown made the first recorded ascent. But they by-passed the principal pitches by a shelf high on the left wall. A direct ascent remained to be done. In 1939 the seeds of discovery germinated in Mackenzie's fertile brain, and one January night, from behind a frothing mug in the depths of MacAlpine's arm-chair, he delivered himself of a revolutionary stratagem.

A direct summer ascent, said Mackenzie, was probably impossible. The overhang seemed hopeless. But in winter, when the gully walls and the four pitches below the amphitheatre were iced, one might carve holds to supply the natural lack. That was a plain enough proposition. Unclimbable summer rock may frequently be climbed by virtue of a snow or ice crust. He calculated, however, that on a short winter's day we could not expect to reach the amphitheatre before sunset. Therefore the remaining eight hundred feet must be climbed by torchlight.

That was a typical instance of Mackenzie's originality. With one bold stroke he cut through orthodox practice. At first the idea of climbing eight hundred feet of snow-bound rock by night seemed unusual; but the more we discussed the plan the more feasible it appeared. We knew by experience that climbing on whitened rock by torchlight is little harder than by day—provided that the proper line of ascent be known beforehand.

And as it happened, we had all made previous acquaintance with the upper face. Therefore the plan was adopted.

Three mornings later (January 1939), Dunn, Mackenzie, and I arrived in the north corrie of Bidean nam Bian. The hills were draped with new snow and a high ceiling of steel-grey cloud promised at least twelve hours of settled weather. We kicked a few hundred steps up a snow-slope to the foot of Deep-cut chimney. It looked grim enough in all conscience. The first three hundred feet were of snow-ice packed between narrow walls, then the angle suddenly dropped and a hundred feet higher the snow spread out fanwise in the amphitheatre. Every pitch was thickly hoared and appeared to hold too little ice to assist us and just enough to augment its normal difficulty. We roped up and Mackenzie took the lead.

The bed of the chimney was choked with firm snow and the vertical walls floured with soft. In one and a half hours we climbed two ice-pitches and arrived at the overhang. Mackenzie cut up to the roof and belayed me round an enormous icicle. I then forced the remainder of the pitch up an ice-coating on the right wall of the gully. We had spent one hour on thirty feet of rock. Thereafter the rock was smothered more heavily than ever and the climbing became very hard and slow. Sweeping with gloved hands and scraping with ice-axes, we gradually forced a way, until at three o'clock, after five hours' climbing, our assault was broken on the fourth pitch. Mackenzie tried again and again to turn its overhang on the left wall. Straightforward methods and his repertoire of tricks and jugglery alike came to naught on brittle ice. He reached within a few feet of the top, but the rest was starkly unjustifiable.

When we turned to the descent we had only one and a half hours of daylight to get down what had taken us nearly five hours to get up. But the retreat ran as smoothly as clockwork, and by using combined tactics and hitching doubled ropes to minute rock-spikes, which were not at all easy to find, we roped down in one hour.

That we had been utterly beaten was of little consequence,

but I was about to learn a valuable lesson, and can now expose a trap from which we narrowly escaped, and thus, perhaps, spare some future party a benightment:

At four o'clock we arrived back at the floor of the corrie, whereupon inner pangs recorded the elapse of twelve hours since our last meal. We sat down on the snow and I opened my rucksack in search of food. There, in the bottom, lay the electric torch on which our climbing plan had been founded, its three-hundred-foot beam reduced to a dying flicker. It must have been blazing full strength for the last six hours or more. When I looked round the corrie at the grey dusk, deepening by little shivering starts into darkness, and saw the cliff loom high and remote behind the murk, I reflected that had all gone well we should now be penetrating the amphitheatre—and upward bound for wide acres of rock and snow, be confidently fetching out our night-light. For once in my life I felt grateful to brittle ice and thankful for a last-minute failure.

The remedy, always to keep torch and battery separate until required, is too obvious to need labouring. It is such attention to detail that distinguishes efficiency from 'bad luck' on mountains.

The First Winter Ascent

Good Friday is always a fine day. In anticipation of this Mackenzie and I planned our final attempt on Deep-cut chimney for Good Friday 1939. We were justified. The stars sparkled from a clear night sky when we left Glasgow at six a.m.; when we reached Glencoe hard frost and bright sun illumined the white face of the mountain world. Neither Dunn nor MacAlpine was free to climb, but otherwise the prospect was perfect. We reached the northern corrie at eleven o'clock with eight hours of daylight before us, and sat down on a warm slab to have second breakfast. I had brought a tin of sardines, and the high traditions of its species were upheld when the key broke. The time that can be wasted on an unopened tin of sardines is phenomenal. Realizing the danger of the situation we attacked with our ice-axes and triumphantly forced the lid while the sun was still high. The sardines by this time were sardines no more, as the rocks for yards around bore witness. But the tin had been opened.

At eleven-thirty a.m. we climbed the frozen slopes under the chimney, and looking up, saw with astonishment what was waiting for us. The character of the route had completely altered. Little rock and no snow save in patches were visible. From top to bottom the chimney was one long ribbon of gleaming ice, blue, grey, and white. We could form no idea whether any of the pitches would go. It looked most unlikely. One could only hope and try.

We agreed to lead alternately and then tied up on a hundred feet of rope. Under the influence of Dr. J. H. B. Bell I had come to suspect that many a stretch of rock or ice, blithely described as perpendicular, is in fact less so than it seems. The theory was probable enough to be worth investigating; therefore I had brought a clinometer with me to measure the *average* angle of the pitches. Thus the first of these was proved sixty-three degrees (I should have thought sixty-eight degrees) and on this Mackenzie opened his innings with half an hour of stylish axe-work. The ability to climb on steep ice with any appearance of grace, when holds must be cut one-handed and one's nose is not more than a few inches from the slope, is rarely seen and can be won only through long practice. Mackenzie at his best, and given good ice, can display a rhythmic motion most fascinating to watch; as Hazlitt says of such art: 'There is something in all this which he who does not admire may be quite sure that he never really admired anything in the whole course of his life. It is skill surmounting difficulty and beauty triumphing over skill.'

When Mackenzie's head came level with the top of the pitch, he stopped. He looked ahead for a few moments and then said that he did not think the second pitch would go. He was doubtful about the result of our climb, for the pitches would all be lengthened by the small depth of snow in the bed of the chimney. He therefore climbed down and asked me to go up and say what I thought. On putting my head over the top I was surprised to find that the second pitch, which had given us hard axe-work on our last visit, was in fact a 'pitch' no longer. It must have been formed before simply by an accumulation of snow and ice where the chimney steepened for several feet. Now it was merely a brief steepening of angle, and the true second pitch was the old third pitch. It looked grim. Height forty feet. The rock overhang was draped with icicles, while the right-hand wall of the gully, by which the overhang must be avoided, looked glazed and nasty. However, I could see no wisdom in retiring without an attempt on it. We had come prepared for severities—and here they were.

Being now above the first ice-wall I took over the lead, and was delighted to find upon the ice a tongue of shallow snow, hard as iron, on which I cut a staircase of three-inch notches, until a hundred feet higher we came to the next impending obstacle—that summer overhang of high renown. The shortage of snow left it much higher than upon our last visit, and the overhang was prominent thirty feet above; but the quantity of ice would have satisfied the most querulous. The angle of the lower half was seventy-seven degrees (without a clinometer I should have said 'vertical'), and we were glad to use specially short axes—slater's picks with the side-claws removed—which we find of great value in the cramped space of an ice-choked crack or chimney, where a swing with a full-size axe is hardly possible. Mackenzie attacked at first with two-handed vigour. His ashen shaft flashed as he opened his shoulders and the well-struck blows went home. A sharp crack as the pick drove in —a gout of white spray. The ice split and splintered. The tinkling fragments flew outward and whirred past my head, their hum rising in pitch as they shot into the void. Whenever he moved on to the first holds balance became delicate; his initial violence gave place to forearm and wrist strokes with the short axe, and as he gained height to a mere patient picking, which accounts for the length of time that such climbing demands. He climbed fifteen feet and retired. I again took over the lead and completed the route to the overhang, where I found a shallow recess of pure ice. I wedged myself between two pillars of ice at the back and brought up Mackenzie. He halted only to remove his rucksack and was then able, safely belayed by myself, to skirt the overhang on the right wall and cut up a curtain of grey ice to the top.

Mackenzie was now in high feather and constantly gave vent to a piercing whistle, whose tune, if any, was too shrill to be detected by merely mortal ears. Meanwhile, I paid out the rope and sat back on the icy scaffolding. There is an undeniable thrill in gazing out, like an eagle from its eyrie, through the slit of a lofty chimney. I felt it keenly as I glanced down to the sun-bright cup of the corrie. That plain view of the sweep of the snow-fields between torn crags is stamped in my mind with peculiar intensity. I can recall it clear and sharp at will, visualize a fragile snowflake on the wall and the sinuous curve of a drift in the corrie, when many a more noble panorama, which I thought unforgettable, has grown dim and misty.

The confined space of a gully may appear at a disadvantage, but within the smaller field of vision, whether the sun shine upon a filagree of frost, burnish a further crag, or flood some distant moor and river, one observes a quality in sunlight that cannot be properly seen in the open; one sees a peculiarly rich and mellow glow, which in open country is absorbed into the landscape and lost to the eye. In fact, one more clearly observes sunlight's inherent beauty.

After brooding by myself for ten minutes I heard Mackenzie call me upward. We had already spent an hour on the pitch, so, relying on his rope-belay, I climbed swiftly on precarious holds to economize time. I discovered him, beaming all over and gaily whisking in my rope round an ice-axe, barely two inches of which were sunk into a strip of snow-ice. It appalled me into a quick heart-beat—until I found that snow tough enough to hold a ton weight. This absence of snow in the bed of the gully added to the tenseness of the climbing. One might never rest at ease between pitches, for the ice-layer was thin and foothold rarely more than a few inches deep. Every step of the climb had to be cut with the axe. We could not tell from one half-hour to the next, when we might be defeated. On the other hand, the brisk air seemed to brace us up throughout the day, and after our first hesitation we felt absurdly optimistic.

The snow in the chimney now became better and we went up speedily to the third pitch. This we regarded as the crux of the climb, since we had failed to get up before. A tape-like runnel of snow-ice, glossy and concave, rose gently from our feet and swept upward, quickly rising to verticality until forty feet above our heads it bent forward in a cornice. Above the cornice was a low rock overhang. There were thus two overhangs, one of snow and the other of rock. Thus far we had passed over many a short bulge not included in clinometer readings, but this forty-foot overhang could be climbed direct only in the bar-parlour of a highland inn.

It was my turn to lead, and no other course being possible, I climbed to the centre of the concavity and then traversed on to the left wall of the gully. Straggling veins of black ice streaked the rocks, which stood out as a cheerful red between the white runnel and the blue sky. Higher up, a left-flanking buttress fell back and allowed the sunlight free play in the more open part of the gully ahead. I felt as though about to emerge from a region 'numbed by the slow snow-breath' into a rocky paradise of warmth and laughter.

The golden promise of the upper gully so filled me with *élan* that I made short work of an otherwise nasty wall, and drew level with the cornice that crowned the pitch. To continue up the wall was impossible. I tried and found that the ice was good enough where it bulged and bad to disappearing point where it did not bulge. The only route open to me was to traverse round a rib on the wall on to the overhang. It was from this particular move that I shrank. Quite apart from mountaineering principles, every instinct recoiled from such a step. To tread upon a cornice near the top of a steep gully is to shout aloud for disaster. Owing to the various shortcomings of the rock, the step was, moreover, a wide one: three and a half feet across the angle of a corner.

I asked Mackenzie what he thought of this predicament. A question purely rhetorical, asked for the satisfaction of making my own violent reply. Mackenzie tried to conceal an amused grin and studiously ignored me; very wisely he would encourage me neither way. I leaned round the rib and prodded the cornice with my axe. Its back, at least, was blue ice thickly hoared. There was a narrow joint between the ice and the rock behind. With all my strength I then hit the cornice a full blow with my axe-head. Not a move. It was like hitting granite.

Provided I could step on to the *back* of the cornice, then for once a rule might be justifiably broken. But the whole difficulty of the move lay precisely in stepping on the back rather than the front; for there were no pull-in holds on the rib to support me while I swung round out of balance. I worked out a method—speed and counter-press—but that cornice did look alarming. Reason said: 'Do it! It 's safe.' Instinct said: 'Don't. The cornice and you will collapse outward.' I tried to rely on detached judgment rather than the instinct of self-preservation. On that I acted. I leant round the rib, drove my axe into the joint behind the cornice, and swung round the rib in a crouching position—balance retained by a press on the rib with one hand and a pull on the axe with the other. Then my foot came on the cornice, my main weight still on the rib. Looking between my legs, my eye went down to our morning snow tracks below the chimney. I let go the rib, flung my whole weight on to the foot on the cornice, at the same instant whipping the axe-pick into a crack in the rock above. There was never a safer cornice in all Scotland. A few more awkward movements and the pitch was climbed. Mackenzie joined me. The way was clear to the amphitheatre.

The most urgent question before us was whether we should find the amphitheatre a cul-de-sac. But our natural desire to quicken the pace was frustrated, for though the gully rose uninterrupted for a hundred feet, the ice in its bed was so thin that everywhere the glazed rock showed through. This unpleasant state persisted until we penetrated to the snows of the amphitheatre, which we found to be a beautiful little cirque ringed by warm brown walls—a hanging corrie in the midst of the cliff. The time was three p.m., and thus far we had spent three and a half hours on the climb, two-thirds of which still lay ahead.

The amphitheatre was filled with downward-tilting snow and backed by a high crag, from which the snowfield had shrunk away to leave a twenty-foot chasm. We stood beside the brink and surveyed the scene.

To our front and left we were truly walled in; the only breach was a forty-foot crack, lacquered in black ice and therefore impossible; to our right, a snowy belt of more broken rock offered a feasible escape over the north-west rim. We were then frankly jubilant and indulged in a joyous half-hour. Sitting like horsemen astride the lip of the chasm, we voraciously consumed our first meal for ten long hours and gave free rein to merriment over past failures. It is an odd thing in mountaineering that misfortune in retrospect provokes more mirth than success; discomfort is but a sorry competitor against humour on the time-track. We wound up the feast with a panegyric on the vanquished chimney and regret at the absence of Dunn and MacAlpine.

When put to the test, our chosen route of escape yielded readily and we emerged at last on the upper face. Projecting everywhere through the snow were bare ribs, broad walls, and low ridges. They were mingled in a general confusion and gave us heavy work but not technical difficulty. The choice of route was wide, but to avoid dead ends it was very necessary to select the way as far ahead as possible. No such care is required in summer.

In one hour we climbed six hundred feet above the amphitheatre. Thus far we had found the appeal of this superb climb to lie in its variety. First, three and a half hours of severe ice in the chimney, then as a pleasant change a long scramble unroped on an interestingly complex face: ice, rock, and snow in perfect proportion. We both thought that this twelve-hundred-foot route ranked next to Crowberry gully as the second-best winter climb in Glencoe.

Mackenzie and I were enjoying ourselves so much that a short way beneath the summit we turned and climbed back down the cliff. Choosing a discontinuous series of shelves, grooves, and gullies on a course further to the north, we made a tortuous descent to within two hundred feet from the corrie; when suddenly the mountain unmasked its batteries.

We were most luckily traversing a ledge under protection of an overhang when there came from above an ominous crash. Through the twilight there whizzed three feet above our heads an enormous boulder. It hummed and sang as it shot into the darkening corrie. A whiff of grape-shot followed; then all was still. One round only. I like to think of it as a shot fired in celebration: to commemorate a first ascent and to mark the close of a year's campaign.

6 *Rubicon Wall*

I HAVE NO WISH to embroil myself in that well-tried topic of the debating chamber: 'To travel hopefully is a better thing than to arrive'; but let me say, non-committally, that whether these words be true or not of the spires of El Dorado, they are not infrequently true of Ben Nevis in summer. A mist-cap and a rain-blanket, ample enough to dampen a Vesuvius, keep the mountain cool, too cool, in the heat of summer, the rocks too often slippery to the numbed hand, and Rubicon Wall unvisited.

By the summer of 1937, no second ascent, since the first by A. T. Hargreaves four years earlier, had been made of the Rubicon Wall on Observatory buttress. The route was classed as 'very severe,' and was thought to be the hardest on Nevis. Its neglect arose from the difficulty in getting the right party on to the mountain at the right time; for Rubicon Wall is throughout a slab-climb, impregnable in rain and amenable only to rubbers on dry rock.

In late July 1937 there came a west highland heat-wave. The right weather had at last arrived, and after an exchange of telegrams the right party assembled one evening in the Nevis hut. Mackenzie and MacAlpine came straight from the Cuillin. They were lean from much climbing and brown as niggers. In place of Dunn I was able to bring with me from Glasgow Douglas Scott, the most beautifully stylish rock-climber who has ever tied himself to my rope. It seemed too much to expect that the weather would hold. Yet the night came warm but not sultry, and the 1st of August dawned with a tropical brilliance.

At sunrise I climbed Carn Mor Dearg to get photographs of the cliffs while the sun was on them. I returned to the hut for breakfast, to find Scott scanning a guide-book.

'What do you think we should climb?' he asked innocently.

We all cleared our throats simultaneously, and save that I was a bar ahead, the answer came in four-syllable harmony.

We turned out at ten o'clock and went up the left bank of the Allt a' Mhuilinn, from which we diverged rightward into the wide bay between the Observatory and Tower ridges. From the back of this bay there arose a thousand feet to the summit the broad mass of Observatory buttress, whose left half constitutes Rubicon Wall. The wall looked very slightly less vertical than the Rannoch Wall of Buachaille; its pale face was coloured the same faint tint of red. There all comparison ended, for Rubicon Wall was twice as high, and here were no grooves or incut holds, but a rumpled sheet of smoothest porphyry.

After a short ascent upon screes we climbed on to a snow-field, which hung like a white apron from the cliffs. So far as home mountains are concerned, an August heat-wave is an odd time for snow-climbing and we had not thought an ice-axe necessary. But as the snow very considerably steepened as we neared the rocks, and as the surface was hard as a board, I found myself creeping sideways on my edge-nails and wishing that I had an axe for braking purposes.

We had aimed toward the left of the wall at a yellowish rib, which marked the start of our route. This lay close to the unclimbed gully that split Rubicon Wall from Observatory ridge. On approaching the foot of our rib we found our way unexpectedly barred by a *randkluft*, a chasm forty feet deep and six feet wide between the snow and the cliff. It circled the whole width of the buttress like a moat around a fortress. Its formation there was probably less due to melting by the radiation of warmth from the rock, for little sunshine ever strikes the base of the buttress, than to a downward sliding of the entire snow-field.

The obstacle it opposed was a serious one. For a while it seemed that we might have to withdraw. The thin lip of the *randkluft* overhung and could not be trusted as the spring-board for a standing jump. Further to the right, where the lip was broken, a jumper would arrive on unclimbable rock. We made a close inspection to see whether one might lower a man into the blue depths with prospect of his climbing the rock from the bottom. We saw, then, that close to our rib the snow-lip was thicker. It seemed likely to bear the weight of a man with a margin of safety. As the lightest member of the party, Mackenzie was delegated to try the jump.

We roped up—myself second, MacAlpine third, and Scott last. I took up position six feet below the *randkluft* and Mackenzie balanced like a tight-rope walker on the upcurled rim. His landing platform was a two-inch foothold, with a handrail of smaller holds on the wall above. He eyed these with pardonable hesitation, braced up and measured his distance most carefully; then again wavered, like a reluctant bather on a cold day. Suddenly he leaped: a perfect landing. He clung for a second, as if surprised at his own success, then moved slightly leftward and more slowly climbed the rib to a stance fifty feet up.

There was room up there for no more than two men at a time, therefore we in turn made the jump and moved up only as accommodation in that transit area allowed. With one exception it was the most commodious stance of the climb and boasted the first of the day's two rock-belays.

We followed the rib, which is distinguished from the mass of the wall not by protuberance but rather by its creamy tinge, for but a short way further. Its trend brought us to a saucer-like stance at the edge of the unclimbed gully, into whose bleak recesses I looked closely for the first time. I saw a series of overhanging pitches, wet, water-worn and in high degree forbidding. As a summer route it seemed blankly impossible. In winter—who can tell? Its ascent will be the most brilliant feat in the history of Scottish mountaineering.

Further ascent on our present line seemed no longer feasible, and Mackenzie traversed along a ledge to our right. It grew more and more narrow, until at last it faded out in a taint score on the wall. When he could go no further I followed after, to give whatever moral support he might draw from my presence; for the place was exposed and there was no rock-belay. He turned straight up on a high-arching slab, with the utmost difficulty gaining five feet in height; but all his efforts were frustrated by the polish of the rock. I had, indeed, never before seen rock of such metallic hardness: when kicked with a boot it rang like the steel plate of a ship. Mackenzie came down and we retired along the ledge until we could again balance without handhold.

'It 's rubbers or nothing from now on,' said Mackenzie, 'and you 'll have to carry my boots as well as your own.'

I shouted 'Boots off!' down the rope. Then we fetched out our rubbers and I stowed our two pairs of boots in my rucksack, which now weighed a good twelve pounds.

The sun was beating full upon us, and one might say reverberated from the rock like sound from a gong. We removed our shirts, and only the already alarming bulge of my rucksack persuaded us to retain our breeches. When all was ready we traversed back to the edge of Zero gully and Mackenzie attacked the refractory slabs from a new angle, this time with complete success.

For the next two hundred feet we described a curving course over the slab-sea, cautiously balancing up from one rounded hold to another, rarely if ever finding a notch and never an edge or splinter for grasping fingers. The principal task of one's hands was simply that of maintaining, by sense of touch waist-high on the rock-surface, one's sense of equilibrium; and for the rest, by down-press of the palms, aiding the feet. As with all true buttresses the rock was indefinite, and the exact line of our route impossible to describe. On Rubicon Wall, however, the rock is everywhere severe, and our problem was not that of choosing the best route from many alternatives, but of finding any route at all. For that reason I believe that we could never have been very far from Hargreaves's original line.

All this while we were moving gradually away from the unclimbed gully until we took to an incipient gully or groove on our right. After climbing a short way up its right wall we were forced to make an awkward stride across the groove to the left wall, then to recross to the right wall and climb a vertical or even overhanging edge. The movements were all airy and nasty ones. One could not tell, from one movement to the next, whether the rock just ahead was climbable.

After two hours of such climbing, during which we met not one belay, I felt thankful that the tail of the party was not less strong than the head; little save purely moral assistance of the rope could have been given to any weaker member of the team. But the greater responsibility lay with Mackenzie; the higher we went the more clear it became that should he lay an incorrect course, and bring his party to an impasse, our plight would not bear thinking upon. Without rock-belays, to rope down was impossible; and to climb down——! Suspense mounted as the issue continued unresolved. I conceived a great respect for those who made the first ascent.

At one o'clock we arrived at the first genuine ledge of the climb. It could not have appeared more opportunely. A traverse had become essential. From furthest east to west Rubicon Wall upreared in a final rampart of a hundred and forty feet. Directly in front no weakness invited assault. One's inclination was to trend toward the unclimbed gully, where the rock, being overlooked by Observatory ridge, wore a less exposed air; but there the ledge appeared to lead only to the base of a rectangular face, high and grey as the hull of a man-of-war. We had no choice but to traverse to the right in search of Hargreaves's route.

In the meantime, MacAlpine and Scott were strung out for a hundred feet on the slabs below. We therefore indulged in the luxury of a seat upon a square-cut block, reflecting that after all we had done well to retain our nether garments, and waited there for the party to reassemble. I watched them critically as they gathered on the ledge. In their tanned skin and tatters, stripped to the waist, three civilized men never looked more like pirates from the Spanish Main. Mackenzie in particular, sitting cross-legged on his stone quarter-deck, had the alert carriage and predatory mien of an Elizabethan sea-captain.

Our situation remained too doubtful to lend itself to free conversation, and after the exchange of no more than a few pleasantries Mackenzie and I departed westward along the ledge. The ledge quickly thinned to a crease and petered out at the centre of the wall on rocks that were none the less still traversable. We stopped. The continuation of Hargreaves's route lay farther to the right, but more directly overhead, on a wall that rose close to the vertical for a hundred and forty feet, were indented two shallow grooves, about twenty feet apart. A third of the way up, each came to a clean-cut end at the base of a swollen slab.

'If we could get up there it would be a new variation,' observed Mackenzie. 'But God knows if it would go.'

'If you like the look of it,' I answered, 'have a try. If ever you were in form it 's to-day.'

Mackenzie cast a brooding glance upward. Suddenly his eye caught fire. 'Come on,' he said, 'it 's in the bag.'

We went up to a small corner at the base of the left-hand groove. It now seemed vertical and not a little exposed, but Mackenzie found a way up until brought to a halt at twenty feet. All further efforts failed. His descent of the groove presented an unpleasant problem; for there were no handholds on which he could lean out to see his footing, while the angle was so steep that to lean out was imperative. He therefore drove in a ring-spike and roped down.

We consulted. I urged him to try again farther to the right, not explicitly suggesting where. We moved twenty feet along to the second groove and Mackenzie climbed fifty feet to its terminus. He gave a loud 'Ha!' of delighted surprise, and shouted over his shoulder, 'There 's a belay!'—the second belay of the day's climbing.

He drew in my rope and I went up to find him ensconced on a foot-plate, which was cut like the half-section of a crow's-nest. It was the only break in the upper face and would take only one of Mackenzie's feet. I placed my own foot on his and clung on while he tied me to a small spike. There followed some intricate contortions while he won clear of entanglement; then he climbed to the slab overhead.

The groove had been difficult enough, but the slabs were of an altogether different quality. Despite his sure movement Mackenzie's climbing of them was, to speak modestly, sensational. I stood on one foot, body and face hard against the wall, and paid out the rope as I watched him balancing above, stealing up the rock, occasionally pausing before gliding onward. Often my only view of him was a pair of heels stereoscoped against blue sky. I saw his body, incredibly foreshortened, only when he turned to one side or the other. As though sighted along a rifle-barrel, my eye lay close to the rope, which after sixty feet hung straight from his waist and clear of the rock, and tapered as does a white roadway into the distance of a plain—an effect that added greatly to his apparent height and loneliness.

He disappeared. Ten minutes of electric tension dragged to an end. Ninety feet of rope had run out. Then from far above came the faintest of shouts. The words were indistinct, but I knew every inflection of Mackenzie's voice, and the tone was jubilant. He was up!

I lost no time in fetching up MacAlpine and in his favour thankfully abdicated my uneasy station. Mackenzie was by then ready for me and I ventured up with high expectations. Nor was I disappointed. The slabs were built up in a series of very severe mantelshelves, widely spaced and usually shaped like inverted saucers, tilting outward. The rock was hard and sleek as marble, so that whatever the skill of a climber no boot-nail could have stayed on the rock. Here was the purest of balance climbing: handholds at discount; complete reliance reposing in the friction of feet and the carriage of head and body.

In consequence I laboured under a disadvantage from the agonizing drag of my twelve-pound rucksack. Four hundred feet below was the gaping mouth of the *randkluft*, and I could see right into it. The typical move, which stays in mind with all the freshness of the day's encounter, was that of hoisting myself up to a mantel by the down-press of my right palm, of lodging the left foot on that same mantel at hip-level, and then, without further handhold, straightening the left leg, my sense of balance preserved by hands fluttering up the wall above and the right toe lifting against the wall below. I discovered, too, why Mackenzie had paused from time to time—to draw a deep breath at the end of each movement.

Rubicon Wall suddenly ended on a broad stone-strewn ledge, from which the last six hundred feet of Observatory buttress fell back to the plateau. My first thought, as I stepped on to the ledge, was to congratulate Mackenzie on a great lead.

Now that our goal of pilgrimage was happily assured, and we might descry the celestial city of our mountain-top, my second thought was to cast off my load of worldly cares—of total weight twelve pounds. 'To bear the burden up the breathless mountain flank, unmurmuringly,' is not a virtue I share with Ruskin's Swiss peasant. My third thought went out in compassion for MacAlpine, perched like a stork on his roost below. I signalled him to take up Scott and come on when ready.

While MacAlpine was climbing I had to stand well back to give him a safe belay; but later I obtained a unique photograph of Scott, climbing, as it seemed, out of the very jaws of the *randkluft*. From above, Rubicon Wall reminds me in some ways of looking down from the great dam at Aswan; the rocks and concrete sweep away in the same clean fashion. Rubicon Wall is less even—but twice as high. Upon this down-rush of slabs Scott climbed with a feline flow of movement that enthralled me. I have seen no man so entirely at home on balance climbs.

I could not help noting the contrast of this route with my climb up the Cioch and Crack of Doom, which likewise abounded in slabs. There we ended weary in muscle from wrestling up on minutely inset holds. Here, after four hours' climbing on a more difficult route, we finished as fresh as paint; for we used not arms but feet—balance, not energy. These sheets of porphyry may be smooth, but they are sounder than gabbro, and any man who falls here falls by no defect of the rock. This is the hardest rock-climb I know on Nevis. The course is continuously difficult. Experience in the leader is as vitally important as high skill.

Whenever Scott arrived we coiled the rope and devoted an hour to talk and tobacco. At last we donned our boots and climbed the upper buttress, now broken like the rapids above a fall. Upon the summit plateau we were gently cooled by the faintest stir of air. We could see Ireland and a blue haze that I thought to be the Cheviots of England. But most enchanting of all was the black bristle of the Cuillin, which leap to the eye of a mountaineer as lightning to steel, so that a hundred encircling hills passed unobserved.

Was this, our El Dorado, a better thing than our hopeful pilgrimage? I experienced something of both that day—and still I cannot answer. I think the question is such a vexed one because it is not, in the first place, legitimate. The goal and the way are one; they co-inhere; they are not to be separated.

7 *Defeat*

A December Night on the Crowberry Ridge

IT IS THE CUSTOM of mountaineers to set on record their most successful climbs, but to say nothing of their reverses. The custom is an unfortunate one; there can be no doubt that one may sometimes gain more genuinely valuable experience from defeat than from the most brilliant series of first ascents. This consideration persuades me to set down in writing an unsuccessful attempt, on 13th December 1936, to make the first winter ascent of the Crowberry ridge by way of Garrick's shelf.

With this high task in view, Mackenzie, Dunn, MacAlpine, and myself assembled at Inverarnan on the night of 12th December. The following morning we drove north to Coupal Bridge in Glen Etive, where we discovered that once again Dunn had forgotten his boots. He drove that seventy miles to Inverarnan and back like a rocket, and we finally set out for the Buachaille at ten-thirty a.m. The hour was now late, yet we adhered to our original plans, although a defeat high up at dusk on a rock-snow-ice climb could hardly be contemplated with equanimity. However, the route was well known to us and we felt confident of success. We were all in excellent physical condition, exceptionally well equipped, and yearning for a first-class climb. These factors overcame our good judgment. The morning was cloudy, with the wind in the west-south-west. New snow had fallen overnight but was not lying in sufficient depth seriously to impede our progress to the foot of Crowberry gully, where we encountered a short difficult pitch that whetted our appetite for bigger and better things. Never was an appetite destined to be more harshly glutted.

We now left the gully and moved up the lower rocks of Crowberry ridge, where we traversed a ledge of steeply shelving snow on its northern wall. This movement brought us under the first big pitch of Garrick's shelf. Here we found a cave large enough to accommodate the whole party, and we gulped down our second breakfast hastily before roping up.

The construction of Garrick's shelf is peculiar. It is a narrow trough running up the northern wall of the Crowberry ridge, parallel to the Crowberry gully. The shelf itself, which is punctuated with steep pitches, terminates in precipitous rock some two hundred and fifty feet below the crest of the ridge. This last section, difficult in summer, ends in a steep scoop that debouches on the Crowberry ridge near the base of the Tower.

We found the rocks well plastered with snow, but ice was present only in small quantity—too small quantity, as we discovered later. The snow-covering on steep rock was not sufficiently frozen to hold, and had to be cleared away as we advanced. Our progress was much hindered by fierce blasts of wind from the south-west, which swept down the Crowberry gully and shelf, bearing great clouds of powder snow that completely filled all the holds after each of us had passed upwards. Woollen gloves froze to the holds, and were sometimes difficult to disengage.

Four hours of continuous climbing on the shelf found us at the top of the fourth pitch, at a height of some two thousand seven hundred feet. At this point I took over the lead from Mackenzie, who retired to the end of the rope for a rest. Henceforth the order on the rope was myself with Dunn as second man, then MacAlpine and Mackenzie. The shelf now began to narrow and steepen, while the snow was thinner and in worse condition than ever. The sun had already set, and the upper reaches of the shelf were pervaded by a grey and gloomy twilight. The need for haste had become urgent, yet the next fifty feet of plain, straightforward gully occupied no less than twenty minutes. The difficulty lay simply in persuading the snow to hold. There was no danger of its avalanching.

Garrick's shelf now ended and merged in the steep face of the final rocks. On our right, the shelf fell perpendicularly into the depths of Crowberry gully; on our left rose the vertical wall of the Crowberry ridge; before us the rocks swept up steeply for sixty feet to a small, rectangular tower. This tower was sheathed in black ice and fog crystals. It lent distinction to the place.

Our first problem was a narrow crack set in a corner and packed with snow. My first two attempts on it failed, but a third and more determined effort proved successful, and I climbed the crack by the lay-back method to a small ledge. The time was now four-thirty p.m. The usual route into a square recess at the base of the tower was unjustifiable, on account of its skin of thin ice, and I therefore made an attempt to force the rocks on the left. After a great deal of manœuvring for position, an outward-tilting mantel-shelf plastered with firm snow lying on ice was laboriously overcome. For a moment the position looked promising; on the left only a short wall barred the way to easier rock running past the tower to the crest of the ridge. But my first movement to the left would of necessity be made without handhold, a 'down-and-out' strain being placed upon the feet, the foothold being a sloping slab coated with *verglas*.

I reported my position and the party consulted. The time was now a quarter to five; the weather was rapidly deteriorating; to retire now would spell immediate benightment with the whole of Garrick's shelf below us. On the other hand, only six feet of rock barred the leader from almost certain triumph. The decision we had to make was a grave one. Should or should not that next, very dangerous step be taken? We decided that it should not, and I retired.

Across the black chasm of Crowberry gully the wall of the North buttress was now growing steadily dimmer in the gathering darkness; already the rising storm was roaring across the upper rocks of the Crowberry ridge. Snow was falling steadily, and this was reinforced from time to time by sheets of drift snow, hurled upon us from the rocks above. The situation appeared to be sufficiently desperate, but the party had climbed too long in combination to entertain any doubt of a satisfactory issue. We carried with us three hundred and thirty feet of rope, a torch, spare batteries, and sufficient food. We resolved therefore to continue to climb downwards rather than bivouac.

The descent of the steep section in the snow gully to pitch four was less hazardous than we had expected. The first three, secured by the rope, enjoyed a comfortable passage. They cheerfully urged me to slide, and trust them to field me if need be. I declined, and the party moved down in strictly text-book style to pitch four. A wide square-cut chimney, all three walls of which were vertical, now presented an interesting problem largely complicated by its invisibility. The solution taxed us for two hours, but we finally dug out a spike of iced rock, from which the others roped down, belayed from above. Having seen Dunn safely down and well established, I followed a thought too gaily. For the fixed rope somehow rolled off its hitch above. Down I went with a rush, conscious only of one fat blue spark where a boot-nail struck bare rock. A split second later I landed astride Dunn's shoulders. He was strongly placed, safe and solid as rock itself, and by grabbing my thighs stopped a farther fall. The party was working now at such a high pitch of concentration that we gave the incident not a thought until later.

We were by this time enveloped in darkness. The snow on the shelf and on the surrounding rock could be dimly discerned as a dull grey mantle, far too obscure to afford any indication of the route. We progressed slowly by torchlight. Creeping circumspectly down the shelf over snow and broken rock, we descended as much as a hundred and fifty feet in one and a half hours. Above the uproar of the wind and the flail of careering snow could be heard some unusual noises, which, had we not known each other better, must have sounded suspiciously like profane language. At nine a.m. we reached an open corner at the top of pitch three.

Here we were unable to rope down. There was no rock-belay, and the snow was too unsound to take an axe-belay, but we contrived a good anchor by jamming our axes in an angle of rock. Thus protected we climbed in turn down steep snow to a point near the base of a rock-face. A distinctly tricky traverse to the right then led, after one and a half hours, to soft snow below the pitch. We could not afford to leave an axe behind us, so I went down without a fixed rope. I was coached over the traverse in brilliant style by Dunn, who employed the effective though inhuman device of ruthlessly skewering his victim with the spike of an axe.

We were now back in the trough, hard against the wall of the Crowberry ridge, and descended very slowly to a short chimney that we failed to remember climbing on the way up. A little disconcerted, we climbed down from axe-belays and found ourselves in a narrow cave festooned with giant icicles. This cave was the most comfortable spot on the whole route, and we felt loath to leave it. I hailed the place with great joy, and after ejecting the rest of the party urged disingenuously that any haste in accomplishing the next section would be most unadvisable. From the narrow recesses of the cave I could speculate as to what was happening below, while I watched, with a certain measure of perverted pleasure, the swirling snow pour in hissing cascades over the roof and down the shelf, where my more energetic companions would literally 'get it in the neck.'

Time sped on. For over an hour there had been a great deal of shouting below and singularly little movement. But at long last a faint call from Dunn summoned me downwards. Sixty feet below, we all congregated on what appeared to be a broad horizontal ledge on the Crowberry wall. An eighty-foot rope had been fixed round a spike on the wall itself and Mackenzie, after prospecting the route at the far end of the ledge, had just announced that farther advance was impossible. He was faced, or seemed to be faced, with a bottomless abyss. We had lost the route.

A good twelve hours had now elapsed since our last meal, and the thoughts of the party turned to hot soup and roast pork. With freezing fingers we then extracted from our rucksacks the handfuls of sodden crumbs that had formerly been jam sandwiches. We reviewed our position as we ate, and came to the conclusion that we were now above Garrick's shelf, on a ledge ending in a cul-de-sac. The torch-beam was therefore directed downwards toward the Crowberry gully. After some prospecting a lower route was pronounced practicable.

Our principal concern was whether the fixed rope would reach to the foot of the pitch. Mackenzie, belayed by the others, set off downwards; he went leftward down steep snow, and then swung into the mouth of a vertical shallow chimney. A long period of suspense followed. In half an hour there was still no movement of any kind from below. The party above gradually became aware that it was being kept waiting—a feeling never absent during the entire descent — and wrathfully inquiring howls were directed downwards. Several minutes later a muffled 'What?' drifted upwards, followed after a while by 'Yip!'—whatever that might mean. We gave it up.

Quite suddenly a shout of triumph assured us that our proper route had been regained below pitch two: the vertical chimney was, indeed, on pitch two itself. In half an hour we were all down. The fixed rope refused to run round the spike and was left behind. A further hour of vigilant toil took us all to a big outcrop of rock, which presented a rectangular face to the lower regions of Garrick's shelf. Immediately below us was the last great step in the shelf. We edged carefully round the right-hand corner of the outcrop, and near its base discovered an excellent spike-belay. The snow here was firm but excessively steep, so we stood face-in during the hours that followed.

Our plan was to attach a thirty-foot loop round the spike, to rope down on a hundred and twenty feet of rope, which we fervently hoped would reach the foot of the shelf, and to secure the first man down with a hundred feet of line. This two-hundred-and-fifty-foot maze of rope and line was thereupon possessed by an evil spirit and became tangled in the darkness. The whole shelf resounded with the most powerfully expressive oaths known to man. Incredible delays occurred. Violent bursts of wind-driven snow still came lashing down the shelf,

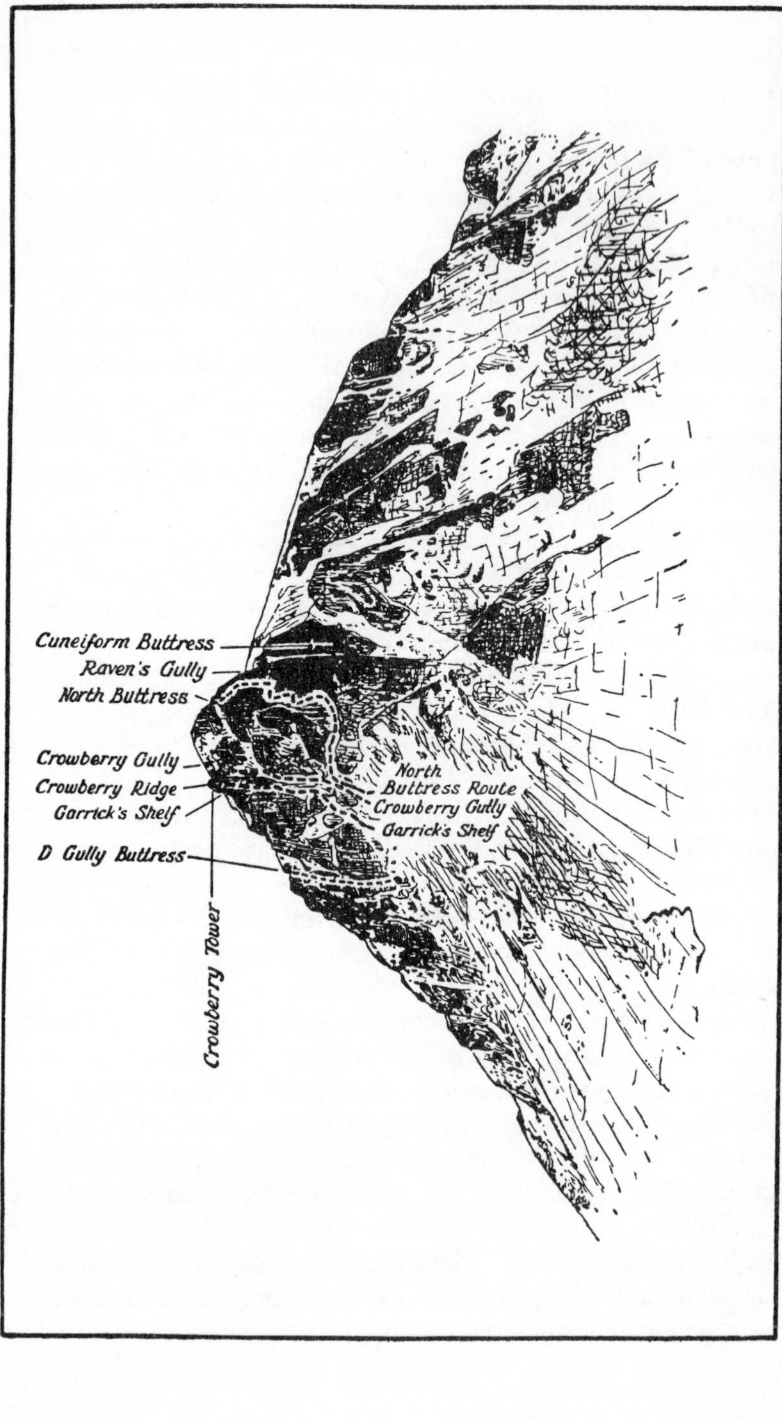

Cuneiform Buttress
Raven's Gully
North Buttress
Crowberry Gully
Crowberry Ridge
Garrick's Shelf
D Gully Buttress
Crowberry Tower
North
Buttress Route
Crowberry Gully
Garrick's Shelf

unendingly, and the last battery in the torch was fading. By wriggling our toes continuously during these halts we contrived to avoid frost-bite.

At four o'clock in the morning everything was ready. One by one we roped down a narrow chimney on the flank of an overhanging bulge. This was appallingly difficult, for the rope declined to run, and our descent resolved itself into an exhausting struggle against friction. The torch was now out of action, so a fitting climax was provided by an awkward left-hand traverse round the bulge from the chimney, a movement that we made unroped, and which led us into the cave below the shelf. Upon reaching the foot of the chimney, I found myself unable to persuade the now obstinately vicious rope to run through the loop. I left it behind, with emotions closely akin to pleasure. When at length I joined the party in the cave, I at once remarked in the bearing and attitude of my companions a striking complacency, the source of which was speedily betrayed by the crumbs adhering to their now incipient whiskers. Thus gorged, these callous people had yet no scruple in demanding bites at my one remaining apple, on the pitiful plea that all their own food was finished.

We roped up on a hundred feet of line. The absence of a torch was a serious handicap, and we experienced no little difficulty in the traverse along the Crowberry wall, where drift snow had piled up on the ledge at a high angle. Shortly afterwards we gained the lower part of the Crowberry gully, where we found our difficult pitch of the previous day miraculously transformed into an easy scramble, but on leaving the gully we unfortunately lost all trace of the usual line of descent.

An hour of prospecting, both up and down, resulted in our finally defying orthodox tactics by committing ourselves to the mercy of an unknown gully, which led us with unexpected ease to the moor. The latter imparted some wholehearted if concluding kicks, and we were all, at one time or another, immersed up to the thighs in bogs. We reached Coupal Bridge at dawn, safe and sound, if not precisely hale and hearty. We had been out for rather less than twenty-one hours, of which fourteen had been spent on the descent.

The moral of this is only too plain. It is one appreciated by none so well as by the party most closely concerned. But our defeat had in no way discouraged us in our determination to make a second attempt under more favourable conditions, when the shelf would be more heavily plastered with ice. By the end of March such conditions obtained and the route was climbed in its entirety.

Garrick's Shelf. The First Winter Ascent

An early start, a small party, good snow and ice, these were essential conditions for a winter ascent of Garrick's shelf. The last consideration delayed our second visit until March blizzards had been followed by a fortnight of sun and frost.

On 28th March 1937 Mackenzie and I arrived at Kingshouse on a perfect morning. A streamer of white mist ringed the Buachaille, whose upper snows were pink in the rising sun. We reached Crowberry ridge to find that from top to bottom, Garrick's shelf was masked in glinting ice—the longest ribbon of clear ice we have ever seen. The ropes we had left behind on defeat were still visible, the cores of transparent pillars two feet thick. We roped up and agreed to lead alternately. We went hard from the start.

In two hours of fast and furious cutting we climbed four hundred feet, passed over four very difficult ice-pitches, and arrived at twelve noon below the crux. This pitch had shrunk to fifty feet. Once again the moderate summer slabs to the left of the pinnacle were glazed and impossible. We attacked to the right on rocks overlooking Crowberry gully. Here, too, the ice was thin; axe-cut holds to the square recess under the pinnacle were painfully minute. Our escape from the recess, made on the pinnacle's right-hand edge, was unusually delicate. Splayed out on this bulging corner we had to change feet on a small sloping hold without handhold, and with a long drop below into Crowberry gully. The pitch was very severe and occupied two hours.

We then arrived in a broad groove which hung over the gully beyond the pinnacle. The groove was choked by an ice-fall of a hundred and fifty feet, twice bulging in fifty-foot pitches, which tried the leaders severely; for the ice was inclined to be brittle and belays poor. At three p.m. we debouched on the crest of Crowberry ridge—a sensational arête arrayed in shark's fins of translucent ice, which we shattered regretfully. Deterred from direct ascent of the Tower by ponderous snows, we traversed southward into D gully and won the summit at four p.m.

Our climb is not one I shall ever repeat in like conditions. It became too exacting. But our day's route led us through snow and ice scenery of deathless beauty. This lives strong in mind, while physical pains and trials, the so-called realities of defeat and victory, have long been forgotten.

8 *Coire Lagain*

I WAKENED AT MIDNIGHT. Although the tent flaps were tied back, I found June air in Skye too warm for a sleeping-bag. There was no moon, but the night was bright. I felt restless, absurdly energetic for such an hour, and had actually struggled out of my sleeping-bag and partially dressed, when I heard the low purr of a car approaching down Glen Brittle. I looked out, and very shortly after heard the swish of tyres and saw headlights glide to a stop two hundred yards away. From the roadway there came an inquiring shout, neither loud nor intelligible, as from one who had no hope of an answer.

I could have sworn that I knew that voice. There flashed upon my inward eye the vista of rock and a white climbing-rope. I pulled on my boots and hastened through the whin to the roadside. To my delight, there stood MacAlpine and his wife! Engaging the Mallaig ferry by telegram, and leaving Glasgow at four p.m., they had come to Skye for a short week-end.

We pitched their tent and brewed coffee. I wish that I could remember now what brand of coffee that was, for no sooner was it down than MacAlpine suggested a climb before breakfast. After his drive of two hundred and forty miles in eight hours, much of it over very bad road, this was more than I had dared to hope. Truly he is one of the elect. We set out at three a.m. for the precipice of Sron na Ciche, and one hour later, in the grey of first light, climbed the gaunt slabs of the Cioch pinnacle.

We returned to camp for breakfast. MacAlpine's visit was a notable occasion—his first visit to the Cuillin. He could afford one day's climbing, and this we had to dispose to best advantage. In other words, where could I introduce him to the Cuillin at their best? I surveyed the entire range, and without hesitation chose the traverse of Coire Lagain. It is the classic short day of the Cuillin, the Cuillin in essence—narrow ridge, distorted rock, 'jagged towers tossed aloft against the sky'—by judicious treatment one of the laziest long days. For our rock-climb to the main ridge we must choose one that combined length with shade from the sun. We had already climbed the gabbro of the Cioch; therefore I proposed the basalt of Sgurr Alasdair.

For a fortnight past the daily temperature had been consistently touching ninety degrees in the shade. We accordingly set off at seven a.m. to reach the shade of the cliffs before the sun grew too hot. We climbed some two thousand feet, passing through Coire na Ciche and crossing the upper lip into a little corrie that cups the green pool of Loch Lagain.

We were now within the most noble rock cirque of Skye. The cliffs of Sgurrs Alasdair, Thearlaich, MhicCoinnich, and Dearg formed a close ring around us, a thousand feet high. Yet there is no gloom in that corrie; rather an atmosphere of gaiety in which has perished many a too arduous plan, checkmated by the care-free waters of Loch Lagain. For though the loch be small, one may dive deep from a rock platform and swim fifty yards; on one side there is even a grass margin—a rare luxury in such a site, charming to the wanderer as the yellow sands of the lotus-eaters. Let a man but once recline there on a hot day, and he will no longer roam.

We skirted the loch and climbed up a long scree-slope to the north buttress. Our earlier notion, to climb by Abraham's route because it was harder, had been censored by the holiday spirit of the corrie. We now chose Collie's route because it was less difficult—and more openly situated. We roped-up and climbed easy slabs, which steepened as the buttress narrowed, until several hundred feet above we went up an abrupt face in whose middle we came upon a small recessed ledge. We sat there, sucked a thirst-abating lemon, and savoured the keen tang of freedom on a mountain wall, from which we looked high over empty space to the jumbled world beneath. Despite the heat the air was fresh and clean. On the glassy surface of Loch an

Fhir-bhallaich, one and a half miles away toward Glen Brittle, we could see the quick rings made by rising fish.

Half an hour later MacAlpine belayed me from the back of the recess, and I gingerly traversed on to the right-hand face. The rock was basaltic and smooth, somewhat exposed but of moderate difficulty. After a delightful little climb we continued steeply to the summit. Just underneath the cairn I was startled into a crouch as an eagle of six-foot wing-span skimmed over the crest. One could clearly see the golden breast-feathers. Eagles were common in Skye that June; one saw them daily, circling round Sgurr Dubh, where it is to be presumed they nested. I never saw more than four in the air at once, and this was the closest view I had yet been allowed.

The summit of Sgurr Alasdair is fairly pointed, but there was room for two of us at the cairn. Our firm intention was to traverse round the rim of the corrie to the Inaccessible Pinnacle of Sgurr Dearg. Meantime, we believed there was no need to hurry. Ten hours of daylight stretched before us. Thus we completely forgot the problem of thirst; for we were now in the full blaze of the sun, and the rocks were already hot to the hand.

We unpacked our rucksacks and disclosed our sandwiches. Within thirty seconds two hopeful gulls hovered overhead. In the Black Cuillin there are none of what an old writer calls 'God's jocund lyttel fowles.' These naked peaks are most frequented by ravens, gulls, hawks, and eagles—above all by the ubiquitous gull. I say ubiquitous advisedly, for a climber in the Cuillin need only stop and open his rucksack, and although not one gull be in sight, within two minutes there will gather a growing congregation to share the feast or pick the crumbs, according as their host keeps open board or niggard.

In such tropical heat our appetite was speedily satisfied, so we descended a few steps northward, and bit by bit threw our surplus bread over the precipice of the stone-shoot, between whose narrow walls a throng of acrobatic gulls performed vertical dives to retrieve the food in mid air. They never pounced as a hawk might, but dropped like stones down the shaft until beneath the falling scraps, when they suddenly stood on their tails, caught the bread, and swooped sideways and out between the gully walls. Not one mistake was made, nor a feather turned wrong.

We returned to the cairn, where I tried to persuade MacAlpine that I could see St. Kilda, the minutest speck on the line where sky and sea divided—a hundred miles north-west. But MacAlpine clung to his privilege as a relative and remained profoundly sceptical. The sea was quite as deep a blue as the Mediterranean in summer. It appeared gently to lean up to the horizon, polished as ice, so that one might well wonder the outer isles did not gravitate back to the mainland. There must have been, none the less, a gentle Atlantic swell, for there were snatches of foam around the shores of Loch Brittle.

A man who has not been to Skye in May or June has not, properly speaking, seen Skye at all; for there is an exquisite quality in the sunlight seen only during the three months after the spring equinox.

The gulls, meantime, observing that no more food was to be had, had taken themselves off and were engaged in harrying the eagle, which now soared over Coruisk. The scene was much like that of fighter aircraft attacking a heavy bomber. The eagle deviated neither right nor left, deranged not a plume nor flapped a wing, but in ponderous calm held to its slow course. The gulls flashed in and out, wove loops, swooped at all angles, at the very last moment changing direction with a flick of tail and wing. Their agility was astonishing. The eagle's impassivity wholly admirable. For it suffered not a few pecks before it passed out of sight behind the Dubh ridge toward Scavaig. Cuillin eagles appear to lead anything but a quiet life. I have rarely seen the wretched birds unharried either by gulls or by ravens.

About one p.m. we began an almost imperceptible drift round the cirque, a sort of northward dawdling rather than scrambling, enlivened by the ascent of Sgurr Mhic Coinnich by King's

Chimney, which ran fifty feet up an open corner to the summit overhang. This last we turned by a traverse on the bare right wall and climbed up to the cairn. Our thirst, which on Sgurr Alasdair had been kept at bay by a lemon, now possessed us ike raging demons.

> O, for a draught of vintage! that hath been
> Cool'd a long age in the deep-delved earth.

It is inevitable that in the gabbro desert of the Cuillin green should most attract the human eye—it is even the green basalt that most strongly attracts the compass needle—and to a thirsty climber there is no more dazzling emerald than Loch Coire Lagain. Looking down upon it from the edge of the main ridge, we saw the cliffs stand round in tall-towered battlements, as though the loch far below were a drop of priceless green nectar that must at all costs be safeguarded. Thus we watched and moved by fits and starts—the long ascent to Dearg became unthinkable—and our last ambition, to scale the Inaccessible Pinnacle, lay in the bottom of the loch with a philosophic brick round its neck. Henceforward, our only possible destination was that green allure below.

Beyond Sgurr Mhic Coinnich the ridge narrowed to an edge. dropped sharply, then broader but riven fell away in a series of high steps to the bealach below An Stac. Some time in the afternoon—one takes no precise note of time in Skye—we launched ourselves down the rapids of the An Stac scree-run, the fastest in the Cuillin, and a few minutes later were projected in a welter of sweat on to the grassy bank of the loch.

We could hardly strip our clothes fast enough, and so parched were our bodies that on going in from the diving-boulder one could positively feel the water soak into the skin, to such effect that our agonizing thirst of a minute before was perceptibly lessened. For half an hour we dived and swam in a wild ecstasy. The delicious sting of chill water reinvigorated our limbs as could no course of massage. I felt that I had never awakened till now to that allegedly familiar quality of water—its wetness. That there was beauty in wetness had hitherto never penetrated my mind. From that moment I have learned the truth, that in fact there is beauty in everything; and that one is not always apt in seeing it. 'A thousand-mile journey begins with the first step,' and the discovery that beauty is in all, and that all beauty is the same beauty, is the first step to the highest peak of the universe.

At length the cold began to penetrate more deeply. We came out, and scrambling up the swelling flank of a slab, basked awhile on the sun-warmed rock. Through half-closed eyes I watched a fleecy cloud sail immeasurably high above the crags. Its snow-whiteness deepened the hue of the firmament, as the grey rock drew out the sheen of Loch Coire Lagain. There was refreshment of mind in the green water, and in the purity of blue sky, rest of heart.

9 *The North Buttress of Buachaille. Winter*

IN EARLY DECEMBER 1937 a great blizzard swept the central highlands. The roads were blocked, the mountains burdened, moor and river buried in deep snow. Then came the frost. On the 12th it broke all records for severity in Argyll. The conditions seemed not yet ripe for climbing in the confined space of rock-ridge or gully, but for MacAlpine and me, attentively hearkening, the hour had struck for a visit to the North buttress of Buachaille Etive Mor. Like Garrick's shelf it is not very difficult in summer, yet in winter conditions good climbing can be expected of it. Here we should not be confined to a narrow shelf but have available for route selection the whole breadth of a buttress. Snow in abundance was inevitable, but on open rocks so early in the season we little imagined that ice would be met in quantity or that any hard test lay in store.

On 12th December we left Glasgow by car two hours before dawn. Despite our wheel-chains and the good work of snow-ploughs in preparing the way, the sun had risen before we swung north-west from the Blackmount, and saw Buachaille. It burned like gold in the furnace. For the sun was still low and glittered across the snow-fields of Rannoch moor, rayed in streaming banners of light over the frozen wind-ripples, leaving blue shadows on the lee-side of drifts.

That was the coldest day I have ever known. The deer stood forlornly by the roadside, or collected in dazed herds around the Kingshouse Inn, pleading to be fed. They were given grain by a stalker. All noise was muffled by the snow, and all the Campbells in Scotland might have marched through the glen and no footfall given the alarm. The world had sunk into a numbed stupor. Even the thermometer that hangs outside the inn had given up the unequal struggle, and after recording its lowest possible, had withdrawn its thin red line within the bulb. Less ancient instruments elsewhere recorded eight degrees below zero (Fahrenheit), and the anti-freeze mixture in MacAlpine's car engine went solid before the day was out. To conclude these curious effects, unusual at least in my own short lifetime, the metal door-handle of the inn stuck to our bare fingers.

Although mercifully spared the usual delay of Dunn's hurtling southward for boots, we lost no little time in examining this strange new world, in photography, and in listening to our curiously muted voices. Ten o'clock was upon us before our preparations were complete and we set off toward Buachaille. The mountain was a uniform white. Not a black spot sullied the glare. We spent the first one and a half hours in wading through snow-fields and threading an icy maze among the lower crags. Not until we traversed towards Curved ridge and the ash-tree did we meet our first and surprising check. Confronting us was the waterslide, upon which one walks unthinkingly in summer, now bulging large in bosses of blue ice. The connecting ledge, which overlooks a drop of twenty feet, was invisible under a mass of white ice inclining from the wall above. We had no choice but to rope up and spend half an hour's step-cutting, and I went at it like a buccaneer digging pieces of eight. Not a moment was wasted.

Beyond the waterslide we moved straightway into the foot of Crowberry gully, which severs Crowberry ridge from the North buttress. Good snow, surface-glazed, led us rapidly upward for a few hundred feet to a fifteen-foot rock-pitch, whose embarrassing defence was frail snow superimposed on *verglas*. In consequence of such delays on the easier slopes of the mountain it was twelve-thirty p.m. before we drew level with the east wall of the North buttress. Not having fed for seven hours, and the cold having put a keen edge to our appetites, we each scooped an arm-chair in the gully and sat down to second breakfast.

Ten feet above our heads a ledge like an unrailed balcony girdled North buttress to Raven's gully, which demarcated the west side. For three hundred feet above that ledge the buttress rose abruptly, then gently curved back on its thousand-foot flight to the summit. Provided that I made no error in route selection we had ample time to pass well beyond the steepest section before sundown, and nearer to the summit we might rely on strong moonlight. Even MacAlpine was satisfied with our prospects, and he is renowned for his level-headed common sense. To climb in his company is a guarantee that a lively breeze will fill the sails of the party all day, but no high-flown ideas, no extravagant propositions cut any ice with him.

At one o'clock we roped up and climbed on to North buttress balcony. It was paved with a thick layer of sea-green ice, which dipped gently outward. The angle was just enough to make walking impossible. I plied my axe for a quarter of an hour, and in one run-out of rope (eighty feet) crossed the ice-band to a narrower continuation of the ledge. It was heavily snow-banked. We traversed to Raven's gully in search of the line of least resistance and finally returned to a corner crack near Bottleneck chimney. The crack was choked with snow. But for previous summer knowledge we should never have guessed that there was a route hereabouts. The buttress wall had everywhere an even coat.

I confess that beguiled by previous visits I had underestimated the whole climb, and was not keyed up to a piece of mountaineering quite out of the ordinary. That first crack gave me a rude awakening. It was hard, very hard, requiring a full hour and a run-out of ninety feet. Those who know the route only in summer will be amused to hear that I found still greater difficulty in finding above the crack any stance to which I could bring MacAlpine. The old roomy platforms were there no longer. MacAlpine, disconsolate below, began to growl a little and I brought him up for company, if for nothing else; his fund of humour could cheer the most afflicted climber.

Having made the best of a bad job and dispensed with a belay, we found that further progress straight up had become impossible, and that we must execute a delicate left traverse across a face. The rope was here no protection and MacAlpine began to calculate the days of grace on his unpaid premiums, but we accomplished the move and the rock began to look easier. This turned out to be an optical illusion. The rock became in fact more difficult. Ten precious minutes were wasted in a vain effort to get up a tempting corner, which would have straightened out our route; instead the trend of the crags pushed us more and more toward the left, until at last we overlooked Crowberry gully.

The mouth of the gully seemed like an icy courtyard, walled and turreted a thousand feet by ridge and buttress. We have never seen the fantastic grandeur of its winter rock scenery matched by any other gully in Scotland. Directly opposite to us Garrick's shelf stirred our recollections of a year ago, and we suddenly realized that this was the anniversary of our defeat. I hastily looked at my watch, but believing that there was still time to spare I described my subsequent ascent with Mackenzie, which was the hardest five hours I ever spent on a mountain. To-day the shelf was burdened with soft snow.

Our ten minutes' reminiscence was not without bearing on our climb: we became too anxious to waste not a further moment in following the route of least resistance, and that soon led to the error we had most need to avoid. Meantime we climbed a short crack and flake and then had two long run-outs of rope, but still there was no sign of the buttress yielding; and the day was wearing on. It became clear that the left flank of the buttress was going to be too much for us. Therefore we traversed ledges back to the centre of the buttress. The walls above rose in either rectangular steps or swelling slabs, covered even where vertical in snow with the sheen and pile of ermine. It was beautiful to the eye, but hardly gladdening, for the labour of cleaning and climbing such rock seemed destined to be lengthy. It was then that we came upon a groove running straight as an arrow up the cliffs. It looked moderately difficult.

I knew from experience that rock faults are often the worst routes. They are always the most inviting; they wear the very aspect of weakness. Into that trap I fell headlong, not stopping in my keenness to save time to reflect that if thin ice were to be found anywhere on the buttress it would most likely be here. Intelligence is as indispensable as an ice-axe in winter. However, one is wise after the event. The fact was that on looking up the groove I could see no ice in the lower part, whereas there appeared every promise of quick climbing. If there were ice further up, why, no doubt I could deal with it. Truly the 13th December is my bad day.

At two-thirty p.m. I started up the groove. From my own point of view all went well for twenty feet, but MacAlpine was not so happily placed. I swept the holds with my gloved hand, dislodging cataracts of snow on to his wrathful head. On the second twenty feet the difficulties mounted and progress sadly dwindled; the rock required study and no little imagination to combine its properties to advantage. On the third twenty feet I at last met black ice.

Melted by the sun, snow-water had trickled into the groove and frozen, spreading over the rock in a thick varnish. However, could I climb fifteen feet further, there seemed a possibility of my forcing an exit from the groove. I chipped out several notches and found them deep enough to support the edge-nail of a boot. I eased myself on to them, using for the hands press-holds against the sides of the groove. The cutting of further notches, while trusting only to a precariously placed boot-nail, which might be displaced by one quiver of the leg, proved an operation more delicate than I liked. To avoid the slightest body movement one had to tap the ice gently as though breaking toffee with a silver hammer. The carving of a hold occupied ten minutes. I cut three and climbed up.

'Ten feet of rope left and the sun has set!' yelled MacAlpine. 'What is it like?'

I estimated another hour to force the exit and get MacAlpine up. Were the ice to thin in the slightest degree it would become impossible. I carried no piton and should therefore be unable to descend in bad light. But *did* the ice thin out? It was furred with snow and invisible. That decided me.

'It is magnificent,' I shouted back, 'but it is not mountaineering. I 'm coming down.'

But that was easier said than done. My lower body prevented my seeing the ice notches, nor could I lean out and look down backward for them. They had to be felt for with insensitive boot-nails after a gentle lowering of the body from a gradually, very gradually bended knee. Widely spaced holds, or a muscle tremor from long standing in one-nail steps, would have earned a summary verdict in the courts of mountain justice. Resisting temptation, I had cut these holds close and happened to be in perfect training. I therefore won acquittal from the ice and faced the trial of the central section—when, like a last-minute galloping of horses and the waving of a reprieve before the aggrieved nose of a hanging judge, there appeared a small spike on the outside wall of the groove. Before the vision might dissolve my rope was round it. A few minutes later I had roped down and joined MacAlpine on the ledge.

We looked eastward to estimate from the closing in of dusk the daylight left to us. Many miles across the moor of Rannoch the breath of frost had lain all day in a transparent haze; in the morning, suffused with sun, like a pall of gold-dust; in the afternoon like faintest pearl; now, with the setting of the sun, it spread from the furthest fringe toward the middle moor, blue as peat smoke at dawn. We calculated that we had still half an hour of good daylight to do something decisive.

MacAlpine must have been almost frozen to death during that last hour and a half, and being a sociable animal, obliged to freeze without company, might without blame have grown despondent and pessimistic. Hope makes a good breakfast but a bad supper. However, as always when I most need support, MacAlpine became most cheerful and confident. Instead of pronouncing for retreat he now backed me up in deciding to make a quick attack elsewhere. It sounded as if long standing on exposed and ice-bound ledges was the chief delight of his life. I was waiting for him to say that I was climbing like a chamois, but he disappointed me.

It was agreed that should I fail to find a route quickly we should begin roping down the buttress in the fading light as best we could. At four p.m. we traversed ninety feet westward with a bout of step-cutting on icy ledges. I chose the face of one high square block and swept off the snow with my arm. Small square holds began to emerge. The route was not too apparent, but neither was ice. I went up, clinging, scraping, excavating, mounting higher and higher until I passed that fifteen-foot wall and the one beyond and the slabs that followed them. It would be hard for me to say how difficult this part actually was; for I had taken the bit between my teeth and was keyed up to the fighting pitch that makes subsequent classification an impossibility. At the middle section I traversed high-angle rock on one-nail foothold without handhold, yet did not find the move awkward; although MacAlpine, who was properly not wasting time when he followed, took a vigorous pull or two on the rope. I was thankful for his workmanlike intelligence.

The light of day was still with us when the buttress became noticeably more broken. The exact art of precision climbing in the groove had no place here; honest hard toil and little more gained us seventy feet of height in thirty minutes. These slabs and walls, so deceptively smooth under fluffy blankets of snow, began to bristle on the slightest cleansing, so that we were soon able to move together, which we did with celerity whenever one-handed climbing had become a bare possibility. Intersecting ledges grew more numerous, one could easily evade obstacles to pick the easier line of advance, and the angle of the cliffs fell back.

Meanwhile the twilight had darkened into night, but before the last light drained from the snow the moon assumed the relinquished task of the sun. We made steady and tortuous progress for a few hundred feet, then stopped to take off and coil the rope. The cold had become extraordinary. I happened to touch the head of an axe with my bare hand, and like the door-handle of the inn, the steel stuck to the flesh as though smeared with glue. Yet in that windless air we hardly felt the cold so long as we kept moving.

From now onward we were able to choose the least troublesome course and move freely about the rock. The moonlight cast our shadows long and thin upon the snows, and before us the buttress swelled in a silver wave to the summit, bearing us up firmly to the starred sky. We congratulated ourselves on our lateness; for there was magic in the air. Towards the end snow conditions changed markedly. Upon every crag and boulder lay accumulations of fog crystals, shaped like fig-leaves and overlapping in massed banks, which must have been a foot deep on the last rock-ring under the summit.

We halted at the cairn to survey the softly shining world far below, and the more brilliant sparkle above, then went south along the glittering summit ridge to the crusted snow-slopes of Coire Cloiche Finne, down which we launched ourselves in a six-hundred-foot glissade on the first stage to Glen Etive.

10 *The First Ascent of Clachaig Gully*

A GREAT ROCK-CLIMB traditionally presents to its pioneers, before they ever set foot on the mountain, obstacles and delays as numerous as those they encounter on the rocks of first ascent; and these last are charged with an air of impregnability, which from the instant of victory miraculously and for ever vanishes. Such facts are rarely appreciated by those who follow after, and who, when the way is known, are often greatly puzzled why the route should have gone so long unclimbed. Clachaig gully was no exception to the general rule. Therefore it seems worth while briefly to preface an account of the first ascent with subjective matters.

From my first climbing days, when I explored the easiest hills with a thrill of adventure, the unclimbed gully at Clachaig, Glencoe, made a most powerful appeal to my imagination. Facing the front door of Clachaig hotel, it splits the south flank of Sgor nam Fiannaidh in a curving gash two thousand feet high—the longest gully in Britain. During the previous fifty years it had sustained at least a score of attacks, several by outstanding mountaineers, all of which met defeat at a great cave-pitch at six hundred feet.

Therefore my early relation to Clachaig gully was much like that of the invalid of whom Stevenson said, 'The mountain-side beckons and allures his imagination day after day and is yet as inaccessible to his feet as the clefts and gorges of the clouds' —a fact which I knew all the more surely after my introduction to rock-work, for then I saw what expert climbers could accomplish on rock, and that seemed so much more than I could ever hope for myself that the wind was quite taken out of my sails. Moreover, when some of these mountaineers, whom at the age of twenty-one I regarded as men of heroic breed, cast in nobler mould than lesser humans like myself, declared in my presence that the great cave in Clachaig gully was impossible, I confess that I gave up hope. But from time to time the gully still lured my mind with the power of the unknown, and gave rise to many picturesque dreams, in which I cannot remember ever reaching the top—but passed always through rock scenery and over obstacles such as never met the eye of living man on mountain.

After a further three years of unbounded enthusiasm, during which I lost but two week-ends' climbing, my knowledge of men and mountains considerably increased, as a consequence of which I beheld them with no less respect but with a more calculating eye. I knew now from my own experience that the opinion of even the best mountaineer of what is possible and what is not possible in rock climbing is five times out of ten worthless, and that the truth of most physical problems has been expressed in one sentence by Nansen: 'The difficult is that which can be done at once, the impossible that which takes a little longer.' Therefore, in the spring of 1938, when I found the vision of Clachaig gully recurring with all its old force and frequency, I gave up dreams and cleared for action.

My first visit was made with MacAlpine and W. G. Marskell on 24th April. We reached the Great Cave, and there, after careful study and desperate effort, we failed. Yet, whatever impossibilities might be waiting in the fourteen hundred feet beyond, I felt sure that the Great Cave could be climbed. No trace of a route could I see, but I sensed that there *was* one. And a more disturbing feeling than that can hardly assail a mountaineer. Like all our predecessors, we retired discomfited. But henceforth my blood was up. As we climbed down to Clachaig in a rain-shower I was already praying for a spell of good weather and longing for the day of return.

Thereafter not a drop of rain fell in Argyll for seven days. By the end of that week I was in agonies of frustration, for as so often happens, the difficulty of getting the right party on to the mountain seemed insuperable. Dunn, whose company is more pleasing than a first ascent, would join us only if we camped and climbed on Garbh Bheinn of Ardgour, a magnificent and little-known rock-peak to which he is passionately devoted. Usually so careless, he was now adamant.

Therefore, on the afternoon of 30th April, Dunn, MacAlpine, Marskell, and I sped by car across the moor of Rannoch—bound for Ardgour. Mrs. MacAlpine accompanied us to share our camp but not our climb. I could never hope to combine a stronger party and better weather for Clachaig gully, but I knew that nothing could halt the westward journey if once we passed Kingshouse Inn. It came into sight, flanked by tall pines, white walls sparkling on the sun-drenched moor, like a quartzite pebble on a sea-drenched sand. We could not pass it by, and swung off the Glencoe road to be given our last chance and respite—and mugs of dark brown beer.

While we quenched our thirst in the lounge MacAlpine and I set about the conversion of Dunn, who was justly incensed in view of prior compacts. I fear that he scored most of the debating points, for MacAlpine's pitiful plea was our heat exhaustion after the long drive from Glasgow—we were too weak to go further—and as for my own, said Dunn, that boiled down to a pig-headed refusal to accept defeat! Climbers had been beaten in Clachaig gully for fifty years, but on Garbh Bheinn an abundance of new routes could be made on a thousand-foot cliffs of gneiss — on rock as good as gabbro. We cunningly stoked Dunn with a host of irrelevancies and fresh supplies of beer, then fanned the flame of debate with the breath of dialectic. Each quarter of an hour that passed carried a load from my mind, and at last the hour became too late for any hope of reaching Ardgour in daylight. When Dunn discovered how he had been tricked his face was a study, and a warning to all mountaineers to drink not a drop but water.

We drove down Glen Etive and camped by the river.

Not more than two or three times each year there comes a

day so fine that one will swear that never before have skies been truly blue, nor air keenly invigorating. Such was the first of May. At ten a.m. our car rolled up to Clachaig Inn in mellow morning sunshine. Far away in the woods lower down the glen we could hear the faint call of a cuckoo, wooing a man to idle sprawling and dreaming as does no other bird-song. But the huge bulk of Sgor nam Fiannaidh rose immediately to the north; and barely five minutes' walk away the Clachaig gully cleft the mountain in two. A more obvious challenge to the mountaineer could hardly be conceived. If this mountain be not the shapeliest in Scotland, it has yet, in the words of Elroy Flecker, 'a monstrous beauty like the hind quarters of an elephant.'

We moved up gentle grass slopes to the start. A cascade of water, flashing in the sunshine, foamed from the foot of the gully, and for eight hundred feet above a forest of small trees sprouted from the flanking walls amidst a profusion of luxuriant vegetation. The final twelve hundred feet were bare and stern. There was good climbing there, and on clean rock, but the lower part looks from a distance like a slice out of central Africa.

We skirted the torrent by scrambling up the rocky bank, then drew close to the entrance of the gully. The water in the bed was easily avoided and great walls rose gradually on either hand until we felt like insects at the bottom of a canyon. Long-cherished aspirations flooded my mind in a wave of enthusiasm for the climb. But could we possibly succeed where better than we had failed? Exaltation subsided to a subdued excitement. I felt as though treading those very clouds that Stevenson alleged to be inaccessible; mind and body were taut.

For five minutes we climbed easy rocks. The high retaining walls, splayed out and far apart in their upper reaches, steepened and came close together as they approached the bed of the gully, where the bare rock was exposed. The trees and vegetation were thus confined to the upper walls of the gully and rarely interfered with our climbing. The rock was now becoming difficult and we halted to rope up. To save time we arranged to climb as much as possible in two parties, myself with Marskell and MacAlpine with Dunn, each party using a hundred feet of rope.

Marskell and I set off first, and continued climbing up good rock through exotic jungle scenery. We had negotiated several mild difficulties, and had climbed some four hundred feet, when we suddenly overtook another party of three climbers. They were men of high repute and well known to us by name.

The leader of the party stood dripping moisture at the top of a narrow vertical chimney, where a waterfall foamed forty feet to a pool below. His second man, an accomplished Alpinist, was jammed half-way up the chimney. Icy jets of water poured down the open neck of his shirt. His breeches bulged and quivered round the accumulating volume, which at last spurted under pressure from the knees. We gaped in silence at the struggles of the victim, whose terrible contortions were at length crowned with success. He emerged weak and bedraggled from the top of the chimney, whereupon the dammed-up water, now released, surged down like a tidal wave. The surpassing frightfulness of the scene put us all in excellent humour for the rest of the day.

The party above disappeared, and it gradually dawned upon me that we must not gaze all day at the waterfall. Marskell, in fact, was already looking at me with a far-away, speculative smile, as though enjoying something in anticipation. Dunn grinned gleefully from ear to ear. 'What about Garbh Bheinn now?' was written all over him. In none save me could be discerned any concern for his own immediate prospects in the chimney. Therefore I turned up my collar and paid the penalty of climbing with men made of sterner stuff than myself.

I edged cautiously round the pool through hissing spray, hesitated, retreated with a sensation of nervous shock in the solar plexus, then stricken with shame advanced more determinedly and found small holds at the outer edge of the chimney. The spray poured over my body, a constantly penetrating spur to hasten me upward. At the very point where total immersion had seemed inevitable, I discovered some rock wrinkles that allowed me to push myself up, back and foot on opposing walls. My head, chest, and feet were thus clear of the main volume of water, which instead poured on to my stomach. In one more minute I was standing on top, damp but delighted, and looking forward to the discomfiture of the others. I was not disappointed. I have paid good money to see performing sea-lions give me a great deal less pleasure.

When all were up we reaped the benefit of the gully's southern aspect. The hot sun flooded in and began to dry our clothes even as we galloped across screes, swarmed up an overhang, and regained the first party below the Great Cave. This most perplexing of barriers, the limit of all previous exploration, was a wall fifty feet high; the left half being scooped out in a shallow cave, in outline like a thin-necked bottle; the right half, a sheet of discouraging sleek slabs. To either flank the gully walls rose two to three hundred feet. We could still see no possible line of ascent and bestowed ourselves on various rounded stones—I tested several by hand to select the warmest—while we discussed the problem over lunch.

Meantime we were still somewhat wet after the waterfall, but our partial ducking had had a pronounced psychological effect. The mettle of the party had been tempered by immersion. Each one of us had struck top form, such form as one finds but once or twice in a year's hard climbing. Therefore, despite the apparent hopelessness of the rock, we were incorrigibly optimistic. 'Where there 's rock there 's a route' is the arm-chair axiom of the climber incarcerated in the plains, itching for rough rock under his hands, doubting not that all things are possible, however smooth the slabs and high the angle; but when great sheets of stone rise uncompromisingly before his very eyes, they usually bring to the mountaineer a more fitting humility. To-day, we seemed to retain that abounding faith that supplies hand and foothold where none have previously existed; almost realizing in action the dream-world of the Kingshouse fireside.

We serenely munched our squashed and drooping sandwiches, dried our clothes in the hot sun, and watched the first party go into action. The cave was forty feet high and topped by a ten-foot chimney. A little torrent burbled down this chimney and splashed the inside of the cave and surrounding rock. Still, this was the most direct line; as such it appealed to the leader, who declared his preference and stepped into the cave. The left wall overhung, but the right lay at a lesser angle, so he climbed the latter till the roof forced him out, when he tried to traverse on to the outer slabs, thus hoping to reach by detour the base of the final chimney.

From the position of his body relative to the rock I could see that even though he successfully traversed from the cave, access to the chimney could be gained only by a brilliant acrobatic convulsion, hardly reversible. Assuming, then, that he found himself jammed in the foot of the chimney, he would have to get up the remainder to preserve himself from extinction; and there was no indication that the chimney was climbable. On the contrary, it bore every visible mark of impossibility. His only line of retreat would thus be a clear drop of forty feet to the screes. When trying that very traverse a fortnight before I had suddenly realized that life was already sufficiently short without such measures being taken to curtail it further. The leader of the first party came to the same conclusion. After due reflection he climbed down again.

The competitive spirit is happily completely foreign to Scottish mountaineering, and although the leader of the first party was fully entitled to make several attempts before allowing passage to our party, he now most generously stood back and invited us to have a try.

The cave route being far beyond my own skill I turned to the right-hand part of the barrier, where merciless slabs converged on a grass corner near the top. That grass corner was the key to the problem—if one could reach it. That no human could climb from directly below I knew but too well from my last visit, when I stuck on rock smooth as ivory. Some other approach would have to be found. Since it could be gained neither from directly underneath, nor yet from the left, there remained but one alternative—an ascent of the right-hand wall of the gully, followed by a traverse round a sharp rib and then ten feet across an almost vertical wall, which looked holdless from below. This wall was our last hope. I had not tried it before.

I changed into rubbers and climbed the gully wall to an enormous boiler-plate slab, out of the middle of which a rowan-tree sprang from a crack. I followed the lower lip of the slab till it heaved up against the rib, which it licked with an up-curled tongue. Delicately balanced on the tip of this tongue, I swung a leg round the rib on to a sloping foothold on the face. To my great relief and delight, I then saw a sketchy line of dimples, which might connect my rib with the grass corner, now looming large as a green oasis in a desert of severe walls. I moved forward cautiously, clinging to in-cut notches with my fingers and more rounded knobbles with my feet, until the holds suddenly became too sparse and I had to stop.

In hope of encouragement I instinctively looked down at the rest of my party, but they now seemed remote and impersonal. Like some medieval theologians, who argued for years how many angels could balance on the point of a needle—their true goal forgotten—they were grouped together and wrangling on the moral justification for using pitons on new rock-climbs.

I turned again to the rock for more material aid, but could find none at first. The direct horizontal line could not be continued. Something had to be done quickly, for muscles were tiring with the strain of too long a halt on inadequate footing. A more anxious scrutiny at last revealed above me a square-cut indentation, just large enough to take two finger-tips. I pulled up at once in combination with a toe scrape, and the two sufficed for a quick lift that earned better holds. In another minute I reached the oasis, a downward-tilting patch to which I clung with hands, elbows, knees, and feet, all of which were used for upward squirms and wriggles, which by spreading the weight of the body over a wide area made such peculiar climbing safe and enjoyable. The grass corner was in truth the key to the rocky heart of Clachaig gully. Only one more bolt remained to be drawn—a four-foot bar of rock, which yielded to patient manipulation. Then I drew myself beyond all verticalities on to the level top of the Great Cave. The gate was unlocked and the barrier down. All the unexplored mysteries of the gully lay open to us.

For several blissful minutes I knew the blaze of sheer delight that follows the fall of a great obstacle on a new climb, firing one with enthusiasm for life and mountains. In small part it may arise from reaction from nervous tension, but principally from the wholesome sense of triumph after hard work—after effort not only of muscle but of mind in application of climbing craft.

I brought up Marskell, then we threw his end of the rope down to MacAlpine and Dunn. They climbed with many exclamations of astonishment. The other party then decided to abandon the climb and managed to force an escape up the western wall of the gully. Meanwhile, I had time to appreciate the unique downward vista, the like of which may not be seen on any other British climb. The rocks we had climbed below were invisible: only the level scree-floor of the gully could be seen above each of the numerous pitches. Therefore the gully appeared to plunge headlong, as though its unsupported screes were an avalanche petrified, for ever menacing the inn at Clachaig. The inn, now small and distant, like a grain of chalk on a green baize cloth, stood neatly framed between the gully walls. These latter were most remarkable. Two vast parallel rock gardens, they rushed down on either side of a steep and stony avenue—true hanging-gardens crowded with slender rowan-trees and birches, cool and green in the burning sunlight, bright with wild flowers and all kinds of vivid moss and fern. Here, too, were many Alpine plants, amongst which I could name only the yellow saxifrage. All mingled in a riotous confusion. One must come in late spring to see this sight at its best.

We hastily pulled on our boots again. The party was now fairly straining at the leash. No one had ever been in this long upper part of the gully, which curved like a scimitar in an eastward upsweep of fourteen hundred feet. What should we find —impossible obstacles or rock too unsafe for climbers with pretensions to sanity? Should we be able to get up without further difficulty, or if we failed, could we hope to escape up either of the retaining walls, themselves rising to three hundred feet? Pulled by curiosity and spurred by difficulty overcome, we set to work on the next passage—a thirty-foot shelf. It was hard and awkward. In a mossy corner near the top I was pounded for five minutes to the joyful surprise of the party below. Elation must fly and sober respect for rock return before one is permitted to pass on from this corner.

Lenient rocks flattered and soothed us for a further two hundred feet. Our minds relaxed in foolish unwariness for several minutes, instead of stiffening in distrust of abating difficulties, which were no more than a lull, a gathering in of the gully's might for another great resistance. In consequence we were unduly startled to find ourselves entering a high-walled cauldron, where we were faced at last by a terrific chimney. It stood seventy feet high, streamed with water, and was circled by rock bulwarks of unusual fierceness.

Our hopes sank to a low ebb. The moment of defeat is never pleasant. We had now been climbing for nearly five hours and were nearly half-way up the gully. Therefore I revolted at the idea of retreat without a determined effort to force a route somehow or other. I examined the encircling walls quickly and critically, knowing that I must spot a line of attack before it was clouded by the mists of prudence.

We stood in the centre of the cauldron, at the upper end of which the stream fell sheer down the chimney from the invisible continuation of the gully. To the left of the waterfall the cauldron overhung in black bulges; whilst to the right the east wall rose perpendicular, the lower part perfectly smooth, the upper deplorably loose—so loose that we thought a loud shout might tumble the rock around our ears. Unanimously, we named it Jericho Wall. Its face betrayed but one weakness.

Running up the lower smooth wall was a narrow corner, steep but not vertical, smooth but not holdless, petering out against the higher Walls of Jericho. Here, then, was a route to try. I replaced my boots with rubbers.

By this time I was again keyed to the calm that inoculates a climber against high-angle rock and exposure, and progressed steadily up the corner on small holds, till I arrived at a platform the size of an ash-tray. Before me was the unpleasant prospect of an upward traverse across Jericho Wall itself. I proceeded step by step, testing every hold and avoiding where possible those that seemed insecure. By good fortune few footholds were dangerously unsound, whereas an unstable handhold could be used by delicately pressing down on it rather than brutally pulling outward. By virtue of this technique, loose holds could, after careful examination, be used with safety, provided due allowance was made for the fracture lines. On getting over the top I found myself stranded on a rolling wilderness of grey slabs, barren of standing ground from which to take in Marskell's rope with security for us both. I therefore went leftward to the waterfall, where there was an excellent stance near the lip.

I then discovered that my hundred feet of rope had been fully used up, and that while I was comfortably placed in the centre of the gully, Marskell, MacAlpine, and Dunn would have to climb well out on the right wall, so that if any one fell, the result would be a terrific pendulum swing against the wet slabs below me. Therefore to follow would be no different from leading. In the past I have climbed often enough with weak parties to realize how helpless must be every leader without strong support in such a position; he must avoid climbs like Clachaig gully. That Marskell, MacAlpine, and Dunn negotiated the hair-trigger holds of Jericho Wall by careful and determined climbing contributed more to the day's success than the leader. All of us cleared away much of the loose rock—Marskell especially threw down large quantities—so that the traverse is now safe and no longer severe.

When we had reached the top we again split into two parties.

It is most unusual for any route to present more than two points of supreme difficulty and we felt confident that the most formidable defences had now been pierced. The character of the gully had completely changed. We were well above the tree-line and there was little or no water in the bed of the gully; the walls were bare and narrower, the rock scenery stern and lofty, and the standard of climbing harder. But there was no passage of outstanding character until we reached a huge red slab, a wet, unbroken sheet of eighty strenuous feet. Immediately beyond, the gully narrowed to a level trough. The walls were nearly four hundred feet high, yet one could touch them both with outstretched arms. This singular formation could not continue far, and the trough in its last agonies gave a sharp double twist and reared in a short chimney. The right wall awkwardly overhung, requiring an expenditure of energy out of all proportion to the chimney's size and importance. We were beginning to feel our seven hours' climbing.

Thereafter everything went so well that once more we unwisely thought that all serious rock-work lay behind. We were transported with delight—at least I was—and imagined the gully as good as climbed. Actually we were little more than three-quarters of the way up.

Then came the next shock. A mass of dull red rock, higher than a city building, towered in front of us. We named it the Red Chimney pitch. A shallow cave, arching thin and high like a great cathedral window, rose thirty feet above the screes. From its apex sprang a narrow chimney, splitting open the walls for twenty feet above and thus overhanging the base of the cave. This wet, gaping crack was in turn crowned by twenty feet of red slabs. Total height, seventy feet.

We had come too far, however, to be easily shaken, and felt that the problem might be solved could we only force an entry into the bottom end of the chimney. Without difficulty I climbed the wall to the right of the cave, and one foot to the right of the chimney found a ledge that seemed specially designed for rest and reflection. The crux of the pitch was to get my body round the corner and jam it into the chimney. It was a most unusual situation; for the chimney being under-cut, nothing but good mountain air occupied the thirty feet of space between its lower end and the screes. Near the top that space would become fifty feet, and fifty feet of a clear drop is never to be sneezed at. At all events, as I craned my neck round the corner to look at the next twenty feet of smooth wet rock, and wondered whether it were climbable, I felt a pardonable anxiety to eschew any step too palpably irreversible.

On the opposite wall of the chimney, at the bottom, was one knobble. I placed my left foot on its hunched back as a provisional gesture, and allowed my back to rest on the near edge of the chimney. In the attitude of a public-house loafer, I was thus comfortably supported over space. Then I swung on to a small hold in the back of the chimney and the problem was solved. But the chimney was stubborn. I had to fight strenuously to reach the haven of two chock-stones near the top. The upper one was loose, was tested thoroughly, and was subsequently used for a strong arm-pull. But winter frosts may undermine its reliability for another year.

Above the chimney was a perfect stance ringed with low walls like a pulpit. One could imagine a lesser rock nesting there in prehistoric days. I had to rest for five minutes until my exhausted muscles returned to normal. On this first ascent I had undoubtedly used more strength than was necessary through an over-anxiety not to fall off. Then Marskell arrived and I tried the final slab. The various nicks and corrugations were not too well distributed and strained muscles, already tired from eight hours' climbing, gave us a higher opinion of the slab than it probably merits. It made a worthy finish to a superb pitch.

There seemed to be no end to Clachaig gully. We continued climbing up and up, and for several hundred feet the clean firm rock gladdened our hearts by its irreproachable conduct. We calculated that we had climbed nearly forty pitches, and as the rock yielded ever more easily we thought more than once that the last obstacle had arrived, only, on climbing it, to find another one ahead. Profiting by previous experience, I became more and more suspicious. The Clachaig gully has a character all of its own, and I felt in my very bones that it would not come to an end tamely. There would be a sting in the tail. I was even prepared for the tail to whip up and utterly rout us at the last moment.

Then we saw it. Beyond doubt the last pitch in the gully. An unspectacular wall of blank red rock. Its first fifteen feet were well broken, its upper fifteen feet so smooth that no holds could be seen from below. A glance at my wrist-watch showed that we had been climbing for nine hours; we were all weary and this last pitch was obviously very hard, assuming it to be possible—so I exchanged boots for rubbers, in hope of easing my labours. The lower half led easily to the smooth section, where bands of slab ran lengthwise across the wall, underlapping, thereby exposing long, thin edges. On these I made an upward traverse to the centre of the gully, feeling most insecure until I could clap my hands on top of the wall and pull up with a last hard effort. I looked upward. The gully no longer rose purposefully before me, but meandered onward, scree-strewn, uninterrupted; the flanking walls, so high and formidable lower down, fell away in low easy slopes.

I could hardly believe it. We had made the first ascent of Clachaig gully. I shouted the good news down to the rest of the party, where it was received with great enthusiasm. But we were too tired to be demonstrative.

We made our descent down the true right bank of the gully, which is quite free from rock. But tired as we were, and urged to haste by hunger and fading daylight, we were first slowed, then brought to halt by the beauty of the westward hills and sea-lochs. The sun was down. There was no splashed colour and blaze in the afterglow, such as one usually sees in May. Between the light-starts on Loch Linnhe near at hand, and a sky of clear lemon in the west, the mountains of Ardgour rose in sharp outline, yet without substantiality. One looked not *at* them, but into them, as through the mouths of caverns filled with purple haze, and still one looked beyond. . . . They delighted not by crude colour, breath-taking as that can be, but with atmospheric subtlety and noble shape. These were the mountains of true vision, not of this world, causing one to mourn his lost splendour during this life of exile, yet rejoicing him with promise of a return. But there is no way of explaining them. . . .

An hour later we briefly celebrated at Clachaig Inn. Then the pangs of hunger, as only the destitute and mountaineers of this country know them, routed us out of Glencoe and back to our camp in Glen Etive. The evening we spent there stands out clear in my memory as one of life's milestones of sheer happiness, when we were absolutely content and had not a care in the world. An ambition of four years had been satisfied; nerve and sinew had been hard tried on a long new rock-climb, and now, in a clearing in the woods, we relaxed our tired bodies on soft grass before a crackling fire—while our food was cooked and served by my sister, Mrs. MacAlpine. We were in high spirits yet quiet, joyful yet wearied out.

Exploratory rock climbing is the best of all.

NOTE. On returning next year to Clachaig gully I repeated the ascent in five hours. Several other ascents have been made in from four and a half to seven hours. Jericho Wall is now safe and sound. I do not recommend the climb in wet weather. Rubbers are no longer required for any of the pitches.

11 *Observatory Ridge in Winter*

DURING THE MONTH of January 1938 great quantities of powder-snow fell in the central highlands, accompanied by dry and bitter winds, which in Glencoe swept the rocks clear and packed the gullies deep with drift. In early February sheets of windslab formed on eastward-facing snows.

Mackenzie, MacAlpine, and I put our heads together to discover what especial benefit might be derived from this state of affairs. It seemed to us likely that if such conditions prevailed in Glencoe they might also hold good on Ben Nevis. Gullies might be either easy or dangerous, according as they were tight-packed or loose, but the great ridges ought to be in perfect order—swept clear of powder and encrusted with old frozen snow. Then Mackenzie had an inspiration. There was no record, he said, of any winter ascent of Observatory ridge since the first by Raeburn, eighteen years ago. We knew of one other ascent in April, but not in genuine winter conditions; the ridge seemed much neglected. Being two thousand feet long and reckoned difficult in summer, it was not a winter route on which one could wander with an old umbrella: we must strike at once while the snow was frozen.

Thereupon I sprained an ankle by slipping in a friend's drawing-room. After seven days' rest I was hobbling with a stick, feeling desperate and vowing like Bill Bones that 'Doctors is all swabs'—while my companions enjoyed a very severe climb, which they described to me in high, astounding terms. That was too much. Sprain or no sprain, my stick went out of the window and I to Nevis with MacAlpine and Mackenzie. We arrived at Fort William on the evening of 19th February. We stopped there to buy a bottle of rum (for my ankle), then climbed two thousand feet by the banks of the Allt a' Mhuillin to the Nevis hut, which we reached at midnight.

Intense cold wakened us at dawn.

We arose at seven o'clock, and our breath made columnar clouds of smoke in the icy atmosphere. Imagine our joy when we discovered a truly perfect morning! Not a cloud in the blue sky. Straight before the doorway stretched the two miles of precipice, crowned with flowing snow-cornices, which blazed in the slanting sun-rays. From our feet the snow-fields swept in a frozen sea to the cliffs, beating like surf against the base of ridge and buttress, leaping in spouts up the gullies. The rocks were laden with snow, but as we expected, there appeared to be less than usual on Observatory ridge. There were countless patches, of course, but everywhere the hoared rock showed through, except high up where the angle eased, and low down where the snow had been swept down by the wind.

One could feel a terrific power to attract in the perfect form of that ridge. It was broad and firmly planted below, but tapered through the first thousand feet to a delicate edge on the last thousand:

> Icy in pure thin air, glittering with snows.

And all this was in accord with our belief that we should not find overmuch snow on the ridge until we were high up, where despite the narrowness of the ridge the rocks became easier. We calculated seven or eight hours for the whole climb. Our judgment of snow conditions, thus substantiated by every visible sign, was in fact wrong, and was destined to involve us in one of the hardest battles we have had the good fortune to wage.

We hurried back to the hut and made breakfast. Shortly before nine a.m. we set off.

The effect of weather upon thought and temper is most profound. And from the crackling air of a hard morning an electric energy seems to flow through one's body. There was no wind to shiver us or to shackle our minds to material things. Well clothed, and thanks to MacAlpine passably well fed, we revelled in the cold, and our spirits leapt to the gay colours of the mountain. Our eyes ranged in delight from ebony towers to pale brown ridges, from the cream of a cornice to the sheen of green ice bulging a buttress, from silver icicles to ice glinting grey in gullies; from the blue sky to the feathery powder squealing beneath our boots like harvest mice. Life is more than merely worth while on a fine morning with stirring work ahead.

We stopped to examine the great unclimbed gully on the right flank of Observatory ridge. Its awe-inspiring appearance compelled a halt. The first thousand feet were a continuous ribbon of unmitigated ice. From time to time a small powder-snow avalanche trundled down the gully and flashed on to the snow-field below. If ever a party tries to climb that gully it will have to be very sure of stable snow above.

We then gave our attention to Observatory ridge and decided that the speediest method of effecting lodgment thereupon was to contour its base into Zero gully, which bounded its left flank, and then make a right-hand traverse on to the crest. Zero gully had likewise never been climbed, and the cause of neglect was apparent when we moved into its lower reaches. High up, higher than we could see, the angle fell back, but the lower visible section bristled with pitches of green, overhanging ice. In point of severity there seemed little to choose between these flanking gullies, and once launched on our climb we should have no alternative to direct upward advance or downward retreat. We turned involuntarily and examined Observatory ridge still more respectfully, but we were no longer in position to see far ahead and our view was restricted to a race of snow-dusted slabs, freckled with dark walls and lined with ribs.

At nine-thirty a.m. we left Zero gully and traversed on to Observatory ridge by a convex terrace swamped with the foulest rice-like snow, which lay poised with devilish cunning above a series of crags. Breaking steps soon imparted the first unpleasant thrill to the day's proceedings. We stopped and roped up, with Mackenzie leading, myself second, and MacAlpine last. The rope gave us much needed confidence, for the snow was so unreliable in quality that one could not put down one's foot secure in the knowledge that one's step would hold—that one would not, if unchecked, accompany the breaking snow over the crags below. This bad snow low down was only to be expected, and we remained confident that conditions would rapidly improve as we went higher. Then we began to wonder if we should ever get higher. Our ledge had thinned to a flake, and in order to escape from the dangerously poised snow, Mackenzie sought the first opportunity offered by the rocks near the crest of the ridge. I tied myself to a spike and paid out the rope while he wrestled with a high wall of snow-speckled slab.

His artistry was delightful to watch, yet he never ran out more than fifteen feet of rope. He tried straight up, to the left, to the right, tried every dodge of body adjustment known to an expert leader, but without avail. Half an hour passed and we were still in the same position.

MacAlpine, impatiently balancing on doubtful steps thirty feet beneath on the terrace, began to question the wisdom of proceeding further if rapid progress were not possible early in the day. For reasons of his own he was anxious to get back to the hut in good time. In fact, we had the not unusual choice between daring and exceeding prudence. On the one hand, I felt that if we were going to turn back at all we had better do it now—it would be our last chance. On the other hand, we had looked for slow progress low down owing to the accumulation of powder-snow, and believed in finding rapid progress higher up to compensate. Lastly, the party was in good form and Mackenzie displaying all his usual mastery; but his skill had to be transferred to climbable rock. I therefore urged him to come down and traverse forty feet to the right. He did this and met instant success. The hunt was up.

Our immediate route lay fifty feet up a truly vertical rib, where splendid holds lay distressingly far apart and exercised our arm muscles more than we liked. I remember that rib with affection as the last safe and solid thing that we met in a long day and night. Above, our troubles gathered thick and fast. Slab succeeded slab, and rib succeeded rib, but all were lightly covered with snow, which when dusted off revealed rocks glazed with frost; all were intersected by ledges piled high with powder-snow bearing a wind-slab crust, which peeled off and swished over the edge suggestively whenever a foot was placed on it. And this snow was invisible from below. It lay on what might be called the corbels of the ridge.

That such accomplished deception was true to the character of big ridges we knew, but on this occasion we had faith that recent winds had swept the rocks clean. Always we were led on and up in the reasonable certainty of mind that conditions would improve, and always we were disappointed. The snow did not improve—it got worse. For some reason the wind had not been getting at it, had not scavenged half as much of it as we had expected. Therefore, we had to go cautiously and take elaborate rock-belays, while we traversed back and forth on the treacherous footing in search of the line of least resistance. Our progress was correspondingly slow and the hours went swiftly by.

Mackenzie fared better than MacAlpine and I on these wretched traverses. Light and wiry, he went first and the snow would often bear his weight complainingly, whereas the further strain placed on it by a second or third man was more than it would endure. At one such ledge I was crossing above precipitous slabs on a ribbon of floury powder banked at a high angle against the rock-face, when my steps caved in without warning. My feet slithered to the edge, but just before the slip developed into a fall I caught two finger-holds on the wall above. Mackenzie was well placed to hold me had I gone further. The rope was an ever-present safeguard. Nevertheless, the possibility of repetitions of this incident was always in our minds and kept us in a state of constant anxiety; and such a strain, prolonged through many hours of hard work and technical difficulty, is at first not easy to bear with indifference. But one improves with practice.

MacAlpine's task at the end of the rope was not an enviable one. He climbed on the shaky remnants of holds left to him by Mackenzie and me—after we ourselves had experienced difficulty—with a superb confidence, most cheering to watch. There was one specially loathsome and slabby gutter, where Mackenzie, balancing with precarious grace on icy wrinkles, made upward progress by using delicate push-holds for the palms of his hands on thin snow frosted to the rock. The failing stability of this snow film just sufficed to see me to the base of a vertical crag: then the film flaked off, scuttered down the gutter, and fell sharply into space. How was MacAlpine to get up without that snow? My only rope-belay was a paltry knob, half the size of a thumb-nail, on the wall above me; my only stance a foothold; these had to constitute the justification for MacAlpine's further ventures.

Mackenzie entrenched himself somewhere above. I stood sideways and with all my strength pressed down MacAlpine's rope against its miserable belay. We both prepared for the inevitable moment when MacAlpine must 'come off.'

As for MacAlpine, he surveyed these preparations with polite interest. When assured that all was ready, and that my belay 'would hold the *Queen Mary*,' he calmly stubbed out his cigarette, carefully smoothed the corners of his moustache, tilted his balaclava, then with stylish glide came up that gutter like a Persian cat to a milk saucer.

But Observatory ridge had harder trials in store for us. Meanwhile conditions improved. For an hour we made sufficiently steady progress to notice our gain in height while we climbed. It was a most encouraging change to feel slab and ledge and face succeeding one another, slipping behind and out of sight as we moved up. We used every possible device to save time: as when Mackenzie, for safety's sake, climbed sixty feet up a thin rib of great technical difficulty, while MacAlpine and I, relying on a tight rope, followed more speedily by an easier parallel groove, which was in a highly dangerous condition. Then the ridge suddenly fell back at an easy angle, as though resting on its haunches before rejoining battle more fiercely. We felt that we had better do likewise. Of one accord we stopped, for by this time the rope was a telegraphic wire linking our three minds. We found an excellent stance, where we could all sit down at once and in such comfort as cold snow affords to the mortal hind quarters.

For ten minutes we ate sandwiches and enjoyed one of those bodily and mental contrasts that mountains grant liberally. The sky was incredibly blue, the air windless and still. Not the faintest noise could be heard. Straight before our eyes on the north skyline, the mountains of Wester Ross were ablaze in afternoon sunshine, a jagged wall of white cutting through lilac horizon haze. At our feet lay the hut, a speck of red roof.

Thoughts of what must be ahead at last hurried us into action again, although even yet we failed to realize just how great would be the volume of unstable snow on the upper part of the ridge, or that under such a covering the crest in its narrowness would prove impregnable. The rocks swiftly steepened and rose in a broad tower, seventy feet high, which we recognized as the last battlement on the middle part of the climb. It completely blocked the ridge and was cluttered with incoherent snow. No frontal attack was possible. Mackenzie worked up to the right across snow that broke away and then stopped breaking, keeping us in doubt from one moment and move to another. He disappeared round an awkward corner and I watched the rope creep out at an average rate of two feet per minute. We could just hear a soft scuffling as he wrestled up a snow-choked crack; an occasional expletive floated down to us through the quiet air; then all was silent save for the whisper of falling snow.

The sun was out of sight, but from the look of the sky it was obvious that the afternoon was wearing on. We waited in growing impatience for half an hour before receiving the call to follow. Altogether we spent an hour on these seventy feet of rock. Now we looked to make steadier progress. The ridge narrowed henceforth and was demarcated by terrific cliffs, but the average angle was less than hitherto. We climbed but a

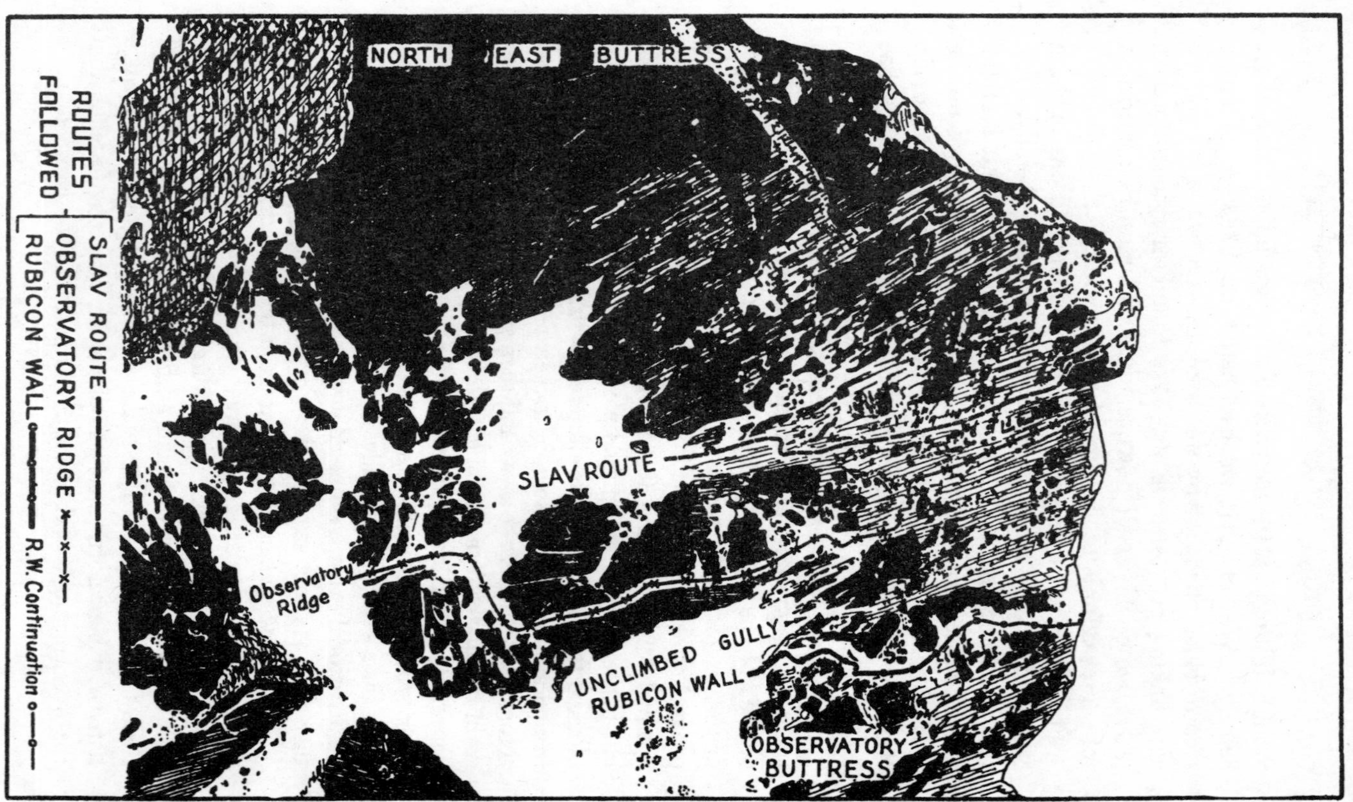
NORTH EAST BUTTRESS
SLAV ROUTE
Observatory Ridge
UNCLIMBED GULLY
RUBICON WALL
OBSERVATORY BUTTRESS
ROUTES FOLLOWED
SLAV ROUTE
OBSERVATORY RIDGE
RUBICON WALL
R.W. Continuation

short way further, however, before we were brought to a standstill. The snow lay on that slender ridge in greater quantity than ever and in even less stability.

The situation was now truly serious. There was simply not enough time to clear this great volume of snow from the crest, and it became painfully clear to each one of us that no matter what we did we were going to have a long and hard fight to win through. The declining sun did little to cheer us on, but there was no gain in standing about, wondering in a flurry of anxiety what to do next. If ever bold and determined leadership was needed on a climb it was needed now, and Mackenzie rose nobly to the occasion. On the face of it the situation was hopeless. To cut away such oppressive thought, to wrest good result from bad circumstance, decisive action was called for and decisive action we got. Mackenzie resolved to abandon tradition and the crest of the ridge, and to make a three-hundred-foot traverse across the western precipice. An upward slanting shelf of snow and ice provided fair prospect of a route, although nothing could be seen of a way to regain the ridge when the shelf ended.

The shelf started unpromisingly with fifty feet of evil powder-snow. Wind-slab was again the danger. The crust broke off in chunks, which swished down the tilted shelf, leapt dramatically into space, hung there for a split second, then dropped out of sight with fascinating suddenness. The entire passage was well belayed, but any fall would have meant a pendulum swing into thin air and great difficulty in regaining the shelf. We trod our subsiding steps with the utmost delicacy. None broke away. Then we cut up an ice-fall and were committed to a traverse from which we could see no hope of regaining the crest of the ridge for a long time to come. We perforce worked doggedly along the face.

Two hours later the shelf spread out fanwise, steepened, and culminated in a knife-edged saddle on which we sat astride in cold discomfort. We took stock of our position. Our saddle was the crest of a subsidiary ridge, which came down at right angles to Observatory ridge, then fell with exceeding steepness to a snow-field under the unclimbed gully. Our route could not have been more clearly defined. We must somehow climb the knife-edge and get back to Observatory ridge. Mackenzie literally swam up these hundred feet, using the dog-stroke to to cleave a passage up the massed powder. Such tactics cleared away the great volume of snow that alone made them possible, and to save time MacAlpine and I used the rope freely. At sunset we gathered once more on Observatory ridge.

We had been climbing for seven hours and thought the worst lay below, therefore we sat back and rested for several minutes. It was well that the truth was concealed from us; for in point of time we were only half-way up that stupendous ridge. The very fact of sunset might be thought disconcerting, yet it overcame all apprehension. From zenith to horizon the colours hung across the sky in broad belts of blue, green, orange, and crimson. The nearby snow-peaks were afire.

After the hard climbing lower down we were peculiarly sensitive to the skyscape. For suspense is not distressing when one is free to act; therefore doubt of the issue stimulates enterprise and perception. Great clearness of mind and an inner calm are part of the many rewards of adventurous mountaineering. The mind is purged of sea-level preoccupations and sentimentalities, stripped of self-seeking, alert to beauty, open to truth, and quick to understand. It is not too much to say that the test of true mountaineering is the presence of adventure and beauty, the criterion of the one being often uncertainty of result, and of the other, always inner purification.

We prepared to start again. Mackenzie retired to the middle of the rope for a well-earned rest and I took over the lead. But the moment I set off there came an almost conclusive set-back. The narrow upper section of the ridge was unclimbable—the rocks were swamped with powder, which was held together by an egg-shell crust. One hundred navvies with shovels could not have cleared those rocks by daybreak. And according to the Scottish Mountaineering Club's guide-book to Ben Nevis it was not possible to escape from the ridge into either of the flanking gullies. Unless we could reconcile ourselves to remaining where we were permanently the guide-book had to be proved wrong.

In the fading daylight we saw that fifty feet above one might possibly cut a route into Zero gully. At all costs that must be done. Once there, we felt sure of getting up by torchlight, even although, as we could see, the gully was decorated with the outward heave of at least three ice pitches. The first essential was to force a route up the dangerous snow of the ridge for another fifty feet. Thus far we could surely go, if no further.

That short stretch of ridge was climbed rapidly, for it was highly precarious and not to be lingered over. We had been ascending or traversing unsafe snow all day, and the continual succession of false alarms that this occasioned amounted in their sum total to a considerable nervous demand on the party as a whole. I myself felt resigned to defeat at this stage of the climb. Unless one cultivates detachment in time of stress, reason responds to tiredness by losing hope in face of further trials ahead, all accentuated by the onfall of night and cold. I drew much encouragement from the example set by Mackenzie and MacAlpine, who appeared to remain supremely calm and optimistic. Whether such an attitude be well founded or assumed, its effect on a leader in emergency is incalculable and irresistible. To feel that the party behind you is strong and has confidence in you is half the battle on a big climb, when it is the strength of the team, not that of the individual, that carries the day.

At five p.m. precisely, as light was failing altogether, I cut my way into Zero gully. To learn our fate I prodded the snow in the gully-bed with my axe and was delighted to find a hard surface. The angle was fifty degrees. Several feet higher the snow gave way to opaque ice, then to clear ice, but I could open my shoulders to this stuff and hit out hard, with the comfortable feeling that I was on safe ground and was getting somewhere. Soon it became too dark to see how the axe was fashioning the steps. I stopped, brought on the others, shortened the rope, and went on again by torchlight.

There was no moon, but the clear sky flashed with stars; nor was there any wind, though the cold was numbing. Thus for a quarter of an hour our plight seemed not so bad as it might have been. Then the gully hit back at us. We ran into powder-snow at least one foot deep and thinly crusted with wind-slab. This abominable mixture continued right to the top of Ben Nevis except where the ice-falls protruded in fat gleaming bulges. When one is hard-pressed for time and energy there is a sore temptation to trust to soft loose snow lying on ice. But any one who yields in Zero gully enters a death-trap. (Especially is this true of Alpine climbs.) The only tolerable way of proceeding was to excavate the powder and cut steps into the icy bed of the gully.

Needless to say we were already tired and cold, perhaps more tired than we knew, for the climbing demanded and received our unremitting care and attention. We climbed in Zero gully without any protection, moral or otherwise, from the rope; for our axes could not be used as belays: the spikes would not pierce the ice stratum and were valueless in the powder stratum. Moreover, having seen the lower part of the gully from below, we were unable to push on with care-free hilarity. We took no chances. A single mistake by any one of us might mean the speedy end of both climb and party. Therefore the step-cutting could not be skimped; the steps had to be well made, not too far apart. This meant heavy labour; digging, excavating, cutting, and at last climbing, until one's arms and shoulders ached with the incessant work, whilst one's mind kept alert to the faultless control of body movement. We grew more and more tired, and realizing it, more and more determined. It was beyond the power of one man to lead throughout, so each of us took turns at going first, flogging out the upward passage, until his weariness resulted in too slow progress, when he would retire in favour of the next man.

In two hours we reached the first ice-wall. Until my days

are ended I shall never forget that situation. Crouching below the pitch amidst showers of ice-chips, I fed out the frozen rope while Mackenzie hewed mightily at the ice above, his torch weirdly bobbing up and down in the dark and the ice brilliantly sparkling under its beam. Looking down, I could see just a short curve of grey snow plunging into the lower darkness, then nothing until the twinkling lights of the Spean valley, four thousand feet below.

The atmosphere was electric; the climbing spectacular. Mackenzie slowly cut his way to the top of the wall, where he dislodged an enormous plate of snow-crust, which flashing past me at high velocity, fell flat on top of MacAlpine's head. The plate smashed to a thousand fragments, which shot with a hiss down the gully. MacAlpine gave a hollow grunt, at which the hairs of our balaclava helmets rose up on end, for he carried the rum (for my ankle) and seemed about to depart with it hutwards by the shortest route.

A further two hours slid by in wearisome cutting and waiting. The waiting was worst of all, for one had time to savour the great cold, and to feel the strain on leg muscles of interminably standing on smallish steps. The slope was steep enough for one's knees to rest on the snow and be chilled and finally numbed by the constant contact. MacAlpine and I had to climb with our torches held between our teeth, for both hands were employed on axe, rope, or holds. Fortunately we both had light-weight torches, but our mouths being frequently open our throats became dry and parched. Mackenzie, no foolish virgin, had his bulb and reflector secured to his head by an elastic band, the bulb being wired to the battery in his pocket.

At nine p.m. we reached the second ice-pitch, the angle of which was about seventy degrees. After so much exhausting work I looked on this obstacle with extreme disfavour. Had the leader been fresh it would still have been very hard. Therefore both Mackenzie and I entered the fray, and thanks to the former we got up, but the effort cost us much reserve energy and MacAlpine took over the lead.

Far off, beyond the crest of Observatory ridge on our right, the dim outline of the Great Tower on Tower ridge loomed through the darkness. Its top lay three hundred feet below the summit of Nevis and we looked across to it every little while to gauge our progress. But the watched pot never boils. We climbed for a solid hour without detecting the slightest difference in our own height relative to the Tower. Each time we looked we felt the same keen pang of disappointment. I began to feel anxious about the life of our torch batteries; these showed us all we required to see and no more, which was sometimes just as well, but they were losing much of their original strength. And somewhere above was a third ice-fall. For all we knew there might be more to follow. These cheerless thoughts were abruptly ended by the appearance of the ice-fall itself, an immense convex boss, a tough morsel whose mastication took half an hour of axe-work.

Up and up we went, digging, hitting, carving, scraping, moving steadily and without interruption for an hour. Quite suddenly, the snow became firm and reliable. On our left hand, stark square-cut towers were silhouetted against the starry sky, and round them could be heard a mighty rushing of winds, the voice of the high and lonely places of the earth. Then Zero gully broadened out and debouched without cornice on the summit plateau. We went over the top one by one, our hearts filled with relief. The time was eleven-thirty p.m.

'Well,' said Mackenzie, 'we 're up.'

I answered 'Thank God!' And for once I meant it. Nothing more was said, then or later. But I had no doubt then, and have none now, that this was the longest and hardest climb in relation to sheer strain that we should ever do. We had learnt that when one stands on the summit after such a climb it is not the mountain that is conquered—we have conquered self and the mountain has helped us.

A bitter east wind snarled across the snow-fields and we hurried for shelter to the ruins of the Observatory. Only the roof and three feet of wall projected through the snow-cap, but we managed to squirm through the top of a window and to wriggle along a tunnel to a snow grotto inside. Once again in high spirits, we sat cross-legged in a circle while MacAlpine, beaming like a lighthouse, broached my bottle of golden rum and decanted it into a thermos flask of steaming tea. The festivities that followed lasted far beyond midnight, while outside the wind howled round the corners of the walls.

Then, bursting with all reserve clothing, we braved the blast and, in brilliant moonlight, descended in two hours by Coire Leis to the hut, where we arrived seventeen hours after our departure on the previous morning. We could hardly keep our eyes open, but were inordinately happy. Much of my own delight I owed to Mackenzie, who had given us that day the greatest lead I have ever seen on mountains. Indeed it was a magnificent and unforgettable spectacle; for he was confronted with well-nigh impossible difficulties, and by strength of will rose far above his everyday self, forcing an issue by bare courage and precision of mind and movement. Each time I look back dispassionately on that performance, my respect for the human animal increases. He has powers within him of which he knows too little.

Note. One year later we repeated the ascent in six hours. The rocks were encrusted with hard snow and there was no powder. The difference in quality of snow alone caused the eight hours' difference in time. The ridge then gave us the most splendid of winter climbs.

12 *The Lost Valley and S C Gully*

The Lost Valley of Bidean nam Bian

IN MARCH 1939 there came, as is customary in Scotland at that time, a great improvement in snow conditions with successive falls, thaws, and frosts. The course of that ideal cycle had kept me for some weeks to hill-walking and the shorter routes, but the frosty climax raised my hopes high and my spirit ached for a kingly climb; therefore I set my heart on the highest mountain of Argyll, Bidean nam Bian, 'The Peak of the Bens,' and resolved to climb if I could its north top, Stob Coire nan Lochan, by the renowned S C gully.

My hopes were shared by Scott, MacAlpine, and T. D. Mackinnon and approved by the weather clerk. We reached Glencoe at ten o'clock of a brilliant morning, the world such a dazzling white as to pain the eye; the air coldly dry, searing our nostrils until we learned to breathe slowly but deep. From where we stood on the Glencoe road, Bidean was out of sight two and a half miles to the south-west, its majesty screened from vulgar gaze by three guardian spurs, known to the world as the Three Sisters of Glencoe. But far behind the cordon, there was permitted an icy glimpse of Stob Coire nan Lochan, thrusting a princely triangle into cloudless blue.

We determined that our approach should lie between the first and second Sisters by way of the Lost Valley. That appropriate name is used only by a handful of mountaineers who are intimately acquainted with this almost unknown glen, the most genuinely remote and in autumn or spring the most beautiful hill recess in Argyll. First, however, we had to cross the river Coe, whose fifteen-mile length bars access to the mountain and helps to preserve the Lost Valley's sanctity.

We went downhill to the river's bank. It was sullied by no bridge hereabouts and we were faced with a knee-deep wade of twenty yards. Luckily the stream was hushed and muffled by the heavy snows closer to the source, and ran here with unwonted sluggishness. Several protruding boulders wore snow-puffs, those subject to splash bearing domes of blue ice. Harrowing as the prospect was, we did not timorously linger on the brink—not when we stood barefoot on the snow. The slippery shores of the river-bed forebade a swift crossing, despite the support of our ice-axes, and we gained the south bank with feet numbed to the bone. Circulation was soon restored on the uphill tramp.

Twenty minutes later we entered the lower reaches of the Lost Valley, where a wooded ravine has been carved out by the Allt Coire Gabhail. At first we kept high on the west bank and then followed a descending track through the trees, whose silver-grey shadows stole across our path like spirits. Where we came to the stream the ravine widened, but the track along the bottom was hidden in soft snow and we picked our way among half-buried boulders. The trees were loaded like the most audacious of Christmas-card scenery; each gaunt branch bent heavily to its burden and every twig hung fat as a rabbit's tail. The last time I had passed this way the glen was a haze of red and gold leaf, and filled with the chatter of a now frozen burn.

The glen steepened. We climbed through a tangle of rock and trees where the burn vanished underground, until we came to an isolated crag under whose foundations burrow a warren of caves. We stopped there to investigate. I had been through the caves often enough before but had no knowledge of their winter condition. As I thought, the rock-corridor and chambers were dry. At any season of the year they afford a sheltered bivouac. A short way beyond the crag the ground levelled. Around the dry bed of some ancient stream a little arbour was formed, an outer porch from which we debouched at last on the true sanctuary, the Lost Valley of Bidean nam Bian.

At a height of twelve hundred feet, it stretched flat before us, a narrow plain walled by the two northward-running spurs of Bidean. The head of the valley was dominated by an unclimbed buttress of the summit ridge, two thousand feet above. All along the western wall icy turrets and battlements caught the sun, gleamed and shone. On these cliffs no climbing has been done, and no doubt with good reason. In summer, the valley floor is a green mountain lawn, at whose farther end the stream draining the higher corries sinks underground—to reappear below the caves. The construction of the valley leads me to think that at one time a loch may have lain there. But now the meadow was covered a foot deep in snow, whose spotless surface, untrodden by man or animal, heightened the valley's loneliness and deepened its silence.

Spring or autumn—for these have greatest charm—a man might come here for a week and be alone. He might pitch a tent on that meadow and be as much out of sight and sound of civilization as if he dwelt at the North Pole. On his side, all the advantage of a noble mountain girdling him about. He might go up to those unclimbed cliffs, seamed with gullies and chimneys, precipitate stairways, and explore to his heart's content; down to the ravine, if he were a botanist; or climbing to the spurs, walk for a dozen miles on the high ridges of Bidean, with breeze, sun, and a hundred hills for company; perhaps he might wander along to one of the Sisters, and gazing over the edge, watch with compassionate eye the fast car of some busy human creep like an ant along the Glencoe road—and then, going down at evening to his tent on the meadow, trim his solitary candle and smoke a peaceful pipe. He would find himself, after all, less alone than in cities.

In short withdrawals from the world there is to be had unfailing refreshment. When his spirit is burdened or lightened the natural movement of a man's heart is to lift upward, and this is most readily done in the Lost Valley, for there it is easy to be still; and there one may approach the state of which Gerard Manley Hopkins wrote:

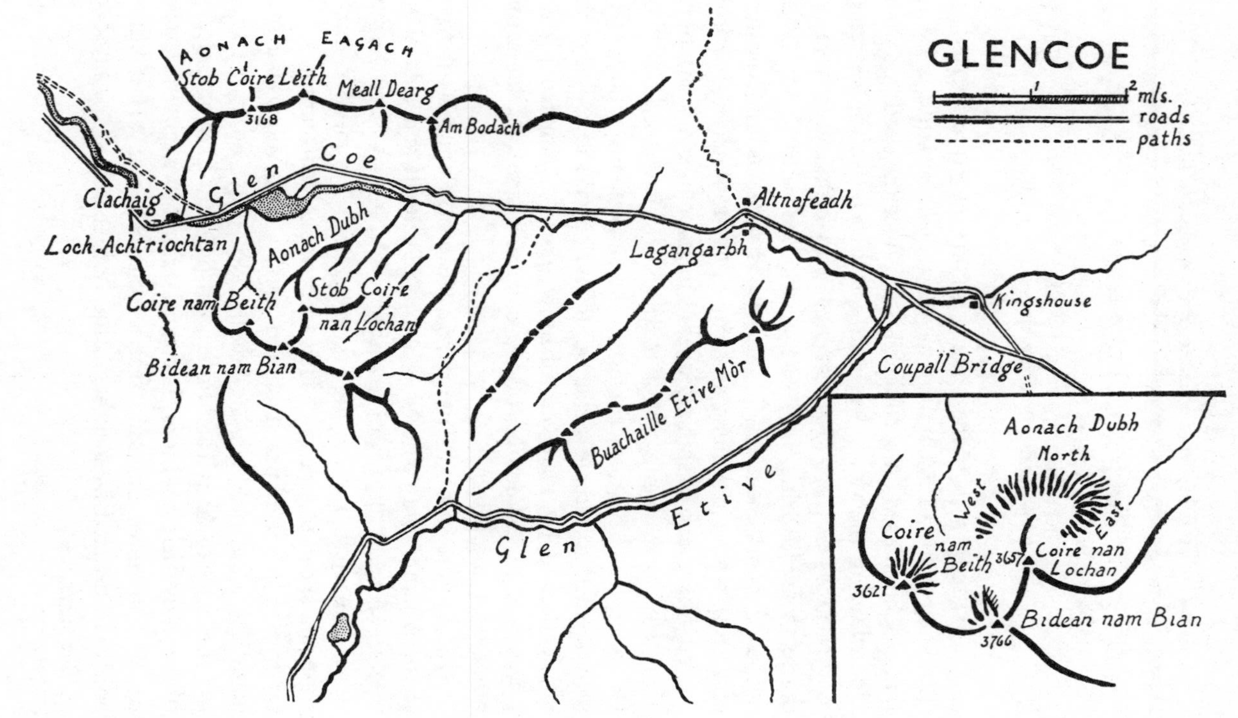
GLENCOE
1
2 mls.
roads
paths
Aonach Eagach
Stob Coire Leith
3168
Meall Dearg
Am Bodach
Glen Coe
Clachaig
Loch Achtriochtan
Aonach Dubh
Coire nam Beith
Stob Coire nan Lochan
Bidean nam Bian
Altnafeadh
Lagangarbh
Kingshouse
Coupall Bridge
Buachaille Etive Mòr
Glen Etive
Aonach Dubh
North
West
East
Coire nam Beith
3621
3657
Coire nan Lochan
Bidean nam Bian
3766

I have desired to go
  Where springs not fail,
To fields where flies no sharp and sided hail,
  And a few lilies blow.

And I have asked to be
  Where no storms come,
Where the green swell is in the havens dumb,
  And out of the swing of the sea.

We passed on over the valley, leaving our track across the snow-field with an uncomfortable sense of desecration, a feeling that quickly passed, as such feelings do, once the deed was done. Upon leaving the valley we bore uphill to the left in search of easy ground: as the snow deepened with height gained so our desire to avoid drifts, into one of which I sank to my waist, deepened commensurately. Our route took us underneath a crag from whose wall hung an array of ten-foot icicles, precisely spaced, like a rack of shining javelins in some medieval armoury. Thenceforward, bearing west to the north-east corrie of Stob Coire nan Lochan, we went up broad snow-fields, whose every flake seemed to radiate a sparkle, a myriad crystal crumbs; the whole flecked by glare and shadow like a hammered platter. I was greatly enamoured of the delicate shade of blue within our deeper footprints.

On the last slope to the corrie we crossed sheets of thick crust, whereon we could walk as on pavement and tack about freely. Across the pit of Glencoe I saw the Aonach Eagach ridge as though for the first time. It ran for miles with the edge and sheen of a razor. Had I not walked and scrambled on its crest a week earlier, I should hardly have thought a man could have balanced on the edge. Not only did it barricade the boundary of Argyll and Inverness-shire, but like some cleaver of the gods fairly cut the air between. After a two hours' ascent to close on three thousand feet we climbed over a last hump, and were ushered by a light northerly breeze into the presence of our peak.

The S C Gully of Stob Coire nan Lochan

The time was twelve-thirty p.m., and we stood on the rim or a shallow corrie seven hundred feet under the summit of Stob Coire nan Lochan. We looked straight upon the side of its north ridge, which confronted us with three buttresses. The south buttress, which was then unclimbed, was divided from the central buttress by the five hundred feet of S C gully. We could see into its white interior, and as invariably happens when a steep winter gully is seen *en face*, it appeared perpendicular. The upper half hung like a silk ribbon from the out-curl of a cornice, the overhang of which seemed to form a complete barrier round the top; in the lower half two snow-pitches were visible. But what most fascinated us was the steel-like glint of a seventy-foot ice-wall in the middle.

One could understand the feelings of a Himalayan mountaineer who was once brought hither by Dr. J. H. B. Bell and who protested that to attempt S C gully was suicidal. And probably it might be were it in the Himalaya. Between three and four thousand feet, however, such a gully may be entered with good heart, although with prospects that cannot be foretold. Although we could see the main features we were quite unable to declare them surmountable. Nor is it possible in winter, unlike summer, closely to calculate the time for a severe ascent; time depends on details of snow and ice, which high on a long rock-climb may by unforeseen quality and quantity add to or remove from an estimate a half-dozen hours.

As our route was short, we guessed four to six hours for a party of two. Since it was already afternoon they might not reach the cornice, another unknown quantity, until dusk—if indeed they could pass the ice-wall. The implication was obvious; and with great generosity MacAlpine and Mackinnon volunteered to stand down.

We all crossed the snow-fields to the cliffs and kicked steps for a hundred and fifty feet up firm snow-slopes to the foot of the gully. The snow hardened there and an ice-axe came into play; after fifty feet of cutting we arrived below the first pitch. This was a great surprise to us. On our first visit in 1937 it had been only a short wall of small difficulty. Now it was twenty-five feet, at an angle of seventy-five degrees (measured by clinometer). Scott and I tied up on a hundred feet of rope and I offered the lead to him, as being a better climber than myself. He refused and I turned to examine the snow-wall. The snow was good—that tough and viscous kind called *névé*, which I refer to hereafter as snow-ice.

I exchanged windproof for woollen gloves; for the former are very apt to slip both on ice-holds and on the shaft of the axe. Then I cut hand- and footholds as far ahead as possible before beginning to move up on them—throughout to adhere to that rule is the prime secret of climbing a snow or ice pitch. Whenever I began climbing I found the wall sufficiently steep to force me into a sideways turn before raising each leg, otherwise the bent knee overbalanced my body. When I was well over the top I drove in my axe to the head and brought up Scott. MacAlpine and Mackinnon thereupon waved farewell, and with a shout of 'Good luck!' glissaded down to the corrie.

The bed of the gully steepened, and we continued, an axe-slash and two kicks to each step, up to the second snow pitch. Its height and angle were less than the first, and where the snow-ice bulged a hollow had formed between the shell and the rock. I could cut the shell, and thrusting in my hand to the forearm, thus counter the outward lean of each step-up. We had climbed one and a half hours from the corrie by the time Scott joined me. He looked quickly past my shoulder. 'This is where the fun starts,' he remarked. And he was right.

The gully at once became sterner. The snow rose sharply in front and hardened. I had to wield my axe in earnest and hew properly cut steps. Then we entered a narrowing lane in the left half of the gully, the right half being occupied by a raised and icy chute—the seventy-foot ice-wall that had filled us with doubt nearly two hours ago. Our lane terminated under a tall overhang, where massed icicles hung like organ-pipes, and beneath which we hacked out a platform in steep snow. Scott entered into possession, tenant of a natural refrigerator. His lease was destined to be longer than we dreamt. He thrust in his axe until six inches down it struck rock. As a belay that was by no means good enough: further excavations revealed a spike in the gully-bed, and to this he tied himself.

Our situation was most exhilarating, for the gully walls rose high and sheer, the outer edges clean-cut. They were clad in breastplate and shield of gleaming ice, festooned with streamers of white powder. But my own attention was most engaged by the ice-chute above me. To climb on to it I had first to surmount its side wall, which was smothered in soft snow. Clearly, my best policy was not to climb up, but to traverse along it till the chute dipped to meet me. I swept off the loose snow and exposed brittle ice underneath; it was laid like wainscot and readily peeled off under the shock of axe-blows. Nevertheless, I spent ten minutes cleaning the wall, slowly traversing on an upslant, before I leaned over the upper lip and cut my first holds on the face of the chute. Then I climbed over the wall and looked up.

Fifty feet above, the ice-sheet thinned to what looked suspiciously like *verglas* filmed with hoar-frost. One could see the faint rugosities of the rock underneath its veneer. It might take an hour to reach as far—and when then? It was useless to speculate. I decided to go on, but in greater doubt of the issue than before. At present I was lodged on good snow-ice, thick and easily cut, but after six feet this gave place to true ice—and to the sting of spiculae spraying into my face at each axe-blow. This cutting was of necessity one-handed, and to save our valuable time I exchanged the long ice-axe for my old friend the slater's pick. Between twenty and thirty feet up I began to experience the utmost difficulty in placing my holds. The ice bulged in conformity with rock underswell; at the very points where I required ice to circumvent such bulges, rock-slabs bared rounded tips. One had need to calculate peculiar body angles and stresses for avoidance moves, and engineer the route to suit.

Between thirty and forty feet up these troubles passed and new ones assailed me. The chute was here rumpled by waves of white ice-plates. If roughly treated, they immediately shivered vertically and left one, in reward for time and work expended, with ice too thin to use but most beautiful to look upon, shining with a dark gloss like calf's-foot jelly. The most paying method was to trace the base of each hold with horizontal strokes, then deepen it with the gentlest of vertical chip-strokes. But occasionally I met a particular brand of pale blue ice that insisted on the reverse process. One quickly came to know the quality of a plate by its outward signs.

After one and a half hours, a period in which one might complete a football match or play half a round of golf, I had carved a line of notches up only fifty feet of iced rock. But like Nelson at Copenhagen, I would not have been anywhere else for thousands. Every moment was intense experience; for body and nerve life lived at the full. I had arrived at the suspectedly glazed section, but the glaze was thicker than I had dared to hope—half an inch perhaps—and much of the rock protruded, dusted as the ice with hoar but quite unglazed. My time was now less occupied with cutting than with a search for natural wrinkles that might be scraped clean. These unluckily led me up to the left to a crux, a sudden bulge that threatened defeat.

I could not progress and remain in balance. Therefore, standing on a rounded knob, I cut one finger-hold on the upmost curl, by its aid embraced the bulge, and stretched up to cut the first hold beyond. I could not stay in position long enough to finish it, for the blood ran out of my axe-arm, and leg muscles ached dangerously. The strain became unbearable. I returned to my knob and rested. Then I tried again and finished the first hold. I withdrew and rested. Three more such efforts were required to cut the second hold. Then I stood back, placed a final two notches in the centre of the bulge and climbed up. This passage was, if anything, too exciting, and I was mightily relieved by the chance of a precarious balance step to the right, where the angle fell back.

I was now close under central buttress in a seam of gravelly rock, from which pricked out one or two embedded stones. They were well frozen in and withstood testing. On these I climbed to an iced slab at the top of the pitch, where the angle of forty-five degrees seemed mild indeed. A year had passed since I had relished so stirring a winter action, but I was full of sorrow that MacAlpine and Mackinnon had not shared the full tide of happiness.

I yelled down to Scott that all was well. But the snow was too shallow to afford an axe-belay. I climbed a further ten feet, laboriously kicking steps to the detriment of my toes, rather than using an axe and so smothering in debris my hard-won holds below. My hundred feet of rope had now run out. I drove my axe two feet deep, and taking a turn of the rope round the shaft, called on Scott to come on.

In the course of his half-hour climb the sun set. Between the vertical walls of the gully I looked out as though between blinkers. Yet that very restriction had merit. It gave to the hills, arrayed in keen edges against a pale green sky, and flaring a more fiery pink with each passing moment, a framed and focused power to strike for all time to the mind. The broader and more splendid panorama, prevailing daylong, confuses the eye with too great a mass of detail—suffers from a diffused interest that too readily fades with time and is forgotten. Moreover, that panorama is not lost through a gully-climb. It comes at the top, a sudden revelation; thus more memorable.

For a few minutes the mountains burned, white and red upon a field of green and gold. In low country one may see so rich and full a glow of colour in the cavernous nave of Chartres Cathedral, when the forenoon sun floods the stained glass and the vast brown flags are flecked by shafts of ruby and blue. But Chartres is not matched elsewhere. To seek such depth of colour, and to find it in yet more noble forms, one must go to mountains. The light died from the ridges and was replaced by a ghastly pallor, as when the angel of death breathed upon the gleaming cohorts of Sennacherib. The green of the eastern sky slowly faded and was invested by night. Below me, I could hear the lonely ring of Scott's axe.

I drew in his rope, inch by inch. Scott is normally a leader, and when second on the rope continues to climb with the care of a leader—a comforting thought for myself. An unsteady partner is as unwelcome in S C gully as brittle ice. His helmeted head at last appeared over the brink—the first I had seen of him for two hours. He climbed to my own level, and then to warm him up after his age-long residence among icicles, I asked him to lead the last two hundred and fifty feet to the cornice. A man long frozen and eager for swift exercise, he cut the slope with a vigour that showered me with chips. By the time he had gained sixty feet the fragments came at me with no small velocity; those that did not register on my head and shoulders whizzed by like shrapnel. I hastily called him to a halt and climbed up. Thereafter we continued on a short rope, and dispensing with belays, moved together to the cornice.

The exit of the gully being fairly small, I had feared a complete cornice and much expenditure of time in cutting through the overhang. And thus it had appeared from the corrie. We arrived to find it sweeping overhead in a faultless volute, six feet high and complete save at one corner, where it joined the top of south buttress. There the overhang had collapsed and left a vertical snow-wall. Five minutes later, and four hours forty-five minutes from the corrie, we emerged on the back of the ridge, our boot-nails rasping on the frozen snow crust.

A bitter wind blew from the north. Twilight was deepening, and sky and mountain were drained of all colour. The peaks of Mamore and Lochaber no longer flaunted their crests with the royal bravado of noon; nor stared, menacing and livid as upon the ebb of the afterglow; but shrank toward the shadowed north, the most forlorn of ghosts. In an hour's time, when the moon and stars shone, they would step forth in coruscating might, triumphant.

We untied and coiled the rope, walked south to Stob Coire nan Lochan, and below the final peak glissaded down an eastern gully to the corrie. We hastened to the further rim, sped toward the distant glimmer of snow-fields in the Lost Valley, and beyond, down to the velvet dark of Glencoe.

13 *Lochnagar*

The First Ascent of Parallel Buttress

THE THEME OF OUR conversation was the illogical preference that most men betray for clean, sound rock. 'Any fool can climb good rock,' said Dr. J. H. B. Bell, as our car topped the Devil's Elbow and nosed down toward Braemar, 'but it takes craft and cunning to get up vegetatious schist and granite.'

I felt no inclination to contest the point: 'Before fording the river,' runs the proverb, 'do not curse the alligator's mother'; and the fact was that we were bound for Lochnagar—the greatest citadel of vegetatious granite. We hoped to climb at least one, if not two, new rock routes there. In the circumstances, a panegyric on lichened and mossy rocks savoured to me of judicious diplomacy.

We turned eastward and followed the track up Glen Callater until we came to an attractive camp site beside the river and within striking distance of Lochnagar's south-west flank. The May evening was well advanced, but all Scotland had been baking under a heat-wave and the air was still balmy. We decided to sleep out on the heather. Only the gentlest breeze stirred on the hill-side and there was no need to seek a sheltered hollow. We chose a springy couch near the track, and pulling a sheet of tent canvas over us to keep off the dew, lay back, with minds passive but alert, and watched

> the gold air and the silver fade
> And the last bird fly into the last light.

Then we set about the solution of those classic problems that have puzzled philosophers for ten thousand years.

Our talk gradually died away, becoming more and more intermittent as the sky darkened to navy-blue. The glow of our pipes grew dull while the first stars, faint and twinkling, grew slowly bright and steadfast. Silence fell. Just a whisper of wind over leagues of heather. And then I saw and heard no more.

We were awakened by the rising sun shining into our eyes. A fresh spring morning—the most joyous thing in life. Our primus stove was purring in no time, and then Bell and I repaired to the river. We found a briskly flowing pool and dived in. Once was enough. The water stung, but we came out glowing. After breakfast we packed up, and taking a couple of hundred feet of rope, set out for Lochnagar.

Our proposal was to go straight up to the summit, make a new route down the cliffs on the Tough-Brown ridge, and then, if all went well, make an ascent of the unclimbed Parallel buttress. The programme was ambitious enough, but nothing seemed impossible that morning. Our progress up the first slope was marked by the whirr and squawk of startled grouse. The cool of night still lingered in the air and the strengthening sun was only now drawing the dew off the heather. But the walk up to Lochnagar from Loch Callater is five miles, with two thousand two hundred feet of climbing, and even though we went slowly we were forced within the hour to strip to the waist. There was not a cloud in the sky. The heat had become intense but not enervating; it cooked the flesh round one's bones without sapping energy. In one and a half hours we topped Cairn Taggart. The stroll over its broad back to the White Mounth was sheer delight. The short grass and heather rustled dryly underfoot, the air shimmered; a sweet scent, enlivened by thyme and bog-myrtle, rose in waves from the warming ground. The scene typified the Cairngorms—an immense and rolling sky-line with snow-splashed peaks to the north-west. Any tendency to monotony in the foreground was sharply counteracted by the sparkle of the Dubh Loch on our right, framed between the crags of its corrie. Over a black cliff a raven glided lazily, yet with an alert poise that suggested a nestful of young among the rocks.

At midday we crossed the stony summit plateau and walked along the edge of the north-eastern precipice. At intervals, a cleft crag or a gully that bit into the brink disclosed dramatic vistas of the corrie twelve hundred feet below. The cliffs ended there in long scree-slopes, which converged on the waters of a glistening tarn. Glancing to the side, my eye swept a mile-long arc of plunging granite. It is alleged that one may see the Cheviots from Lochnagar—a distance of a hundred miles—but the farthest views had already been obscured by heat-haze.

At the top of the Tough-Brown ridge we halted, rested, and prepared for the climb. At twelve o'clock we began, unroped, the first phase of descent. The first hundred feet were well broken up. Then we diverged from the original route, which swung eastwards, and continued straight down. The angle quickly steepened, and tiers of vertical slabs, intersected by grassy ledges, obliged us to rope up. Our purpose was to find a more direct line of descent than that of the original route.

Throughout the central portion of the ridge we were entirely successful. The very nature of the rock lent itself to descent. It is less troublesome to drop down a series of short walls than to wrestle upward against granite and gravity. At first our new line involved a certain amount of traversing to and fro in search of the best route, then in search of any route at all, and latterly we were pushed off the crest until we overlooked Raeburn's gully at the western side of the ridge.

We had a simple choice before us: either to descend the west wall into the gully or to try to force a way down the true crest of the ridge. Our first desire was the crest, and we made a determined attempt. Only two hundred feet lay between us and the screes—two hundred feet of convex granite slabs, devoid of any excrescence that might serve as a rope-belay. Like the lower part of most ridges, this was the steepest part of the whole, where convexity achieved its maximum inclination. There were no intersecting ledges.

We made trial and reconnaissance, in the course of which I found myself stranded on one-nail rugosities, with insufficient handhold to lean out and prospect for further footing; with the disturbing awareness, moreover, of no good rope-belay and a two-hundred-foot drop beneath. Even Bell, tough as granite and long in the tooth, cast a ruminative eye over these proceedings. He declared definitely for the gully.

The gully wall gave us a good climb of a hundred feet on sound rock. It brought part one of our programme to fair success and ourselves into Raeburn's gully, a hundred feet above the base of the ridge. The gully was snow-filled.

We were now in the sun again, and hotter than ever. It was then that our eyes caught the liquid glitter of Lochnagar. Its colour was deep-sea green. I doubt if a loch can actually beckon to parched climbers, but most assuredly it can merrily laugh and seductively smile. In a few minutes we were pulling off our clothes by the shore. A granite block made an excellent diving platform. I curled my toes round the edge and plunged deep for the bottom.

Then up I bobbed, to float in hydraulic comfort, while watching small white clouds cruise across the blue sky, or studying possible new climbs on the stupendous mass of rock above. Thereafter we basked like a couple of idle seals on sun-warmed boulders, until at length the trumpet-call of duty sounded clear and insistent.

Before leaving the loch I looked more critically at Parallel buttress. It lay midway between Eagle buttress and Tough-Brown ridge, from which it was separated by Parallel gullies A and B. Both of these gullies were unclimbed. Between them the broad base of the buttress tapered as it soared, until six hundred feet up it narrowed to a slender ridge, which curled to the summit. The total height was seven hundred feet. There seemed to be a particularly nasty section about five hundred feet up—a short tower placed at one of the narrowest points of the ridge. If one reached so far there seemed little hope of by-passing that tower, and a problematical chance of climbing it direct. The thought of failure so high was disturbing, but doubts such as these are the spice of mountaineering, lending suspense to the climb and zest to success—and if one be philosophical, consolation to defeat.

At three p.m. we started the climb up steep rock immediately to the left of gully A. After a short ascent we made an oblique traverse across gully A on to Parallel buttress. Bell went ahead, working his way up grey sheets of granite while I selected my own route twenty feet behind. We had agreed to climb unroped until either of us felt the need of moral support. This lower part of the route was typical of the true buttress—broad fields of rock with plenty of scope for variation. For the first two hundred and fifty feet our ascent continued obliquely toward the centre line; then, as the rocks curved more and more precipitously, we were once again forced from the crest, this time toward B gully. Needless to say, the rocks were lichened and peppered with tufts of sparse grass. I shudder to think what the climb must be like in wet weather. There is a notable paucity of belays, and slime-coated granite, I should imagine, would give pause to the stoutest heart.

Our way was now blocked by a ring of impending slabs, which circled the whole breadth of the buttress. Our only hope was to turn them by a right-hand traverse along a thin and vegetatious ledge to the extreme edge of the gully. There, on the actual brink, we found a breach in the defences and climbed for a moment with our heels projecting over the gloomy depths. A short upward scramble, a slanting traverse up a long scoop in the gully wall, and the crest was ours once more.

From now onward the buttress tapered quickly, the crest became definite, and our choice of route narrowed to a single inescapable line. In short, the buttress was all set for a 'showdown'; the conditions were ripe for the uprise of one supreme obstacle, which could be turned by no backstairs cunning, that 'dark sanctuary of incapacity,' but must be won by frontal assault or not at all. We knew in our hearts it must come, and in due course come it did: in the shape of an ugly tower, the same that from far below had looked but a short wall.

The honour of leading the first attack was bestowed upon me. While we roped up I stood back and surveyed the situation. We stood on secure footing on the narrowest edge of the ridge, from which the rocks fell sharply on either hand into deep gullies. The tower rose thirty feet, its head shaped like a blunt diamond and bent gently forward, so that the last ten feet slightly overhung. This arrow-head was set upon a high bust of slabs.

I looked around both flanks in hope of detecting some weakness. They were perpendicular. Frontal attack was the one course open. But running up the left side of the bust was one exceedingly thin crack. It ended twenty feet up at the left edge of the arrow-head. There was just a chance that from there one might traverse below the final overhang to the right-hand side overlooking B gully, at which point it looked possible to climb on to the top angle of the diamond.

I failed on the crack. Eight feet up was the most I could make. After that there were no holds, not even a down-scrape on lichen or a pull-up on a tuft of grass. Bell tried next, but a brief examination convinced him of the worst. However, we still had one last card to play.

Bell dug into his rucksack and produced—I wish that one could write in a whisper—two pitons. Their use is frowned upon by many British mountaineers. Like the queen of Spain's legs, a piton not only ought never to be seen, but must not be supposed even to exist. Its use, in fact, should be sparing and reserved for exceptional circumstances. Bell and I solemnly declared that this was an exceptional circumstance. It qualified with honours.

Armed with his pitons and a small hammer, Bell climbed the wall as far as he could. Where the holds vanished he hammered a piton into the crack until only the ring protruded. Using the ring as a handhold, he pulled himself up, contrived to get one foot on it, and by a movement curious to watch, stood erect. He drove in the second piton and this he used as a handhold only. the rest of the crack was wider, still demanding a high output of energy, and then he reached a little niche at the left side of the arrow-head.

When he saw what remained to be done he wisely decided not to move further until I had joined him. On my way up I was able to remove both pitons and so leave the rocks in their pristine condition; which meant that I had to dangle like a marionette on the rope, ever a wounding experience for the ribs. There was little room on the niche and before I quite reached it Bell had to move out. While I settled in and coiled the rope, Bell removed his boots. There is nothing so comforting as stocking-soles for a traverse on smooth slabs, and this is Bell's frequent method of dealing with them.

He needed all the security he could get. When I watched him edge out on swift-dipping granite below the arrow-head, which tended to thrust his body out of balance, I realized that he trusted only to the friction of feet, for my belay would have been of doubtful value had any sudden strain come on the rope. However, the last trump had not yet sounded. He reached the right-hand side of the arrow-head, scrambled on to the sloping roof, and disappeared. I waited patiently, prepared to hear of some new horror beyond; then I heard a voice say, 'Well, I 'm up,' in the detached tone one uses for 'Good morning' at Monday's breakfast table.

To save time I told Bell that I should keep on my boots and might therefore require a pull on the rope. He assured me his belay was a good one and I began my crab-like crawl. I was right—with boots I required a constantly tight rope. In a few minutes I was again by his side.

The very air seemed brighter, more full of good cheer above that thirty-foot passage—a reaction, I suppose, from difficulty overcome. Peering over the blunt tip of the arrow, my eye went straight to the gleam of the loch. Three hours ago I had wondered whether a bathe before a climb were too good a thing on a hot day; it often tends to make one lethargic. But to-day that was not the effect on me, nor on Bell, whose performance at the crux, alternately exhibiting furious vigour and delicate balance, bore striking testimony to the virtue of Lochnagar water. Were the full truth known, this matchless tarn might become a national Lourdes.

We crossed a narrow neck behind the tower and climbed a steep nose, which turned out to be a threat without substance. Then we stopped, and with an upward glance saw that no further tower barred the way to victory. The ridge meandered onward, narrow, shattered to blocks, but after another hundred feet no longer standing out in distinguished isolation, more a part of the general mass of the cliffs, into which it finally merged just below the plateau. We united and coiled the rope, then followed the riven crest, whose unresisting crags seemed to welcome us at each turn. At the very end was a knife-edge of frozen snow.

At five o'clock we stepped on to the summit and passed, as it were, into another realm. Far beneath our feet a mighty expanse of tawny hills and plains stretched to the utmost fringes of the earth, and faded there in unfathomable blue. Over all hung the breathless hush of evening. One heard it circle the world like a lapping tide, the wave-beat of the sea of beauty; and as we listened from our watch tower and looked out across the broad earth, our own little lives and our flush of triumph in climbing a new route became very trivial things. They were suddenly measured for us against eternity and the real, and in such perspective vanished away, of no moment. Yet in that same instant our climb on the granite crags, the bare summit and the lands below, were with ourselves idealized as though in a point out of time and exalted in oneness. We began to understand, a little less darkly, what it may mean to inherit the earth.

14 *Tower Ridge in Winter*

IT IS NOTEWORTHY how often the red-letter days of our mountaineering come as a complete surprise. One such December day I spent with Dr. J. H. B. Bell and Douglas Laidlaw on Ben Nevis.

We passed the night of 16th December in the S.M.C. hut below the cliffs. For once we had made no definite plans, feeling that at such a place and time they might be an undue tempting of providence. At eight-thirty next morning we therefore stepped from the hut in a mood of mild suspense, wondering how much of the world would be visible. Westward, across the Spean valley, golden moors glowed in the early morning sun; but the upper glen of the Allt a' Mhuilinn, where the hut lies, was deep in snow and the blue shadow of white cliffs. The sky was full of wind and sun.

The snow conditions appeared excellent and we discussed the possibilities over breakfast. There was a wide choice before us, but in truth our minds had already been made up for us by the stirring challenge of Tower ridge; two thousand three hundred feet high, triple-towered, encased in snow and ice, it stood forth from the mass of the cliffs, the most splendid feature of the mountain. We set off with rope and axe at nine-thirty a.m.

Within five minutes the first surprise of the day was sprung by Bell. He proposed a direct ascent of the Douglas boulder. This boulder is seven hundred feet high and forms the first tower of the ridge. It presented toward us a huge face of slabs, which never having been climbed in winter condition would therefore make an excellent appetizer for the main course ahead; or so we thought, such was our innocence.

The first phase of operations was staged on a broad expanse

of intermingled slab and rib draped in masses of powder-snow. At the end of one hour I doubt whether we had managed to climb as much as a couple of hundred feet. It was more than well, perhaps, that before we were too deeply committed we came to *verglas*, which forbade further progress. Eleven o'clock, therefore, found us once more at the foot of Tower ridge. Whatever the others thought of such an appetizer, I myself felt akin to that Scotsman described by Byron, who having heard that kittiwakes were excellent whets, 'ate six of them, and complained that he was no hungrier than when he began.' With all speed we repaired to the eastern flank, and climbing by snow-slopes and broken rock came at eleven-thirty to the crest, a little way above the Douglas boulder.

The ridge was here slender but level. In front of us it rose abruptly for several hundred feet to the 'Little Tower,' whose midway bastion guards the narrow ascent to the main keep—the Great Tower at four thousand feet. The rocks were everywhere inundated with snow, which clung even to vertical walls. The climbing to begin with was not difficult; a sweep with a gloved hand disclosed good holds. Our first and foremost enemy was time. In the previous winter a good mountaineer had spent sixteen hours on Tower ridge; we had now only five, and must hope for better conditions to reach the Great Tower before sunset. We thought we could do it, but even then there was no guarantee that we should find the Tower passable before dark. At that height accumulations of snow and ice would be much greater than on this lower part of the mountain, and the quality would be altogether different.

Meanwhile, Bell forged ahead by himself. Laidlaw and I roped up and followed behind. This procedure saved time and we made fair speed up the first section of the ridge. Each ledge held a steep pile of snow and each square-cut block wore a tall bonnet. But the snow was good and held an in-driven foot firmly. For the most part Laidlaw and I were able to climb together, thanks to excellent rope management by Laidlaw. Following twenty to thirty feet behind, he climbed with several coils in his left hand, his ice-axe in his right, ceaselessly letting out rope or drawing it in as distance between us altered, simultaneously taking his own holds, deftly whisking the rope clear of obstacles, and never allowing it to trail on the rock. A perfect demonstration of rhythmical rope-work, accompanied by delighted grins of pleasure in the climbing.

After an hour of such climbing we arrived below the Little Tower. Strictly speaking it is not a genuine tower, but an abrupt steepening of the rocks appearing as a tower from underneath: no cleft separates it from the continuation of the ridge. To-day it was muffled up in a thick fur coat, in the unbuttoning of which we spent much time. The holds then displayed were small and glazed, most difficult to detect and scrape clean. Ninety feet up Laidlaw joined me on a ledge; we traversed leftward round a corner and discovered a much-perplexed Bell. He was held up by a vertical wall of unusual obstinacy. When at length the problem was solved I noted that a full hour had been spent on the last hundred feet.

After some more very hard climbing on the east face over glazed rock we regained the ridge above the Little Tower. The rocks then assumed a more benign angle. Nothing could stop our reaching the crux of the ridge. For one more hour we kicked, swept and cut our way up encrusted blocks until at three o'clock we were brought to a halt under the ponderous mass of the Great Tower. Two more hours would decide our fate. Meantime, we had still no conception of what difficulties lay in wait. A few years before, Bell and F. S. Smythe had been turned back at the *farther* side of the Tower at sunset, and Bell was not looking forward to a second defeat. However, no winter climb is ever the same climb twice: and therein lies the superiority of winter over summer mountaineering in Scotland.

The Tower rose almost sheer for a hundred feet above our heads. Its armour of snow and ice plate was complete. Not a chink showed anywhere. But circling round the eastern wall and overlooking the chasm of Observatory gully, there is, in summer, an easy ledge by which one may walk and then scramble up a slab until one comes to a face of sixty feet, which may be climbed to the top of the Tower. This eastern traverse was now banked with hard snow at an exceedingly high angle. It looked a mere frieze on the wide wall that dropped far out of sight into the gully.

Still unroped, Bell began step-cutting on the eastern traverse, until twenty or thirty feet along he was stopped by the first down-twist in the ledge. The snow thinned out there and it looked sensational. Bell looked at the twist, looked down at the gully, and waited for Laidlaw and me. He then tied himself to the middle of the rope; therefore I took over the lead and continued cutting until we came below the summer route.

The whole face was congested with heavy bulges of pale blue ice. Bell was against my trying the route at all, on the ground that I should take an hour to get up. However, no other route was likely to take less than an hour, and being obstinate in the face of such challenges I made an attempt. The ice was laid down in stout boiler-plates, awkwardly angled and linked by high steps of more thinly iced rock. Five minutes' cutting sufficed to show me that one hour was an underestimate; nor was I getting any encouragement from below. 'It 's a waste of time,' said Bell repeatedly. 'This should be our last resort, not our first.' It was absolutely essential that we should be across Tower Gap before dark. Some other way must be found.

At three-thirty p.m. I withdrew from the ice and we decided to prolong the eastern traverse, if we could, on an upward-slanting line for a couple of hundred feet. We might then be able to climb back to the crest just before Tower Gap, whose U-shaped gash cleaves the slender ridge between the Great Tower and the main cliffs.

We moved a few yards further along the Tower wall and found our way obstructed by a twelve-foot flake of rock, split from the main mass by a crack just wide enough to admit one leg. The flake gaped like a partially opened clam and tilted outward toward the gully. With aid from Bell, who gave me a push from behind and then held me in balance, I managed to wriggle up the slippery film of the edge and find a secure stance on top. Indeed, I could not have found myself a safer position on the whole mountain, for I stood chest high within the crack as though wedged in a rock pulpit. The others came up on a tight rope and I vacated my pulpit to Bell, who was thus well placed to protect my more dubious operations beyond.

From the rim of the flake I climbed to the wall above, where a jutting corner made the first step or two troublesome, then I passed out of Bell's sight and emerged upon the white face of a long cliff, seamed by thin and icy ledges. Much step-cutting was required, mostly one-handed cutting with the left arm: to retain balance I had to use handhold on the wall above. Being not insensitive to exposure, I remained constantly aware of Observatory gully yawning hungrily at my heels.

I made slow but steady progress. To Bell and Laidlaw, the long delay, approximately an hour, was thoroughly exasperating. They could not see what I was doing, nor what the difficulties were, but could hear the metallic ring of the axe and occasionally glimpse the scurry of ice-chips into the void. The inch-by-inch movement of the rope stood in horrid contrast to the swift flight of time. The eastern sky was growing coldly pale in prelude to night.

From time to time I heard low growls, urging me not to dawdle, or muffled barks of alarm, drawing my attention to the revolution of the earth and the corresponding need for speed by climbers. But I felt greatly cheered when I thought what my taskmasters would say upon treading these ledges themselves. Eventually the hitherto impossible wall above me lay at a climbable angle and I started straight up for the crest. The rock was thickly fluffed with snow, which I laboriously scraped off with my axe, disclosing slabs wrinkled like the hide of an elephant. I found woollen gloves of great advantage over bare hands, which would simply have slipped off the rock; whereas the wool lightly froze to the wrinkles and gave a fairly secure hold. I crawled twenty feet up the slabs and drew level with the crest ot the ridge. The coping of snow was wind-moulded to a delicate knife-edge. I popped my head over the top and looked down the other side.

A strong westerly wind smote my face. The corrie was roofed by an even fleece of cloud, which lapped against the wall of the ridge several hundred feet below and ran down the full length of the Allt a' Mhuilinn glen, where the surface was sunset-fired. The red-gold of the sky, coming so suddenly after hard climbing along an ice-clad wall, literally stopped my breath. Knowing how fleeting such a wonder may be, I was filled with anxiety lest the others should miss the full splendour. I scrambled to the crest, called to Bell to come up quickly, and driving my axe into the snow, took in his rope round the shaft. Carn Mor Dearg and the Aonachs were rose-pink against a bright green sky.

After his long wait Bell required no exhortation to hurry, but by the time he joined me the most brilliant hues had quietened. None the less the effects were still hectic enough and Bell's astonishment gratifying. As Laidlaw arrived, a more rare phenomenon occurred. The sun on the far side of Nevis was right down on the Atlantic, and the shadow of the mountain was now projected like a gigantic gnomon across the face of Scotland, devouring at one stroke the breadth of Inverness-shire, until the apex not only reached the utmost rim of the world but climbed into the fringe of brume above. The effect was then not of a shadow thrown by the mountain toward the horizon, but of a broadening beam of dark directed by the apex in the sky toward *us*. For a few moments it hung there in the guise of an anti-sun, radiating not light but darkness. None of us had witnessed this phenonenon before, and only once had we known it reported —by Leslie Stephen—of a sunset on Mont Blanc. Then the anti-sun vanished. At one stroke the earth was in twilight.

Immediately after sundown the wind grew in strength each minute and we hastened to attempt the crossing of Tower Gap before the last light died. Between the Great Tower and the upper cliffs the ridge hung like a tight-stretched curtain, but the snow-blade was comparatively soft and for twenty feet we stamped it underfoot. Then we came to the brink of the Gap. It made the most savage cleft I had seen on Scottish mountains. The icy flanks dropped sheer into deep gullies, and on the far side, rising twenty feet, was a frost-hoared wall shaped like a canine tooth. The wind tore through the open jaws with a pulsing roar and thunder-beat, like a charge of cavalry, intermittently relenting only to rush again with increased force.

'This is where Smythe and I were beaten last time,' Bell shouted in my ear. 'I don't want a repetition now!'

'It looks tough,' I replied. 'Give me a tight rope till I'm down.'

I climbed into the Gap. The floor was curved and edged like a sickle. I kicked out a platform. But when I attacked the wall beyond I could make nothing of it. The tooth was enamelled in thinnest ice, which bore a top-dressing of fog crystals. In perfect calm I question whether it might have been climbable: with a half-gale tearing at my body and the rope billowing over Tower gully, I could not even effect lodgment on the lowest rock, nor could I see any method of dealing with it. Despite the limited standing-room both Bell and Laidlaw joined me; for the situation was serious. We tried each flank of the tooth without success. Every movement was made highly precarious by the wrenching wind and the thinness of the ridge. After half an hour of vain effort we were no closer to any solution and dusk had fallen.

I faced the unpleasant facts and began to think out ways and means of retreat, swiftly speculating whether we could climb down the eastern wall on to the tilting snow-fields below Tower gully—a long, steep, and uneasy procedure—or had better follow Bell's old line of retirement by the secondary Tower ridge. I asked Bell what he thought. He looked down the east wall and shook his head. 'Not that!' said he. 'Better go back as I went with Smythe.' But the idea of returning along the eastern traverse dismayed me. Quite apart from darkness, the cold had become piercing.

It was then that Laidlaw suggested lassoing the tip of the

ROCK

W. H. Murray on Buachaille Etive Mor

AGAG'S GROOVE, RANNOCH WALL

THE OBSERVATORY RIDGE OF BEN NEVIS

Observatory ridge in centre. North-east buttress on left. Observatory buttress on right

BUACHAILLE ETIVE MOR

SOUTHWARD FROM SGURR ALASDAIR

THE CLIFF

Route I, Rannoch Wall

GARDYLOO GULLY, BEN NEVIS

THE BRAERIACH PLATEAU

tooth. I was doubtful. It seemed a waste of precious minutes. We were not cowboys. However, the alternatives were bad enough to make it worth one trial. I untied my rope, doubled it into a loop, and climbing half-way up the short side of the Gap, cast the rope high and hard into the teeth of the wind. At this very first attempt the loop whipped neatly round the top of the wall. Life is like that. At another time in such weather one might spend an hour in fruitless effort.

Bell was now tied to one end of the doubled rope, the other being in my own hands. 'He was scant o' news that telt his faither was hanged,' say the lowland Scots; but in the highlands a man can string up a friend and be unashamed. Feeling very much like Mr. Ellis, the public executioner, I hauled at my own end of the rope, while Bell went skyward. In ten minutes he was up and the day was saved.

Laidlaw followed next. While he was climbing, my attention was drawn to a sudden, visible ebb of the twilight, several times repeated. The snow-swamped mass of the upper cliffs retired into thickening night; the rocks took on a gaunt and ghastly aspect, until one might say most aptly that 'Echo, here, whatever is asked her, answers Death.' The scene returns with faultless definition to the mind in after-days, although at the time, in a freezing wind, but a quick impression seemed to be registered.

In all, I had spent one hour in the Gap before my turn came to follow. Almost paralysed by cold, I partly climbed and was mostly dragged up the hoary skin of the tooth. The remaining three hundred feet of the ridge gave a straightforward climb in knee-deep snow, but care was required to avoid being caught on the wrong foot by the greater gusts. We skirted the last riven crags by a steep snow-slope to the right, then with a final tussle scrambled on to the summit plateau at six p.m. Our climb had lasted seven hours.

To our surprise we found ourselves in calm. For the wind, baffled, struck upright from the cliffs. Before us stretched vast snow-fields, shining frostily under the stars; beyond, rank upon rank of sparkling peaks. A great stillness had come upon the world. We seemed to tread air rather than crusted snow; we were light of foot; we walked like demigods in joyous serenity. The intensity of our exaltation seems peculiar to the following of a great rock-climb to a climax of supreme beauty. After the hard fight on Tower ridge we were elated, by the miracle of sunset, steadied; for in profound beauty there is more solemnity than gayness; so that our faculties were in balance yet highly keyed, therefore abnormally alive to the deep peace of the summit. Its grace flowed in upon the mind with a touch soothing and most delicate. We need feel but once the spell of that enchantment to understand Schumann's declaration that the true music is a silence. In the quiet I felt something of the limitation of personality fall away as desires were stilled; and as I died to self and became more absorbed in the hills and sky, the more their beauty entered into me, until they seemed one with me and I with them.

Later, while we walked slowly across the plateau, it became very clear to me that only the true self, which transcends the personal, lays claim to immortality. On mountains it is that spiritual part that we unconsciously develop. When we fail in that all other success is empty; for we take our pleasure without joy, and the ache of boredom warns of a rusting faculty.

At last we turned toward Achintee and went down like fallen angels, with an ever-mounting reluctance, from a spiritual paradise to the black pit of Glen Nevis.

15 *Cir Mhor*

THE EVENING OF THE FIFTH OF AUGUST 1939 found R. G. Donaldson, M. Mackinnon, and me toiling with swollen rucksacks up Glen Rosa to the high pass that looks down to Glen Sannox. We had come to the Isle of Arran for two days' rock-climbing and ridge-wandering. In tribute to the notorious properties of Arran granite, whose 'cyclopean walls' make high demand of time and energy, we proposed to camp fifteen hundred feet up in the north corrie of Cir Mhor.

It is not my policy to 'rough it' on the mountains unnecessarily, for hard times need no seeking; therefore, in addition to much climbing equipment we were heavy-laden with tent, sleeping-bags, eggs, bacon—the luxuries of a comfort-loving world, when hard tack and a couch on the heather might have served our turn as well. I kept remembering a certain climber who had lived for ten days in the Cairngorms on peasebrose alone; at which I warmed with indignation, telling myself that pseudo-toughness had roots in laziness. But I thought wistfully of iron rations and the light load they entail as the sky darkened and dusk closed upon us on the long windless slopes below the Saddle.

These symptoms of weariness may bear on a phenomenon that arose later. Donaldson, brimming over with vitality, inspired no doubt by this being the start of his summer holidays, had reached the pass ten minutes ahead of me. I could see his tall figure on the rim of the ridge against the night sky. He was staring eastward and I automatically followed his gaze when I stepped up beside him. Before me, the waning moon was just clear of the far rim of Cioch-na-h-Oighe, and thus perceptibly rising. A few stars peered and twinkled round the fringe of a travelling cloud. Even the sea, visible only as an inky blackness, had a motion felt rather than seen. Everywhere that sense of movement.

After two hours of uphill tramping in sultry air I felt released in a world lively and free, which awakened in me the illusion of watching the spin of the earth and its flight through interstellar space. This sensation sprang from both sight and touch: the brush of the wind on my cheek, the lift of the moon, the glide of some wisps of cirrus, and more especially of the stars, which seemed to race behind them. From the lofty pass I watched this sweep of the earth through a chartless universe with the added sense of a majestic rhythm of movement, which may best be likened to the greatness of rhythm in a Beethoven symphony. The illusion lasted half a minute and disappeared with the arrival of Mackinnon. On reflection, I remember no other mountaineers reporting that experience, which on subsequent nights I have tried in vain to recapture. Yet so naturally did it come and go that I thought nothing of its rarity at the time. And my attention was at once claimed by the hard work in front.

Half a mile away on our left crouched Cir Mhor, beneath whose ebony wedge the north corrie lay like a dark pool, screened by Cioch-na-h-Oighe from the low moon. We went down to it by a long traverse of the mountain-side, groping our way in pitch blackness through a confusion of heather and rock outcrops. A man's opinion of this world sadly deteriorates if he gets much of such work. My thoughts, so exalted a short while ago, sank very low indeed.

Many a time Mackinnon and I stopped on the lip of some drop, which for all we knew might be five feet deep or fifty, or sat on some obstructing boulder, and comprehensively cursed. We cursed the mountain, the moon, and in particular Donaldson, whose most heinous crime was that of being alive and visible—and in front. At the end of a tiring day I have at other times known weary men unwisely keep silent, allowing vague and baseless resentments to gather over the party like a thundercloud. A discharge of invective is to be heartily recommended at such times. It clears the air. Most salutary of all is a friendly word; but most difficult.

We arrived in the corrie at midnight and pitched the tent on a patch of turf midway between the cliffs and a small stream, whose plentiful supply of water made the corrie a first-class base. Inside the tent our cramped quarters were soon reduced to the cheerful chaos that attends supper. At one o'clock I disentangled myself and went out for a last look round. The moon stood well toward the zenith, and infinitely far below drove a golden furrow across the jet expanse of the sea. The sky was swarming with stars; and Cir Mhor, which an hour before was no more than a painted shadow lurking in the background, had taken a great stride forward; its cliffs now rose directly over us like the palm of an uplifted hand, raised not in threat but in benediction. Everything seemed propitious for the morrow and I pulled on my sleeping-bag with that delicious sense of work past and pleasure before, which yields a present of pure content.

I know few mountaineers who are good risers. It was broad daylight before we bestirred ourselves and not till nine a.m. did we set out and take stock of the day's battleground. It was a glorious summer morning and every detail of the cliffs stood sharp in clear air. The huge granite slabs lapped upon each other like the plates of a suit of mail; even in photographs Cir Mhor may be distinguished from all other rock-peaks by this unique armoured façade. Our plan was to attack the slender buttress named B C rib (thus styled from the B and C gullies that flank it) and thereafter follow a direct route on the upper face to link with Bell's groove near the summit. This course would give us the longest rock-climb on the mountain.

I was anxious to investigate B C rib. Many years ago, in a paper read before the Alpine Club, this rib had been described as the most dangerous of Scottish rock-climbs, mainly, I think, on account of a paucity of belays. However, the times change and I felt certain that the stigma could no longer be held true: we hoped to find the climb of great interest yet not severe. So far as we could judge from below, the main difficulty lay in the smoothness of slabs in the central section and an unavoidable overhang at the finish.

A short uphill walk brought us to the base of the rib. We roped up with a hundred feet between each man, myself as leader and Donaldson second. By cutting out a long preliminary ascent of the lower mountain, our high camp should, in theory, have brought us to the rocks fresher and better able to deal with them. As now, I have generally found this belief a partial fallacy, inasmuch as one is neither warmed up nor worked into that smooth upward rhythm of movement as essential to good rock-work as to hill-walking. I began to climb the easier rocks like an old cab-horse, and on the more difficult bestowed too great an output of energy. After sixty feet I was stopped by an awkward corner at the right-hand edge of the rib. Its tall grey wall bristled with unsuitable projections, whereon I struggled like one in an evil dream; until of a sudden I struck form. Eye, mind, and muscle co-ordinated, and I felt myself drift up the cliffs like smoke. It is a delightful sensation and one of the incidental joys of rock-climbing.

When I reached the stance above and watched Donaldson climb, and again from a still higher ledge when I looked down like a roosting gull while he brought up Mackinnon, I saw from the smooth progress of their tousled heads that each was in good climbing mood. The knowledge reassured me. For the principal obstacles were drawing close. Should belays be few and far between, not the form of the leader alone, but that of the whole party, must determine safety or danger. Shortly afterwards we came to a tilting grass platform, and there, hard before us, sprang the great slab which had drawn my suspicious eye from the corrie.

The pitch was an unbroken sweep of granite, shield-shaped, bare of feature save for one long groove, too thin for hold, which ran diagonally from the low left to the top right corner. In this shallow score were lodged at intervals a few tufts of coarse grass, whose cushion might accommodate the edge-nail of a boot. On these, it would seem, must depend a climber's further progress and 'the continuity of his cervical vertebrae.' With a quickened interest I instinctively cast round for belays. Not a spike, not a knob however diminutive, gladdened the prospecting eye. Donaldson, who as second man was most affected by this deficiency, was trustfully unconcerned. He was clearly sustained by those twin pillars of mountaineering faith; belief in the axiom that the leader does not fall; and more practically, that if he does, then the most secure of all belays by a second man is his sitting down on a ledge, whence he may feed out the rope round his waist—*not* round the rock.

Conscious of being safely belayed, I stepped very gently on to the first tuft, and before it might think of subsiding passed with stealthy tread to the second tuft. And so swiftly on till at length I glided over the top. There is no real difficulty in the pitch, but the grass must be tenderly treated and the foot set down as though on egg-shells. Nothing would persuade me to venture on it in wet weather.

A Lakeland climber to whom I described this simple slab was horrified. To place trust in grass-holds seemed to him a dangerous flouting of first principles. But this is not so. Grass and loose rock are natural inhabitants of the mountain precipice, and mountaineers must be able to use them; like snow and ice, their condition may be judged in advance—with practice.

When Donaldson and Mackinnon had rejoined me we climbed without further incident to the final overhang. There was a little recess to the left of it, like the niche for a saint under the eaves of some cathedral spire. I am uncertain of the height of cathedral spires, but our own niche was about two hundred and fifty feet above the screes, say four times the height of a city tenement. The ascent of the overhang, therefore, promised aerial thrills. But of this I was confident: there must surely be some very fine handholds as yet invisible to us; for it is manifest that no overhang may be climbed without them. Donaldson tied himself to a stout rock-spike at the back of his niche, and although lamentably unsaint-like, gave me a seraphic smile and the word to go forth.

I edged out to the right on small notches, taking my handholds low down to preserve arm strength, then went straight up until the overhand stopped me. At this vital point I found an undercut hold at waist-level, on which I was able to lean out of balance and stretch the left hand over the top. My hurriedly groping fingers at once closed round the ideal handhold, the same that has ever charmed my dreams, but which never till now materialized in the living rock—a jug handle. One vigorous pull up and my chest was over the brink, legs dangling in thin air; then with a few press-holds I pushed myself up to the easy rocks beyond. Like many an impending obstacle in life, it fell at once when boldly tackled; and the joy of swarming over this brow of space was out of all proportion to the technical difficulty. One's blood spins and the spirit sings. No melancholy in a man can survive such rock.

It is to be noted that at no time throughout the route had I climbed without a good belay. The standard of climbing was very difficult.

The whole upper rock-face was now at our disposal, like a splendid book stored with secrets of varied lore, of sudden beauty and essays in brisk adventure, of which, most sadly, we had time to read but a chapter and that quickly. We were, in fact, free to select one route from numerous alternatives, for the rocks were much riven and abounded in hidden nooks and crannies, and tantalizing corners with who knows what beyond. The face demands several days' exploration.

The line we ultimately followed led us tortuously to an inclined passage, which bored into a sudden upheaval of slabs. It appeared that we had reached a cul-de-sac and must turn back, but a disappearing tunnel called aloud for examination. We discovered that it ended in a rock chamber roughly shaped like a beehive. Fifteen feet above the down-tilt of the floor the arched roof was pierced by a hole—a hole wide enough to admit the body of a man. I caught a glimpse of blue sky and the white flash of a gull breasting the sun. They drew one's spirit upward, but to raise the flesh even to the foot of the chimney seemed beyond the ingenuity of man. No abundance of good holds could serve our purpose. None the less, and despite the plain evidence of our eyes, some intuition of a practicable solution held us there.

The problem was an intellectual one, and as such had its fascinations. We examined the construction of the chamber in a spirit of detached speculation, with something of that purely objective curiosity by which Galileo, observing the pendulum swing of a chandelier above his cathedral pew, surprised and formulated one of the fundamental laws of physics. The analogy would appear unduly flattering to Mackinnon and me, for this objective thinking bore fruit only in Donaldson.

There was a crack at one point of the wall, and where the roof began to overhang the crack held a chock-stone. Donaldson climbed up and threaded a rope through it and we viewed the situation anew. My own attention wandered again to Donaldson, who is at all times an absorbing study. He is much given to reverie and had fallen into a long abstracted stare, his lips slightly apart, as though breathing had momentarily ceased. Then his face suddenly warmed as the glimmer of a secret thought, rising like a bubble from the depths, broke through his eyes in a smile. At once he was alert. The rope hung clear to the floor; he seized one end and tied a loop there, adjusting the rope till the loop hung midway between floor and ceiling. The top end he tied securely to the chock-stone: after climbing the crack to the chock-stone he pulled the loop toward him, inserted one foot, and then with a powerful lunge catapulted himself from the wall. The forward and upward swing of the pendulum carried him close below the hole in the roof, whereupon he let go the rope and, swift as thought, grasped handhold in the opening. In a trice he had jammed his chest and shoulders in the chimney. After a noble struggle of some minutes he squirmed up and was free in the open air.

Had this feat of acrobatics been performed twenty feet above sawdust in a circus, it might have brought down the house in applause. High up on the face of a mountain cliff, it passed off with no more than a cheerful 'Good work!' Belatedly, I pay tribute to the quality of Donaldson's mind, for imagination and realistic thought rarely correlate. The actual acrobatics looked spectacular, but in fact were of little merit, for I had no difficulty in repeating them. An end of the rope was then thrown up to us by Mackinnon, who tied himself to the other end but had no way of joining us by his own volition. We therefore pulled him up like a sack of coals to the chimney, and thence like a cork from a bottle.

There seemed to be no serious barrier between ourselves and Bell's groove, so we sat a little in the sun and coiled up the rope; then continued, each to his own line, up the pale grey lanes of granite, whose flanking crags were sweeping in more closely to the final cone. I imagine we must have been following one of the joints in the armour, but we were too close to the vast scale of things to know this certainly, as an ant in a jungle, perhaps, may doubt whether it crawls in a track or a clearing.

A short way beneath the summit we made a descending traverse to the right and were confronted with our last pitch, Bell's groove: a great slab cleft by a diagonal crack. I recall no definite holds. The friction of cloth and skin and the jamming of the right boot in the crack were the means of adhesion and propulsion. Thinking in our folly that we could climb Arran rock without using our knees, we had this day discarded breeches for the greater freedom of shorts, and in much the same way as we had disgorged pier dues to land at Brodick, so here a toll of cuticle was exacted at the gate to the summit. Thus, each in turn spread his body over the edge of the groove, and wriggling like a caterpillar, forced his way up by inward pressure of foot, knee, and forearm. Feeling slightly the worse for wear, we left the groove behind and mounted the last few feet to the cairn.

Cir Mhor has one of the sharpest tops in Scotland. There was no room for three of us, so we went a little way down on the far side and enjoyed a spell of sun-bathing. An hour later we felt compelled to traverse the A' chir ridge to Beinn Tarsuinn.

The A' chir ridge is the finest in Arran, and has attained much fame by virtue of the sensational photographs which may be taken at the *mauvais pas*. I myself, never having traversed the ridge, looked forward to it with high expectations.

At one o'clock we set off. The air was still and a hot sun beat upon the crags. We therefore went shirtless and enjoyed one of the most invigorating ridge-walks that have fallen to us in summer. The 'bad step' resolved itself into an easy stride across a cleft in the thinnest part of the ridge. Throughout we walked in the authentic mountain atmosphere, where a climber feels poised in the middle air between heaven and earth, and knows himself most close to the former. The crest was narrow and bold, like some of the less riven parts of the Cuillin; the rock clean; deep glens fell away on either hand and carried brawling streams to the sea, which in return sent wheeling round the hills a sparkling halo of gulls—those birds of inhuman beauty, whose wild eye and stainless plume seem to me to have been evolved from the world expressly to embody the true spirit of seaward mountains, and by their cry, forlornly echoing among the rocks, to sound the inner music.

At three p.m. we came to the summit of Beinn Tarsuinn. Half-drugged by sun, I curled up on a rock beside the cairn and, closing my eyes, let my mind take me where it would. I soon balanced gloriously at ease on a spar of granite, and like a wizard on a broomstick, drifted far over the western isles with white gulls for escort.

16 *The Cuillin Ridge and Blaven*

I ARRIVED IN SKYE for the first time in June 1936. I hardly knew what to expect. I had heard much of the Cuillin and read more, and my imagination had run riot. It speaks volumes for the character of the range that my wild dreams fell short of the wilder reality. Climbing from Glen Brittle to the summit of Sgurr na Banachdich on a clear day of great heat, I saw them at last, by myself. Twenty peaks of naked rock shimmered in the heat-haze; a horse-shoe of light grey spikes linked by a six-mile ridge of gabbro and shattered basalt, narrow, rarely sinking under three thousand feet. Eastward, beyond the main array and across the deep, long-running valley of Glen Sligachan, the bulk of Blaven rose high above wisps of whitely curling mist, which glided up the west buttress and vanished. From its summit a sharp and pinnacled ridge fell and swept up again to the curving crest of Clach Glas. After an hour of silent admiration I took a wider sweep with the eye, disclosing a feast of sunlit seas and distant islands, and still later, a still wider sweep to embrace skyscapes that rocked the mind with wonder. Time spent in failing to fathom a blue sky is never spent in vain. Let the mind soar like the highest-mounting bird, self-surrendered to the infinite, and an infinite spirit seems to flow into one. This is the law of grace. Thus seeds are sown from which a rich harvest of philosophy may be reaped in its season. But I was too inexperienced to reap then.

Nor was I elderly enough to find in beauty an excuse for inaction. In fact that day inspired me to plan more tumultuous outpourings of energy than ever. How doubly excellent, I thought to myself that night, would be a combined traverse of both eastern and western Cuillin! Like many great rock-climbs of the past, the one-day traverse of the Cuillin Main Ridge was long held to be impossible (it involved ten thousand five hundred feet of ascent) until in 1911 it was accomplished in twelve hours by Messrs. Shadbolt and Maclaren. Since then it has been many times repeated. But twenty-five years had elapsed without any attempt on the traverse of the whole Cuillin. For although the Main Ridge traverse of the western Cuillin is now acknowledged to be the best day's mountaineering in Britain, and the traverse of the eastern group, comprising Blaven and Clach Glas, gives four thousand feet of the best mountaineering in Skye, yet the two had not been combined. East was east and west was west, and Glen Sligachan lay between. Such was the position in 1936.

The varied attractions of the double traverse fairly jostled for attention inside my mind. Firstly, the course lay through the grandest mountain scene in Britain, and granted the prerequisite to success—skill to maintain the steady rhythm of climbing movement that slowly annihilates height and distance—then, no matter how long and hard the day, we should lose nothing of enjoyment, then or in retrospect.

Secondly, I was fascinated by the problem in mountain-craft. One must inevitably start or finish in darkness; therefore to turn ground to best advantage, where should one start and where finish? Should one bivouac on the ridge beforehand? And where descend after—to Sligachan, Broadford, or a previously pitched tent at Coruisk or Glen Sligachan? Should food and water be cached on the ridge, and what kind of food had best be used? What bodily training would be needed in preparation?

Thirdly, since success must depend on untested qualities of mind and body, the issue would remain in doubt till the day was nearly done. The great physical strain would afford valuable data concerning one's ability to master an exhausted body, to discipline temper and judge calmly under stress. I thought then, and now I know, that everv man should have such knowledge of himself. And in 1936 I had no idea what my own limits were. Thus there was a double problem to solve, strategic and personal.

But above all, it was a good climb.

The first practical difficulty was to convince my own mountaineering friends that the proposition was not an impossibility. And for three years I was unsuccessful. 'It can't be done,' is a phrase one hears too often. One cannot stop its impinging on the ear-drums, but one should refuse it admittance to the mind. For it is demonstrably untrue. I had no inclination to attempt the ridge by myself, and had to find a companion who was not only an excellent rock-climber but an enthusiastic mountaineer into the bargain. The problem continued unsolved until December 1938, when on one of the luckiest days of my life I met R. G. Donaldson. He was very quiet and reserved. My first impression was that I had met a man in whose company no unwholesome thought could exist. It was not an experience I had had before. He had the reflective, unusually clear and steady eye of a man who can dream and plan boldly, and act with energy. Moreover, he actually entertained the idea of trying the two Cuillin ridges! I was astounded. Within six months I knew him for what he was—my plans for an Alpine holiday were discarded in favour of Skye, and mid August 1939 found Donaldson, M. Mackinnon, and me encamped in Glen Brittle. Mackinnon decided not to accompany us on the ridge, but most generously helped us in other ways.

We imposed on ourselves no special training, and our first ten days were spent in climbing ourselves into good form. Most of our excursions involved long traverses on the Main Ridge, preceded by a severe rock-climb and followed by a gargantuan feast at the base camp. Huge as our meals undoubtedly were, the abounding hordes of midges dined still more sumptuously. Skye in August is no fit place for man or beast. The entire island falls into a state of midge-ridden anarchy. Life in camp was often wellnigh unbearable, and almost every night witnessed scenes of disorder and sounds

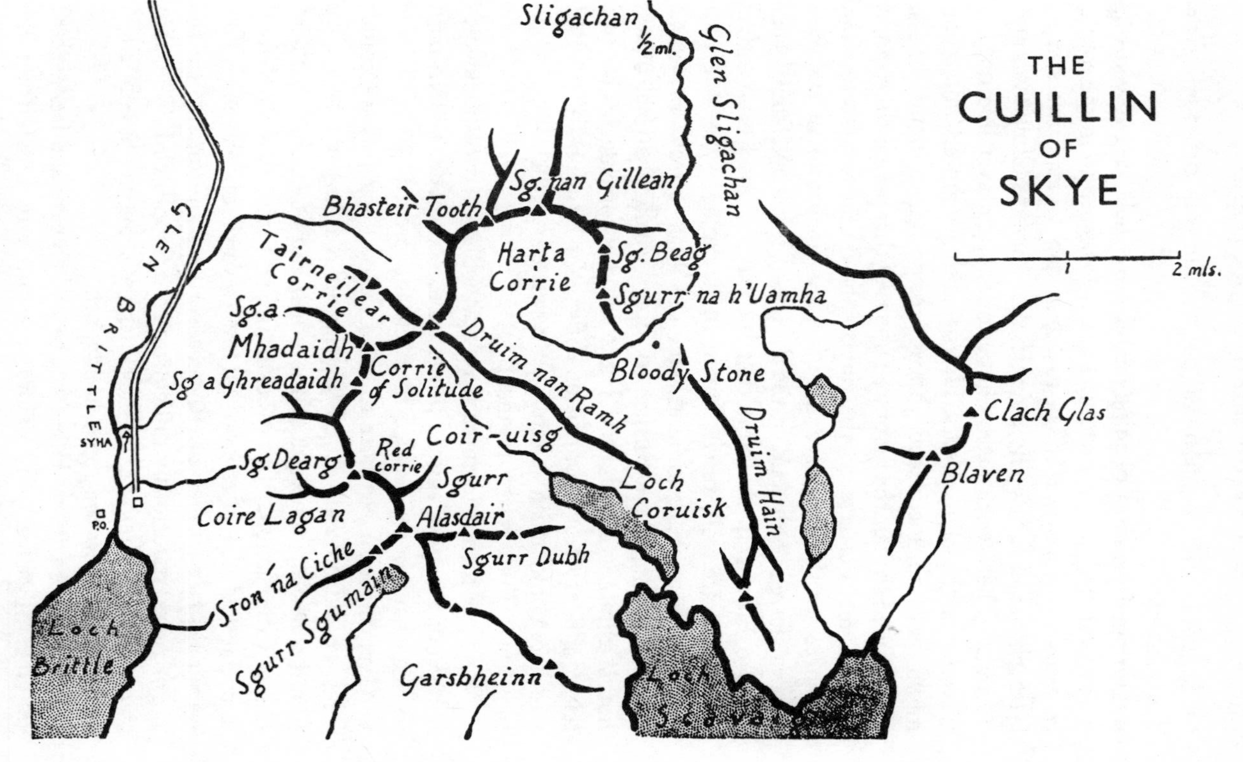
THE CUILLIN OF SKYE
1
2 mls.
Sligachan
½ ml.
Glen Sligachan
Sg. nan Gillean
Bhasteir Tooth
Harta Corrie
Sg. Beag
Sgurr na h'Uamha
Tairneilear Corrie
Sg. a Mhadaidh
Druim nan Ramh
Bloody Stone
Sg a Ghreadaidh
Corrie of Solitude
Coir-uisg
Druim Hain
Clach Glas
Blaven
Sg. Dearg
Red corrie
Sgurr Alasdair
Loch Coruisk
Coire Lagan
Sgurr Dubh
Sron 'na Ciche
Sgurr Sgumain
Garsbheinn
Loch Brittle
Loch Scavaig
GLEN BRITTLE
SYHA
P.O.

of torment, dire enough to pour balm on the soul of a Torquemada.

During these days of mingled bliss and hell we evolved our plan of campaign. We should start at Garsbheinn in the south, traverse the ridge northward to Sgurr nan Gillean, descend to Glen Sligachan for two hours' rest, then traverse Clach Glas and Blaven. There were sixteen hours of daylight available and the traverse might take twenty hours—perhaps more. Thus we might have to spend four hours' rock-climbing in darkness. We decided to allot the first three hours of that period to reaching the first real obstacle on the ridge—the Thearlaich-Dubh Gap—where we should arrive at dawn; the final hour of the four we transferred to the end of the day, to the traverse from Clach Glas to Blaven, in the hope that by making good time earlier we might, after all, reach Blaven in daylight. The ascent to Garsbheinn at the beginning, and the descent from Blaven at the end, might take a further six hours, making a total of ten hours' climbing by night. The total was formidable, but we felt confident of overcoming all difficulties by torchlight. Bad weather would mean failure. We trusted to the happy combination of luck with judgment.

Were we fortunate enough to reach Blaven, we should certainly not care to stagger up five miles of boulder-strewn path to Sligachan, so we decided to pitch and provision a small tent in Glen Sligachan, as near to the foot of Blaven as we could. This we did on 22nd August, a day of roasting sun, when we found a perfect camp site at the north end of Loch an Athain, below Coire Dubh. We stocked the tent with two days' food and devoted the afternoon to the traverse of Blaven. This reconnaissance was essential, because the route-finding on the north ridge, notoriously difficult in mist, would be hopeless for two exhausted climbers did they strike mist and night combined, unless they knew the route in advance.

Furthermore, it was important to find an easy and fast descent to Glen Sligachan. Therefore, on our way down from the summit we reconnoitred two routes. Donaldson went straight down the west buttress and I down a gully to Coire Dubh. We consulted afterwards at Loch an Athain. Either route was direct, but the ground too awkward for easy negotiation by night, and we knew that our descent from Blaven after fourteen thousand feet of climbing would be a somewhat harrowing experience. It seemed best to find an easier route, even though it were longer. Therefore, Donaldson suggested the long, easy ridge running southward to Camasunary, a route that led not toward our tent but two miles in the opposite direction. Then we should return up the path in Glen Sligachan, thus defeating exhaustion by rhythm. I baulked for a while at choosing any route that took us so far out of our way, but the alternatives seemed even less attractive. We decided, reluctantly, that our descent should lie down the south ridge. The decision was a bad one, and would not have been made had we known the mountain better. Having omitted to bring any food, we then retired speedily on Sligachan.

Our next two days were spent in skirmishing with the weather. The first day was cloudy and we made no move. That was a great misfortune. For the aurora borealis roused us from our sleeping-bags before midnight. Directly over the Cuillin one of the gateways to heaven had swung loose, and beams of celestial light swept back and forth across the earth. This wonderful display lasted for hours. How we wished we had been up on the ridge that night! But the next morning was again cloudy, and we spent the whole day resting. We were anxious to avail ourselves of a clear night. For the moon was waxing in the second quarter and we should have good illumination. There is added delight in the climbing when black peaks point to a starry sky.

Then, at eight o'clock, the cloud-cap lifted. Could we now rely on the weather for a day or two? For some days the wind had been south-easterly. In Glen Brittle a movement of the wind from south-east to south brings rain, but there was no sign of change. I therefore proposed an immediate start. Our decision was sudden. We ate dinner and packed our rucksacks.

We had decided not to cache food or water on the main ridge, therefore in addition to the usual sandwiches we carried a one-and-a-half-pint water-bottle and vita-glucose.

We left our tents at ten p.m. We had each looked forward to this night from our first climbing days, and as we moved slowly uphill in the gathering darkness we felt that tenseness of mind and body that enlivens the opening hour of a long-delayed venture. For the wind and weather conditioning our efforts were as unpredictable as our ability to stay the marathon course.

Our first misfortune was not long delayed. Mist had been gathering round the mountains, and as night fell the clouds sank into the corries and obliterated the peaks. The moon, which had given promise of lighting our four-mile walk round the base of the Cuillin to Garsbheinn, was now obscured. The wind had moved to the south and the weather had won the first round. We moved slowly, not only to conserve strength, but because boulders, heather, and deep-cut streams were so inextricably mixed that we could not with safety move fast.

After an hour and a half of disagreeable walking we crossed the lower slopes of Sgurr nan Eag into the western corrie of Garsbheinn. The prospect was bleak and gloomy. Far below, a flashing lighthouse on Soay exposed the island's flat outline against the darkly crawling sea. It was hard to believe that men lived on ground so bare and desolate. In front of us, scree-shoots rose into thick mist. Fifteen hundred feet of perpendicular scree (I had no clinometer) in mist at midnight is a realistic foretaste of what awaits climbers in another world.

We climbed in silence, in stony silence, for my part inwardly cursing mountains and this the foulest of them all. The ascent seemed interminable, and the fact that we reached the top merely put us in worse humour, for we arrived there at one-thirty a.m. in a keen moist wind. Somewhere in front lay twelve thousand feet of climbing, and already we felt too spent to put one foot in front of the other. A crag below the cairn gave us shelter while we pulled on gloves, balaclavas, and sweaters before settling down to rest. Shivering with cold and crouching on damp rocks below the cairn, we were surrounded by a thick wet mist, which precipitated a fine, just perceptible drizzle; and far away in lonely Coruisk the staccato bark of foxes roused mournful, lingering echoes.

At two o'clock in the morning we dragged ourselves to our feet and stumbled sleepily down through the mist to find the ridge to Sgurr nan Eag. Donaldson had been unable to get a fresh battery for his torch before leaving Glen Brittle, and was soon forced to rely entirely on mine. I therefore went first. We slowly scrambled along the narrow crest while grey tentacles of mist writhed and twisted round our bodies, diffusing and blanketing the powerful beam from the torch, so that little advance choice of route was possible. Donaldson followed as best he could in the feeble back-wash of light, but as always he made no complaint, although the effort to follow for three hours in semi-darkness without stumbling must have been an irritating strain. I have yet to hear him utter a disparaging word of any man or mountain.

We reached Sgurr nan Eag at three a.m., which was later than we had hoped. The level walking on top was a great relief after the long ascent, but if we were already tired enough to find relief in a little level walking, when we had barely started our day's work, then our prospect of success was surely not very bright. The fact of the matter was that we both felt despondent; that I was not outspokenly bad-tempered as well was probably due only to hard exercise. Human vitality drops to its lowest ebb in the hours before dawn, and no mountaineer is ever cheerful at three o'clock in the morning in mizzling cloud. If he were, his maddened companion would push him over the edge.

We struggled down to the col above Coire a' Ghrunnda, climbing automatically, but failing in darkness to strike that rhythmical movement so vital to long-distance mountaineering. Befogged in mind as well as body, we were almost trapped into the ascent of a rectangular tower, which overhung on its far side. We side-stepped just in time by traversing ledges on its west wall and began the gruelling ascent to Sgurr Dubh. We reached the top thirty-five minutes behind schedule. A halt was essential, and we stopped for some food and water. Throughout, we were determined to go no faster than we found natural.

On the descent from Sgurr Dubh to the col below Sgurr Thearlaich the inconvenience of having but one torch between two became most apparent. At every crag or boulder I had to stop and shine the torch backward for Donaldson. This reduced our speed to a crawl and we went as slowly as though tied together on a ten-foot rope, each impatiently waiting for the other to climb up or down the crags before he himself could move. I became more and more convinced that our expedition would end in failure, unless by a miracle the weather cleared and we received impetus from awakened vigour.

Meantime we floundered up the ridge to Sgurr Thearlaich, until the broken slabs and scree steepened into solid rock. We swarmed up a gabbro tower, traversed a level ridge, and were faced with a vertical wall of basalt, wet and grey in the gloom. We tied on the rope. I adjusted my head-lamp and placed the battery in my trouser pocket. The ridge was narrow here and fell away with great steepness on either hand. Directly in front the wall was unclimbable. I traversed a few feet to the left, and had gone half-way up when, unluckily, just as I reached for a handhold, the rucking-up of my breeches switched off the electric current. The hold promptly vanished, leaving me to grope in blackness for a substitute, while my body contorted in the effort to retain a sense of balance. This happened twice in quick succession before I reached a stance where the angle eased off. Donaldson, with no torch at all, climbed here with less fuss than I, for his eyes had become used to the bad light.

The mist was lifting slightly from the hills by now, and the darkness was lessening. But we were still climbing in heavy twilight when we reached the Thearlaich-Dubh gap. On its lower short side a basaltic wall fell thirty feet to a horizontal edge, the flanks of which plunged several hundred feet to deep-set corries. On the upper side was an eighty-foot face of gabbro, split for half its height by a crack, the sole breach in its defence. This great gap, the first of four principal obstacles, causes no hesitation to competent rock-climbers, but no one may deny that in twilight hours the gap is spectacular. To save time, we adopted time-honoured tactics by roping down the cleft. There we tied on the rope, squirmed up the crack on the long side, crawled up the slabs above, and reached the top at daybreak.

The rocks became easy and we made good time to the top of the Alasdair stone shoot, where we broke off from the main ridge to climb Sgurr Alasdair. At ten minutes to six we reached the cairn. We were very far behind schedule, but the miracle for which we had prayed was now enacted before our very eyes: the last shreds of white mist were stripping off the peaks, and the sun was up and out. The sky steadily grew more blue and cloudless, a cool breeze blew—*from the south-east.* And as the sun, low, but shining clear, lifted the last rays of morning mist for the light wind to scatter into nothingness, so it lifted our mental fogs for the mind to whip away all lethargy of body. We were stung to action by the freshness of the morning. The joy of life returned to us.

Donaldson led off with a speed that interpreted our change of mood, and within six minutes Sgurr Thearlaich was behind and Sgurr MhicCoinnich in front. Moving rhythmically at last, we sped along the clean slabs of the ridge and swung down the steep drop to the MhicCoinnich col. Like an enormous cobra with its head extended, the summit tower reared two hundred feet overhead. Up we went, eighty feet to the base of the tower, where a right-angled corner, sixty feet high, was topped by a great overhang. We roped up and climbed the corner by King's chimney, a narrow crack adorned by small jammed stones. Upon nearing the overhang we traversed out on the right wall, where a sweep of slab avoided the projecting head and brought us speedily to the top.

Donaldson was revelling in the climbing. He led the way along that ridge and up the south rib of An Stac at such a steady pace that I was forced to concentrate on the rotten rocks to avoid getting left behind.

At last we strode over the crest of the Stac and arrived at our third point of difficulty, the Inaccessible Pinnacle of Sgurr Dearg. We climbed the pinnacle by the eastern arête, which by an old tradition, from which no man may depart, is ever to be described as 'a knife-edged ridge, with an overhanging and infinite drop on one side, and a drop on the other side even steeper and longer.' We roped down the perpendicular west side.

The time was seven a.m. and we had gone so well from Sgurr Alisdair that we felt free to halt and feed. We were tired, but were cheered by our good luck. We had time in hand and were graced by perfect weather. Half an hour later we started on a long easy ridge, curving like the sharp rim of a bowl to Sgurr na Banachdich. As we left Sgurr Dearg behind us I could not help looking back with some emotion to the plunge of the north buttress, where the overhang collapsed beneath my feet two years before. I seem to have had a most efficient guardian angel, and I never withhold a word of congratulation at the scenes of his master-strokes.

We arrived at Sgurr na Banachdich at eight-fifteen a.m. Our camp in Glen Brittle, a tiny cluster of tents in a green field, still lay in shadow; for the sun had not yet rounded the southern spur of the Cuillin, and no sign of life could be seen anywhere in the grey glen. Up on the ridge we climbed in golden sunshine, feeling a genial superiority to our bed-bound brothers and sublimely forgetful that our own earliness afoot was hardly habitual. The peaks and pinnacles of the Cuillin, no longer black but steely grey in sunlight, surged eagerly into a light blue sky. Across the Minch the Outer Hebrides were strangely near and clear-cut. But they lost none of the aloofness that has ever entranced men of sympathetic mind. Where they rose from the sea, earth there was transfigured and its form eternal, and the searching light of morning failed to disturb this sacred mystery; which is not, though seen here most readily, of them alone; nor, as is said so often, is it peculiar to the cloak of their atmosphere, infinitely variable to hour and season, responsive to wind and cloud, rain and sun; but a thing steadfast through change, in everything that is.

The Cuillin, and all that one may see from them, are at their best in the early hours of a fine morning. The stillness and silence have a profundity unknown to any time of night. For at no time does the earth sleep less than at night; then more than ever it is contemplative and expectant. But at sunrise the mountains are enrapt, like Wordsworth's nun, breathless with adoration.

We were now half-way along the ridge and had reached the first great bend in the horse-shoe, which here changes direction from north-west to north-east. An hour of steady climbing took us over the slender needle of Sgurr Thormaid and the long thin edge of Sgurr a' Ghreadaidh on to the thrice-cleft comb of Sgurr a' Mhadaidh. By this time we were most definitely tired—as yet a pleasant muscular tiredness: we had maintained rhythm and were buoyed up by the keen air and wind. Where the ridge was cleft our minds found interest in the choice of route over wall and rib; or where the ridge was easy, on the ever-changing face of Coruisk, where drifting cloud shadows mottled the blue water of the loch. Nevertheless, our tiredness grew as we approached Bidein Druim nan Ramh, and was only held at bay by the delight of grasping the rough gabbro of the triple pinnacles, so that when at last we hoisted ourselves on to the summit-tip we felt that a short rest had been well earned.

The time was ten o'clock. Looking south to Garsbheinn, we seemed to have covered an enormous chunk of the ridge, but Blaven, our ultimate goal, looked distressingly high and distant as ever. The secret of an easy mind on the big days of one's mountaineering, as elsewhere, is to concentrate on the work immediately in front, not to let imagination run riot on hazards far ahead, for that way lies discouragement.

I dragged my thoughts back to the present, and an excellent present it was. The three pinnacles of Bidein lurched out of the ridge in close company. We were squatted on the apex of the trident's centre tooth. To the north, and contrasted with the throng of peaks to each side, was that most exalting of panoramas—a vast and uninterrupted sky, towered with lofty clouds and melting into a gossamer horizon-haze in faultless graduation of blue to silver. Half an hour passed. During that time I doubt if Donaldson and I exchanged more than a word or two, nor had we done so since leaving MhicCoinnich. Save in special circumstance, conversation and mountaineering go ill together; the more one breaks the precept the less contact is there, other than physical, between the mountains and oneself; and thus the best part of mountaineering is not experienced. The worst companion one may have on a hill is a talker.

We left Bidein at ten thirty-five and launched ourselves at the long expanse of ridge toward Bruach na Frithe. Good scrambling on the descent to the col was followed by an interminable ascent, more than an hour of hard drudgery in sweltering heat. The wind had died, and for the first time we suffered from 'a thirst like that of the Thirsty Sword.' Our growing exhaustion was marked by slow progress on short obstacles and weariness of muscle at the top of them. On the long scree-ridge below the summit our legs had to be driven to their task by conscious effort. Bruach na Frithe is one of the easiest mountains in the Cuillin; its summit one of the finest view-points. At a glance we absorbed the wild sprawl of gabbro architecture, from the boulder-spattered desolation of low corries to the soaring beauty of sun-washed ridges—a moment's glance that has endured through years. The sun was standing still at high noon and we pressed onward to Sgurr Fionn Choire, our minds centred on a little oasis of bright green moss in Fionn Choire: 'Go but a little way over the ridge . . . thou wilt find bubbling through the fountained rock a spring colder than northern snow.' These words of Leonidas describe the spring we found shortly after midday.

Sitting together on each side of the pool, which was no bigger than a chalice, we filled ourselves up with the purest and highest-sited water in Skye. It never fails to give me a severe pain across the forehead, yet I am never truly thirsty without thought of longing for it. We stopped no more than ten minutes. Before climbing back to the ridge we each ate two tablets of vita-glucose, which we had carried for refreshment before attempting Naismith's route on the Bhasteir tooth. Their effect, normally unnoticeable, was on exhausted bodies immediate. Within ten minutes there was distinct improvement of muscular efficiency due to the refuelling of the blood with sugar. Later in the day, when our exhaustion was much greater, the effect of glucose became still more prompt and powerful, acting as quickly as brandy but lasting no more than half an hour. Glucose was the only food we carried during the remainder of the expedition. We consumed between us twenty-four tablets, taking two each at a time before long ascents or short difficult obstacles. They improved our time by cutting down the length and frequency of halts.

We regained the ridge under the Bhasteir tooth—

> The peak that stormward bares an edge
> Ground sharp in days when Titans warred;

it threatened us like a battle-axe, the uneven edge opposing advance with an overhang of a hundred and fifty feet. Its savage appearance will rarely fail to intimidate tired climbers. We were glad of our glucose, still more so of the rope. After roping up we traversed several feet from the overhang across the south face of the tooth. The almost vertical cliff above could then be climbed by Naismith's route. We enjoyed that climb. It was more sensational than strenuous, and the last few airy feet, where one trusts to edge-nails on a shelving ledge, freshened us not a little.

Abutting against the tooth were the higher crags of Am Basteir. We worked up them to a ten-foot overhang, normally of small account, which made us pant for the first time that day. At one p.m. we passed the summit and rattled down to the col below the famous west ridge of Sgurr nan Gillean. The ascent of this ridge is the craziest section of the traverse, reminding one of the Bridge of Sirat, which according to Attar spans hell with a hair-line. The crest grows steadily more acute until it thins to a hanging tapestry, leaps in fantastic pinnacles, then swirls up and onward to a finely sculptured peak. At one-thirty p.m.—eleven and a half hours after leaving Garsbheinn—we stood together at the cairn. Our traverse of the main ridge was ended. The speculative part of the day had begun.

We rested a short while, then followed the ridge southward toward Sgurr na h-Uamha. We soon found that we had to contend with reaction, and by the time we struck down An Glas-Choire to Glen Sligachan our pace had been reduced to a painful crawl. The sun was blazing, hotter than ever before, and there was no wind. However, we struggled down by slow degrees, the boulder-strewn floor of the corrie stimulating exasperation until the wearisome descent seemed far worse than it really was. And then, down in Glen Sligachan, where the moorland quivered through the warm air-currents, there was the long rough walk across heather to our camp at Loch an Athain. I reached the tent at four p.m., and Donaldson, who preferred a slower pace, arrived an hour later.

I had waited for him rather anxiously. Until now I had been sure of him, but we had reached a stage beyond which he had never been tried, for this was the testing time, when bodies fatigued with ten thousand feet of rock-work come whining to the inner self to be left in peace, and strength of will was tried by the luxury of camp on one hand as against a further four thousand feet of scree and rock on the other. The first thing that Donaldson announced when he joined me was his determination to continue with me on the traverse of Clach Glas and Blaven. He looked as cool and unconcerned as though talking of a short stroll before lunch. How he does it I can't imagine.

Mackinnon welcomed us with hot chicken soup, followed by chocolate. It was delicious to lie flat out in the sun, one's mind a pleasant blank, recording nothing but the body's gratitude for rest and food. After Donaldson's arrival we enlivened our diet by consuming between us one pint of 'Mummery's blood.' This mountain elixir consists of equal parts of navy rum and Bovril, served boiling hot. Its effect on both mind and body is nourishing, warming, strengthening; it lowers angles, shortens distances, and improves weather.

At five-forty-five p.m. we set off for Clach Glas. Our route lay up Coire Dubh, notable even among the corries of Skye for its evil mixture of stone and heather. But the black ridge far above, ruffling round the head of the corrie in a great arc between Clach Glas and Blaven, gave us heart to face the preliminary toil. A man would have to be dead before pleasure failed him there.

The evening had grown close and sultry. With so much climbing behind us we had expected this further ascent of three thousand feet to be the hardest part of the whole day. Our surprise was therefore all the greater when we felt ourselves climbing comfortably and with more dispatch than during the ascent of Garsbheinn at the very beginning of the expedition. The truth is that fatigue is rarely caused by tiredness of body; almost always by tiredness of mind, which is not to be refreshed by a mere flogging of the will. The will is indeed no great asset until it be fired by feeling—whereupon all things become possible.

Meanwhile, evening clouds were gathering in a dark pall over the Western Cuillin. We felt some anxiety lest mist should fall round Blaven and complicate the route selection before we could get to grips with the last uprush of its ridge. The food and rest we had had at Loch an Athain stood us in good stead as far as the north col of Clach Glas, then with weakening effect along a tormented ridge that broke in a spray of pinnacles against the slabs of the summit spire, which rose like a lighthouse from a stormy sea. The climb up its wrinkled slabs reduced us to our pre-camp state of physical exhaustion; but nevertheless there was a difference. As we stood on the rocky top and looked across to the Promised Land of Blaven, we had the knowledge, denied to Moses on Mount Nebo, that the goal could be won in our own lifetime.

We left Clach Glas at eight p.m. and enjoyed an effortless rhythm of climbing movement down the saw-toothed ridge to the col below Blaven. We stopped there to refuel on glucose, for seven hundred feet of rock lay between ourselves and the summit. Our anxiety on the score of mist was now removed and we had no trouble in zigzagging up the lower crags to the vital chimney cutting the central cliffs. Above and beyond all was plain plodding. We had drawn the last tooth of the Cuillin hills. At nine p.m., exactly nineteen hours after leaving Garsbheinn, we walked up the screes on the open brow of the summit and sat down thankfully beside the cairn.

The clouds which has been gathering two hours earlier had now vanished. The sun had set behind the bristling back of the main ridge, and all surface detail was lost in the dusk. But each bold peak of that far-flung chain, every great cleft and tooth, was painted clear and black against the faded blue of the evening sky. As the eye followed the incredible silhouette, from the far and lonely outpost of Garsbheinn, mile upon curving mile of splintered edge and spurting crest to the noble climax of Sgurr nan Gillean, it won a reward exceeding anything for which we had paid that day in physical energy. Later, when we came back to earth, and looked again, it seemed beyond belief that two infinitesimal animals, standing a minute six feet high, could pace out the length of that vast and jagged outline. We gaped at the ridge and wondered if our day had been a dream after all. The cold fact of the matter was swiftly supplied when we rose to go down. Only once before on a mountain had I been so physically tired; Donaldson never. Our feet felt flayed and raw, although they showed not a blister when examined later.

We had chosen for descent the long easy ridge running south to Camasunary, but the boulder slopes prevented us in our exhausted condition from striking anything resembling rhythm. We crept jerkily downhill, every step costing an effort of will. Dusk gave way to night before we were half-way down that endless ridge. Our mistake in not choosing the more difficult but short descent into Coire Dubh became more and more evident. We despaired of ever getting anywhere on our present route, and at last had recourse to our map for some way of shortening our purgatory.

Direct descent to Glen Sligachan was barred by the western precipice, but some way further on an easy route cut diagonally across and down the face. The difficulty was to find this short cut in darkness and past experience of short cuts should have warned us against the doubtful attempt. We judged our position on the ridge from an angle on the corner of a loch in Glen Sligachan, and then, at what we imagined must be the correct spot, struck sharply off the ridge on to the cliff. A too innocent scree-run lured us down steepening rock into a chimney. We scrambled down by torchlight over several pitches. There was more scree at the base of the chimney, then blank slabs plunged in an ever-quickening fall to the black abyss of Glen Sligachan. On either hand were deep, inaccessible gullies. We were now faced with the appalling prospect of climbing several hundred feet back to the ridge, or of stopping where we were till daylight. Had there been the slightest weakening in Donaldson I should willingly have bivouacked, for the night was good. But his spirit was indomitable and the vote was cast for retreat.

We rested for a few minutes and ate some glucose. The light from our tent a mile or so up Glen Sligachan gleamed brightly and tantalizingly through the night. Roast chicken and eiderdown sleeping-bags waited for us there! The thought was too much to bear. We rose, and somehow reclimbed those weary leagues to the ridge. Thereafter we literally staggered downhill to the south, stopping every five minutes to rest. A further blow fell upon us when we ran into a cordon of slabs, only to fetch up against yet another when the first had been avoided with difficulty. We stopped involuntarily. Donaldson confessed that unless we reached easier ground at once he would be unable to keep going. I myself felt likewise and we could hardly stand erect without swaying. We did not reach easy ground at once; yet we did keep going. If the spirit is willing the flesh can be driven, weak or not.

We had lost the normal route off the end of the ridge, but we broke through the ring of slabs at last and gained slopes of heather and bracken. Even these seemed relentless, jolting, jarring, jerking our feet and bodies on the everlasting downhill climb. Donaldson, nevertheless, had sufficient inward command to make nice calculations and subtle deductions concerning the nearest whereabouts of the path in Glen Sligachan. For a flashing moment I was glad we had come down that ridge. It was a heartening discovery, of present value and future comfort on mountains, that Donaldson knows no limits; he will go till he drops.

There came a time when the slope grew level under our feet, followed later by a second of intense relief when the narrow line of the path materialized—a miracle, in the white glare of the torch. We finished our last tablets of glucose, then tramped, so it seemed, mile upon endless mile along the stony highway, our bodies aching under the strain of maintaining an upright posture. The dull gleam of Loch an Creitheach dropped behind us and the moorland was broken in turn by the waters of Loch an Athain. We left the path and rounded the head of the loch. The cheerful light of our tent shone but a hundred yards away. We reached it at one a.m. and our day was done.

The roast chicken was demolished with remarkable speed, but with less enthusiasm than one might imagine. Sleep, not food, was what we sought most eagerly; nor could all the hastily devoured fowl in the world have stemmed the tide that shortly engulfed Donaldson and me.

The next day was warm and sunny. We slept till noon; then the midges found us—insolent, rapacious midges. They bit us into wakefulness (a remarkable feat), they bit us on to breakfast, they bit us into the laughing brown loch, and then, when we came out, they bit us all over. At four o'clock we struck camp, and fleeing up the glen, came down like ravenous wolves on Sligachan. We dined there when the bats were about in the cool of evening. That was a meal we shall not forget. But we remember it well less for intrinsic merit than as marking the end of the longest and grandest day's rock-climbing that we shall ever carry out in Scotland—or elsewhere in the world. One was left only with the recollection of pure colour, form, and movement. Not an ache remained, not an effort lived. Here, if you like, was the Greek catharsis. So much so, that we opened a bottle of champagne—and toasted the scree-slopes of Garsbheinn, the foxes of Coruisk, and the long, easy ridge of Blaven.

[Note. The first traverse of the Cuillin ridge plus Blaven was made by I. G. Charleson and W. E. Forde in June 1939.]

17 *New Year on Ben Nevis*

Hogmanay on the Plateau

THERE IS MORE THAN one way of observing the New Year in Scotland, and it may be that the devout pub-crawler alone knows true wisdom. Wherever the truth may lie, R. G. Donaldson, G. R. B. McCarter, and I, in a fit of ascetic resolve on Hogmanay, severed all ties with the triumphs of 1939 civilization in order to mortify our flesh on the icy summit of Ben Nevis.

On 30th December we met in a black frost at Bridge of Orchy. There we decided to pitch a tent on the Nevis plateau. A preliminary reference to the Scottish Mountaineering Club guide revealed that winter hurricanes on Nevis could reach a velocity of a hundred and fifty miles per hour. It seemed too much to hope that we should enjoy the privilege of such an experience; but in midwinter all things are possible on Nevis. Our imaginations leapt to the conception that our tent with ourselves inside might be uprooted at midnight and hurled through Cimmerian darkness to the two-thousand-foot contour in the Allt a' Mhuilinn. Therefore, we planned to countersink our tent in the snow-cap by excavating a two-foot pit and building a two-foot wall above. As insulation from the snow we procured light sponge-rubber mats (not a success), four single sleeping-bags, and one double bag. Our tent was a high-altitude model, weighing ten pounds, with sewn-in ground-sheet.

We proceeded to Fort William, and at noon on the last day of the year sallied forth from Achintee. Our rucksacks weighed thirty-five pounds each. We followed the path for two thousand feet, and thenceforward snow lay heavily. The sun shone from a cloudless sky and tempered the freezing air to a choice crispness, so that we could walk slowly and breathe deeply, drinking the cool air as the thirsty climber drinks his beer. After three and a half hours we arrived on the summit plateau, where the great snow-fields were surfaced with an icy crust, the whole awash with the fire of sunset until we seemed encompassed by seas of live flame, as though not only Nevis but every summit of Scotland had reverted to red-hot lava. The sky had become a riot of all colour from palest green to scarlet. The beauty was agonizing, yet there was no feature describable. We watched, hardly breathing, until the colours began to fade. We felt dazed, as though the eyes of the soul had been blinded by too great a wonder.

'I 'd rather be here,' said Donaldson slowly, 'than have done the best rock-climb on Nevis.'

He meant so much more than that—but what more, or what less, could one say?

The weather was now so settled that we abandoned our plan of excavating a pit, and without more delay pitched our tent south of the Observatory ruins, whose walls projected six feet from the snow. Therefore the snow-cap must have been six feet thick. From the door of the tent the snow-slope dipped sharply to Glen Nevis, so that we could look straight across the twisted spine of the Mamores to Glencoe, past the Blackmount and the hills of Crianlarich, until the eye came to rest on the dim outline of Ben Lomond, twenty-one miles south.

The cold was now intense. There was not a breath of wind. With three of us there was no tent-space for rucksacks, so we left them beside the Observatory and took into the tent only food and sleeping-bags. Before tying up the door I took one last look out. The horizons were everywhere dull and dark with night, but far out to the west there lingered one long, thin, and blood-red streak.

Both the doors and ventilators had been completely sealed, so that after preparing a meal we found it warm enough inside to sleep with only one bag. But we paid dearly for this comfort later in the night. The temperature in the tent was too high in relation to the extreme cold outside, with the result that condensation of body moisture reached enormous proportions. The sponge-rubber mats on which we lay gave poor insulation; water-vapour condensed in such volume on the groundsheet that our sleeping-bags were soaked right through. We roused ourselves toward midnight and drank in the New Year from a communal mug filled with 'Mummery's blood.' The moon was up by this time; we could see it shining through the tent fabric. We put on our boots and went out to the open snow-fields—out into such a splendour of moonlight as one sees but rarely in a lifetime.

I took my axe and wandered alone toward the North-east buttress. My shadow moved thin and black along the glistening snow-crust, which crunched quietly underfoot. For twenty miles around me the world was a storm-sea frozen, inundated by a pure, even light, the heavenly grace outpoured to earth. The sky was crowded, shining with stars that were steady and did not twinkle; and four thousand feet below in the depths of the Spean valley, wrapping the foot-hills in a light transparent vapour, hung a fine white mist, which the moonbeams pierced.

I cannot believe that any human could look long and alone upon that pale-faced night and not be stirred by awe—stirred if with naught else by despair at his insufficiency, by the sternness of the trials that must lie ahead before it be possible for his mind to contain the true beauty; by awareness that for such attainment no sacrifice could be too much. And should thought be confused, none the less he will know that Masefield was right, and that beauty, the intangible, can take a man by the throat.

Donaldson and McCarter joined me. From the top of North-east buttress we admired the rock scenery of the cliffs, then separated and prowled about the plateau in silent delight. After a while each went to the summit cairn, returned to the tent, and slept uncomfortably until eight-thirty a.m.

The darkness was noticeably lessening when McCarter opened up the tent to get snow for breakfast. He looked out and gave a shout of astonishment. 'Another damned dawn,' I thought.

But sleepiness vanished and cold was forgotten when I saw the sight for myself. Across the entire length of the east horizon, from farthest north to south, ran a broad crimson bar, fading to orange in its upper fringe, then melting into pale-blue sky, which darkened and deepened toward the zenith and became navy-blue in the west, where night still hung over the frost-bound land. Very long, very thin, unsubstantial streamers of cloud hung about the sky, and these were caught and fired by great beams of light which radiated from a central point in the crimson bar. The whole made a perfect geometrical pattern like a vast cobweb, of which the threads were jets of orange and pink flame suspended across the vault of the sky.

The mountains of Wester Ross, incredibly wild and icy, dominated the north. They looked like the original Alpine range of ten thousand feet from which they are reputedly descended. Now the most aged mountains in Europe, and but the stumps of their former selves, they still display their old nobility in the sharp lines of ridge and peak. Farther east the Cairngorms bulged against the sky in huge rolling domes, like 'frosted cities of infinite sleep.' But the absorbing subtleties of this northern panorama were soon swamped by the stirring crudities of the eastern skyscape, where like a cannon-ball white-hot from the forge the sun came flashing, streaming, blasting up in a glory of blinding light; higher, higher, until we could no longer with level eye look squarely into its face. The colours vanished from the sky, which became an even blue; the icy sparkle of the snow-peaks changed to a growing glare.

Gardyloo Gully

After breakfast we sped south-east to the Carn Mor Dearg arête, and thence toward Coire Leis, down steep snow-slopes. The too icy surface forbade a glissade and instead we were embroiled in several hundred feet of rapid step-cutting. The descent went with a fine plunging swing, for a one-armed slash burst the crust.

At ten-thirty a.m. we surveyed the long array of cliffs from the Allt a' Mhuilinn. Hardly a rock showed through the snow plaster. I was sure that none of the great ridges would go in the six hours of daylight left to us. Perhaps not in double that time. Yet we felt incumbent upon us, since we were first-footing the cliffs, the pleasant duty of climbing a route worthy of the occasion. My eye travelled up Observatory gully, a broad snow corridor between Tower ridge and Observatory buttress, until fifteen hundred feet overhead the gully was split by the unclimbed Gardyloo buttress. The right fork was Tower gully; the narrow left fork Gardyloo gully, an excellent climb, very severe in summer, which might now be anything from difficult to impossible. 'That,' said I to the others, 'is the very climb for us. We can get down to-day if it won't go.'

We crossed the Allt a' Mhuilinn and climbed for an hour up Observatory gully. The snow there was soft and powdery, and we frequently went in up to the knees. Whenever we passed the tilting snow-field that slants toward Tower gully, the angle of the slope greatly steepened and we entered the deep slit of Gardyloo. Thus far we had been able to kick our foothold with ease, but henceforward every step had to be cut with pick or adze. We stopped to rope up, and being honoured with the lead, I placed Donaldson second and McCarter third.

While we were roping I noticed that the wind was loosening snow on the sunlit upper buttresses, and intermittent trickles of powder were tumbling over the walls and hissing in serpentine streams down the centre of the gully. Before I had run out a rope's length the stream grew to a cascade, and the hiss to an insistent swish. The angle of the slope rose to sixty degrees and the snow gave place to an unusual type of snow-ice—dark grey, indeed most often black, yet without the clearness of pure ice. It was gluey. My pick stuck after horizontal strokes. However, I could slice it vertically with a strong blow of the axe and the crunch that sped from shaft to hand was like that of slicing dried clay with a spade. But the delight of working such excellent material was spoiled by eddying clouds of powder, which caught by down-draughts of wind, filled the gully from wall to wall with a whirl of spiculae, whitened us from head to foot, iced the neck and stung the cheek-bone, infiltrated through every crack in our harness, and at times so blinded me that I could see neither Donaldson twenty feet below nor the slope three feet before my face. My axe-shaft became as slippery as an eel and each step cut was a Pyrrhic victory, for each was promptly swamped by spouting powder and had to be hunted for and cleaned out afresh by my followers. With thought dwelling on defeat I made the steps capacious, but the worse conditions became the more stubborn I grew, and swore that if we turned back now it should be for nothing less than a technical impossibility.

After a savage struggle of two hours we suddenly won clear of the blinding dust and found ourselves in calm air beneath two great boulders bridging the gully. The slope eased to forty degrees under the arch, but immediately beyond was a thirty-five-foot chimney and cave, draped in clear ice from top to bottom. The lower chimney was vertical, but only ten feet high; the cave above was narrow, its floor sloping and glassy, its entrance pillared by a tall icicle, one foot thick, and its left wall, by which any route must go, curtained in shining blue folds. I have never seen a nobler ice-pitch on Nevis, but we admired it with dismay. Donaldson was the first to break the silence. 'Perhaps we 'd better go down,' he said. 'We may not have time to get up, but there 's still time to get out.'

Did I feel unequal to the task his words were designed to give me a good excuse to withdraw; but in my heart I knew that a pitch so well iced should be climbable. With that sinking in the pit of my stomach, which I am more used to associate with the last ice-pitch of Crowberry gully, I said I 'd try. Thereupon I took a grip of myself, and once any climber does that the rest is sheer enjoyment.

I set to work on deeply fluted ice on the lower chimney. Although very difficult it fell in ten minutes, whereas the more technically severe cave was destined to consume considerably more than an hour. The ice was exceptionally hard. At the first few blows of the axe it merely changed colour from bleak grey to white. Then the chips came out. I hewed a stance in the cave's floor, and resting my back on the right wall, faced left and spent five minutes thinking what to do next. The broad tactics were plain: Traverse the blue curtain until clear of the roof and then force a route up the open wall of the gully. The detail, that is the siting of individual holds among the folds of the curtain and round the pillar, was highly complicated—so much so that later Donaldson had acute difficulty in locating my trail, for the combination key, so to speak, was known only to myself.

At first I despaired at the great amount of cutting to be packed into the hour or so available, but the prospect brightened when at last I reached the pillar. I wrapped an arm round it, and leaning over the gully, carved half a dozen holds round the corner. Then I swung round the pillar to the outer wall. Its face bore an even layer of ice, inches thick. I worked my way up, wrists and arm-muscles red-hot with the one-handed swing and cut, the familiar ice-spray exploding in my face at each blow of the pick. On this upper wall I had to fashion the holds so that I might raise my legs with the knees turned sideways to avoid their jamming on bulges. At four p.m. I passed beyond the roof and thirty feet above found anchorage in firm snow.

After thus spending nearly one and a half hours on the last seventy feet, I was shameless enough to urge the others to hurry. For the sun had set half an hour ago, the light was failing, and there was still a cornice to negotiate. I could now have kicked myself for lack of foresight in not cutting down a portion of the cornice during our stay on the summit. There is record of one determined party, who, failing to tunnel such a cornice before nightfall, retired to Fort William and returned next day to finish the climb. Such a heroic course was now closed to us. Despite exhortations, forty-five minutes raced past before my companions were able to join me, each arriving with exclamations of amazement at the involutions of the ice.

Donaldson now took the lead and cut the last fifty feet to the cornice. The overhang was twelve feet thick, but our luck rose superior to our deserts, for there was a less than vertical passage on the side nearest Gardyloo buttress. At five o'clock, five hours from the foot of the gully, we clambered on to the summit.

Between us we travelled over a thousand miles to reach Nevis at the New Year; we carried one hundred and fifteen pounds of equipment through a vertical height of four thousand four hundred feet; we spent an uncomfortable night on the snow-cap; our car was frozen when we returned to Achintee. For all this work and unpleasantness we have, say the Philistines, nothing to show except one gully climb. Nothing to clink in our pockets, so to speak. Nothing but a memory. A memory of the wide, silent snow-fields crimsoned by the rioting sky, and of frozen hills under the slow moon. These have remained with us.

NOTE. The time required for a winter ascent of Gardyloo gully varies greatly. As a general rule, longer time will be taken in December and January than at Easter: the less the snow the harder the climbing. In April 1937, after heavy blizzard, I climbed the whole gully in one hour. Both the arch and the cave were then obliterated.

18 *High Camping in Winter*

OUR PURCHASE of a high altitude tent had proved on Ben Nevis to be the best investment that Donaldson and I ever made. The first month returned dividends of several thousand per cent. But our preliminary experiment, a week prior to New Year, was somewhat disastrous, and even on Nevis the foremost problem of camping on Scottish snow mountains with very light equipment, namely, reconciling avoidance of water condensation with reasonable warmth, remained unsolved. Therefore, I think that our experiences upon first encountering such problems, and in finding a correct solution, may interest mountaineers and campers.

Our purpose in procuring a high altitude tent was threefold. We intended to employ it in winter in the Cairngorms, at whose heart a base camp would save a daily walk of eighteen miles or four and a half hours' time. The Cairngorm bothies were dark hovels and their site was fixed, whereas a tent was cheerful and its mobility gave greater freedom. Secondly, we proposed to indulge more often in the delights of moonlight ridge-walking. But where one is obliged to return valleywards for sleep after a moonlight night, his descent, rest, and reascent usually involve a loss of time that debars the mountaineer from a good route next day. That limitation could be removed by a tent on a summit or high corrie. Lastly, and less practically, there is a pleasure in camping on mountains inexplicable to the unbeliever, but which will be at once apparent to any one of imagination.

For our safety no less than our comfort it was essential that we should have a tent able to withstand the most violent of Cairngorm blizzards. In fact, nothing less than a high altitude tent would meet our requirements, and from Messrs. Burns of Manchester I obtained the ideal article.

The tent was made of reinforced cambric, fawn-coloured, with sewn-in groundsheet, and at each end a circular sleeve-door and ventilator. A ventilator in use could either hang outside like a small wind-sock or be drawn inside—a point that proved of great importance. The poles were bamboo and the tent-pegs aluminium, broad-bladed for snow. Around the outside ran a broad canvas skirt, on which snow or boulders could be piled up and the tent anchored independently of pegs. The guys were of stout rope. The tent's total weight was ten pounds, and the size four feet high by seven feet long by four and a half feet broad. It was testified that the tent had withstood hurricanes of a hundred m.p.h. in the Himalayas. The price was six pounds ten shillings.

In honour to unknown craftsmen, I feel bound to say that not only was the fabric flawless and the whole beautifully made, but that to come suddenly on to a mountain plateau, and there to see its lonely splash of fawn between silver snow and blue sky, was in itself enough to lift up a man's heart.

However, I never have taken and never will take any article of mountaineering equipment on trust. Before using the tent on Nevis, Donaldson and I agreed to a trial camp on the summit of Clachlet (three thousand six hundred feet), between the Blackmount and Glencoe. Were the moon favourable we might accomplish the famous winter ridge-walk from Sron na Creise to Stob Ghabhar. This very first experiment revealed one appalling weakness, no fault of the manufacturers and easily remedied later, which gave us one of the most shocking nights we have ever spent on a hill.

We arrived at Kingshouse Inn on Christmas Eve and received a royal welcome from Mrs. Malloch, who very pardonably believed that we had come to stay the week-end. Thoughtlessly, we said nothing of our intentions, and after enjoying an excellent dinner our embarrassment was considerable on hearing her announce, in the charming accent of the western isles, that our bedroom was ready for us. Mrs. Malloch, moreover, is of commanding presence and one of the great characters of the

Scottish highlands, and my heart quailed as I gulped out my confession. Donaldson, whose eye I vainly sought for moral support, was convulsed with suppressed laughter as he watched the very different expressions of myself and our hostess—Mrs. Malloch, head high and hand on hip, incredulous; and myself, apologetic and very conscious that every word I uttered must sound to her like the most youthful folly. I have no doubt that the latter saved us. Mrs. Malloch is accustomed to young mountaineers; but she let me see by a subtle expression of eye that she had thought more highly of me than this. She flung up her hands in horror.

'A tent on a mountain-top!' she exclaimed. 'Who ever heard the like? And this Christmas Eve with snow on the hills, whatever, and maybe more to come! My, but *you* 're not frightened!'

Being at heart genial and grand of manner she had mercy on us and allowed the matter to rest there. But she was soon to taste the sweets of revenge, and in after days, whenever any of my friends called at Kingshouse, she would recall that night with the opening words, 'There 's Mr. Murray now—*he* 's not frightened! . . .' adding with shattering inconsequence at the end of the tale—'and these breeches of his, all torn and patched, why, they must be nailed up on my wall as a trophy one day!'

We left Kingshouse at nine p.m. and went one mile down Glen Etive. It is not generally known that Argyll can boast a funicular railway, of modified type perhaps, spanning the river Etive below Clachlet. The contraption is a wooden box, suspended on wheels from two wire ropes. The river was fast-flowing and broad, and the box, needless to say, on the far side. I threw off my heavy rucksack and made an enthralling traverse of the swaying wire, which at night one might classify as 'exposed but moderately difficult.' I returned in the box and Donaldson stepped in with both rucksacks. The total load was then about thirty stone and the wire considerably sagged, giving us a downhill run to mid stream, whence the box refused the uphill gradient. It began to look as though we must camp overnight in mid air. But eventually, by tremendous straining at the wire, we managed to haul the squealing truck to the landing-stage.

During the two hours' ascent by the western corrie the sky grew ever more cloudy and the moon nebulous. The air was unexpectedly mild. At midnight we arrived at the summit and pitched the tent on the snow-field near the cairn. The snow was a foot deep and soft, but when stamped down gripped the tent-pegs like concrete. In any event, the weight of snow banked on the outer skirt held all secure. The moon was now obliterated and the clouds rolled thickly overhead. Our hopes of ridge-walking had to be abandoned and we withdrew inside the tent for supper.

After supper we unrolled our eiderdown sleeping-bags and placed underneath them two sponge-rubber mats, whose purpose was to insulate us from ground-cold and thus to prevent condensation of body moisture, which must result from a direct contact of our sleeping-bags with the groundsheet. I had anticipated the condensation problem by using whatever intelligence God had given me. And I was right. Unhappily I had not been given enough intelligence to foresee the solution. We rapidly discovered that whatever that solution might be it was certainly not sponge-rubber.

We had closed both doorways, but the wind was rising, and I tied up one of the ventilators. Then we wriggled into our sleeping-bags, and had almost fallen asleep when the wind began fiercely clutching at the cambric, which aroused us sufficiently to notice that the sponge-rubber was already, within two hours, damp with condensed water, which was beginning to penetrate the eiderdown. However, there was nothing we could do now, and we were beginning to doze again when the rain came down in sheets. Within a few minutes we felt a fine spray of water on our faces. I thought it must be coming through the open ventilator, which I promptly closed. But to our dismay, a few more seconds sufficed to show that the spray came from the roof. The incredible truth at last dawned upon us. Our tent was snow-proof in a hurricane at twenty thousand feet, but was not rain-proof in a half gale at three thousand six hundred feet. In fact, it had not been intended for use at altitudes where rain was possible.

Donaldson and I lay back and laughed weakly—very weakly. We had been well and truly caught out, and nothing remained but to take our punishment as it came. The wind was fairly howling outside, and each time it seized and shook the cambric a shower of half-atomized rain fell on us. Within an hour the tent was swimming in water, which could not escape off the ground-sheet; our sleeping-bags were drenched and their wretched occupants soaked to the skin. The rubber mats were now worse than useless, simply sopping up water and passing it on to us. In the end they were submerged.

The remainder of the night was indescribable, but any one may sample the same experience in his own house. Let him step fully clothed into a cold bath at two a.m. in midwinter, and recline there with a cold shower playing overhead until eight a.m. He will then know, like Donaldson and me, what it means to be grateful for the dawn. At eight-thirty a.m. we struck camp, a process of which it might be more truly said that we weighed anchor.

When we returned to Kingshouse Inn Mrs. Malloch's eye gleamed rather brightly; but she said nothing. Not just then. She waited until we had done justice to a hot meal, and fortified by tall mugs, 'with beaded bubbles winking at the brim,' were arm-chaired before a blazing fire. Then some other mountaineers arrived and, for the first but by no means the last time, we heard those introductory words: 'Now, there 's Mr. Murray and Mr. Donaldson—*they* 're not frightened! . . .' Mrs. Malloch on top form is matchless: she soon had us helpless with mirth. It is remarkable how a few hours can change the bleakest misery into matter for jest.

A week later came our New Year camp on Ben Nevis. That was one of the greatest of our mountain days. Our practical experience there was that of camping on snow in an exceptionally low temperature, minus sixteen degrees centigrade. There were three of us inside, and by sealing up the tent we kept warm during the night. The result was the choicest kind of fug, which is not in itself a bad thing. But our breath and body moisture condensed in such volume that our sleeping-bags were literally soaked. The amount of water exhaled by the lungs and exuded by the skin during one night is extraordinary. I had never understood how great until I saw that moisture condense on the groundsheet in pools. The sponge-rubber was again a failure, but so far I had had no time to find any alternative.

However, we were now completely converted to the frequent use of a tent on winter mountains—provided we could stop condensation and yet keep warm. It was a double problem of which one half could at any time be solved; for whenever we opened one of the doors the groundsheet starred with ice, the cambric hoared, the condensation at once ceased; but although we were fully clothed inside eiderdown bags the intense cold robbed us of sleep. The choice then before us was to spend a dry night frozen or a damp night warm. We hesitatingly chose the latter. It is interesting to note that recent Greenland expeditions found exactly the same problem and chose likewise; one of their nightly discomforts being permanently wet sleeping-bags. None the less, I remained convinced that all such discomfort could be overcome by experience.

We were determined to solve the problem, but Donaldson had to leave Scotland shortly after New Year. The great frost slackened for a space and intensified. In town the very buildings stiffened with cold; in Glencoe the temperature fell on the 20th to minus fifteen degrees centigrade. Meantime, I had been lucky enough to enlist Douglas Laidlaw, with whom I decided to place a tent on the crest of the Aonach Eagach ridge in Glencoe. It had always been one of my ambitions to make a moonlight traverse of the ridge in winter. This we could do and still have ample time to settle the vexed question of water versus frost.

We sat down to a council of war several days in advance, and decided that our new tactics must be comprehensive. Firstly, a more effective insulation than sponge-rubber must be found, and the material must be very light—an inflatable mattress was out of the question on the score of weight and bulk, as was everything else I could think of. Laidlaw supplied the right answer from his greater experience. It was a very simple one —a sandwich of brown paper and tar. The sheets were light, easily folded in a rucksack, but were they effective? I was sceptical.

Secondly, the tent *must* be properly aired by the full opening of one or both ventilators according to the wind and cold without; for the lower the outside temperature the more fresh air was required (within limits), and the higher the wind the less the opening of ventilation sleeves. With condensation thus eliminated, but no more, by fine adjustment of ventilation, the problem boiled down to the simpler question of keeping warm: to counteract the admission of freezing air within the tent a single sleeping-bag was not enough. Therefore, I bought a larger sleeping-bag, which could be pulled over my ordinary bag, or be used as a mattress, or be occupied by us both. Experiment would soon decide which was best.

Thirdly, for the size of tent three men were too many, the condensation from their bodies too heavy to be avoided save by opening one of the doors. That not being practicable, for no man in his senses will tolerate being frozen needlessly, then more than two should not be admitted.

We arrived in Glencoe at ten p.m. of 21st January. On our way northward there had been every promise of a bright moon, but when I brought my car to rest under the east end of the Aonach Eagach the sky was again clouded. A moonlight climb is truly the chanciest of all mountaineering propositions. Deep snow lay to the roadway and the glen was rigid with windless cold. When I drained the car's radiator the hot water froze upon the instant of touching the ground. Therefore the degree of cold that must prevail three thousand feet up on the summit of Am Bodach, where we intended to place the tent, was a matter for the most satisfactory conjecture. Could we keep dry and warm this night we could conclusively say that we had cut the claws of one more mountain lion. But I was not optimistic. Despite Ben Nevis, Clachlet took a bit of living down.

At twelve-thirty a.m. we reached the summit of Am Bodach. Upon the northern rocks, which were clad in hard snow, we found a little way under the cairn a ledge just large enough to accommodate the floor-space of the tent, which we pitched broadside to the ridge, with the guy-ropes shooting out at strange angles to rock-spikes and boulders. From this site we had an unobstructed view to the moor of Rannoch, where the sun would rise, to the crest of the Aonach Eagach, which we should traverse, and to the north, where all the mountains of Lochaber stood before us.

The moonlight was locally strong, but by reason of the cloud-film visibility had fallen from upward of twenty miles to barely five. In such conditions a moonlight traverse offered no charms to rival those of daylight, and we postponed our climbing plans to the morrow. We retired to the tent and sealed the doors. Although enormously strong at the reinforced corners, the fabric of the roof was sufficiently fine to allow ample light inside, and in this respect held great advantage over most high altitude tents, which are perforce distressingly coffin-like. In cloud-diffused moonlight we lit a candle inside for the sake of cheerfulness, and not as essential lighting.

We brewed tea, had supper, and went to bed. We began the night with one open ventilator. Condensation showed signs of winning. Therefore we opened both ventilators and discovered that by leaving one sleeve outside and drawing one sleeve inside, fixed parallel to the roof, a current of air across the roof could be induced and yet no draught fall to our own level. The cambric quickly whitened and condensation on the ground-sheet stopped; yet the decrease in temperature was not remarkable. The final test was at hand. Could we now keep warm and sleep comfortably? For the first time it began to seem certain that we could.

Unlike the sponge-rubber, the tar sandwich was astonishingly effective. It gave us excellent insulation against ground-cold, provided that two layers of down sleeping-bag interposed between one's body and the paper. In other words, inside my two bags I could now rest in comfort—not too warm, but feeling no cold that could interfere with sound sleep.

We tried other arrangements, which gave the following results. By using the large bag as a mattress, one has good insulation against ground-cold but too little against air-cold to permit true sleep as distinct from dozing. By using ordinary bags as mattresses and both sleeping inside the large bag the greatest warmth was developed and sleep easy.

Our problem of high camping with light equipment was thus solved. But there must be borne in mind this fact, that condensation and cold are overcome at low temperatures not by one method, but by four, which are complementary:

The ventilation current must be confined to the roof area. There must be effective insulation from ground-cold. The tent must not be overcrowded. There must be effective protection from air-cold. This last means that each man must either have two sleeping-bags or else have one as a mattress and both share a third double bag. The former is preferable for greater comfort; the latter, since it involves three bags instead of four, for economy in equipment. But the double bag is less desirable for a long-term camp. For a short camp it is tolerable; there is no room for childish sensitivity on a mountain-top. Each party must make its own choice. Lastly, these measures apply to severe cold and not in mild weather. They break down where the weather is so foul as to prevent ventilation.

After we had settled down we slept so well that dawn failed to waken us and we were roused only when the first blaze of sunrise shone through the frosted roof. We looked out to find the sky clear and blue and the sunrise splendid as from Nevis at New Year. We dressed quickly—simply a matter of pulling on boots and windproof jackets—and made breakfast. A small tin of milk had frozen solid overnight and we had to carve the contents with a knife and spill the splinters into our tea; otherwise our breakfast was not inferior to that of most highland hotels.

At nine-thirty a.m. we seized our axes and rope and stepped up to the summit of Am Bodach. There was no wind. Down on the moor of Rannoch and in all the valleys of Lochaber a thick ground-mist lay motionless all day. The Aonach Eagach ran one and a half miles westward, its south flank forming the north wall of Glencoe, its narrow and rocky edge blinding white in the sunshine. We made a sharp descent on snow-smothered rocks and walked past the crags of the Chancellor until the crest dipped to a col, whence we ascended the main peak of the ridge, Meall Dearg. Thenceforward the ridge became more slender and craggy, and we had repeatedly to ply our ice-axes in short spells of step-cutting. At the narrowest stretch we came to a *gendarme,* whose glazed rock forced us to rope up and move singly. Immediately beyond we cut hand- and foothold up an icy wall to a higher continuation of the ridge, where double cornices, projecting on the left over Glencoe and on the right toward Kinlochleven, made the safeguard of a rope still more imperative. Between the two overhangs we trod where we hoped the ridge might be, and our divinations were happily correct.

In three hours from the tent we came to Sgor nam Fiannaidh, which marks the western end of the Aonach Eagach, although the ridge continues to the Pap of Glencoe. We lazed inertly in a rocky corner and sunned ourselves while we lunched. Beyond the pointed Mamores the North-east buttress of Nevis was particularly clear and icy. We hoped it was not going to waste and that some lucky men were climbing there! Above all, the flowing line of the summit plateau drew my eye, dispensing time and again a pang of nostalgia.

At one-thirty p.m. we set off eastward, regained our tent in two hours, and had packed up by sunset. Then we heaved on our rucksacks and returned to the crest.

The sun had sunk into a dense haze, which screened Ardgour and Morven in bright orange. There was little of the variety of colour that usually distinguishes a west highland sunset in winter, but the effect upon the white flank of the Aonach Eagach was unique. I had in the past criticized mountaineers who print snow photographs in sepia. Who, I asked, ever saw brown snow—who ever heard of it? Certainly nobody I had ever met. Crimson, pink, gold, silver, blue, orange, and violet snow are common enough in Scotland. But never brown. Yet before our astonished eyes the orange north wall of Glencoe darkened, until for miles to the west its snows were rich chocolate.

When twilight had turned all to monochrome we set off downward. Later the moon rose, and when I turned to look for the last time at the ridge above, flung a phantom sheaf down to a frozen tower. Facing us across the glen, the vast corrie under Stob Coire nan Lochan was in cold, pale-blue shadow; then the many peaks of Bidean nam Bian lit up one by one, and burned. The whole majestic cluster scintillated like a candelabra. In sheer height, silent aloofness, beauty of form, it filled me with that despairing awe that comes to us all occasionally. Merely to have seen that beauty for a few minutes, to have felt as I felt then, seemed worth any sacrifice and hardship.

Our plan for a moonlight traverse had been mistimed by twenty-four hours. But we were well content. We had made high winter camps a pleasure in themselves, quite apart from any opportunities they offer for mountaineering, by the removal of the worst discomforts, and had therefore given ourselves incentive for their frequent enjoyment.

That dire penalities may lie in store for the inexperienced I have shown at my own expense. But knowledge comes quickly and makes one free as the mountain wind. One gains nothing worth having on mountains without paying for it; beyond the snowline minor hardships will always be met in a small tent, and the sooner a man is trained to rise above them the better. In the end they are far outweighed by the joys of dwelling for a space on snow-fields close to the sky, where the dawn and sunset come like armadas in slow and solemn grace, and the very air has a beauty, which we call purity.

19

Raven's Gully and Crypt Route

THE NORTH BUTTRESS of the Buachaille Etive Mor is cleft asunder from the Cuneiform buttress by a straight gash of four hundred feet. Since the mountain first uprose from the hardening earth, or more likely from recent times, in the seventy thousand years after the fourth Ice Age when its towers were hewn by the chisels of time, the recess of that fierce stroke has bred the cloud and later the raven, and to these remained sacred until our own day.

The inviolate state of the sanctuary was acknowledged by the Scottish Mountaineering Club when they most appropriately named it Raven's gully. Attempts at penetration failed. At last, in June 1937, J. B. Nimlin led a party up the gully in nine hours. During the next two years, several attempts to repeat the ascent were repulsed—twice violently repulsed, when expert rock-climbers from England fell from the overhang at the fourth pitch, the angle of which allowed to each leader a fall of twenty-five feet clear of obstructing rock. And since the rope held, neither suffered injury. Around the gully there closed once more an aura of impregnability. One might say that the raven perched upon the fretted crags, and like Poe's bird of omen, croaked its 'Nevermore.'

In June 1939 I began to feel that a visit to my friend the raven was long overdue. To call on her soon after the breeding season seemed mannerly; in fact I had no choice. So long as the rock had been wet I had determined not to set foot on the fourth pitch. I could afford no handicap where better men than I had failed; but by 12th June not a drop of rain had fallen in Glencoe for a fortnight. That same evening I arrived at Kingshouse with MacAlpine and W. G. Marskell.

A cloudless morning followed—one of those light-hearted mornings peculiar to spring, windless yet fresh, when colours shine with a brightness of fairyland. We drove first to Lagangarbh, on the Glencoe road, and walked thence across the moor to Buachaille. Two thousand feet up on the north face, Raven's gully looked an absolutely perpendicular slash, as black as midnight. That closer acquaintance would dispel those illusions we knew; but many an otherwise willing climbing party must have been turned away by that gape of gloom. It is an unfortunate and misleading effect of distance—an effect that lessens the closer one approaches up the boulder-strewn slopes of heather, until at last one enters harbour between the towering flank of North buttress on one's left and the lower tongue of Cuneiform buttress on one's right, and finds, before one's upturned face, a gully clearly lit, enticing.

We roped up and were almost tempted astray by an obviously possible line for a new route up the slabby wall of North buttress: an ascent of which has since been made. We gave it a moment's consideration, but my heart was set on Raven's gully and would turn to no other lure. Like all good gullies it rose in steps, approximately ten in number, all of which were not as yet visible. Rarely elsewhere have I seen such a vista of overhangs crowded within so short a distance. The gully bristles. As it cut back into the rock so the flanking walls, pearly-grey on North buttress, sea-grey on Cuneiform, projected further and rose higher, gaining wildness of outline as the gully grew in splendour of height.

However, if we had come visiting we were not as yet admitted to the entrance hall. The gully started straight away with a ten-foot overhang, discomfiting as the stare of a barred door. The raven, it seemed, was not 'at home.' Moreover, despite the fine weather the rock was wet. Since we had all exchanged boots for rubbers I avoided the damp rock by climbing on to Cuneiform buttress, and from there gate-crashed by a traverse into the gully's interior.

A red pitch of fifteen feet rose in front. I was glad to observe it was only vertical. One must be grateful for these tender touches in Raven's gully. We relished a strenuous climb up its right corner and strolled across a level scree-floor to the most notorious tier, from which recent predecessors had retired in haste.

The gully was here twelve feet wide and rose in a step thirty feet high. Recessed midway up the face was a low-roofed cave, from which the upper half of the step overhung the gully floor. Misguidedly I began to study the rock and to speculate. Such a place grows worse, and the pale cast of one's thought more appropriate to Elsinore than Glencoe, the more one looks. Action was demanded unembarrassed by reflection. I climbed up to the cave.

To avoid the overhang there was but one possible route—up the dull red wall of the North buttress. From the floor of the cave one might traverse out over the gully on a yard-arm of rock. I edged out to its tip and looked up the wall. That was a dismal surprise if ever I had one. The wall was bare of holds. I returned to the cave and considered tactics, which began to crystallize round an excellent spike in the cave's back. My companions would have to work their passage. They both joined me and I asked Marskell, who was middle man, to go out to the end of the yard-arm; MacAlpine, who was last, to sit in the back of the cave and tie himself to a spike—to which he also tied Marskell and then gave me the safer belay around his own waist.

The grouping of the party made a simple tableau of man's progress through the ages: with Marskell balancing on his spar as the Java ape-man; MacAlpine squatting on his rock floor as the Neanderthal cave-man; and myself as *homo sapiens* about to ascend over their shoulders to the higher life. I thought the fancy appropriate, but my friends were blind to these similes. Every one sees the world in his own way.

I traversed out beside Marskell and climbed up his back until I stood on his shoulders. His poise over the gully was by no means too secure, but he maintained a Dunn-like immovability, which tempted me to linger longer than I ought. By my right side a snout of the overhang jutted downward, leaving a widish crack between snout and wall. I tried to avoid the constriction of the crack by climbing a few feet up the face, hoping thereafter to traverse to the top of the pitch. That was an error of judgment for which I met condign reward. The sole foothold lay well to my left, the only handhold a thin score to my right. My body thus lay on a slant across the wall, and the moment I tried to move higher my legs swung under the overhang. I found myself forcibly doubled round the snout; a mortifying moment for one with only a shirt between stomach and rock. Being helpless to move, I was obliged to come down.

To Marskell and MacAlpine my venture on the wall had appeared much more precarious than to myself; as a man driving a fast car is more at ease than those who sit behind. When I returned to the cave they were doubtful whether a second attempt should be made, but were loyal when I determined to try again. For although the first attack had been foiled the reconnaissance had been successful. I knew now exactly how to climb that fourth pitch.

Marskell again trod the yard-arm and again I went to his shoulder. I stepped on to his head and transferred straight into the crack. With a most bitter struggle I somehow forced my way up by counterpress and friction. I again found the finger-tip score, but this time came directly underneath it, and by its aid wrenched a further inch or two. When nothing more in this way could be done I stretched up my right arm and my grasping fingers closed on a magnificent notch above the bulge. With a violent pull on one arm I dragged myself up. More holds appeared. The roof of the overhang fell back. I was up. That I believe to be the hardest fifteen feet of rock in Glencoe—as nearly unclimbable as anything I have yet ascended.

A sharp incline of running scree rose from the sloping edge of the overhang. It looked highly dangerous. I shouted to Marskell to take shelter. Whenever I set foot on the scree a shower of stones slipped over the edge and flashed like hail before the crouching cave-dwellers. I climbed ten feet up the gully but could find no belay, therefore I settled myself ankle-deep in the delicately poised scree and informed Marskell that I could hold, but not pull without dislodging both myself and the gully bed. The problem was therefore how to pull up the last man to offset his lack of the initial 'shoulder.'

We solved the nasty problem by bringing the last man up second. He sent up an end of his spare rope on the slack of my own rope, and thus protected, climbed up with his ever safe and steady deliberation. Marskell was now left below, tied to both myself and MacAlpine. In addition I sent down my own end of rope as a handrail. Then MacAlpine pulled, I pulled, and Marskell pulled, all quite gently. By good fortune Marskell has a special aptitude for high-speed climbing, and whether a pitch be hard or easy makes singularly, one might even say startlingly, little difference. In five minutes he was by my side, pale from effort, and breathing hard. We rested awhile from our exertions.

Without more ado we went up a short way until the scree ran into the tall cave of yet another overhang, a more courteous sentinel than we had met hitherto; for it leaned to the right half of the gully, granting access to the left half by way of a strenuous chimney. We went back and knee up its smooth walls, worked outward to a chockstone, and thence up a very steep groove. Still higher we arrived at the most satisfying rock of the climb —a twenty-five-foot wall, which I need hardly say was vertical. It was bestarred with minute holds, curiously arrayed, reminding me of the Tennis Court wall of Scafell. Save that the latter is difficult and this severe, the two share the same technical charm.

Thenceforward the gully narrowed, and high above was spanned by a fallen crag. We climbed a broad uproll of brown rock, and passing under the great arch came at last to the true heart of the gully, the inmost sanctuary where the overhanging wall of the Cuneiform and the loftier tower of the North buttress achieve their climax of might. Before us the gully forked: on the left, rising in a sunlit shelf high on the North buttress wall;

on the right, extending long and straight, flagged with loose stone, a twilight aisle into a vast cavern.

I swithered at the cross-roads for a few minutes. But I was filled that day with a single-minded determination to climb Raven's gully. Such fits come over me from time to time. As I had turned from a new route below, so now I turned from the distant cavern, which threatened a cul-de-sac. I climbed an exposed rib on to the lower end of the shelf, where the gully fell from our feet with unusual steepness. We continued by Nimlin's route.

For some days thereafter I never regretted a decision more. Had I only borne right for a few hundred feet, along that brown aisle and beyond the architrave, what wonder might I not have found? A grotto, like the glimmering nave of some old Gothic abbey? Or merely a dripping hole? Most likely of all, if I can judge of rock formation, a subterranean chimney to the top of Cuneiform buttress, like those within the bowels of the Church Door buttress and Bhasteir tooth. I lost that opportunity of exploration; with a quite unconscious wisdom I threw it away. It remains an aspiration: 'a possession,' says Stevenson, 'as solid as a landed estate.' Thus no less than heretofore Raven's gully entrances me with that siren song of the Unknown. Assuredly I shall go again.

The shelf rose convexly for a hundred and fifty feet. We moved slowly on and up, the members of the party still climbing only one at a time, until we looked far over the ponderous crag, which bridged the lower gully, to the desolation of the moors east of Mamore. At length I arrived on a platform where the shelf ended at a last short wall. Immediately above lay the trough between the two buttress-tops. I sat down and sunned myself in a sheltered corner, while one by one the others came to me. I could see straight down the plunging gully and felt disappointed at seeing no sign of the raven; but her shyness was pardonable. Then I heard her croak.

Thus pacified, I turned to the wall and forced my way up a crack. At one p.m., two and a half hours after entering the gully, we made our exit at the top. We were seven hours earlier than I had any right to expect, but we made the ascent under ideal conditions and I was encouraged from behind by a powerful party, on a day when each one of us suddenly struck top form. The climb was very severe. Provided there be good ice at pitch four, it is my firm opinion that Raven's gully will provide a thrice-royal route in winter.

A sudden accession of good form is a pleasant and usual experience for a leader, but sudden loss of form on a hard rock-climb is one of the most frightening things that can happen to him. The experience is rare and has assailed me but twice. The circumstances that give rise to it are well demonstrated by my first visit to the Crypt route on the Church Door buttress of Bidean nam Bian.

Upon the north face of the buttress an arch two hundred feet high overhangs the screes. The normal route goes by a flake to the right of the arch, then up and across the roof to Raeburn's chimney, by which one gains access to the upper buttress. Now this arch was pierced by two holes, and it had long seemed to me that a direct route might be made by climbing straight up the wall under the arch and going through one of the holes on to the roof. Therefore, on 5th June 1938 I persuaded Marskell and MacAlpine to go with me to Bidean nam Bian. None of us was aware that this route had already been climbed by an English party and entitled 'Crypt route.'

We went to the buttress, which is situated in the northern corrie directly under the summit, on a day of careering mist. The crags emerged like a great castle on a promontory, clothed in silvery purple light and backed by storm-cloud. Starting from a snow-gully below the arch, we climbed seventy feet up a chimney, then penetrated by a stepped corridor into the bowels of the buttress. We came to a dark chamber at the end of the passage and thought we could go no further. I groped my way round the left wall and discovered a shaft boring upward through solid rock. We forced our way through and arrived in a second and much darker chamber, which a flaring match revealed as not unlike the king's tomb in the heart of the Great Pyramid, but smaller.

Again I thought we could go no further, until above me on my left the last flicker of the match revealed another hole. This led to a third rock chamber. A faint streak of light betrayed a final tunnel, which must surely take us to the open air. The tunnel was so small and tortuous that I spent almost half an hour struggling on my stomach; to gain admittance I had to take off my rucksack and push it in front of me, greatly wondering what surprise would come next. Had Dunn been with us our climb would there and then have failed, for his broad shoulders would never have fitted into the aperture. I myself fitted rather too nicely, and only by the most strenuous propulsion of forearms and boots could I wriggle forward. I should say that this route is the safest in Scotland, for though much effort is required to get up, it is equally difficult to fall down.

Since the rucksack in front blocked the light I could not see where I was going, but knew that our route had now spiralled inside the buttress so that we must be facing Glencoe. Suddenly I found my head and shoulders projecting from a window in the face of the cliff. I looked directly down to the snow-gully and outward across the corrie, now dismally curtained in sleet, from which I was protected by the arch close overhead. It was good from this shelter to see the clouds wildly driving around the crags. Reluctantly, I pulled myself out of the hole and found foothold on a slab, where I waited for Marskell. He had a hard struggle—in fact he was obliged to go back and remove his clothes before he finally wormed through the tunnel. Thereafter I climbed open slabs to the lower hole in the arch, where I found an easy way to the roof.

Our only remaining task was to cross the arch and go up Raeburn's chimney, which is difficult and slightly exposed. I had climbed it often before without finding trouble. But three causes now combined to throw me quite off form. Firstly, we had been climbing constricted chimneys in the safest of rock-climbs; therefore the change to more exposed rock was sudden and unwelcome. Secondly, we had come to try what we thought was a new route—the issue had been much in doubt and our arrival on the arch a triumph; therefore I felt that the climb was finished, and with success came reaction. Thirdly, I waited for thirty minutes in paralysing cold for the others to reach the arch.

The psychological result was complete loss of confidence. I traversed the arch and uneasily mounted a slab to the foot of the chimney. With every movement that followed I felt a dreadful qualm in the pit of my stomach, and not since I was led up my first rock-climb had I been at such a loss what to do next or so dominated by a strange environment. Half-way up I found myself, for the first time in my life, pounded—unable to move either up or down. Time passed. I could do nothing but watch flakes of sleet alight and melt on the wet rock before my nose. My fingers lost all sensation. At last it became evident that should I stay where I was a moment longer I must fall. Whereupon I rallied my strength of will and forced on myself one more movement. At once the invisible fetters fell away and I climbed perfectly. Curiously enough, Marskell saw nothing alarming in my climbing save that I had been unconscionably slow; but the escape had been narrow and I was unhappy even on the moderate rocks above the chimney.

When a mountaineer sees two or more of the above forces combine against him he should keep a sharp look out and pull himself together. The danger lies in his being caught unawares, but he will have no trouble if he be mentally prepared. Loss of form is not usually a sudden thing, and a good party in top form has to reckon with only one subjective danger—carelessness on easy ground. That more than anything will bring a climber to disaster; but nowadays mountaineers are so well warned of easy rocks of descent that they automatically increase in watchfulness when they come to them. In consequence, I have been in less trouble on mountains than in valleys. But I learned a salutary lesson in Glen Falloch.

I had climbed that October day on Buachaille with Mackenzie and T. D. Mackinnon. On our way home we visited the falls of Falloch, which were in full spate and a sight well worth seeing. Above the topmost fall was a long and narrow gorge, through which the congested waters dashed foaming to leap with a thunderous roar to a rock cauldron. At one point the gorge was narrow enough to challenge one's sporting instinct. Was a leap possible? We measured it up with the eye. It would have to be a standing jump from spray-drenched rock.

'Easy!' scoffed Mackenzie, and with one bound was across.

One by one we jumped safely. The gut was narrower than it looked. We had been too impressed by the fury of the water. Thus, I was just a trifle less careful in making the return jump; my foot slipped off the wet rock and down I went into the gorge. I struck my head against one of the walls and was already half-stunned when I hit the water. My body was seized, whirled round, shot along the gut and hurled twenty feet down to the cauldron.

I came to the surface with bursting lungs, but was pinned under the fall and gulped in more water than air. Each time I strove to swim out a powerful up-current threw back my body like a twig. I tried to each side in vain, and everywhere that current tossed me back, until I grew dazed by the pounding of the fall and my breath was battered from my body more effectively than by iron bars. Within five minutes (I had really no conception of time), my violent struggles to swim out became a more desperate struggle to keep afloat, for the weight of my clothes dragged me down and the surface was churned so high that I could not breathe without swallowing great draughts of water. My struggles grew weaker, then stopped through sheer exhaustion. Immediately I went under.

Meanwhile, Mackenzie and Mackinnon were helplessly watching from the edge. They could not reach me, for the rock wall was high and undercut all round. For any one to plunge into that boiling cauldron was a madness likely to result in the drowning of two men instead of one. Notwithstanding—when

Mackinnon saw me go under he could contain himself no longer, and forgetting even to remove his hat, dived in. I came up again to see him striking out hard for the fall, but powerful swimmer though he was, he could not get near me. The current spun him round and cast him up on a shoal at the low end of the cauldron. A most noble effort.

When I saw that no help was possible I truly thought that my last minute had come, but nevertheless made a last fight. I think that that is one of the most shocking moments in a man's life, when he knows that his life is lost but is not yet resigned to death. He has a feeling of despair not pleasant to look back upon. A man in that state is capable of superhuman exertions, and although 'exhausted' I tapped hitherto unsuspected reserves of energy. But the forces against me were too great; for the last time my struggle weakened; then I surrendered, and sank.

My past life did not flash before my eyes. Save for one thing of which I cannot write, I thought only that I had chosen a foolish way of ending my life, which might have been expended to a worthier end on mountains, where one seeks beauty, than in horseplay at a waterfall. The instant I was reconciled the peace of complete detachment came upon my mind. I discovered for myself, once and for all, that in approaching death there is nothing to fear. It is pleasant. Like the release from prison to freedom—a little strange at first.

A few minutes later Mackinnon and Mackenzie were pulling me ashore at the low end of the cauldron. I had gone to the bottom, been driven sideways by an undercurrent, and then propelled to the surface beyond the grip of the great back-eddy. Thereupon I drifted by the side of the cauldron down to the shallows.

For half an hour I lay on the bank and vomited water while Mackenzie thumped my back. By the time they had stripped and dried me I was sufficiently alive to resent the fuss. But seven days afterwards I was still too exhausted to rock-climb. The only serious result was the loss of Mackinnon's hat, a stylish and expensive model, newly purchased, which he would not allow me to replace. Like a true Scotsman he blamed only himself for not having had the presence of mind to take it off!

Who will wonder that I feel more at home on hills than in low country? The higher the safer. We should all remember that Edward Whymper fell off a platform at Birkenhead after lecturing on the Matterhorn.

20 *Crowberry Gully in Winter*

AT THE END OF JANUARY 1941 I received orders to join the Middle East forces in Egypt. The occasion clearly called for one long last climb on the Buachaille Etive Mor. I had already made seventy-nine ascents by one route or another, and each had but strengthened my conviction that Buachaille was the most splendid of earthly mountains. I was destined not to see it again for four years, and therefore can never be sufficiently grateful to R. G. Donaldson, a true friend, who cut his own work at Cambridge and came north to climb with me. We selected Crowberry gully as the best winter route in Glencoe, and one that would give us all that we bargained for and more. In this hope we were shortly to be confirmed by events. Crowberry gully rarely yields so early in the season.

We drove up to Kingshouse Inn at two o'clock in the morning of 1st February. A quilt of new snow covered the ground, the sky was heavy-burdened, and large flakes fell twisting through the beam of the car's head-lamp. After our long drive through snowstorms on Rannoch moor, the old inn looked a true outpost of civilization. Nor, despite the unearthly hour and the profitless trouble we had caused her in past years, did Mrs. Malloch fail us. A fire, hot tea, food, and beds—all were waiting for us—even a gift of that strange substance, more precious in war than blood—Pool petrol.

Five hours later we wakened to a perfect morning. At nine o'clock we went down to Coupal bridge. While we plodded over the snow-clogged heather the sun rose clear over Rannoch moor. A cloud-flock hovered overhead, but was fast disappearing before we reached the iced boulders of the lower slopes. Towering high in front, so that we stopped with our heads well back to look, the walls and slabs of Buachaille, muffled in new snow, dazzled our eyes where the sun struck. The mountain looked like a fortress of ice, its summit diamond cut deep into a royal blue sky.

It was this last that held us there. It was not alone the confusion of snow-turret and bastions, nor even the ridges racing up and up, drawing in to the white blaze where the last rocks leaped against the blue; not grace of design, nor colour, nor height—none of these things alone—that charged our minds with wonder. These beauties were indeed endless, but were brought to unity and fulfilled in that austere and remote line dividing snow from sky. It was the signature of all things. It held us spellbound. It is hard to know why, until we know that it is the most simple things that most deeply impress a man. Until we know that we shall not hope to know the true beauty. Up there, nothing stirred. Not even 'the sigh that silence heaves'; only a breathless stillness. A bright light. A pureness of beauty above all that eye can see, or ear hear, or it can enter into the heart of man to conceive. One may say nothing of it that is not somehow false or misleading. For the truth that can be spoken is not the truth. Yet on the heights of truth one never climbs in vain.

We continued slowly uphill, delayed from time to time by short ice-falls. While cutting a step below the main cliffs I struck a powerful backhand blow with my axe and snapped the shaft near the head. We had now but one axe between us for such big game as Crowberry gully, and the question arose whether we should go on. I had another very short axe for cutting on ice-walls. This could stop a slip on hard snow but had no value as a belay. However, I recollected that the big pitches in Crowberry gully spring from shallow caves, where the second man can find stances to give the leader body-belays. The leader, therefore, would carry the large axe and all should be well. I did not like this arrangement, but the reasons for retiring so soon were not good enough. We continued upward.

At eleven a.m. we traversed into Crowberry gully. It began

invitingly. The angle was low and the slope wide. We were still in sunshine, and a bend in the gully hid the verticalities above. But a climber is no more satisfied with snow than a farmer with weather. An inch or two of new snow lay on old hard snow, and the top layer kept slipping on the lower. We floundered inelegantly, trying to avoid step-cutting so early in the day on so easy a slope, until at last exasperation overcame ingrained laziness. We are unsophisticated enough to find step-cutting a joyous art. But one grows impatient if time be scarce.

An introductory pitch of snow-clad rock, then a long and concave slope, led to the first bend, whence we had our first view of the climb as a whole. It appeared as a thousand-foot shaft, splitting deeply an enormous expanse of snow-plastered cliffs. To its right lay the North buttress, to its left the Crowberry ridge. Between these close walls the gully soared tier upon icy tier to the gentle curve of a far-away snow ridge, where one wisp of cloud idled.

The gully quickly steepened to the first shallow cave. From here to its end Crowberry gully rises in a glorious crescendo of difficulty, each pitch in winter being noticeably harder than the preceding one. The crux, and the final cave pitch that immediately follows, share the honours in severity. This mounting difficulty has disadvantages. Certainly it tunes one up for the final onslaught, but if either crux or cave pitch is unclimbable one is defeated late in the day with all the gully tc climb down again. I have never seen any belays on the gully-walls for roping down. Therefore it is not difficult to get oneself benighted.

From now on each of us led alternate pitches. Donaldson started off. The first three obstacles all involved the same glazed slabs and snow; each was separated from the others by one or two hundred feet of hard snow surfaced with new, in which every step had to be cut with the adze; none was exposed but each ran true to form, the long groove of pitch two and the overhang of pitch three being respectively more difficult than its predecessor. On this last pitch Donaldson had a stiff struggle.

Half-crouched below the overhang of frozen snow, to which he clung with one hand while leaning out at an alarming angle over the down-race of the gully, he scraped and picked at the frosted flank of the North buttress in prolonged and repeated efforts to find or fashion hand- and toehold. He won his way in the end. But these pitches consumed much time. It was three-thirty p.m. before we reached Thin Crack chimney, a feature of the gully in summer. Here we paused and considered.

In front lay three notable pitches. We could see them framed between giant white walls. Three hours of daylight remained, if one counted late twilight. Yet the last two pitches might themselves take one and a half hours each for the leader alone; this excluded Thin Crack chimney, a very hard thirty feet when the chimney was blocked with snow, as it was to-day, and the climber was forced on to icy slabs to its right. Our decision was that unless we were over the crux by four-thirty p.m. we must turn back.

We lost no time. In thirty minutes the Thin Crack was behind us and we drew to a standstill in Crowberry junction. At this crux in the climb Crowberry gully branches. The left fork is a chimney shooting up to Crowberry Tower gap—it had not yet been climbed. The right fork, beginning as a broad belt of slabs which have never been climbed in summer, runs up to the climax of the cave pitch and debouches on the open brow of the mountain a hundred and fifty feet below the cairn. Between these two forks stands an unclimbed buttress. Amidst this welter of unclimbed rock the summer route winds its tortuous way, twenty feet up the unclimbed chimney, then across the unclimbed buttress into the right fork above the slabs. This route is not difficult, but in winter had never proved possible. Then one relies on a good coat of ice over the slabs of the right fork. The work there is severe, even exposed, and requires a hundred-foot run-out. To-day there was no ice on the slabs. Their only coat was thick powdery snow. We had, after all, come too early in the season to find ice in good quantity. Such was the cheerless situation.

I reflected with pleasure that this was Donaldson's turn to lead, but I tried the slabs myself out of curiosity. They were impossible. From past experience of Crowberry junction I thought that our only hope of finding a route was in forcing a way up the angle between the central buttress and right fork. For such a hazardous task some simple rope mechanics were essential. To this end I repaired to a snowy stance about twenty feet up in the depths of the left fork. The chimney was hereabouts arched by a square crag, over which, after several abortive efforts, I cast an end of rope to which Donaldson tied himself. Then I anchored myself to a thick pillar of clear ice. The position thus was that if Donaldson came off on the first fifteen feet he would not fall, but would merely suffer a harmlessly sensational swing across the gully. In face of this improvised gallows Donaldson remained as unperturbed as an aristocrat on the scaffold. If the rocks were climbable at all he would get up. I was sure of it. Yet he did not get up. He made ten feet, after which not all his tenacious ingenuity could get him higher. We both came down to the junction and changed places on the rope.

I tried to force the passage where Donaldson had failed but could find no adequate hold. The rope came to me at too wide an angle to be of assistance, but I thought that there were possibilities of readjusting the rope to allow a more direct pull. Meantime, my arms and wrists ached with hanging to minute holds and I prepared to climb down. At this instant a small powder-snow avalanche, discharged from the North buttress at a great height above, came trundling down the gully, poured over my head, and swamped the rocks around. Large quantities of freezing powder shot down my neck and formed a waist-belt of liquid horror. This discomfort was quickly forgotten, for the small holds by which I had ascended thus far were obliterated, and try as I would I could not find them again with my feet. Handhold was too sketchy to allow of leaning out to prospect. I realized that I should be bound to come off, and warned Donaldson accordingly. Nevertheless, I contrived to climb down a few feet before the rock and I parted company. I swung across the gully, feeling like a parachutist, and keenly aware of the thinness of climbing-rope. A few seconds later I came to rest on the gully-bed, and after unroping joined Donaldson above.

The time was four-forty p.m. By previous agreement we should now have turned in our tracks and hastened down to avoid benightment. We agreed that the game was almost up—but not quite up. The sterility of pessimism had not yet descended upon us, whilst the fertility of optimism suggested, first, an attempt at the summer route, and if that failed, then a readjustment of the rope over the chockstone to afford a more direct pull on the corner route. We had only to think of the difficulties below to be fortified in these decisions.

I set to work on the summer route by traversing 'back and foot' to the outer edge of the chimney. But I failed to start the traverse across the buttress. The rock was slabby, thinly iced, and engulfed in powder-snow. However, I changed for the better the rope running over the chockstone and made my slow way back to Donaldson. A third attempt on the corner route was now our only hope, but I had to confess to Donaldson that I was temporarily too muscle-weary to try. He then climbed down to the junction and again took the lead.

Once he was launched on the rocks I could not see what was happening, and a long period of suspense followed. Like myself, Donaldson is not communicative on a climb. Twice I was enjoined to hold the rope tight, from which I gathered that he was luxuriating in more than moral support. The rope moved no more than a few inches in twenty minutes. I passed the time by scrutinizing the retaining walls below with an eye to a traverse out of the gully. In all the wide acres of rock on the North buttress I could detect not a single line of escape. The Crowberry ridge through almost all its length was overhanging, and in any event an escape there would be one from the frying-pan into the fire.

My eye wandered back to the rope: little movements were to

be seen that indicated something alive at the far end of it. Then, gradually, still inch by inch, the rope snaked—upward! I could hardly contain myself. The tempo of rope-movement steadily quickened, often going out a foot at a time, until a hundred feet had scuttered over the snow-encrusted chockstone. A faint call of 'Come on!' floated down to me. To any future climber, belayed after sunset to a pillar of ice in the left fork of Crowberry gully, I guarantee that these hackneyed words 'Come on!' will stir his spirit like a flourish of trumpets.

I reached Donaldson at five-thirty p.m. A little more cutting, a little more kicking of steps, and we arrived below the final cave pitch. Its appearance shocked us. Having come so far, and toiled so hard, we were in no mood for spectacular severities. But the cave arched forty feet overhead, thrust down at us a tusk of red rock, and looked impregnable. Our natural reaction after the crux, combined with a grey twilight, lent a degree or two, as it were, to the verticality of the flanking walls. Donaldson settled in his frost-lined cave and gave me a belay, while I used the failing light to search out a weak spot on the North buttress side, where a layer of black ice spread over the rock like tar. It is unlikely that I could have solved the problem of starting at all but for two lucky chances. At a height of four feet, and again at ten feet, a clump of frozen snow adhered to *verglas*. Both occurred where there was no other vestige of hold. Either might break away without warning, but each was sufficiently low down for the risk to be taken safely. When put to the test, both clumps held and did not break until later.

After reaching the second clump I could at first see no way of getting higher. The ice was still too thin to use save as a last resort. The protruding bones of rock were glazed and badly spaced. For a moment or two I leant my back against the tusk and allowed my gaze to wander downward. I gained rest and lasting memories at the same time. Beneath my heels Crowberry gully plunged in a grey cataract, and far below disappeared in a sea of darkness, which slowly and surely seeped up the gully like a flowing tide. The sheeted walls and snow-banked ledges of the North buttress had long ceased to sparkle, and looked unspeakably bleak. I know nothing more merciless than frost-bound cliffs at dusk. After the setting of the sun, grimness is their keynote and their hymn hostility.

Donaldson by this time was making anxious inquiries about conditions ahead, to which I replied with the usual non-committal noises. I managed to move up a foot, then, unexpectedly, another foot. The ice became thicker. There followed three-quarters of an hour of continuous cutting—a race with ebbing light. The angle was too high, and therefore balance too delicate, to permit any weight behind these axe-blows. I had to peck away, using one hand from the wrist, trying to hew holds wherever allowed by rock bulges and brittle ice, which cropped up, with a kind of inevitability, always in the wrong place. This was one of those pitches that wring from a climber, when he is half-way up, a hasty declaration that never again will he set foot on iced rocks, and when he is up, a solemn oath that never in all his life will he forsake them. And so it turned out. I reached the top with aching muscles and a joyful heart.

I had to cut some further distance up shallow snow before finding sufficient depth to sink half my axe-shaft for a belay. Donaldson's position was now an unenviable one. The extra cutting had discharged rivulets of chips over all the holds carved so laboriously. It was becoming too dark to see details of rock or ice for delicate climbing movements. However, I shouted down, 'I'm up!' and after the conventional interval, 'Come on!' Donaldson, frozen stiff with his long wait while night closed round, and uncertain of our prospects, welcomed the order with delighted liveliness; and that, with a tight rope and his own great skill, carried him up the pitch within fifteen minutes. He gave a remarkable exhibition of resolute climbing.

Our only anxiety now was the bad state of the snow in the last stretch of gully—powdery stuff lying on old granular snow at a high angle. We continued to move one at a time from axe-belays. A small awkward pitch of ten feet caused trouble;

beyond was a hundred feet of plodding to the snow-ridge where the gully ended.

We stepped on to the open mountain-side at seven-fifteen p.m., and came face to face with a cloud-racked, starry sky. The ring of low crags under the summit, the ground beneath our feet, and all the rocks around were buried deep in fog crystals. Although night had fallen, yet up there so close to the sky there was not true darkness. A mysterious twilight, like that of an old chapel at vespers, pervaded these highest slopes of Buachaille. We stood at the everlasting gates, and as so often happens at the close of a great climb, a profound stillness came upon my mind, and paradoxically, the silence was song and the diversity of things vanished. The mountains and the world and I were one. But that was not all: a strange and powerful feeling that something as yet unknown was almost within my grasp, was trembling into vision, stayed with me until we reached the cairn, where it passed away.

We went down to Glen Etive for the last time, and I fear we went sadly. The moon shone fitfully through ragged brown clouds.

21 *Cairngorm Blizzard*

ONE DAY IN MAY I fled the noise and tumult of cities for the peace and quiet, as I thought, of the Cairngorms; and thus once again there was demonstrated the truth of those oracular words of La Fontaine:

> On rencontre sa destinée
> Souvent par des chemins qu'on prend pour l'éviter.

Had I only known, when I arrived at Aviemore that afternoon, what in fact lay in store for me on the morrow, I should have thought twice before stirring from the Great North Road. Doubtless I should have stirred none the less. Men prize most highly what they win hardly.

I had come alone to indulge in a little hill-walking. It is good for a climber to go off by himself from time to time; a practice greatly to be encouraged—it sharpens up his mountain-craft; his feeling for the hill scene is heightened and his eye for detail quickened—but a practice to be discouraged in the Cairngorms in spring or winter: hills that command my respect more than any other range in Scotland. Moreover, when I looked south to their distant swell, it was manifest that I should be lucky to see anything save a compass-dial. A pall of cloud hung over the mountains, its underside lurid from the reflected glare of the snow plateaux.

My plans were accordingly modest, until an evening stroll by the shores of Loch Balladern introduced me to a fair-haired youth of quiet eye and upright bearing, who stood dripping before me on the shingle after a swim in the loch. While he dressed he told me his name was Mortimer. I liked him on the instant, and with no more ado asked him to climb with me next day. He welcomed the idea and I shared a meal in his tent by the loch-side. We laid plans for the morrow. We should go nine miles to the head of Glen Einich, five more to the

Devil's Point, then northward to Braeriach we should enjoy a five-mile walk at a height of four thousand feet—a total round of thirty-one miles.

Now that I had a friend with me the wicked look of the weather already offered consolation. A course of compass-work is never amiss; for the one way efficiently to handle map and compass is by practice, and the Cairngorms are said to be the best training-ground in Europe. I suggest that such an opinion puts the cart before the horse; one had better train elsewhere and leave to the Cairngorms the final test. That their heart lies ten mountainous miles from human aid has been realized too late by many an ill-equipped climbing party; for the range is sterner in foul weather than may be found anywhere at a like latitude, and a Cairngorm blizzard can be the last word in natural savagery.

However, we were particularly well supplied with food and clothing. We assembled this gear in the tent, and added to the pile a coil of Alpine rope, which in the end came near to saving our lives.

Next morning we were up at six a.m. and away at seven. The first stage of our journey went by twilit tracks through the forest of Rothiemurchus. There had been high wind and rain during the night and we marched to stirring music, 'The sea in the pine-tops murmuring.' The branches still dripped and swayed, and the fallen drops gemmed the tangle of undergrowth, from which arose a moist breath, so fragrant that to this day I can recapture the emotion it aroused. I can well understand the sentiment of that Scots soldier in Iraq, who, according to John Buchan, described his camp site as 'twa miles on the Rothiemurchus side o' Baghdad.' At the furthest fringe of the forest we crossed a barred gate in a deer fence, where a battered notice-board warns the free Briton that he is liable to be shot. There was an ugly sky behind us.

From now onward we began to lose touch with the human world. We had reached a no man's land, where the outpost of the Cairngorms, Carn Eilrig, and the last pines of the broad Spey valley, confront each other like rival sentinels on a frontier.

The furthest tree dropped behind and our track drove its lonely scratch over a wilderness of heath and stone toward the dim recess of Glen Einich. Meantime, the growing commotion of the sky forced itself on our notice. The whole north-western horizon was congested with gathering storm-clouds. They had flung out slate-grey skirmishers, which even now were racing in squadrons overhead, throwing themselves athwart the mountain bulwarks. Down in Glen Einich there was no more than a spit of rain, cold and ominous.

Seven miles out, at the lower bothy, we took shelter and asked ourselves seriously whether it were worth while going on. There seemed a promise of big developments in the sky; but the day was too young to be termed hopeless, and if need were we could descend from Cairn Toul and cut the second part of our programme. Good reasons, no doubt, for going on—but the truth is that human nature is happily perverse, and the delight of wrestling a fall with the elements an exhilarating prospect.

We covered the next two miles to the upper bothy in record time; for the rain gave place to hail, which came down harder each moment. This ramshackle hut of blackened wood is perhaps the most famous refuge in the Cairngorms. A haven where many a storm-tossed climber has been thankful to ride out a blizzard. We found the inside to be damp, gloomy, and indescribably dirty. Despite such minor drawbacks we derived a thrill of snugness from the devil's tattoo of the hail. Everything pointed to this being our last chance to eat in comfort, and we settled down to second breakfast. The time was nine a.m. Then my eye was caught by an array of carvings on the wall. On looking closer I was surprised and delighted to find the engraved names of several mountaineering friends. The bothy was so lonely, so deeply buried in the mountain fastness, and therefore my finding of these old names so unexpected, that for a minute my imagination ran away with me. 'All the wistful past waked in one glance,' and I could fancy that friendly voices and the laughter of former days still echoed through the hut.[1]

[1] The upper bothy has recently been destroyed.

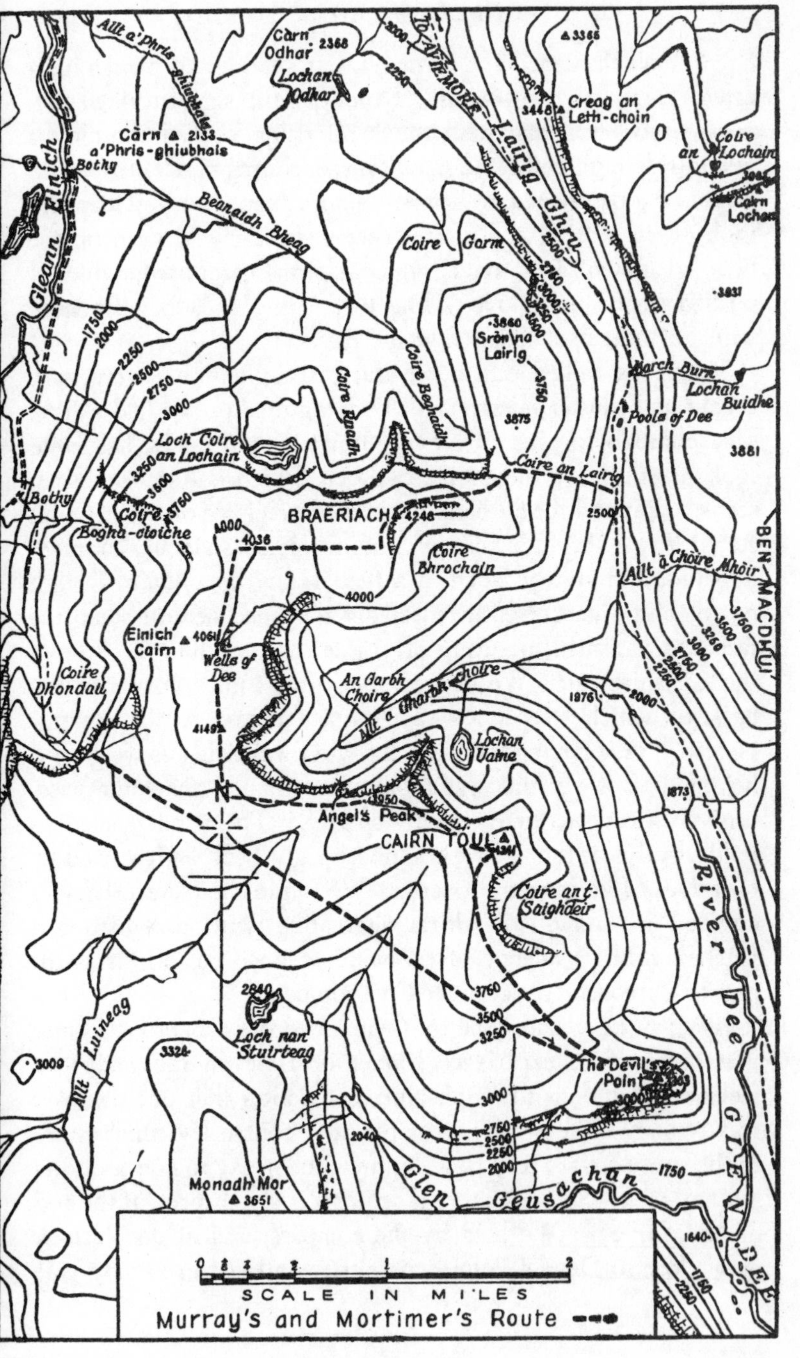
Murray's and Mortimer's Route
SCALE IN MILES
BRAERIACH
CAIRN TOUL
Angel's Peak
The Devil's Point
Lairig Ghru
To AVIEMORE
River Dee
GLEN DEE
BEN MACDHUI
Glen Geusachan
Gleann Einich
Monadh Mor
Loch nan Stuirteag
Lochan Uaine
Wells of Dee
Pools of Dee
Einich Cairn
An Garbh Choire
Coire Bhrochain
Coire an Lochain
Coire Garm
Coire Ruadh
Coire Beanaidh
Coire an t-Saighdeir
Coire Dhondail
Coire Bogha-cloiche
Loch Coire an Lochain
Beanaidh Bheag
Càrn a'Phris-ghiubhais
Allt a'Phris-ghiubhais
Càrn Odhar
Lochan Odhar
Creag an Leth-choin
Sròn na Lairig
March Burn
Lochan Buidhe
Allt a Chòire Mhòir
Allt a Gharbh-choire
Allt Luineag
Bothy

The hail slackened and went off, but shuddering planks indicated a strengthening wind. I thought the sign excellent, for my opinion was that with the wind rising so fast the clouds would ride high before noon. Thus encouraged, I set to work. I applied a protractor to the one-inch Ordnance Survey map and took every bearing and distance we were likely to need on the hills. I noted these on a piece of stray cardboard, which I pushed inside my glove. The map could thus be dispensed with during the remainder of the day.

When we sallied out at ten-thirty the glen was lively with breeze and bluster, every top cloud-engulfed. We had a five-mile climb before us to Devil's Point, but the first half mile took us south by the shores of Loch Einich. A most dismal scene. Beyond the far bank the hoared precipice of Sgurr Dubh stared down through veils of shifting mist—suddenly loomed, lingered, and slowly faded in a regular rhythmic cycle. High on the cliff a darker gash repeatedly remained behind when the face had vanished, destitute of visible support, like the grin of the Cheshire cat. We steered south-east into a corrie, at the back of which steep snow-slopes gave access to the summit plateau. As one might expect, the wind was rising as we gained height, but as yet this was more an assistance than otherwise. Our progress was unexpectedly speedy. The wind pushed us uphill, and near the top we could lean right back on it and allow ourselves to be carried forward. We found the plateau heavily covered in snow, soft drifts alternating with case-hardened patches. The tendency of the wind to push us too far south had to be constantly corrected by compass.

After an hour had gone by there arose the dangerous feeling that most of us experience sooner or later on mountains—a feeling tantamount to an absolute conviction that our compass was wrong, quite wrong, that the true course lay much more to the south. It is easy to yield, dreadfully easy to compromise, but any man who does either is set for a nasty surprise at the end of his journey. We held by the compass, and at one o'clock drew close to Devil's Point, where the wind was exceeding gale force in short gusts, some of which must have approached a hundred miles per hour. We had to crawl on hands and knees over the last twenty yards to the cairn, for we were unwilling to be picked up and hurled down the Lairig Ghru face. For a moment we were tempted—the first of the day's three great temptations—to find a route down to the Corrour bothy in the Lairig Ghru. But this seemed too gross a betrayal of our day's expedition and we let the idea go—reluctantly, for the wind was bitter.

After we topped Devil's Point we began the real work of the day, our six-mile journey northward. That we might have to spend more than five hours on it was not at this stage credible, and all went well on the first mile and a half to Cairn Toul. On our right hand, the parallel rift of the Lairig Ghru, just visible as a blur of gloom, was a sure guide in case of need. But the wind was now against us. Although no snow was falling, twisting snow-devils were racing across the surface of the plateau and hurling handfuls of powder and spiculae into our faces. Often these gusts were too violent to bear and we had to turn our backs and wait for them to slacken.

We were thankful now that our bearings were ready beforehand, for in such a gale map-work would have been highly troublesome. A compass check on direction was occasionally essential, less on account of mist, which had cleared a little since Devil's Point, than of clouds of flying drift. On top of this major irritation came the minor difficulty of breathing. The wind literally flung our breath back between our teeth. To avoid its impact on the mouth we had to go head down to it.

In half an hour these terrific gusts eased off and became infrequent. We had easy walking for a while, and when we came to steeper slopes the wind was much less violent, although the height was now three thousand five hundred feet. At the end of an hour we began to feel the intoxication of filling our lungs with Britain's purest air, the supreme property of these high-level plateaux. To that was added the zest of fighting a wind that was no longer implacable, that was yielding with no worse than a stout resistance. One had the pleasing sense of being detached from one's own body. One drove it over the plateau as though wielding a weapon in battle. One had the mastery and exulted. When one halted the feeling was different; then one dwelt in the body as though in a tent for a brief bivouac, the real self or soul being no more confused with the body than the camper with the canvas and pole. On a wind-swept plateau we may drink the living waters of freedom and learn of our heritage.

When we started on the last rise to Cairn Toul there came a wider clearance than usual. Suddenly Mortimer gripped my arm and pointed uphill through the mist chasm.

'Look!' he exclaimed. 'Two men crossing to Glen Einich.'

Upon looking up the slope I was duly surprised to see two climbers a long way ahead of us. And we had thought ourselves early on the mountain, and considering the weather, almost brazen! I watched them traverse a full fifty feet from east to west across the snow-slope, one about ten yards in front of the other. I hailed them, but the wind tore my voice in the wrong direction. We advanced and saw them halt, apparently to wait for us. At a hundred yards' range they turned out to be two black boulders. So great was out astonishment that we failed even to laugh at ourselves. It was a perfect illustration of the eye's absolute need of some framework before it can distinguish a moving object from a stationary.

We had found the long plod to Cairn Toul arduous, but had little to complain of, for the snow underfoot had been pounded into hard sheets. When we passed four thousand feet the clouds were rapidly receding before our uphill advance, and we arrived at the cairn with a sense of enlarging sky and broadening vistas. The day showed every sign of turning out exactly as we had hoped, a strong shouting day—fierce but harmless.

Leaning sideways to the breeze we were lucky enough to get a superb view of the eastern Cairngorms. Here and there a hail shower trailed like crystal tapestry over their rolling domes. For the most part they stood clear, in truth 'palaces of death and frost.' The cloud ceiling continued to rise, fast-pacing as ever, until the giant back of our plateau lay bare. Its outflung limbs stretched far toward Inverey and Rothiemurchus, Cairn Toul brooding over the one and Braeriach the other. Between lay leagues of snow.

The sense of our minuteness on these empty wastes became acute. I felt a tiny speck swallowed up in an environment incomprehensibly great, like the flicker of earthly life amid the uncountable galaxies. Here we knew what it meant to be alone, yet to feel distant kinship with the gods. One might imagine that the human spirit would be cowed by the inhuman majesty of the scene; but this need not be so. Although he be alone, many a man will find the contrary to be true. Whatever there may be of greatness in a man's mind will grow and go out in sympathy with the greatness of the mountain world: whatever is little will shrink. So that where one man is intimidated another is ennobled.

There is, too, something in the plateaux that makes appeal to man's restless heart, an appeal that seems to be felt by people of all countries. For I found it again in the course of twelve months' travelling in the deserts of Syria, Iraq, Egypt, and Libya. There I discovered the same bold sweep of horizon and sky, the bare and boundless distance, the wind and desolation. The same simplicity. Despite all barrenness and hardship, the deserts stir deep instincts of the human mind, the impulse to rove and explore, the love of quest that betrays the yearning of the race. These powerfully urge us across the mountain plateaux and the lonely summits.

Our correct prophecy of the cloud clearance had immensely pleased us; and as erring humans will, we began to assume our judgment infallible. Uttering our grave opinions like a bench of law lords, we declared that the wind, though moderating, would keep the tops clear all day; we could safely press on with part two of our programme. Yet be it noted, the cloud ceiling remained close overhead. At three p.m. we started north-west by the brink of the cliffs to Angel's Peak.

Then, most surprisingly, before we had gone any distance, the wind died away. An uneasy silence fell. At the gentle slopes of the col we stopped and watched a great change overtaking the sky. In every direction, as far as eye could see, stretched an unbroken mass of dark storm-clouds, rapidly pressing down upon the mountains like a leaden canopy. White flakes were beginning to wander high overhead. We hurried into action again. Ten minutes later we were enveloped in dense mist.

This calm prevailed through the journey from Cairn Toul to Angel's Peak. We were just underneath the top when as suddenly as the wind had died it returned. It came from a point more to the west, loud and shrill, buffeting the west flank and spinning streamers of snow around us. The light turned an ugly yellow and then darkened to iron grey. Down in the lowlands, the stories of the Grey Man who is alleged to haunt the neighbouring summit of Ben Macdhui is a fit subject for derision. In threatening storm it is less incredible, and when I suddenly saw a great grey shadow loom through the murk, a blurred figure taller by far than human form, I confess that for one moment I was startled out of my wits. Then my Grey Man materialized as Mortimer on the cairn above me.

The renewal of the wind persuaded us that although the cloud could not be broken up, at least foul weather might again be staved off until sunset. If so we had time in hand, and since our bodies had been hard punched by the weather we sheltered for thirty minutes on the lee-side of the peak, where we pulled on all reserve clothing, ate food, and checked our bearings to Braeriach.

We were determined henceforth not to try to follow the line of the cliffs, but to keep well clear of them. I know of one party of four climbers who in thick weather gaily walked over the edge of the north corrie of Cairngorm. They were properly tied on a short rope, but when the leader dropped through the cornice the second man was caught napping and was plucked like a straw into the void. The others promptly followed.

Most luckily they missed the rocks and struck steeply inclined snow, which glanced them downward for several hundred feet. By a miracle, not one of them suffered fatal injury. Therefore, to preclude chance of a similar fate, we made our route on three bearings—half-mile west to the head of the Garrachoire, a cliff-ringed corrie deeply breaching the plateau, then one and a quarter miles north to the north top, point 4,036, and lastly three-quarter mile easterly to the summit.

At four p.m. we set off. If the sky monsters had scowled on our trespass before, it was not until now that they roused themselves in good earnest. It became obvious that a thick snow-storm must at any moment close down on us. The flakes came faster and faster, at first fat and whirling, then driving and vicious, applying an icy lash to the cheek. We had gone half-way to the Garrachoire when a blizzard came down like the wrath of God.

More intensely than on Cairn Toul we now felt much alone—a feeling that did not so much intimidate as rally one's inner resources; for the fact that civilization might as well be a hundred miles away for all the difference it could make in emergency, lent the mountain fury an inspiring quality unknown on more accessible ranges. The rough hair of our woollen balaclavas was shortly a mass of icicles, especially around the mouth. The wind-proof cloth of our breeches went stiff as a board and our chests were encased in breastplates of white armour; even our eyebrows and lashes were iced, and we felt thankful we had no moustaches.

To add to these discomforts we began to have trouble in navigation. Our compasses especially caused us vexation of mind, being unreadable on the move and hard to read at the halt, against the battering of the wind. At the head of the Garrachoire, and despite my compass having a floating dial, I seemed to spend hours (they were probably minutes) helplessly watching its gyrations. The visibility had fallen to almost nil, and for twenty minutes thereafter we could not see beyond our boots. Below, above, on all sides, was the impalpable writhing whiteness, which left the eye nothing to focus on, nothing to which one could relate one's own body. The result was that our sense of balance was quite upset. We had the sensation of floating rather than walking, an illusion repeatedly shattered as the heel jarred into invisible depressions or the toe stubbed on hummocks. At the moments when visibility improved we had great difficulty in distinguishing large objects far off from small ones a few yards away. The compass by itself was thus well-nigh useless.

We met the situation by Mortimer's halting in front, when I took bearings on his figure, or in his general direction when he disappeared. Then I went forward on the correct line and passed him by thirty paces. He, meantime, had rejoined the proper line and was sighting on my own figure. We thus advanced one at a time. The system was slow but the alternative was aimless wandering.

We passed what we hoped was the south top, and were henceforth moving above four thousand feet and exposed to the full wind force. To give the eye a focusing point the first man threw snowballs in front, but they were not satisfactory and occasionally we found a rucksack better. When cast ahead it could be seen as a darker blur through the whiteness. On the other hand we had to be careful not to lose it, for when we had recourse to this device the plateau was seething. The noise deafened us. Added to the pulsing blast of the storm on the mountain flanks, now louder in one place and now lower in another, was the fierce instant *swish* of loose powder sweeping across the snowfields, rising in pitch by hoarse shocks, then diminishing to its *swish—swish—swish*.

In these conditions, and wading through a snow morass, we found accurate compass-work excessively trying. There was sore temptation to skimp the task and take a chance—say to take bearings only once in five minutes—but we stuck to our wearisome routine determinedly. At what he thought was close to the second top Mortimer stopped and shouted in my ear:

'Back to Garrachoire—wind behind us—down to Corrour.'

That was the third and last of the day's temptations. The Corrour bothy lay low in the Lairig Ghru. We could rest there until the following morning, for we had food enough for two days. Such a move was alluring, for the wind was not merely violent but unconscionably cold. I wore a woollen vest, a flannel shirt, and four sweaters beneath a windproof Grenfell jacket, and still felt frozen. The wind pierced my balaclava, which had to be reinforced with a scarf. My hands were numb under two layers of heavy woollen mits. And Mortimer, who delayed putting on his second pair of gloves until too late, suffered later from frost-bite.

We very nearly took the lure, for the uproar of the storm seemed to hammer all thought out of our heads, and only by an effort of will could we bring our brains to reason. Presently, however, sanity prevailed and we saw the situation in its true light. We were experiencing not a winter blizzard but a spring blizzard, which would last only a day. To stampede down to Corrour would be childish. The true Cairngorm blizzard blowing for several days from the south-east was a very different matter; even then the bothy could be more a trap than a refuge; for down there, surrounded by high mountains and hourly deepening snow, with increasing cold and a dwindling food supply, we might simply be weakened and then caught by a second and killing storm. That had happened to Baird and Barrie—and to others. It is best to fight a battle when one's vigour is unimpaired.

We pressed on and had travelled one hour forty minutes from Angel's Peak when we began to feel anxious about the north top. For the last mile from the south top I had been counting my paces to avoid overshooting the mark, point 4,036, which we assumed to be only an undulation on the rolling plateau. Mortimer in addition had kept a time check, reckoning our speed at a little more than a mile an hour. In view of our staggering and broken progress we had disturbing doubts of these calculations, without which we should yet have been lost. When we had gone the correct distance there was no sign of any top. Visibility was thirty feet. We went further, returned, went off at right angles. No use. It was suggested that we separate and search independently, but the proposal was vetoed. Our search for the top might develop into a more anxious search for each other. There was nothing for it but to bestow full confidence on our own estimates. There being no top in sight anywhere around, we agreed to assume that we stood on it.

Our final bearing was now three-quarters of a mile easterly. A small northerly error in angle subtended thus far would lose us the summit. Therefore to avoid landing in trouble by passing it to the north, we decided to bear south of it to the broad target of the eastern precipice, from which we could follow a sure line to the cairn. We left the north top at five-forty p.m. Fifteen minutes later we stopped to rope up; in thirty minutes I reckoned we were very close to the cliffs. They must be less than a hundred yards away.

I happened to be in front just then, and it became my chief duty not to fall through a snow cornice. Therefore I began to sound any doubtful step with my axe-spike. Whenever Mortimer saw what I was about, he stopped me and said that his hands had become too dead to hold a rope in emergency. I had already guessed that and was not alarmed, for I could trust myself to find a cornice when I came to it, but to ease his mind we switched the rope and I went to the rear. At first he was able to continue without probing, then visibility shrank to a few feet as great waves of wind strove to sweep us off the plateau. As though prospecting for crevasses on an upper glacier, he now thrust in his spike before each step. Five minutes later I saw him stop and retire a pace. He turned to me with a yell and a flourish of his axe. He had found the cliffs, and as it happened, saw the lip from a distance of three feet. We turned north to the summit.

As daylight ebbed the snow-fields were pervaded by an unutterable gloom, like the grey twilight of interstellar space. We wasted no time at the cairn, which we reached at six-fifteen p.m. A storm by day in the Cairngorms is a hard experience.

A storm by night would have killed us. Rarely have I been more exhausted and numbed with cold, which now gripped not only the extremities but the whole body. Our one anxiety was to get off the mountain. The snow had stopped falling before we turned down the long east ridge to the bealach, but the fury of the wind had no whit abated and the whole world for us was a raging chaos of wheeling and scudding drift. That anywhere on earth there could be such cheerful comfort as a hot bath, an old arm-chair before a fire, or better by far, urns of steaming tea, seemed but the golden fantasy of some Miltonic Eden. We felt the gross illusion that here were the only realities of a mechanistic universe—bleak rocks, bitter wind, snow, and withering cold.

We had gone five hundred feet down the ridge when its east flank fell back sufficiently to allow an easy route to the Lairig. The edge was heavily corniced. I smashed the overhang with an axe and cut a foothold or two on the wall below. Five minutes later we went careering down the snow slope. Our blood spun to the swoop of standing glissades, but the surface was rough and we suddenly reverted to the vulgar sitting position, which gave an increase in speed and a decrease in pleasure, for our boots sprayed an icy back-wash into our faces. In a gratifyingly short space of time we were sitting on a boulder in the Lairig Ghru. We rested only long enough to untie the rope, then climbed to the top of the pass. The time was seven-thirty p.m.

That nine-mile descent to the Spey!—it went on for ever, down—down—down everlastingly into depths of increasing darkness. When we reached Rothiemurchus it was with something of wonder, a weary surprise rather than thankfulness. Down here the wind merely snuffled round the boulders, but a rousing blast, discharged at judicious intervals, served to jog the memories of three hours ago. Already the wild turmoil far above our heads seemed infinitely remote; and the Braeriach plateau, like some lost continent of the skies, but a legend of a bygone age.

22 *The Evidence of Things Not Seen*

THE MOON WAS NEW-RISEN. It balanced like a yellow apple on the black barb of Schichallion. The flood of its mellow light poured far across the moor of Rannoch. Driving north from Bridge of Orchy I was obliged, for the first time of my life, to wear sun-glasses at night. I can truthfully say that in three years divided between Asia, Africa, and Italy, each famed in story for its bright nights, I have seen but one comparable to this that I shared with Douglas Laidlaw in December 1939.

Our intention was to climb the Buachaille Etive Mor by its eastern cliff and we had chanced on the ideal conditions. By the time we reached Kingshouse the moon had swept the sky clear; neither cloud stemmed nor star survived the torrent. At a quarter-mile's distance the inn appeared to float upon the moor, 'whiter than new snow on a raven's back,' and the tops of the pines were silver-tipped.

After an hour's delay we went down to Coupal bridge in Glen Etive, whence we crossed the moor to Buachaille. I had imagined I knew this mountain under every whim of the elements, yet here was something more than new: for though we may not postulate absolute beauty of things material, the Buachaille was less clogged with the pollutions of mortality than is normally granted to an earthly form. Therefore let us speak of the unspeakable, for there is no speech so profitable. The east face was washed by intense light, so searching that no shade was cast by ridge or buttress. All detail merged in the vastness of one arrowy wall, pale as shadowed milk, impregnably erect. At the remote apex, a white crest broke like spume on the high seas of infinity:

> So shalt thou see and hear
> The lovely shapes and sounds intelligible
> Of that eternal language which thy God
> Utters, who from eternity doth teach
> Himself in all, and all things in Himself.

But I lacked the quick vision of Coleridge. To my unaccustomed eyes the scene at first bore an appearance of unreality; yet the more I gazed, the more surely I knew that I saw not an illusion greater than is usual, but truth made manifest: as though our everyday world had been a dull image in the crystal mirror of Shalott, only here woven on the magic loom by an artist, one of true intuition, who rejecting inessential things had selected in masterly economy those precious to the truth, thus throwing into high relief the hitherto obscured beauty that underlies the world. Unlike the Lady of Shalott, I failed to break the spell and gaze straight upon the ultimate reality; yet the hills that night were big with it; its signs unmistakable.

It is this that Goethe calls 'the open secret.' It is this that mountaineers style 'the mystery of hills.' Put more broadly, it is the mystery of the universe, of which the forms of man or mountain may be likened to veils that reveal its being yet mask its very essence. Ask Nature what she does and we are answered, as Faust was answered:

> So at the roaring loom of Time I ply
> And weave for God the garment that ye see Him by.

If the answer be taken to heart our understanding of mountains is broadened and deepened toward the understanding of all things created; but the point of its last line strikes home only when applied to oneself.

Our destination was the base of D gully buttress, where we arrived at eleven o'clock. We swarmed up the first few hundred feet, and roped where the plinth narrows for the upward drive. All around the rocks were stark, scrubbed clean as the decks of a battleship, the shade of palest ash. Near at hand they sparkled with a coarse crystalline glitter, never seen by day. It is affirmed by Chesterton that one is sometimes uplifted as though by trumpet-call not so much by the beauty of Nature as by her generous and defiant ugliness. 'Has the poet,' he inquires, 'for whom Nature means only roses and lilies, ever heard a pig grunting? It is a noise that does a man good.' This paradox rejoices the true rock-climber. He is no mountaineer who can look upon the ugly face of those age-gaunt crags, and fail to feel their rough honesty go straight to his heart, there to kindle sympathy to a flame of delight. In their mere proximity there is happiness. A contentment of the same kind, if less high, as that where the friendship of two men ripens until the delight of simple companionship removes the need of speech.

We met no rock-work that posed a problem greater than that of daytime. But the cold, steadily growing since sunset, gripped the world in frost, which we countered by wearing gloves as far as the one severe pitch of the ridge. Bare hands and numbed fingers were then the order of the night.

The remainder of the ridge took shape as an attenuated staircase. Half-way up the weather changed abruptly. An icy wind whipped out of the north, and a great cloud mass, which must have been piling up unseen to the north-west, suddenly tumbled over the summit. With one mighty roll it engulfed us. Snow began to fall, at first idly, with a soft crepitation, then fast and silently. The wind rose.

The light above the buttress was still surprisingly good, so we traversed northward on to the crest of Crowberry ridge. With mist writhing about us and snow shrouding the rocks, we flitted up the Tower like phantoms in a phantom world. On top of the Tower the wind died and the snow stopped. The fog hung dense and still. Well, I thought, we had enjoyed a splendid night-climb, but we must now forgo all hope of a still finer prize. However, we had come for the mountain, not for the rock-climb alone, so down we went to the Tower gap and up the lofty brow to the cairn. The mist at the summit was bright and pearly. It seemed to be thinning, and our dead hopes stirred in the first pangs of resurrection. Perhaps . . .? Who knows . . .?

We sat down to it.

Just a quarter of an hour: then the clouds began to stir uneasily, rent by deep internal stress. Caverns, vast as mountain corries, swirled open and closed. Yet not a breath of wind touched my cheek. The effect was tantamount to the supernatural: I understood as not hitherto what strange emotion quickened the Ancient Mariner when his sails filled and no breeze blew. The caverns widened—deepened—the mist sank to the Tower and the clear moon burst from a clear sky.

The cloud bank was now stabilized at three thousand feet, its spread fleece flowing to every horizon save the south. We looked out upon the glimmering surge as though from 'magic casements, opening on the foam of perilous seas, in faery lands forlorn.' Through the swell of the tumbling billows projected the iceberg islands of Argyll and Lochaber. As the Corellian devil observed, hard frost, like hard times, brings noble work into prominence. And this blanketing of intervening country, combined with the dazzle of their frozen snows, drew all the peaks unnaturally close in a fantastic optical illusion. Nevis looked but a stone's throw, and Bidean nam Bian a practicable leap.

Within an hour the cloud-sea broke up. When the preliminary boilings and heavings had subsided, the surface caved into maelstrom, spraying up streamers of shining mist, which shrivelled to tenuous wraiths, and like the ghost in *Hamlet* 'shrank in haste away.' On every hand the entire mass then dispersed and swiftly rose far above our heads. The final state was a high ceiling of widely deployed cumulus, still as becalmed galleons. But the Mamore and Nevis peaks retained their own bank, and seen now in correct perspective, looked for all the world like a flashing necklace, flung down carelessly on a cotton-wool pad. Nor had we ever realized what teeming waters spatter the moor of Rannoch, until we saw these hosts of white eyes upturned, calmly looking to the moon. Like them we waited:

> With heart as calm as lakes that sleep
> In frosty moonlight glistening,
> Or mountain rivers, where they creep
> Along a channel smooth and deep
> To their own far-off murmurs listening.

That was our heart's desire—to wait, to wait for we knew not what. Nor did our instinct err. For we had yet to learn that from this inner stillness, which lifts the mind far beyond the imperfect offices of prayer and praise, comes the great flight of the spirit: and its apprehension of glory and beauty eternal.

But the wings do not grow of their own accord.

Toward four o'clock in the morning we returned to Glen Etive. Our most sanguine expectations had been met; our eyes feasted and our hearts elated. We had set out in search of adventure; and we had found beauty. Thus we had found them both in their fuller sense; for in the architecture of hill and sky, as in great art and music, there is an everlasting harmony with which our own being had this night been made one. What more may we fairly ask of mountains? None the less, I came down from the summit filled with the acute awareness of an imminent revelation lost; a shadow that stalked at my side ever more openly among the hills. Something underlying the world as we saw it had been withheld. The very skies had trembled with presentiment of the last reality; and we had not been worthy.

Those fairest forms of the mountain way—are they all that is spread out for us to read on the high places of the earth? Something in that night cried out to us, not low, nor faltering, but clear, true, urgent—that this was not all: that not half the wonder had pierced the clouds of our blindness; that the world was full of a divine splendour, which must be sought within oneself before it might be found without: that our task was to see and know. From the deeps of the earth to the uttermost star above the whole creation had throbbed with a full and new life; its music one song of honour to the beautiful; its word, 'Holy, holy, holy, Lord God of hosts, heaven and earth are full of thy glory. . . .' And we knew, as surely as men know anything on earth, that the implacable hunter had drawn close. Turn where we would, there was nothing anywhere but He. One's ear caught the ringing of His footstep; and one's eye, 'gleams like the flashing of a shield.'

> At last I heard a voice upon the slope
> Cry to the summit, 'Is there any hope?'
> To which an answer peal'd from that high land,
> But in a tongue no man could understand;
> And on the glimmering limit, far withdrawn,
> God made Himself an awful rose of dawn.

23 *Rocks and Realities*

I HAVE ALWAYS FELT that Leslie Stephen's celebrated shaft missed its mark when he identified as 'the one point of superiority' of Scottish mountains their leagues of heather. There are two hundred and seventy-six mountains in Scotland. To any one who sees them at all seasons, their unique virtue becomes that wedding of rock and water portrayed to such perfection down the western seaboard from Cape Wrath to Arran; less perfectly but still notably among the rivers and lochs of the central and east highlands. In heather there is much to admire; of its season I have no good to say. The climax arrives in August, of all months in the year the most noxious to Scottish mountaineers, when the great midge plague has stricken the valleys and every hill is oppressed by a sultry atmosphere. That season, thank God, is brief! The Atlantic and the lochs, on the other hand, are with us at all times, of all mountain settings the most brilliant, matched in none of the twenty foreign lands I have seen for myself, and the true point of distinction.

The varied charms of water make deep and universal appeal. And they are common to all hill country. Whether it be water storming in frolic under a highland bridge, or at peace in brown rock-pools, or an evening tide-rip ablaze with sun-start, or morning hills in a still tarn, the endless forms of contrast are met in the valleys. One need not climb to see them.

But if not more subtly, yet still more greatly moving is the sweep of sea and loch that greets a man treading a western mountain-top. His wider view I hold more noble than the valley scene. It is the setting of Scottish hills amid broad or winding waters that gives rise to a particular form of beauty which I have given up all hope of seeing equalled.

However, it is by our physical presence on the cliffs and ridges, by the exploration of their gullies no less than by wandering the plateau and wooing the waters, that we come fully to know these mountains and win the high reward of intimacy. To him that hath shall be given, always it is thus; through the very steps that a man takes by reason of his love of hills, there is added to him the joys of a sport.

Thus it is of vital consequence to note that though mountaineering abounds in healthy adventure, it implies to a mountaineer much more than sport. If he is a young beginner, as I was, or not much given to thinking, he has not the slightest idea what that 'more' is. He cannot imagine what has happened to him. He feels only a great hunger to know mountains wholly, in their every aspect; he is urged from within by some overpowering need, which in its earliest stages, when he is walking the hills for the first time, can make him truly sick with the mountain fever. For mountains can be at first all life to him. He is driven to explore every part of them, in their every mood, and in doing that he schools himself in the technique of climbing: which is undoubtedly a sport. Moreover, that sport is packed with fun, excitement, skill, and the sternest kinds of test, the most soothing rest of body and contentment of mind. Who will blame a fallible man if he lose sight of the further goal, or falsely identify it with the sport? He may even be so led astray as to contract a disease, whose symptoms are a man's 'peak-bagging' with an eye to records, or his making new routes with an eye to his reputation. The instinct to explore is here perverted.

Of what real benefit is the original, overmastering desire? To what good end is it directed? By what way do we get there?

It is no adequate answer to say that we get there by mountaineering. If a traveller should ask us the way to Cape Wrath, he is little wiser if we reply: 'By travelling.' Yet, however much like a traveller to the unknown, a mountaineer in his early days is given, at least once, a sure indication of the way. For his journey's end is like a magnetic pole to which instinct is a sensitive compass needle.

That first blind instinct to know mountains wholly is, I think, both good and true. But the most obvious implication is most apt to be missed: that a man has need of a catholic taste if he would arrive at his end. Here analogy breaks down. For the ways are not one but many, and I hope clearly to show that all should be followed. On moor and plateau and upon summer rocks the ways are widely known. Therefore, as a first step, I wish to shed more light on the snow and ice way on the cliffs —it is grievous that the best mountaineering in Scotland should be greatly neglected. I shall be practical. Thereafter we may arrive as it were upon a promontory, from which we may see the ways and the end and find our questions answered.

I cannot claim to know mountains better at one season than another. However, I have not disguised the truth that I prefer winter to summer mountaineering; for it is in winter that the Scottish hills excel. No one who has seen the skyward thrust of a snow peak, girdled by its early morning cloud wisp and flushed with the low sun, will dispute with me. Follow a long ridge of encrusted rock to its sunset tower, tread the summit at moon-rise; and you will agree that without that intense experience your life would have been a poorer thing. Such an ascent calls for a technical skill and knowledge more considerable than that demanded by summer rock-work.

To the art of rock-climbing there is added, firstly, the judgment and treatment of snow and ice. As a general rule Scottish snow is surprisingly coherent and not much given to avalanche —one may often ascend soft snow massed upon the crags at angles that would be dangerous in the Alps. One's greatest difficulty is then persuading the snow to support the foot; there is rarely danger of the mass sliding. When the danger is present an experienced mountaineer is protected by an instinctive feeling for the state of the mountain, but that is of no comfort to the beginner. What every one must avoid like the plague is very wet snow or very dry powder lying in bulk upon ice or slabs. I know of one man who has lively recollection of climbing the Castle buttress of Nevis and finding the upper slabs heavily covered with powder bearing a wind-slab crust. How innocently silken, how inviting it appeared to the unsuspicious eye! He threw a boulder on to the middle surface. For three seconds there was silence. Then he heard the ugliest sound that a mountaineer can hear, a noise like the cutting of cardboard with heavy scissors—and a crack opened across the snow sheet. But crack or no crack, one retires.

A more usual danger is the collapse in spring thaw of waterlogged cornices, whose bombardment, with stones intermingled, once routed me from Coire Ardair in April. I was attempting a first ascent of the Centre Post with Dunn and MacAlpine. The day was warm, yet the snow of the gully seemed firm enough. But whatever its appearance of safety we *felt* the mountain to be thoroughly dangerous; every cliff has an atmosphere of its own, and that of Coire Ardair had this day passed out of sympathy with us. Such was our unease that after climbing the first hundred feet without difficulty we unanimously agreed to withdraw. We were later walking down the corrie when the cliffs seemed to tumble like a pack of cards. We had to take to our heels and fly for our lives.

The cornice menace especially applies to Nevis, whose summit lies close to the level of perpetual snow, and where cornices may attain a thickness of forty feet. But they are infrequently higher than ten feet at the gully exits. The conditions under which they collapse are unmistakable. The mountain drips. And under such conditions I once saw two Welshmen dance upon the cornice of Tower gully in June. The mist was dense, and they were inclined to resent my remonstrances, until they discovered that the drop below was not ten feet but upward of two thousand. The fall of cornices is not necessarily delayed till spring. As a general rule they are safe while frost prevails, but are always liable to collapse in whole or part after heavy snowfalls. They become overweighted, have not time to consolidate and freeze, and down they come. Several accidents have been caused by climbers going to the gullies too promptly after blizzard.

In theory, it is a straightforward matter to pass judgment on doubtful ice. Either it is too thin or too brittle or it is not. In practice, there is sometimes acute difficulty in deciding whether the danger signal has appeared. In a groove below the crest of Crowberry ridge, for example, I suffered a minute's agony of doubt at the base of a thirty-foot wall of brittle ice. Ten feet underneath, Mackenzie belayed me with an ice-pick driven into a four-inch tongue of snow-ice, and close behind him the groove bent over the chasm of Crowberry gully. I resolved the doubt, and went up with a safety margin as fine as one can justifiably accept. This situation is unusual, but that problem is not; each man must judge for himself, and the moment he feels unable to give a verdict he is defeated. He must acknowledge defeat and go down.

In these several incidents we may find a simple guide to action after judgment. Prudence is not a goddess, to be worshipped—least of all in youth: or sea and air would yet be unnavigated, no man ever have shared his last crust, or climbed a mountain. But there are times when we must pay her tribute, when to do otherwise is stupidity. It is the greater honour to a mountaineer if he retire rather than overreach his skill or his day's form, or presume upon the forbearance of a mountain in bad order.

In the treatment of high-angle ice, technique varies according to the quality of the ice; upon that I touched lightly in describing S C gully. Elaboration of the problem can serve no purpose; one can learn to cope with iced rock in only one school. The delight of such climbing springs both from exercise of muscular skill and deliberate engineering of the route, a craft that gives satisfaction to mind and body alike, that strengthens mental energy and self-reliance—craft exercised both in detail on gully pitches and in greater scale over the breadth of a snow-bound ridge or buttress. Upon these, the best winter route may follow a line of least resistance very different from the best summer route. Errors in the art of route selection have led not a few parties into benightment or near escape therefrom, even upon climbs well known in summer. I have described such an error and escape of my own on the North buttress of Buachaille, which as winter rocks go is not hard, and the moral of which is that in winter a mountaineer has much greater need of an alert intelligence, especially where no difficulty is anticipated.

There is further added to summer rock-work the winter merit that no route is the same twice. The accumulation and condition of snow and ice vary enormously from month to month. The most remarkable change I have seen was the transformation of Garrick's shelf between my first visit, when the rocks were swamped in soft snow, and my second three months later, after blizzard, thaws, and frosts, when the shelf was a mass of clear ice five hundred and fifty feet long. Likewise, on our second visit to the Deep-cut chimney of Stob Coire nam Beith, we encountered an ice ribbon of two hundred feet. The change from snow had occurred within three weeks. Conversely, a short severe gully may by heavy snowfalls become in a few days an easy and straightforward snow slope. I have seen such a fate overtake Gardyloo gully, normally a very hard climb. In short, one can state no rule about the effect of snow and ice on rock. Impossible summer rocks may become climbable; moderate rock unclimbable: a week later the reverse may hold good.

Each winter ascent thus affords to the mountaineer a pleasure fully equal to the rare ascent of a new route in summer. He sets out in the morning to explore unknown difficulties, amidst scenery more splendid than in summertime, and ever new; he is awakened by suspense quickly to see and long to remember a score of details, hitherto unregarded, of beauty near and afar; his is the joy of a hard-fought climb, and when doubt of the issue is at last removed, the elation of winning the only true victory—one that cannot be taken for granted.

Suspense lends keen interest to the shortest route, but is there naturally of short duration, and if need be retirement is simple. On the long gullies and ridges, say between six hundred and two thousand feet, in which Scotland abounds, doubt of the issue raises serious consideration of time. Let a mountaineer have as much experience as you please; he will be able to form a general estimate of snow and ice conditions, but he cannot foresee their detail at the various points of a long route. He cannot say that a fifty-foot groove, a thousand feet above, is lined with frozen snow and not brittle ice, that the slabs beyond it are coated in snow-ice and not thin glaze. Therefore, upon what he finds but could not foresee may in extreme case depend success or defeat, or whether his climb take five hours or fifteen. And on winter days there are only eight to twelve hours of daylight.

Consequently, where a man frequents long hard routes he is sooner or later bound to complete one or two of them in darkness. In that event he has nothing to fear; should he be unfortunate enough to lack moonlight he has nevertheless a competent party, electric torches, and spare batteries. Without these no winter ascent of rock should be ventured.

By means of torches a strong party can climb by night well-nigh anywhere—provided the line of the route be known. That applies less to summer rock than to snow and ice, upon which torchlight is adequate as sunlight. The snow shines brightly, every detail of an ice-pitch stands clear, and one can no more make a mistake than in broad day. Climbing in a gully by this method is particularly simple, elsewhere it is slower. Yet these facts are not widely appreciated. It is to be borne in mind that a torch is of no avail for route selection on the indefinite rock of a difficult buttress. The route may indeed be very hard, but must be well known or clearly defined.

Only twice have I been obliged to complete climbs by torch-light. The moon has favoured me. I have more frequently begun climbs by torchlight, when sun or moon were laggard in rising. Need of a torch at the day's end is often avoidable by an early start; one hour lost in the morning, which never seems important at the time, can most readily lead to the loss of several hours in darkness. But not all the precepts of the Stoics have ever got a man out of bed sooner than his nature inclined him. One makes pious resolutions. Always one will improve next time. But in fact, only the certainty of a good climb does the trick.

These latter sentences do not apply to the Alps, where snow conditions greatly worsen in the afternoon.

If a younger climber with hopes set on winter ascents should read some of the routes I have described, he may be visited by qualms on the score of danger. My very last wish is to discourage him. From what I know of his breed there is little risk. I can assure him that some of the climbs were hand-picked for description because the prevailing conditions were unusually difficult; that there is no need to go straight to the hardest routes and every need to start on the easier. The ability to cope with advanced winter climbing derives simply from training and practice. Undoubtedly it has sometimes every appearance of danger, which I regard as an unmixed blessing, for danger is a good teacher, and as Hazlitt says, 'makes apt scholars.' It is that which at first we cannot do which in the end is done to perfection. We improve by constant practice.

In Scotland there are easy snow gullies by the hundred. When, and not until, a climber can conduct himself safely both on summer rock and on straightforward snow like that of the centre gully of Beinn Laoigh, or many of the Nevis gullies, he can hardly do better than visit such snow-covered rocks as the Curved ridge and the North buttress of Buachaille, the crags of Stob Coire nam Beith and the Aonach Eagach ridge. In almost any high corrie he will find a well-iced crag or boulder, upon which he can first practise, as I did, cutting holds in ice.

He will find the work fascinating and not so hard as he thought; he will speedily learn how to space his holds, and that he must never impatiently outstrip his handhold, leaving himself on foothold only—the frequent and fatal error of the novice. Then let him go with a good party to the upper couloir of Stob Ghabhar in the Blackmount. He will, between January and April, find an ice-pitch there, which may vary in size from ten to thirty feet, and can watch his leader cut ice for anything from twenty minutes to one and a half hours. It is a very good gully, but too short to rank as a first-class winter ascent. On no account must he neglect practice in the arts of roping down and climbing down. With such experience behind him he could well be led up the big climbs by a strong party.

Where the members of a climbing team have followed such a course of training, it is difficult to see that any element of danger peculiar to winter climbing need arise. Danger is a relative conception—relative to the strength of the party, to its skill and judgment. Crowberry ridge, for example, is never dangerous in winter. But a weak or careless party might commit suicide by going to it when a strong one would be safe as though strolling in a public park, and that whether it meet success or defeat. As with snow and ice, so with the grass and loose stones of summer rocks; in themselves they cannot be considered dangerous: one may say only that one party has the skill to deal with them, and that another has not.

The real or objective dangers on home mountains are rare. A falling stone may come at any man—Nevis is again the prime culprit. No judgment can forecast the date of collapse of a Cuillin overhang. It has been there for fifty thousand years, perhaps, and who shall say it will fall to-day at two-fifteen p.m.? Yet, one collapsed within a minute of my passing over it. The fall of a cornice is sometimes unexpected, but the cornice that sags over a gully in thaw is not truly an objective danger, inasmuch as it is avoidable by any one with eyes in his head.

Therefore, if any climb be free from falling stones and snow, to describe it as 'dangerous' is to make an unmeaning noise. One may say that a named route would be dangerous for a named party, but that is a very different thing. My conclusion is that for a well-trained climber acting within his powers, which is simply common sense, there is little danger in Scottish mountaineering.

Everywhere, however, there is the appearance of danger. He is indeed an unimaginative man who, upon the last pitch of Crowberry gully, can look a thousand feet down the snow-caked walls and not think what would happen if he let go. His finger, thereupon, tightens on its ice-notch, for there is no doubt that he loves life. Notwithstanding, he has come to one place where vigorous elasticity of nerve and precision of movement are required to preserve life. It is plain that if he love life he still more loves living—otherwise he would keep to a steam-heated room, eat to diet, and at measured intervals perform physical jerks to forestall the atrophy of his precious limbs. The joy of life will never be measured in terms of comfort and security, nor will the debased currency of the latter buy a true friend. Let us admit, therefore, that together with many another important element, seeming danger ensures that on mountains, more than elsewhere, life may be lived at the full.

Of all apparent dangers, there are none more boisterous and bracing than swift weather changes. The Scottish mountains afford a man ample opportunities of testing his body to the limits of endurance. In the Cairngorms high cloud can change in an hour to low cloud and a snow-laden hurricane. In Glencoe, Lochaber, Skye, and Wester Ross, I have seen changes little less violent occur in less than half the time. They often come at sunset, when mountaineers are nearing the top of a long route. If a party should then be beaten by glazed slabs, a rare misfortune so high, then each man will speedily discover of what stuff he and his comrades are made. If he is blessed with such companions as I have had, he is not likely to be disappointed.

When a leader turns down from the last impossible rocks, and hears the rising wind buffet on white-veiled cliffs, fast fading into night, and on looking down, watches his party again and again enveloped in clouds of drift-snow, torn from storm-swept ridges, he may feel, as I have, an instant's suspicion that the prospect is somewhat grim for hope. An instant later, his rope reminds him that he is tied to men of high heart, that whatever the outcome, they, at least, will not falter. And in that instant the battle is won. Everything that is best in a man is called forth by faith in his companions, no less than by storm. For a fit youth is a fighter and a challenge stirs him. He will shortly exult in the struggle. And the course of later years will prove that rope 'the surest bond life yields of friendship.'

On the other hand, many a Scottish climb will turn out milder than a climber expected and disappoint him with an anti-climax. Many a normally hard route may become astonishingly easy, or fall quickly. Tower ridge has gone in sixteen hours and four and a half hours within the space of the same month. Still more instructive are my two winter climbs on Observatory ridge. In 1937 we were occupied there for fourteen hours: the rock was smothered in powder-snow. One year later we went up in six hours; the rock was encrusted with frozen snow. Now, on that second visit the ridge was of great difficulty. I shall ever remember a groove at three thousand five hundred feet that Mackenzie, the undauntable, was inclined to think not justifiable and which wrung startled exclamations even from Bell. We moved quickly and saved eight hours' time by sole reason of the snow's firmness—especially after entering Zero gully. Where previously we had had to excavate a foot of powder and for seven hours hew a clear ice-bed, we now met hardest snow. By changing the lead as each man tired, we in turn cut fast and hard from the shoulder—one and a half hours to the plateau.

It is worthy of record that in the opinion of Bell, who has more than thrice my experience, that climb ranked with the best of his life. On the several occasions I have tried to write of it, despair at its perfect beauty has consigned my effort to the waste-paper-basket. The splendid opportunities provided by the Scottish rocks for winter mountaineering are known and used by a mere handful of Scottish climbers. Once more we are brought to the need of a catholic taste. Indeed, I can hardly pretend to myself that a man is a true mountaineer unless he knows his mountains winter and summer, on cliff and summit ridge, by day and night, in fair weather and foul. For until then he understands them incompletely; he is still in his novitiate, however expert a specialist.

Of these eight very different aspects and their permutations, it is in winter and by night that the mountains are most studiously avoided, despite that when the peaks are snow-capped and the moon full, visibility of twenty to twenty-five miles is by no means exceptional. Just think what that means. Choose, then, a clear and crackling winter's night; traverse the Aonach Eagach ridge in Glencoe, and you will find there an experience for which you would sacrifice most of your daylight climbs. Better still, if you are alone, as you should be sometimes, go up to the main ridge of the Mamores and walk the shining snow waves that link Stob Ban to the spire of Binnein Mor; only your boot-nails sound on the frozen snow-crust, so that when you stop to listen—and listen—you can hear an utter silence that no one has ever heard in company . . . you will know more of the world's song than may be set forth in books.

The snow specialist, the cragsman, and the hill-walker have chosen to devote themselves to one branch of mountaineering. But the beginner should avoid the trap into which they have fallen; for theirs is not the freedom of the hills, which can be earned only by a true mountaineer. To earn the freedom of mountains one must be able to climb on both rock and snow. Those who hold Bach to be the greatest composer do not for that reason refuse to hear Beethoven. Likewise, the hill-walker should not deny himself the pleasure of rock-climbing, nor the cragsman of snow-climbing. Should they do so, one of the best parts of the mountain world must remain to them unknown.

Rock-climbing is no esoteric sport, and skill is arrived at by simple practice. Difficulty is relative to skill. Thus, if he be accustomed both to difficult rock and the rhythm of long ridges, a climber will scramble on moderate rock with little output of either nervous or physical energy—then, indeed, he may claim the freedom of summer mountains: then there is open to him, by way of example, the greatest day in Scottish mountaineering, the traverse of the Cuillin main ridge. The most enchanting views of corrie and peak, loch and sky, sea and islands, change throughout that epic day with a rapidity unequalled on other ranges, so that again and again one catches beauty unawares. This infinite variety is made possible by the compactness of the twisting ridge, whose sharp edge, tossing in spires or dropping into clefts, acts as a natural curtain, constantly rising and falling to hide and reveal dramatic scenes on either hand; and to which it provides in itself a most noble foreground.

That day cannot be enjoyed by one not a rock-climber in hard training. For such to attempt the ridge is not entirely vain. But he will be robbed by bodily distress of mental reward. His achievement will be a feat. His lost opportunities, countless.

I seem to remember hearing, more than once, that mountaineering serves no useful purpose—and remember, too, rejoicing thereat. It does not increase our bank balances. On the mountains we know ourselves and others for what we are; and, as Scott said of the Antarctic: 'Here the outward show is nothing, it is the inward purpose that counts. So the "gods" dwindle and the humble supplant them. Pretence is useless.' On mountains a man is brought face to face with his own strength and weaknesses, and these latter he may learn, if he wish, to correct; indeed he has little choice; he is compelled to internal honesty and self-discipline. His body is trained in subordination to the will; for there is no chisel more quick to shape character than storm, hunger, and hard work outfaced. In mountaineering, as in no other sport, his adventures are of the mind as much as of the body. The two go hand in hand. To the music of tinkling ice-chips and scrape of clinkers, and the silence of the summits, together they drive free and are tautened—are relaxed—find peace after toil. And when his mind is toughened he will come clearly to see that defeat is not failure: from the first he reaps wisdom, but the second he does not acknowledge.

Life is seen detachedly and in proper perspective from the mountain-tops. Whoever climbs cliffs to a summit cairn will find that the joys and sorrows of his everyday life have been left deep below in the valleys; they have not ventured with him to the foot of his mountain; they have been shed off like a husk; and he, the new man, may survey as from afar his daily round of thoughts, errors, resolves, and behaviour with the inward calm of a critic inspecting a stranger. And it is wonderful what a different complexion is then put upon affairs that he thought of consequence. The true is sifted from the untrue, the real from the unreal. In the quiet of this inner detachment his higher self is awakened; it rises above fatigue and discomfort to enjoy beauty, breaks the fetters that enslave it to bodily desires and environment, rules inwardly. Were a man to achieve little else in his life he would none the less, in achieving this, possess a pearl of great price—an undivided mind and the peace that is true freedom. For though we talk much these days of freedom, rare indeed is the man who bestows it on himself.

Even so, not until the threat of war in 1939 did I realize to the full what a wealth of friendship, care-free adventure and beauty the mountains had granted me on my own way, nor what knowledge of other men. Such discoveries came to me again with a strong sense of gratitude on the battle-fields of the Western Desert, and later, in the prison camps of Italy and Germany. Between the vertical crags of Scotland and the horizontal sands of Africa there might seem to be little relation. Yet the discipline I learned on the former applied with value to the latter. As an infantry officer in the shambles of defeat and the prolonged rearguard actions of June 1942, I found no call upon stamina equal to that demanded by Garrick's shelf in the winter of 1936, nor strain of suspense to match that of Observatory ridge in 1937.

But these latter considerations were not what I had in mind when I spoke of gratitude. In the worst days of war there shone most often before my eyes the clear vision of that evening on Nevis, when the snow plateaux sparkled red at sunset, and of Glencoe, when the frozen towers of Bidean burned in the moon. In the last resort, it is the beauty of the mountain world in the inmost recesses that holds us spellbound, slaves till life ends.

In three years of squalor in overcrowded prison camps, where misery gnawed at men's fortitude, these stored memories heartened me like 'a light for memory to turn to when it wants a beam upon its face'; and youth, somewhat crushed in warfare, revived hope for the future from inexhaustible mountain springs. That through mountains I have been given not only vivid memories but lasting joys and friendships more priceless than accumulations of gold is no idle theory invented in credulous days of comfort and security, but a sure knowledge won in adversity.

To what end may the mountain way lead?

Strictly, I am entitled to answer only for myself, but being an unexceptional man, I imagine that what I have found true should hold good for others. Therefore it has been my endeavour to say by what many roads, at unexpected moments in mountain days, one may win fleeting glimpses of that beauty which all men who have known it have been compelled to call truth. Such, for me, has become the end of mountaineering to which the sport is a means.

Is this an uninspiring or unlikely goal, do you think—is beauty too insubstantial to move a rational man? Let him behold it but once and thenceforward he must ever seek for it—only in it, wherever it be on hill or low country, can be fulfilled his deepest need; for without beauty his spirit can no more live than his body without food. Let him be starved of beauty and at once he declines from real being. The most fleeting glimpse has the power of divine fire to cleanse and to temper; the more lasting, to fill him with this resolve: that henceforth he will take the only way by which he can hope to know its full splendour and to live in its presence. Then must he become practical: *then*, as on hills, he must give up dreams and clear for action. For his hope can be realized.

Mountains here discharge their highest service. A man of balanced intelligence will not make a religion of mountaineering; neither will he fail, by mountains, to be brought face to face with it. Wisdom standeth on the top of high places. From our promontory we look up to the cloud of unknowing that wraps the last height, and from its radiance we know the summit is in sunlight. The way and the goal are before us. To one of exploratory instinct action is irresistible, and he takes to himself the axe of single-mindedness and the compass of his love for beauty. His further ascent is severe, more adventurous than any physical one, dangerous if the route be lost, and the issue sometimes in doubt. In his every upward step is a joy surpassing all that mountains offer. Such a man has understood the schooling of life, and is destined to its fullness.

'I do not say unto you, "Believe this, for it is so," but "Do this." Little by little, as when a man climbs a mountain the earth unfolds beneath him, so for yourselves ye shall see and know, needing no testimony from another, no, not even from ancient scripture. . . . For the Kingdom of Heaven is within you.'

When I looked to the mountains of the future from behind barbed wire, I thought not only of ends but of the ways of striving, for the one adds lustre to the other; not only of solemn hours but of the familiar joys of mountaineering, for in these too there is beauty: dawdling under a blue sky up the crest of a sun-warmed ridge; the irrepressible gaiety of rope-mates, forcing wet slabs in mist and windy rain; stimulating doubts upon the blue ice-bulge in an unclimbed gully; the plunge into a shining tarn; the crackling fire in an inn after blizzard—the beauty of living and of life itself. Of all such days I thought, and before I knew what I was about, of these I found myself writing. In truth, I wrote with no dark design of enlightening others, but because I could not help myself. Bloodshed was forgotten awhile; once again I revelled in wholesome days, when the very air I breathed, in the company of Dunn, Mackenzie, and MacAlpine, of Bell and Donaldson, was that of rollicking adventure; when our mountaineering dreams were turbulent and our hearts high.

On a crisp winter's morning, the advance across Rannoch moor with trusted friends, to attack the snow-bound cliffs of Buachaille Etive Mor, until the axe-shaft, yellow in the sunshine, flashes to the frozen snow below some high gully—and many hours later the steel pick glints in moonlight as a weary arm hews the black ice, not so *very* far from the top; or four thousand feet up, on the north precipice of Nevis, fighting in a gale at dusk to cross the icy gash of Tower gap: there lies the true joy of battle, in exhilarating contest with the elements, upon mountains that may be won, yet never conquered; shared by companions who may be defeated, yet whose spirit I have never seen shaken:

> They have the secret of the rocks,
> And the oldest kind of song.

INDEX

UNDISCOVERED SCOTLAND

UNDISCOVERED SCOTLAND

Climbs on rock, snow, and ice

BY

W. H. MURRAY

CONTENTS

PHOTOGRAPHS

between pages 86 and 87

MAPS AND DIAGRAMS

1 *The Undiscovered Country*

THE EXPLORATORY URGE moves every man who loves hills. The quest of the mountaineer is knowledge. He is drawing close to one truth about mountains when at last he becomes aware that he never *will* know them fully—not in all their aspects—nor ever fully know his craft. Like the true philosopher, the true mountaineer can look forward with rejoicing to an eternity of endeavour: to realization without end. I have climbed for fifteen years and have hopes of another forty, but I know that my position at the close of my span will be the same as it is now, and the same as it was on that happy day when I first set foot on a hill—the Scottish highlands will spread out before me, an unknown land.

The yearning to explore hills was born in myself in 1934, when I, a confirmed pavement-dweller, overheard a mountaineer describe a week-end visit to An Teallach in Ross-shire. He spoke of a long thin ridge, three thousand feet up, with towers and pinnacles and tall cliffs on either flank, which fell to deep corries. And from these corries clouds would boil up like steam from a cauldron, and from time to time shafts would open through them to reveal vistas of low valleys and seas and distant islands.

That was all he said, but the effect on myself was profound, because for the first time in my life my exploratory instincts began to stir. Here was a strange new world of which I had never even dreamed, waiting for exploration. And unlike so many other dreams, this was one that could be realized in action. At the first opportunity, then, I went to one of the few mountains I knew by name—the Cobbler at Arrochar. It was a fine April day, with plenty of snow on the tops. When I stood by the road at Arrochar and looked up at my first mountain, the summit seemed alarmingly craggy and blinding white against blue sky. How I should ever get up I could not imagine. I picked out a route by the line of a burn, which vanished towards a huge corrie under the summit rocks. And what then? I felt a nervous hesitation about my fate in these upper regions. Had I been entering the sanctuary of Nanda Devi I could have felt no more of the sheer thrill of adventure than I did when I stepped off that road on to the bare hill-side.

Later in the day, when I entered the Cobbler corrie, I recognized that I *had* entered what was, for me, true sanctuary—a world of rock and snow and glossy ice, shining in the spring sun and, for the moment at least, laughing in the glint and gleam of the world's joy. I too laughed in my sudden awareness of freedom. Had I thought at all I should have said: 'Here is a field of free action in which nothing is organized, or made safe or easy or uniform by regulation; a kingdom where no laws run and no useful ends fetter the heart.' I did not have to think that out in full. I knew it instantaneously, in one all-comprehending glance.

And, of course, this intoxicated me. For it was a great day in my life. And at once I proceeded to do all those wicked things so rightly denounced by grey-bearded gentlemen sitting at office desks in remote cities. I climbed steep snow-slopes by myself. Without an ice-axe or nailed boots, without map, compass, or warm and windproof clothing, and, what is worse, without a companion, I kicked steps up hard snow, going quite fast and gaily, until near the top I stopped and looked down. The corrie floor was now far below me, and black boulders projected out of the snow. If I slid off nothing would stop me until I hit something. I went on with exaggerated caution until I breasted the ridge between the centre and south peaks.

At that first success a wave of elation carried me up high walls of sun-washed rock to the south peak. That rock had beauty in it. Always before I had thought of rock as a dull mass. But *this* rock was the living rock, pale grey and clean as the air itself, with streaks of shiny mica and white crystals of quartzite. It was joy to handle such rock and to feel the coarse grain under the fingers.

Near the top the strangeness of the new environment overawed me a little—nothing but bare rock and boundless space, and a bright cloud sailing. Nothing here but myself and the elements—and a knowledge of my utter surrender to and trust in God's providence, and gladness in that knowledge.

On the flat rocks on top I sat down, and for an hour digested all that had happened to me. In being there at all I had, of course, sinned greatly against all the canons of mountaineering. But I did not know that. This was my Garden of Eden stage of purest innocence. It was not till later, when I plucked my apple in search of knowledge, that I read in text-books 'Man must not go alone on mountains'—not when he is a bootless novice. Meantime I looked out upon the mountains circling me in a white-topped throng, and receding to horizons that rippled against the sky like a wash of foam. Not one of these hills did I know by name, and every one was probably as worth exploring as the Cobbler. The shortness of life was brought home to me with a sudden pang. However, what I lacked in time might in part be offset by unflagging activity.

From that day I became a mountaineer.

Upon returning home and consulting books I learned that there are five hundred and forty-three mountain-tops in Scotland above three thousand feet. They cannot all be climbed in one's first year. This thought did make me feel frustrated. I once received a book after waiting long and eagerly for its publication. Like a wolf coming down starving from the mountains I gulped the courses in any order, reading the end first, snatching bits in the middle, running here and there through the pages in uncontrolled excitement. I wanted to know it all immediately. In the end I was sufficiently exhausted to sit back and read whole chapters at a time. That was exactly how I felt about mountains.

In my first year I sped all over Scotland—going alone because I knew no one else who climbed—snatching mountains here, there, and everywhere. As it happened I could not have made a better approach. The best and natural way of dealing with mountains is the way I luckily followed: before starting any rock-climbing I spent a summer and winter on hill-walking only. Rock-climbing, as a means of penetrating the inmost recesses and as sport, should not come until later. Thus I made a wide reconnaissance by climbing several peaks in each of the main mountain districts. This preliminary survey gave me a good idea of their differences in character, which are surprisingly wide, and showed what each had to offer.

When I went from the rolling plateaux and snow-domes of the Cairngorms, mounted among broad forests and straths, to the sharp spiky ridges of Wester Ross, set between winding sea-lochs, I had the sensation peculiar to entering a foreign country; a sense not to be accounted for by any material changes in scenery, but one that is none the less shared by all men. I can travel from Inverness to Sussex and feel only that I have moved from one part of Britain to another. But Wester Ross is another (and better) land. Again, when I came from the Cuillin pinnacles and the stark isles of the west to the heathery swell of the southern highlands I returned from vertical desert to grassland, although still hungering like a camel after its dear desert.

Between such different areas Glencoe and Lochaber held a fair balance. They had everything: peak, plateau, precipice, the thinnest of ridges, and green valley, all set between the widest of wild moors and a narrow sea-loch—they were Baghdad and Samarkand, at once home and goal of the pilgrim.

Then I joined a mountaineering club. For the course of that first year's wanderings showed plainly that no man can have the freedom of mountains unless he can climb on rock and snow. The mountains are under snow for several months of the year. Indeed, they excel in winter, offering a sport and beauty quite different from those of summer, a sport harder and tougher, and a more simple and pure beauty. The plateaux and the summit ridges, the great cliffs and the snow-slopes, these are four facets of the Scottish mountains none of which can be avoided, except the cliffs, and these only if a man is content to walk on mainland tops.

In the Cuillin of Skye the rocks are not a facet, they *are* the mountains. Cliffs must not be thought of as blank cliffs. They are cathedral cities with many a spire, tower, turret, pinnacle, and bastion, amongst which a man may wander at will, and explore and adventure, upon which he may test qualities of character and skill, and by aid of which conquer nothing except himself.

In succeeding years the wider my experience grew the more clearly did I see that however much I might explore this unknown country called the Scottish highlands, I should never plumb the Unknown. To know mountains we must know them at the four seasons, on the four facets, at the four quarters of the day. The permutations are infinite. For the variations in snow and ice and weather conditions are inexhaustible. No winter climb, say on the north face of Nevis, is ever the same twice running. Its North-east Buttress, for example, is on each visit like a first ascent. If we go to the Comb of Arran in autumn frost, on a day of still, crisp air when distant moors flame red through a sparkle of hoar, we shall not recognize it as the mountain we knew when clouds were scudding among the crags and the hail drove level. I have been a hundred times to the top of Buachaille Etive Mor in Glencoe. In unwise and sentimental moments I am apt to think of it as an old friend. But I know full well that the next time I go there the Buachaille will surprise me for the hundred and first time—my climb will be unlike any that I 've had before.

Treasures of reality yet unknown await discovery among inaccessible peaks at the ends of the earth, still more on the old and familiar hills at our very doorstep, most of all within each mountaineer. The truth is that in getting to know mountains he gets to know himself. That is why men truly live when they climb.

That heightened quality of life on mountains naturally enough came foremost to my mind in war. In 1942 I made an after-dinner speech in the middle of the Libyan Desert. The toast of 'Mountains' had been put to me by a young German with whom

I shared the meal. In my reply I managed to say all that I have to say about mountains in three sentences. But first of all let me explain how the situation arose.

Just one hour before I had been sitting in the bottom of a slit-trench. My battalion had been whittled down to fifty men, and we were waiting, with the rest of our brigade, for an attack at dusk by the 15th Panzer Division. My battalion commander, with the perfect frankness that such gentlemen have, had said to me: 'Murray, by to-night you 'll be either dead meat or a prisoner.' Thus I sat in the bottom of my slit-trench and went through my pockets with the purpose of destroying anything that might be of use to an enemy. I smashed a prismatic compass, tore up an identity card and my notes on battalion orders. Then I came upon an address book. I flicked over the pages and read the names. And suddenly I saw that every name in that book was the name of a mountaineer. Until then I had never realized how great a part mountains had played in my life. Most of the names belonged to men who are very much alive and active to-day. While I read over them I also realized, again for the first time, how much I had learned from these men, and been given by them, and how little I had been able to give in return. The same had to be said of mountains. And while I sat in the trench I had a clear perception of the two ways of mountaineering that mean most to me.

The first is the exploratory way, the way of adventure and battle with the elements. I could see storm winds and drift sweeping across the plateau; long hours of axe-work on ice, among sunless cliffs; the day-long suspense on rocks that have never before been scratched by nails. These show the harsh aspects of reality, of which a man should know—of which he *must* know if he 'd know mountains and know himself. Rock, snow, and ice sometimes claim from a man all that he has to give. Sometimes the strain on body and nerve may be high, discomforts sharp. But the mountaineer gets all the joy of his craft; his mastery of it is, in reality, the mastery of himself. It is the foretaste of freedom.

I made no effort to think in that trench. Ideas came and went of their own accord in a matter of seconds. I saw the other aspect of mountaineering—for the sake of mountains and not for sport. I could see a great peak among fast-moving cloud, and the icy glint where its snows caught the morning sun. There were deep corries and tall crags. All of these were charged with a beauty that did not belong to *them*, but poured through them as light pours through the glass of a ruby and blue window, or as grace through a sacrament. These show an ideal aspect of reality, of which a man should know, of which he *must* know if he would arrive at any truth at all about mountains, or about men.

At dusk the German tanks came in. When the shambles had ended a German tank commander took charge of me. It was bright moonlight. He waved a machine pistol at me and asked, in good English, if I didn't feel cold. Now the desert at night is often exceedingly cold, and without thinking I said: 'It 's as cold as a mountain-top.' And my German said: 'Good God! do you climb?'

He was a mountaineer. We exchanged brief notes about mountains we knew and liked in Scotland and the Alps. After that there was no end to what he would do for me. He gave me his overcoat, and asked when my last meal had been. I said: 'Thirty-six hours ago.' So he took me over to his tank and produced food. We shared a quick meal of British bully and biscuits and German chocolate. After that he fetched out a bottle of British beer and knocked off the top.

'Here 's to mountains,' he said, 'and to mountaineers—to all of them everywhere.' He took a pull at the bottle and passed it to me. I drank too. I felt moved to reply.

I said: 'There are three good things you get out of mountains. You meet men and you meet battle and beauty. But the men are true, and the battle 's the only kind that 's *worth* fighting, and the beauty is Life.'

I smashed the bottle on the German tank.

2 *The First Day on Buachaille*

THREE YEARS in central European prison camps. Release, April 1945.

During the fine weather of May I was unable to climb. At first if I walked for more than ten minutes I felt faint, and so felt no desire of mountains. My love of them was platonic, requiring of the body no act of outer expression. Four weeks later a first instalment of accumulating energy began to clamour for employment. My last climb in 1941 had been the Buachaille Etive Mor, and my first now could be none other. That is, if I could get up, which was exceedingly doubtful. My thoughts flew at once to Mackenzie. He was back in Glasgow. If any man could get me up Buachaille he could. So to Glasgow I went on 2nd June 1945.

After six years of war I could see no change at all in the Mackenzie—still lean and upright, hawk-eyed and brusque. He too was keen to get back to Glencoe. He had spent the last year or two in the School of Mountain Warfare, but not once had he enjoyed a good rock-climb. I told him gently that he could not get one now if he went with *me*. We must go up by the easiest possible route, go very slow, and not seriously expect to get to the top.

We left Glasgow in my old pre-war Morris eight very early in the morning. And a wellnigh perfect morning it was. As the sun spread over Rannoch the genuine golden air of the good old days spread over the miles of moor (I had begun to wonder if my memories of such days were simple feats of imagination), and the liveliness of all spring mornings again entered into me. I felt now as Mackenzie always used to feel when the first snow of October came on the hills—days when MacAlpine drove us north from Glasgow, usually under rain clouds that boded ill for the week-end, but which had no damping effect on a Mackenzie wild with enthusiasm. His first sight of the snow-capped hills in Glencoe would conjure forth song and piercing whistles. 'Bound along, Archie!—or the snow will be away before we get there!' and similar exhortations inspired the driver.

So I ventured to suggest to Mackenzie that we must aim after all at getting to the summit. No half measures would do on a day like this. I would get to the top or drop dead trying. We came round the famous bend from the Blackmount—and there was Buachaille.

The day was again 8th September 1935, when the final entry in my diary reads: 'I think that for me the most vivid experience was my first view of Buachaille Etive Mor. In the clear morning air every detail of the enormous, pointed cliffs stood out sharp. But the most striking moment was turning a corner of the road and seeing the great shape, black and intimidating, suddenly spring up in the moor. To me it was just unclimbable. I had never seen a hill like it before and my breath was taken away from me.'

Days of innocence! Maybe. But that was precisely how I felt now. As always before, we went straight to Coupall Bridge in Glen Etive, put on our boots, and started. It is the great advantage of this starting-point, as against that from Altnafeadh in Glencoe, that the long approach over the moor is lightened by the shapeliness of the peak, inspiring one from the front, drawing one on and up. Every crag and each long ridge points to the summit-cone. It is a symbolism not lost on the climber. What delight to the eye that was! To see again all the detail of the rocks, every crag of which I knew so well. The delight of recognition—a recognition of form, beauty, character, the lines of weakness and strength, every wrinkle, pit, and scar, on cliffs dove-grey and terra-cotta. From a distance only is the Buachaille black.

An avoidance of the cliffs, such as we contemplated, now seemed to me miserably inappropriate. Surely we might manage to get up an easy rock-climb? A very easy one—say Curved Ridge, if we roped? I made the suggestion somewhat timorously, for I feared to burden Mackenzie with a hundred and forty pounds of human baggage. He agreed and grinned. We changed direction slightly. The moor was drier underfoot than I ever remembered it—our very boots took on an unaccustomed bloom to the brush of old heather, and the *swish*, *swish* of the boots was a song of old, an heroic poetry and new live drama all rolled into one after the dead mud of the prison compounds. I reminded myself from time to time that I was free to go in any direction I wanted. I could turn right round and go right home. Glorious thought! So on I went, breathing in great draughts of moorland air, a free man with a free wind blowing on his right cheek, and sun smiting his left, the scent of the year's new thyme at his nostril, and the swish of dry heather round his boots. Rock in front. I stopped. 'Bill,' I said, 'maybe we could manage Central Buttress?'

'Ha! *now* you 're talking!' exclaimed Mackenzie. 'We could manage it if we kept to a V-diff.' We changed direction.

We scrambled upwards over heathery outcrops to the base of Central Buttress, and moved rightward to the north face. We roped. I hesitated for a moment over the bow-line knot, but tied it first time. I was greatly relieved. It would have embarrassed the Mackenzie to have had to tie it for me. He started up the first pitch and ran out about sixty feet. Then he turned and was ready for me. Now was the test. I looked at the rock, light-grey, crystalline, very rough—and so very steep. I stood back and chose my holds. What would happen? Was the old skill lost?—rock-climbing a thing of the past? I gave myself, as it were, a prod, and climbed.

At the very instant my hands and feet came on the rock six years rolled away in a flash. The rock was not strange, but familiar. At each move I was taking the right holds at the right time—but no, I did not 'take' the holds—of their own accord they *came* to me. Hand, foot, and eye—nerve and muscle—they were co-ordinating, and my climbing was effortless. I reached the top feeling trust in rock and, what in the circumstances was far more wonderful, trust in myself. And also, I should add, gratitude for the Mackenzie, from whom ten years ago I had learned much of my rock-snow-ice climbing.

The lower part of the north face goes up by a series of rough walls to the Heather Ledge, which divides the buttress about three hundred feet up. The last wall on this lower part is split near its top by a short crack at a high angle. The crack was my next important test—the test for exposure. For although the holds are good the body is forced out of balance over a long drop. When I came to make the move it certainly scared me, but the point was that I could control myself. I got up. The true testing question, of course, for progress in rock-, snow-, or ice-craft is not 'Did you get up?' but rather 'Did you *enjoy* getting up?'—if not always just as the moves are made, then very shortly afterwards. I was able to answer 'Yes' to my test, with the appropriate qualification. This meant that we could safely deal with the steeper and more difficult upper buttress.

We had a choice of four routes and I left the decision to Mackenzie. He chose his own Slanting Ledge route, which starts right in the middle of the buttress. This would certainly be less exacting than a continuation by the north face climb, the difficulties being not less in standard or exposure, but shorter in length.

On Heather Ledge we lay back and rested a while. It is the great merit of Central Buttress that it faces south-east—the sunniest cliff in Glencoe and Glen Etive. And Heather Ledge is a balcony, wide of prospect and fit for philosopher kings, where the governments of the earth are measured against the government of the firmament, and fall into perspective, and are made humble. To me, on the Heather Ledge, the fruits of the first were pitiful masses of humanity still crowding the barbed-wire compounds of Europe, and of the other, the mountain world. Everything that is wide and boundless and free, and which is therefore dear to the heart of a mountaineer, is here exemplified; the skies seem vaster than elsewhere, stretching to horizons too far to be identified. The very winds blow more fresh and clean. They purify—give health and life and power to the souls of men imprisoned in flesh and bone and long walled-up in the concrete of the barrack cities. They are purifying winds of the free firmament. To their influence aspire multitudes of men, ringed by the red-rusted wire of mud compounds, beyond and below the rim of the horizon, where governments of the earth sow and harvest. To such men they are true symbols of the winds of the spirit.

All men do not like mountains. It may be that many hate them. But they all love the free adventure and beauty to be found on mountains—or should I say to be won——?

'Time 's up!' said Mackenzie. We walked to the highest point of Heather Ledge. On the nearly perpendicular face above, a ledge ran forty feet diagonally left. We climbed without much difficulty to its top end, where we turned a corner on to a face somewhat less steep. This wall had good holds, on which we climbed until the increasing angle forced Mackenzie to make a long right traverse on rocks little less than vertical, and most exposed (as much so as anything on Rannoch Wall). He halted; then climbed straight up, advancing slowly and obviously having trouble in getting suitable holds. I remembered that on the first ascent eight years ago Mackenzie had nailed the pitch twice. But that was during a rainstorm in the late afternoon, and the pitons had been removed. I watched him closely, saw him resist the temptation to hug the rock, and deliberately force his body away from it, so that he could go up in balance on holds that were not good enough for the grasping and wrestling technique so fatally comforting to the unpractised climber. His rope hung clear of the rock, swaying towards me in a white and rifled curve, beautiful in the sun. A rain-bleached rope—pre-1939, I reckoned, on which wartime moths had dined too well. However, it would hold a second man. The Mackenzie vanished—upwards.

My third test was at hand. A very difficult and exposed pitch at a high angle. I did not pass this one with flying colours.

When I made the right traverse and looked up I felt as weak as a kitten—the drop, the angle, the lack of holds—frightening! but healthily frightening, and not like lying flat in a midnight cellar listening to a bomb whistling down like a grand piano, nor like going into a bare room to chat with the Gestapo—here one had chosen the route, was free to act sharply amid sunny rock and air, to rely on oneself. I remember Mackenzie's studied self-mastery, and pushed myself out from the rock. The moment I committed this act of trust everything went well. Up I went, treading precisely, taking my press-holds for the hands in the right relation to feet and angle. But I confess that I had to do this at high tension with set teeth. I could no more have led that pitch than flown in the air.

What a reaction that was when I reached the top! I mean the rejoicing and being able to give thanks for it all—the joys of coarse-grained rock sun-warmed to the hand and firm to the bite of the boot-nail, the elation of mastering nervous limbs and of flooding their muscles with energy, of using them in a practised craft, fighting, winning—and sharing such adventure with a friend.

'What did you think of that?' asked Mackenzie when I joined him.

'Not bad,' I said. 'Best climb for years.'

'Now, are you telling me!' exclaimed Mackenzie. 'Indeed—who would have thought that!'

'Best climb I 've had too,' he added a minute later.

Our climbing was by no means done, however. A stretch of easier rocks led to the top of the buttress, whence we traversed north on to Curved Ridge. I suggested that we now descend a little and climb the Crowberry Ridge Direct, but Mackenzie employed his veto. He swore he was feeling too tired. It is not like my Herr Mackenzie to be so tactful! It is rather his appalling habit to speak the truth *always*. Yet on this occasion I wonder . . .

So up we went by the Curved Ridge, and then by the Crowberry Tower, at last to plod rhythmically over the last brow to the cairn. I knew well how every stone on the cairn should look, and for a moment was wrathful to see that a few had been rolled away. Still, it was just the same cairn, and I clapped my hand on its top, suddenly remembered the blank despair with which I had last made the same movement, and laughed to myself at the folly of such days; for despair is only for the very young or the very old, and either way it is still foolish. I looked out to Schichallion eastwards, and followed the north horizon round to Mull in the west. All was as it should be. I had returned. I knew these hills so very well that they startled me into no transports of ecstasy—not even after long absence—but they had the greater power to bestow a content that I cannot name, save in terms that must seem vague to any one without a practical knowledge of them—the Recollection and the Quiet. Peace, one might call it?—but again, how many men *do* know what peace is, as against the sympathetic experience of dimly perceiving it outwith themselves? Not many, I fear. It might then be asked whether I mean that mountains are necessary to happiness or to the true completion of any man. Quite to the contrary. So little are they necessary that one of the happiest years of my own life was one of three spent in a prison camp. It would seem that whether mountains contribute to happiness or its reverse depends entirely upon a man's own attitude of mind and heart. They contribute happiness in so far as they elicit a man's love, at first it may be only of themselves, but in the end of the All of which they are just a part.

However, it is fatal (and impossible) for a man to be philosophic about such love at the time of union. The heart and will leap out to it, his mind grasps. In a second it is done. That is all.

'The one thing that matters among mountains,' said Mackenzie, looking out to blue and receding hill-ranks in the north-west, 'is that we enjoy them.'

Simple words. Greatly overlooked. They embody the whole secret of successful mountaineering.

3 *The Great Gully of Garbh Bheinn*

SINCE THE BEGINNINGS of mountaineering in Scotland Garbh Bheinn of Ardgour has presented a double challenge to climbers: hard access and virgin cliffs. Ardgour has always been relatively unknown country, lying far to the west across Loch Linnhe—one of the greatest sea-lochs in Scotland; thus hardly accessible at week-ends. In addition, being one of the best rock-peaks in Scotland and yet so rarely visited, Garbh Bheinn has remained rich in unsolved problems for the rock-climber. In 1946 the most notorious of these problems was the Great Gully. Its earliest history had, in broad outline, been much like that of the Chasm and Clachaig Gully of Glencoe. It had repelled assault over a long term of years, been declared impossible by a past generation of climbers, and finally been once again declared impossible so late as 1946.

The first notable attempt was by Messrs. Hastings and Haskett-Smith in 1897. They were defeated before the half-way point by an eighty-foot cave-pitch, bristling with overhangs. Subsequent parties met the same fate, so that around this pitch there settled a magic halo of impregnability. At close quarters the halo might intimidate, but at long distance it flashed like a lure. While I entertained no foolish hope of having skill enough to climb that gully, still—it was unknown—a gully presenting a challenge. Response had to be made. On 8th June 1946 good weather and a strong party set me westward bound for Ardgour. My companions were Douglas Scott and R. G. Donaldson.

On passing Glencoe village we had our first view of our mountain across Loch Linnhe, from which it rose two thousand nine hundred feet. By virtue of form rather than height it dwarfed all the other hills of Ardgour. A splendid rock-buttress, twelve hundred feet high, gave a free and noble lift

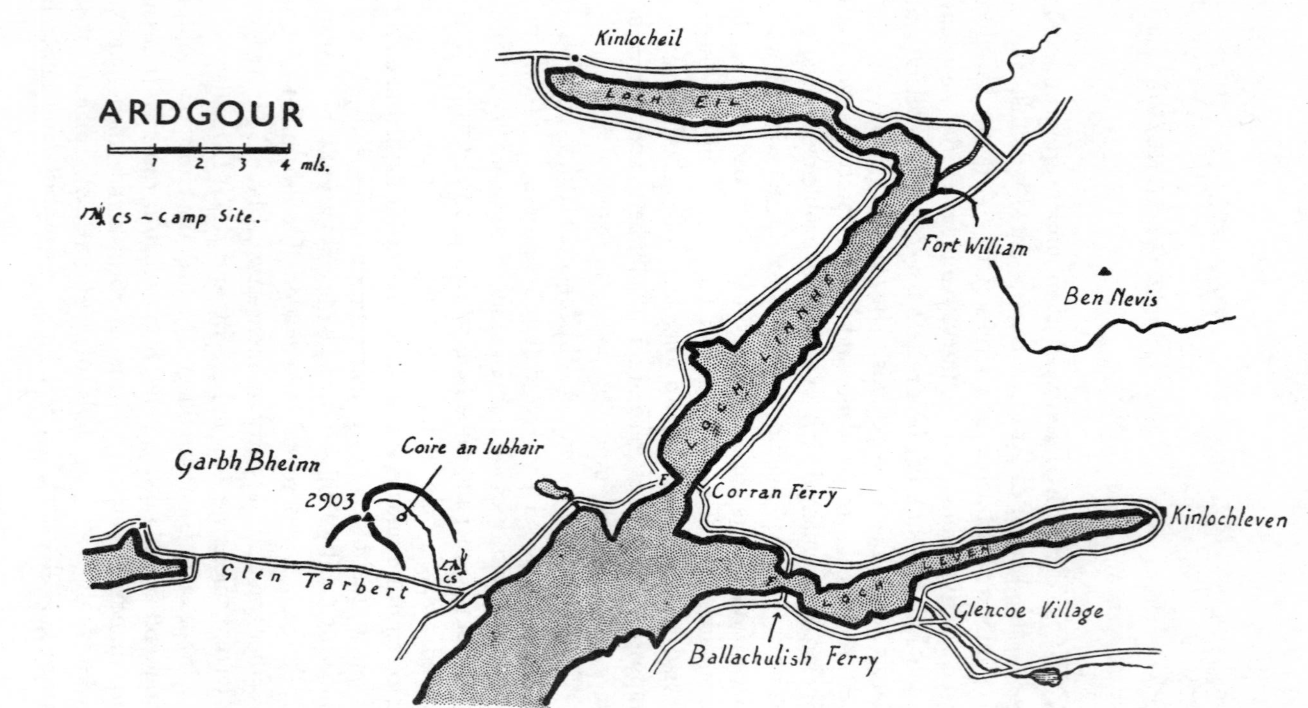
ARDGOUR
1 2 3 4 mls.
cs – Camp Site.
Kinlocheil
LOCH EIL
LOCH LINNHE
Fort William
Ben Nevis
Garbh Bheinn
Coire an Iubhair
2903
Glen Tarbert
CS
F
Corran Ferry
Kinlochleven
LOCH LEVEN
Glencoe Village
Ballachulish Ferry

to the summit. That clean grey tower, standing between a silver tide-rip and a dappled sky, was our battle-ground for the morrow. When we looked closely we could see the dark score of the Great Gully directly under the summit, splitting the buttress from top to bottom.

We crossed Loch Leven by the Ballachulish ferry and Loch Linnhe by the Corran ferry, and then drove seven miles south to Garbh Bheinn. That evening we camped in the lower part of Coire an Iubhair, a trackless glen running for two and a half miles beneath the eastern face of our mountain. A quarter of a mile from the main road we found flat dry ground and plenty of firewood beside the burn; so that we had our supper that night before a log fire at the water's edge.

The site was ideal. The true mountain atmosphere was ours. We were ringed by hills; all around us their crests stood in relief against the clear night sky. The burn flashed and glowed to the leap of flame from the fire. And there was neither sight nor sound of civilization. There was no distraction. Thus we had true contact with the hills; not the mere physical contact of sight or touch, but an effortless sharing or mingling of their presence and ours. That is the direct communion, which we lose utterly amid the distractions of hotels, barely sense in the traffic of hut or hostel, and know truly in a camp or bivouac. When at last we fell asleep before the open door of our tent we did so with a feeling of intimate friendship with mountains, the product of which, being unsought for itself, was happiness.

The dawn broke from a clear sky. At nine o'clock, however, we walked two miles up Coire an Iubhair under locally gathering cloud. Showers and sunshafts struck us alternately, and long wreaths of mist curled and swayed around the summit of Garbh Bheinn. Behind this dark veil the rock of our buttress looked most forbidding and inaccessible. But after we had reached the upper corrie, from which the final peak springs in one great cliff, the clouds lifted and the sky turned blue. The party now split. Donaldson wanted to reconnoitre the only once climbed North Buttress a mile farther up Coire an Iubhair, reckoning the collection of data for a new route there to be more profitable than our visit to Great Gully; for Scott and I were not so audacious at this stage as to say that we were going to climb the Great Gully. We were only going to look at it. At 11.30 we moved into its foot.

The first two hundred and fifty feet were easy and featureless, and we preferred to scramble unroped up the rocks of the north flank, until a sudden deepening of the gully warned us to traverse in. We climbed a high but easy pitch, then the gully deepened, widened, and at last was divided by an almost vertical rib of a hundred feet. The right-hand branch was a mere cleft with wet walls, steep as the rib itself. So we tried the broader left branch; but this started with an overhang on which we both fought and failed. The preliminary skirmish and repulse had one good effect: it woke us up. We put on the rope and metaphorically spat on our hands. I tried to climb the rib. The rock was a coarse gneiss, and came clean to the finger-tips; but after thirty feet the already scanty holds became too few and far between, movements of body too difficult to calculate in advance, so that the chance to traverse into the right-hand cleft came as a providential relief—to be quickly regretted when I entered the damp and dim interior and looked around. The inner wall was green with loathsome growing things, and the side walls moistly sleek, clean enough, but perpendicular.

Scott joined me on a narrow grass ledge. The remaining seventy feet of the cleft looked ugly, but when put to the trial gave me holds nearly all the way; when they failed I bridged—back on one wall and feet braced hard against the other—and wriggled up. The cleft ended suddenly on a thin saddle attached to the central rib on our left. We scrambled over the rib into the left fork, which was now imposingly deep and broad and the true line of the gully. With that cleft in our rear we no longer thought of just looking at the gully. We were going to force a route to the limits of our ability.

A hundred feet of scrambling brought the most notorious pitch of Garbh Bheinn into sight. There was a long level approach, allowing time for its full, disconcerting effect on the mind, and allowing the gully to bite into the cliff, at last to rise up in one eighty-foot step—a step not merely vertical, but starting with a sixty-foot overhang. The flanking walls appeared to lean towards the centre. One would have sworn they were unclimbable. People had thought so for fifty years: they would think so for another fifty. That was our first verdict.

We walked to the foot of the pitch and adopted tactics that once had proved of high value to me in the Clachaig Gully: we did not look at the rock for several minutes—we had lunch. During the course of it we developed an awarenesss that the left wall was not truly overhanging; it was only vertical with a bulge in the middle. I at once abandoned lunch and climbed to the bulge on in-cut holds. Then the holds gave out, and I had to come down. We resumed our lunch.

There remained the right-hand wall, the lower half of which truly did overhang. We munched bread and cheese and looked at that wall contemplatively. If one started sixty feet out from the inmost cave, possibly one might climb the overhang by means of a projecting flake, then make an upward traverse above the line of the overhang to the top. Any such move would be very hard and exposed, and the rock was slabby. I took off my boots and started in stocking-soles.

Two strong arm-pulls on the flake took me up the first overhang, only to be faced with a second but lesser one. Again providence supplied a jug-handle hold on rock that would otherwise have been hopeless. Many a party capable of climbing that wall must have turned away in the past without a trial. The route selection became hard. One had to find a way through the local bulges by balancing delicately across slabs and pushing upwards by shallow grooves. When sixty feet up I became alarmed by the holdlessness of the rock, and halted on a tuft of grass. I had already climbed the height of a city building and the next forty feet looked worse than anything below; it might easily be too much for me, and my ability to climb down was becoming suspect. Such uncertainty of the issue makes a first ascent seem very much harder than any subsequent one. Knowing this, I refused to scare myself further by thinking about hazards ahead, and henceforth lived only from one move to the next. By making good each hand and foothold as it came to me, I duly found myself at the top of the pitch. I had run out a hundred feet of rope and was only two yards from the gully-bed. The climb had not been more than severe.

Scott climbed in boots, and I should lead in boots on a future occasion. Meantime we rested a while in one of those exhilarating situations in which the upper part of the Great Gully abounds. Wide rock walls framed the sunlit summits across Loch Linnhe —the high sweep of the Lochaber plateaux, the pointed Mamores, and the swell of Appin. The land was pure and fresh after the swift showers of the morning; its myriad hues were clear despite their delicacy; deep-toned in the shadows, bright in the sun. For this was the spring sun 'that strikes branch into leaf and bloom into the world.'

Body and mind, we had been wakened up by that rock climb, and its demand for a full vigour and alertness; and so now the beauty of scene awakened us in spirit. We relaxed and rested, with a much more joyful awareness than at any earlier time that day of our good fortune in treading this earth. Below us the supreme obstacle had been vanquished, but up above there remained all the promise of the unknown upper gully, and outwards the broad lands glowing in the paradisaic light. Here, one could have sworn, on a planet such as this there could hardly be sin or suffering, and certainly not disease. The light fell warm and glowing and the things of the earth shone in their full response. We as men, as beings one with that universal whole, and on no account making any choice for ourselves of separation, shared in the full health of its glory. Where there is union there cannot be disharmony, and where there is wholeness—there alone and to the full we have happiness.

The scene below was nothing but a sign, I fear, of things that may be, but as such it gave us cause enough to rejoice, and the faint foretaste of participation, which to beings as weak as ourselves, seemed strong in all excellencies. Men may live and die even in the distant recollection of such promise, and be of good cheer whatever befalls. For the Way is before them and the End assured, if that is their will.

Once again Scott and I turned to our rock climb. We could not guess what lay ahead; for although the gully continued several hundred feet, the alignment of the walls prevented our seeing into it. The day would go hard with us now if we met defeat. I could not help reflecting that our baseless and chronic optimism, so frequently justified on long climbs in the past, must one day draw to its term, and our bluff be called. Shortly after the resumption the gully narrowed to an open chimney, where the route went forty feet up the slabby left wall. For a few dreadful minutes I thought that our final check had come, simple as the pitch appeared, because Scott, now leading, failed to get up. And he is a climber from whom I have a great deal to learn. As one might imagine in the circumstances I took to these slabs in a most energetic and business-like manner, which was luckily what they required. The holds were small and delicate, but they had to be used determinedly. After a short struggle I reached the top. Scott had only been off form and followed with ease. I breathed again.

Thereafter a long stretch of scrambling brought us to the main fork, about two hundred feet from the top. The true continuation of the gully was the left branch, the last hundred feet of which sprang up in a vertical chimney, capped by an overhang. Our success here would necessitate a very special dispensation of good luck, in no way inferior in quality to that enjoyed by us at the Great Cave. That we should receive such a blessing twice in the same day, even in the same year, was not to be imagined. However, we summoned up our energies once more and tried again to look determined. The walls were sheer and three feet apart. I accounted for the first seventy feet by leaning my back upon one wall and using foothold on the other, until eventually I came under the overhang—a projecting rectangular block, tilting down. At this very point the walls had become too wide to allow me to jam myself back and foot. For nearly half an hour I experimented with ways and means for attempting a direct ascent over the front of the block, but the holds were just not there. The sheer drop underneath me forbade the chancy tactics of 'smash and grab.' One may sometimes force slabs and walls in a movement unaided by visible hold, employing a technique called 'balance-climbing'; but on overhangs the laws of gravity are inexorable. 'Find holds,' they say, 'or fall.' And their still small voice is persuasive. Had there been one good hold on that block I could have pulled myself over it, but alas, there was none. I eased myself cautiously down.

In the right-hand branch we could see no difficulties, indeed no climbing of any interest, but right beside us, in the centre of the fork, stood a tall buttress of pale and beautiful rock. The craggy frankness of its face captivated our hearts; so we stood back and selected a route up it. The cliff was a hundred and fifty feet high. Scott led. We went fifty feet up its right-hand side, until holdless rock forced us into a long left traverse, at the midway point of which the rounding of an awkward rib made us swing out over space on the strength of an under-cut hold—a delightful out-of-balance movement. Coarse and reliable rock beyond led us steeply to the top of the Great Gully. Our climb had taken four hours.

We had suffered two minor defeats during the day: at the left-hand wall of the Great Cave and again at the left fork. These defeats have merit; for although the first ascent of the gully has been made, any future climber who can open up the more direct route at the cave and the direct line at the fork will have virtually remade the climb, and transformed a very good gully into an altogether excellent one; the thought that someone may yet enjoy this triumph, that its very possibility is there, gives Scott and me delight.

At the summit of Garbh Bheinn we found Donaldson. If he had inadvertently lost a great climb, he had spent the last hour enjoying one of the great panoramas of Scotland. On the one hand ranged a vast array of the mainland mountains, stretching in line of storm from the farthest north to the south horizon; on the other the Atlantic Ocean and the small isles of the west. This truly is the combination to which the Scottish hills owe all worthiness—rock, water, and the subtle colours of the seaward atmosphere. The part played by heather is small. Our senses were engrossed and our minds won by the free spaciousness of this land—the wide skies and broad waters, a cloud-winged host of mountains, and brisk winds. Such was Ardgour—its freedom and ours.

4 *Affric*

IN ALL THIS EARTH does there live one satisfied climber? It is not possible. If satisfied he would not climb. My winter season of 1945–6, for example, had been extraordinarily successful—every week-end good, without fail! My list of hard climbs done—a satisfying one. Yet I found myself a dissatisfied man in April. Too much time had been spent upon cliffs. Rocks are all very well, I grumbled, but unknown hill-country, where cliffs are admired from a respectful distance and thought of as obstacles to be turned one side or the other by lines of least resistance, *that* kind of country is true mountain-land; its exploration gives to many a man a satisfaction he needs—as deep as he will find on rock if not deeper.

Happily there is no dearth of unexplored hill-country; for it is only necessary that it should not be known to oneself. Now there was one particular bit of country of which I was ignorant, and which had weighed heavy on my conscience for years. I had never been to Glen Affric, never even seen a map of it, nor read as much as a chapter. Rumours reached me of its being the most beautiful of all Scottish glens, and I knew in a vague sort of way that Affric was one of the great hill-passes of north-west Scotland. I knew rather less about it than I knew of some of the Himalayan passes in eastern Tibet. (Although I had not been there either.)

I explained this sorry state of affairs to my friend Donald McIntyre, whom I met one morning in mid-April at Fort William. To my great delight his frame of mind was much like mine. Glen Affric? Yes, he 'd love to go there. But did he know anything about it? Well, only that Gladstone had once been taken to the end of Loch Beneveian and there been so affected by the view that he 'd raised his top-hat.

'Donald,' I said solemnly, 'how long have you got?'

'About ten days.'

'Well, let 's go for seven. But we 'll need a tent.'

The man most likely to part with a tent, we calculated, would be the minister of St. Andrew's Church. Our choice of benefactor was an excellent one, for not only did he part with a tent, but finding us also destitute of petrol gave us enough for the sixty-mile journey north. Unluckily no provisions could be bought in Fort William—it was one of the innumerable fast days for which this town is notorious. However, we sped gaily northwards with our tent in a general state of unpreparedness for which a boy scout might have been stripped of his badges. We had one primus stove but no paraffin oil, and although we had matches, this was not by forethought. However, the weather was perfect as only it can be when it has not been considered for one instant.

At Spean Bridge we bought in the oatmeal which was to be our staple diet for seven days (bread for that period is too bulky for a rucksack), also sausage and kipper. Our halt allowed us to look at our map with a planning eye. From Kintail, on the west coast, Glen Affric runs thirty miles north-east to merge with Strath Glass, which continues to the Beauly Firth. The glen and strath form one great pass running coast to coast across the breadth of Scotland. We decided to make for the eastern gateway, where glens Affric and Cannich join Strath Glass. There is a tiny village called Cannich at the junction, where we arrived that night.

We camped at the edge of the River Glass, near the house of Fasnakyle, at the very entrance to Glen Affric. Our curiosity fetched us up early next morning. A touch of frost during the night and cloudless skies at sunrise helped us to get moving quickly. Our unusual plan was to have no plan at all, save to walk fifteen miles up the glen and then see what we could see. As for the rest, we should accept what the gods offered, and do what seemed right in the circumstances. This readiness to receive whatever might befall was a wise policy in view of our lack of supplies and knowledge. In addition, it gave us so marked a sense of freedom as we marched through woods by the River Affric that we wondered whether such an attitude of mind might not be the best for all life. We resolved to sow no troubles for the future by too rigid planning and the setting of our wills against providence.

Our first half-hour's walking was uphill work on a narrow road. Our rucksacks being weighty with seven days' food we were open to any temptation to halt, so that sounds of a waterfall made us turn off the road to the river, which was hiding among trees. Thus our good fortune brought us to sloping rock at the edge of the famous Dog Fall. It is a very short fall. Its fame, we concluded, must lie either in the power and volume of congested water, which hurtles down the throat of a small gorge into a cauldron gouged out of solid rock, or else in its beauty. The power of the fall is indeed extraordinary but not so great as to bring fame of itself. What of its beauty then? So simple that it can scarcely be made intelligible. And therein is the Dog Fall's secret and abounding fascination in the eyes of men: a thick column of water, pulsing with a sort of fierce life; yet seemingly frozen, and white like ice. The fall's frozen curve, combined with that fierce vibration within the curve itself, gripped our minds. For opposite extremes of stillness and motion were made one form. Beauty is born of such a union.

After half an hour's admiration we continued our walk, while the river widened and the glen opened out. There was no leaf on the trees, which in the lower glen are deciduous, so that every branch was bright in the sun's flood and our Golden Road awash. However, no cause had been given us to think Glen Affric superior, say, to Glen Lyon in Perthshire, until a bend in the road brought us on to the shore of Loch Beneveian. Groups of well-grown Scots firs clustered on the banks. Through a clearing came the blaze of sun-struck hills reflected in utterly calm water. Its richness of varied colour gave it the likeness of an ancient stained-glass window, but no window ever glowed like that loch. I had no more doubts of Glen Affric. Its attributes were made manifest.

We continued three miles along the sill of the magic window, then beyond its west end to the broad river. Grassy banks and the sun's heat were there too much to be resisted. I stripped and plunged, swam, and with McIntyre sun-bathed on the grass. Later we pressed on by a second and smaller loch.

Less than a mile beyond, or eight miles from Fasnakyle, we came to the end of the roadway at a whitewashed cottage. I still think this house to be one of the most remarkable in Scotland. It is built on the low ridge dividing Loch Affric (as yet invisible to us) from the small eastern loch by whose banks we had come. White walls fit peculiarly well into the highland environment. They are appropriate. Perhaps the cottage had been newly washed? Because now, in the sun's striking, it shone; the emerald grass before it shone; and the loch shone blue. The house was a focusing point of a shining world. And far back from the open strath and its wide-stretching waters and far-spaced pines, mountains, snow-capped, shone in the blue of the sky. All were focused in the eye of the white cottage: a wholeness of mountain scene.

A house standing alone in wild country always appeals profoundly to McIntyre and me. It suggests to us peace, beauty, the perfect freedom from interruption that gives a chance of understanding the things we love. Reason prevents me from picturing a New Eden now, in terms of the concrete. Should I ever do so I should picture something like the stalker's cottage in Glen Affric. My unaided imagination could conceive no more delightful home.

However, such a picture of freedom from worldly concerns is a symbol, not to be mistaken for reality. I often meet people living amid scenes of peace and beauty whose hearts share neither attribute. At first I used to be puzzled, dismayed, and even made miserable at finding them not only dissatisfied with their lot and disgruntled with society, but worse still, given over to disparagement of their neighbours. The breeding of ill will had become a chosen task. But true peace, that blessed by-product of an integrated heart and mind and will, depends on no scenery. It can be had everywhere—when the means are known.

The Affric cottage, I thought, looked well outwardly. Did peace live within? In any event to pass it by without a friendly word would be too barbarous an act. I knocked at the door.

The stalker was out on the loch, but his sister welcomed us with a most charming kindliness. No trace of ill will in *this* house! She hailed us into a clean and spotless kitchen, and gave us hot buttered scones and tea, and thoughtful concern for our prospects out in the glen. We, in return, gave news of the outside world, which seemed not too choice an offering. The outside world might call the cottage in Affric 'far from civilization,' when, in fact, it is one of civilization's first fruits.

We went on our way by a rough track winding through stone, tree, and heather above the northern shore of Loch Affric. The hill scene had greatly changed: we were right in among high mountains. The snow-peaks of Sgurr na Lapaich, Mam Soul, and Cairn Eige rose close above us to the north-west. This change had been a gradual one, but a more abrupt change, affecting the whole character of the glen, occurred at the west end of Loch Affric. We had travelled fifteen miles to the mid-way point. That eastern half had been a perfect combination of mountain, wood, and loch; the western half was perfect deer-forest—treeless. Before us stretched bare grassy moorland and the thin thread of a river winding between snow-peaks.

We pitched our tent on a high bank by the river. We had arrived. On every hand were mountains that we had never seen before, and of which we knew nothing. They looked delightfully mysterious. That night was bitterly cold and starry, with a touch of ground frost. On the other hand, we had plenty of wood, and ate a piping-hot meal beside a good fire. Having no plates we ate straight out of the pot, keeping pace with each other in spoonfuls. In its detail this way of feeding gives illuminating glimpses into a man's character. A valuable essay could be written on the subject, with a long and learned title.

Our next day's plan was to get a bird's-eye view of the whole area, so that we might know better what we were about; to this

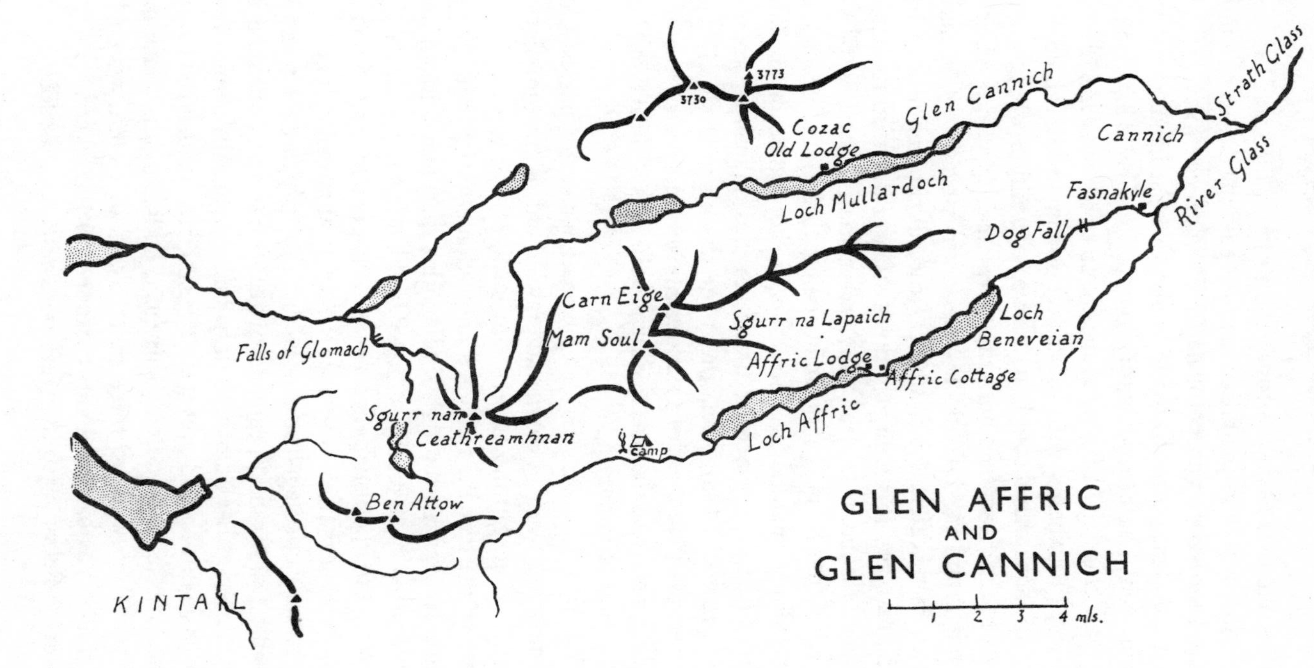
3730
3773
Cozac
Old Lodge
Glen Cannich
Strath Glass
Cannich
River Glass
Loch Mullardoch
Fasnakyle
Dog Fall
Carn Eige
Sgurr na Lapaich
Mam Soul
Loch
Beneveian
Falls of Glomach
Affric Lodge
Affric Cottage
Sgurr nan
Ceathreamhnan
camp
Loch Affric
Ben Attow
KINTAIL
GLEN AFFRIC
AND
GLEN CANNICH
1
2
3
4 mls.

end we climbed Mam Soul and Cairn Eige, which are both above three thousand eight hundred feet. Again the day was cloudless, and we looked down upon a dappled sea of mountains extending from the Cairngorms to the Cuillin. Close at hand, to the west, Sgurr nan Ceathreamhnan (pronounced *Kerranan*) looked a most alluring hill: a far-flung mountain of ten tops and five great corries, all spattered with snow. It dominates the whole of this part of Scotland through its strategic position on the watershed; for its rivers feed both the North Sea, by way of Affric and Cannich, and the Atlantic by the River Elchaig. The highest source of the Elchaig lies well up towards the summit of Ceathreamhnan, and this tributary flows straight down to the Hidden Falls of Glomach on the north-west foothills. The falls are famed as the longest in Britain, being three hundred and fifty feet. They and the mountain lie in the middle of an almost uninhabited part of Scotland, and are thus difficult to reach and unfrequented. Our plan, then, for the morrow should be to traverse the long crest of Ceathreamhnan, find this source of the Elchaig, and trace the stream down to the falls. That would give us a round of twenty miles.

We made our descent over Sgurr na Lapaich. On the following morning I rose at dawn and crawled out of our thin tent into a thick white ground mist. But so light was this bank in its upper fringe that the reddened snow-dome of Sgurr nan Ceathreamhnan towered through it to heights that human imagination would never have dared to raise it. That is a not unusual effect of mist; but the usual effects were exaggerated by the contrast of its shining whiteness against the crimson crown. The crown was stereoscoped against a saxe-blue sky, which gave to its impossible height an appearance of reality that overwhelmed me. If we or any other humans weighed down with the clumsiness of flesh and bone should ever walk over the crest of that red flame in the sky we should surely be shrivelled up like moths. Yet midday found us walking three miles along that crest, which had materialized as hard and stony ground with cold snow lying in pockets. Below us to the west were a maze of sea-lochs.

After we had crossed over the summit we had a most fascinating glimpse into the west corrie of Ben Attow, which splits Glen Affric with a six-mile wedge. The corrie was ringed by rock-buttresses, perhaps ten of them, and not one had been climbed.

We passed over the north-west top, and descended two miles beside the river until the valley floor fell away from our feet in a great cliff, at the left side of which the Falls of Glomach went roaring over. But what constituted their 'hiddenness'? We peered over the edge and caught a glimpse of a great gorge. The falls were indeed invisible. The cliff to the right of the falls was exceedingly steep, yet we thought it might be climbable, and lowered ourselves tentatively over the edge. After coming all this way we must see the waterfall! We had climbed down sixty feet when our position became dangerous. The rocks were loose and rotten, and the falls still invisible behind a projecting column. An attempt to round that column was needful, but invited disaster. We turned and climbed back to the top.

The right-hand side of the gorge was a precipitous slope crossed by tilted ledges. On these ledges we were able to traverse far out until the whole of the Hidden Fall was revealed. The water came over the cliff in one bound of a hundred feet, hit a crag, and split into two falls, which made the final bound of two hundred and fifty feet. At the bottom a dark, deep cauldron was clouded by grey spray soaring high. The two long leaps of water struck the rock with a roar and rebounded. A fearsome sight, it lacked the beauty of the tiny Dog Fall of Glen Affric. None the less one could watch it for hours; the beat, the roar, the long white flash, spray soaring—they hypnotize the mind: one slips into reverie and time wings on.

We bestirred ourselves after an hour and returned to the cliff top. On our ten-mile walk back to camp a flight of wild swans gave us escort, flying from loch to loch as we passed through the glen.

We rose early next morning, being now in excellent training. I think that on any other occasion we should have gone to explore the rocks in that western corrie of Ben Attow. Instead we felt a peculiarly strong desire to explore Glen Cannich. I wondered what awaited us there. Accordingly we crossed the high pass between Mam Soul and Sgurr nan Ceathreamhnan to the upper part of Glen Cannich, which turned out to be treeless like its Affric counterpart; and like Affric the scene completely changed by the time we had gone four miles down to Loch Mullardoch. We had re-entered woodland. Most surprising of all, countless lizards idled on the road or darted across. I had not imagined that lizards in quantity were to be found in Scotland.

Half-way down Loch Mullardoch, just before we came to Cozac Old Lodge, we began to look for a good camp site, and saw a broad, tree-grown point projecting into the loch. At the toe of the point we found a most wonderful site. A big carpet of grass lay between a wooded knoll and a shingly beach. The water was still, deep blue, splashed by white patches of reflected snow-mountain. We pitched the tent and found beside us unlimited supplies of dried bracken for kindling and sticks for fuel. Day and night we enjoyed a red and roaring fire for our meals.

The following day was again hot and cloudless. We stripped off our shirts and sun-bathed all morning on the soft grass by the tent. I swam in the loch occasionally, but for the most part we just looked. The loch being absolutely smooth, reflections were brilliant, the white of each peak sharp amidst the blue. The mountains started from the water, dazzling us like those of the sky. The sunlike beauty of the scene radiated through the eye and mind, evaporating mental lethargy. We felt alive and alert and at one with the whole environment.

After looking out to the hills and water for a whole morning I noticed that while their radiant power of beauty grew their outer form ceased to matter. What indeed did it matter if a hill-slope ran this way or that, or a copse stood here or there? The foreground, in fact, was conspicuous by its absence, and the farther shore cut the middle of the picture: much of aesthetics was shown to be a vain rationalizing after the event. From the mountain-land burst a power of beauty subject to no bond of reason. The material aspect or vehicle had performed its service, and now effaced itself. I saw and recognized an imageless beauty, of which material things are outward signs, receiving from it their being and manifesting it as their purpose.

Next day we struck camp, and withdrew ten miles to Strath Glass. Instead of narrowing the field for future exploration our days in the two glens had expanded that field immeasurably. So that I am still not a satisfied climber—and know that I never will be. Life is short, the mountain infinitely high, but the route goes.

5 *Twisting Gully*

IT WAS A DARK, wet night in December 1946. Douglas Scott and I peered through the wind-screen of our car to see the croft of Altnafeadh, at the east end of Glencoe, loom up through the drizzle. We parked the car under the lee of the byre, and started down the quarter-mile track to Lagangarbh Cottage, which belongs to the Scottish Mountaineering Club. I had a bad cold in the head, and should never have been there at all had we not agreed to meet Jim Cortlandt Simpson at Lagangarbh.

'And the trouble is,' I said, as we picked our way by torchlight, 'that Jim has come six hundred miles for a good climb—something hard and icy. God help us. He'll be bursting with enthusiasm. He *always* is.'

'He'll just have to burst,' grunted Scott.

A lamplight emerged from the cottage and moved quickly towards us. It was Simpson, bursting with enthusiasm. We shook hands vigorously all round, and swore through the haze of rain that this was a joyful moment.

'What shall we climb to-morrow?' asked Simpson eagerly. 'Do you think Crowberry Gully would go? Perhaps the snow will be good high up. *Or* we might climb something new?'

'Crowberry Gully is out,' I said firmly, 'and new routes are *right* out, and I'm nearly out too. If we do anything at all we shall do something very gentle and soothing—something nice.'

Scott, I knew, was grinning through the darkness. But in a little while we were roasting before a great fire in the kitchen and drinking Simpson's hot soup. Mountains began to seem less forbidding. Simpson certainly *was* in good form. However detachedly I might regard his warmth of spirit the fact was that I could feel it thawing out the closed parts of my mind.

'The whole of Glencoe is smothered in a wet blanket,' I said. 'We won't get a good climb at this end of the glen—the climbs don't lie high enough. Snow will be just slush. But we might get a climb on Bidean nam Bian. After all, it's three thousand seven hundred feet, and Coire nan Lochan nearly three thousand. It often has good snow and ice when there's thaw everywhere else.'

'You get a big choice of climbs in Coire nan Lochan,' assented Scott. 'Everything from easy to impossible. We'd better go there.'

Simpson agreed.

We went early to bed. I prayed earnestly for a pouring wet morning so that we might lie long. But the weather turned dry in the morning and Simpson had us up at dawn. Before midday we reached the rim of Coire nan Lochan, the great north-east corrie of Bidean. The two lochans had vanished under a thick snow-quilt. The shapely peak of Stob Coire nan Lochan rose to our left side among lowering cloud. Its northward-running ridge faced us across the corrie with four buttresses and gullies, all about five hundred feet high. The rocks were heavily snowed up, and the glint of ice could be seen here and there. My own contribution to the day's decision was purely negative.

'Whatever we do,' I said, 'let's rule out everything difficult. I could never get up a hard pitch.'

We examined the cliffs in silence for a few minutes, then Scott drew our attention to a great unclimbed groove on the left flank of South Buttress. It was a narrow and shallow gully with a slight twist in the lower half. In neither winter nor summer had a route been made there. It did seem to be a line of weakness on an otherwise unpromising cliff. About one hundred feet up a small crag divided the gully. In the right fork was a monstrous pitch of white ice. The left fork was no more than a chimney of twenty feet petering out on the buttress. It looked vertical, but then we were looking at it *en face*, which would make the angle seem worse than it was. We could form no sure idea of its difficulty without closer examination. We accordingly crossed the corrie and moved up to its foot.

My head was still heavy with cold and I felt like death. Thus I had no intention of climbing that gully: I went only to look at it. The old familiar phrase should have warned me. Meantime every advantage was to be gained by climbing as far as the fork, if no farther. We should at least garner information for future use. I refused the lead and tied myself to the rear end of the rope. Scott went first. From the start he found himself involved in step-cutting on a steep, hard slope. Solid chips began to bounce off my head and shoulders. The South Buttress rose sheer on our right and our eyes were led upwards along lines of shallow grooves, which might conceivably be climbed in summer. It was that faint suggestion of weakness, the invitation of it, that made them seem so unspeakably ugly. The rock had a vertical stratification, dull black but frosted; the snow was bleak and without sparkle, the ice lustreless. The buttress on our left was much more heavily snow-covered on the crest, being at a lesser angle, but all that we could see of it now was the bare wall of its flank, partly overhanging.

All our hopes thus flowed in the gully-bed, drawn by the moon of reason, by whose light angles seen *en face* are lessened. But the ebb-flow set in at the fork. The true line of the gully twisted rightward under a down-plunging crag of the left buttress. The twist took the form of a mammoth icicle, not snow-ice, but frozen water, opaque, glossy, and as far as we could see fifty feet high—there might be more above. At a guess I should say the angle was seventy-five degrees. The leader of any attempt on such severe ice would have to spend on it one and a half hours' one-handed cutting, and even the followers would have trouble. I have no doubt that my silent dissent crept up the rope and affected Scott. Strongly held feelings, although unexpressed, are conveyed unerringly round the party on a hard climb. Scott turned away from the ice-pitch and looked at the left fork.

We were now able to confirm that this left fork was not truly a fork. The buttress protruded a crag sideways, and the 'fork' was merely a short vertical chimney running up the angle towards the crest. The chimney was completely choked with soft snow, and its black walls were slightly ice-glazed. Simpson thrust his axe into the hard snow beneath and belayed the rope, while Scott tried to force the chimney. He very nearly reached the sloping slabs at the top. I could see his hand hurriedly groping for non-existent holds. Then the angle beat him and he came down. However, his work changed the whole course of the day, for his excavations in the chimney had revealed an unsuspected cave almost half-way up. It was small—no more than a hole, but a hole big enough for a man to stand in. That opened up fresh possibilities. For one thing it gave a perfect stance and belay for the second man. Simpson climbed up and disappeared head first into the cave. He managed to right himself somehow, and at last his enthusiastic face appeared at the window. He beamed and directed the battle. Whatever happened, the party as a whole was now secure, and Scott made a most determined assault on the upper chimney. He neared the top and was motionless there for a long time, while his fingers searched sensitively over every inch of reachable rock. But again hold was refused him; he had to come down before strength failed.

Simpson, meanwhile, had been staring out of his window on to the left wall of the gully, which overhung. He could see what I below could not see well—that an out-dipping ledge, steeply banked with soft snow, ran ten feet across the overhang to the outer face of the buttress. He drew my attention to this interesting fact. The question was: could a man edge his way along the soft snow of that ledge *despite* the out-thrust of the overhang above him? And then, what would the crest of the buttress be like? It was invisible. There could be no answer to these questions without a trial. I did at last begin to feel challenged by the climb. What lies beyond? It is a question a mountaineer cannot resist. My cold in the head would have to be nursed later in the day; meanwhile I began to feel like Epstein's *Adam*, arising mightily from thick bogs of flesh and the world, a man aspiring upwards. Scott must have sensed the change. He asked me to lead.

I grasped my axe and moved up. I still did not propose to myself that I should climb the pitch. I was going to try to traverse that ledge, just to see if it were possible, and to find out what lay beyond—all this for future use. Simpson encouraged me at the outset by making alternative suggestions each time I failed to climb on to the inner end of the ledge. The surrounding rocks lay at awkward angles. The mind had to be gripped and stirred to find ways and means to force on the body. But at last it was done. And yes, it was possible to edge along under the overhang! My only trouble now was whether the soft snow would hold on its out-tilt of rock. The point was doubtful, and only Simpson's perfect stance made me risk the trial. I was not yet above him, and he could hold me with ease if the snow peeled off. Step by step I crept cautiously to the outer edge. Then I stepped round the corner on to a good foothold on the face. The change from a narrow gully to open rocks was too sudden—I felt an unwelcome sense of exposure. The rocks held a shiny glaze of ice where they protruded from the snow of groove and ledge. The buttress plunged to the corrie. However, eyes and nerves quickly adjusted themselves. I studied the rocks in front but their riddle remained unsolved, the answer buried under sheetings of snow-ice. They *looked* unclimbable, but if I cut the snow away what might not be revealed underneath?

I set to work with the axe, cut a foothold, moved up a step, and made experimental clearings through the ice above me, exposing grey rock and a few glazed holds. They were arranged rather like the direct start to the Holly-tree Wall on Idwal Slabs in Wales. Whether it were possible to make the initial moves, which included raising the body by the down-thrust of a clenched fist on a pocket of rock, while the rocks were frost-bound, was another matter. I made the move, and once made it seemed to me highly desirable not to reverse it. Twisting Gully would have to be climbed to-day.

On that first ascent of the pitch every move was an unknown quantity. It was not possible to say if the rock were climbable

Twisting Gully—Stob Coire nan Lochan

until stripped of its frozen plating. After the first severe moves the rock went well. Sixty feet up I found anchorage in a snow-filled groove. Simpson and Scott joined me. It now seemed to our advantage that we should continue up the buttress for a couple of hundred feet rather than make a more difficult and immediate traverse into the gully. We accordingly cut our way up snowy channels and over short rock-outcrops, swinging first to the left and then back to the right on a long upslant to avoid impending crags, until at length our route converged with the gully, about a hundred and fifty feet from the top.

The gully had now steepened and narrowed to a long throat below the fan-shaped mouth. Snow-ice lay here at a high angle; none the less it was straightforward ice, requiring common skill but uncommonly hard work. A way was carved through it to the final fan. The snow deepened and softened. It lay so heavily in the fan, at so steep an inclination for its bulk, that I began to feel uneasy at thought of its avalanching. I made a track straight up it. At the half-way mark I saw a crack open noiselessly right across the slope. As fast as I could drive myself to move I climbed about fifteen feet above the split and drove in my axe to the head. But the snow seemed to be too well bound to start cascading down the throat of the gully. The shape of the fan served to hold it. In another year, if the snow lies in such bulk, but in bad condition—either too wet or too dry and powdery—the avalanche risk will be real.

Simpson and Scott joined me below the cornice. It overhung throughout its leftward curve, but the rightward half was only vertical. I traversed right and brought Simpson to the base of the snow-wall, where he belayed me and was in turn belayed by Scott. For the snow was soft enough to kick and the holds thus made might break. I moved cautiously up the wall until I could get my forearms over the top, then with a quick jab drove my pick into the tough snow beyond. One pull up—and the climb was done.

Simpson, on arriving, inquired courteously how my cold was keeping. All trace of it had gone, never to return. It had vanished in a matter of minutes while I was dealing with the crux. The concentration of all the nervous and bodily powers to one end had unified the personality and thrown the cold out. I have known the same phenomenon in war, when men would go into action with minor ailments—chills or sickness—and cast them off in a few minutes; also in religious mystics in prayer: and all for this same reason—an integration.

When Scott pulled himself over the edge I could see from his preoccupied eye that our new route was forgotten. He was making a swift all-round search for photographs. But conditions were poor. Loch Linnhe reflected glassily the layers of high grey cloud, the sunless cliffs of Bidean stared frostily across Coire nam Beith, the glens were lifeless, the snows flat, the mountains stripped of every material thing that adorns. They were stark. There was nothing to catch the eye save bare and essential mountain. Perhaps that explains why they looked so mountainously noble. But their undiminished beauty could be caught in no photograph.

Scott looked distressed for a minute, then his face brightened. 'Well,' said he, 'that *was* a good climb. Four hours up.'

6 *Night and Morning on the Mountains*

THE MOST ACUTELY difficult expedition to achieve on mountains in this country is a moonlight climb in winter. Not that the difficulties are technical. A full moon among snow-mountains will normally provide visibility of twenty-five miles—if the sky be clear. And that is the root of the problem: to combine leisure with a full moon, a hard frost, and a clear sky. Success needs patience, long and persistent patience.

I had been waiting seven years for a chance of traversing by moonlight the Aonach Eagach, which forms the north wall of Glencoe. Its name, which means the Notched Ridge, is especially given to the rocky crest extending one and a half miles from Am Bodach in the east to Stob Coire Leith in the west. This ridge is the narrowest on the Scottish mainland. Throughout its total length of nearly two miles there can be no escape in winter down its precipitous flank to Glencoe, except at one end or the other. Thus its traverse under a plaster of snow and ice is by day a memorable expedition. By moonlight I hoped for a double ration of mountaineering bliss.

I made my first abortive attempt with Douglas Laidlaw in 1940. The war intervened. But at last the record frost of February 1947 brought the long-sought opportunity. One Saturday evening I arrived at Altnafeadh in Glencoe with Donald McIntyre. We stopped at Lagangarbh cottage for a meal and awaited moonrise. It came up at last over Rannoch Moor, gigantic as a melon—dwarfing the earth. We waited for an hour until it rose well above ground haze, by which time it shrank to normal size and its light power doubled.

Then we set out, not yet for the Aonach Eagach, but for a two-hours' prowl of delight up and down Glencoe. We went

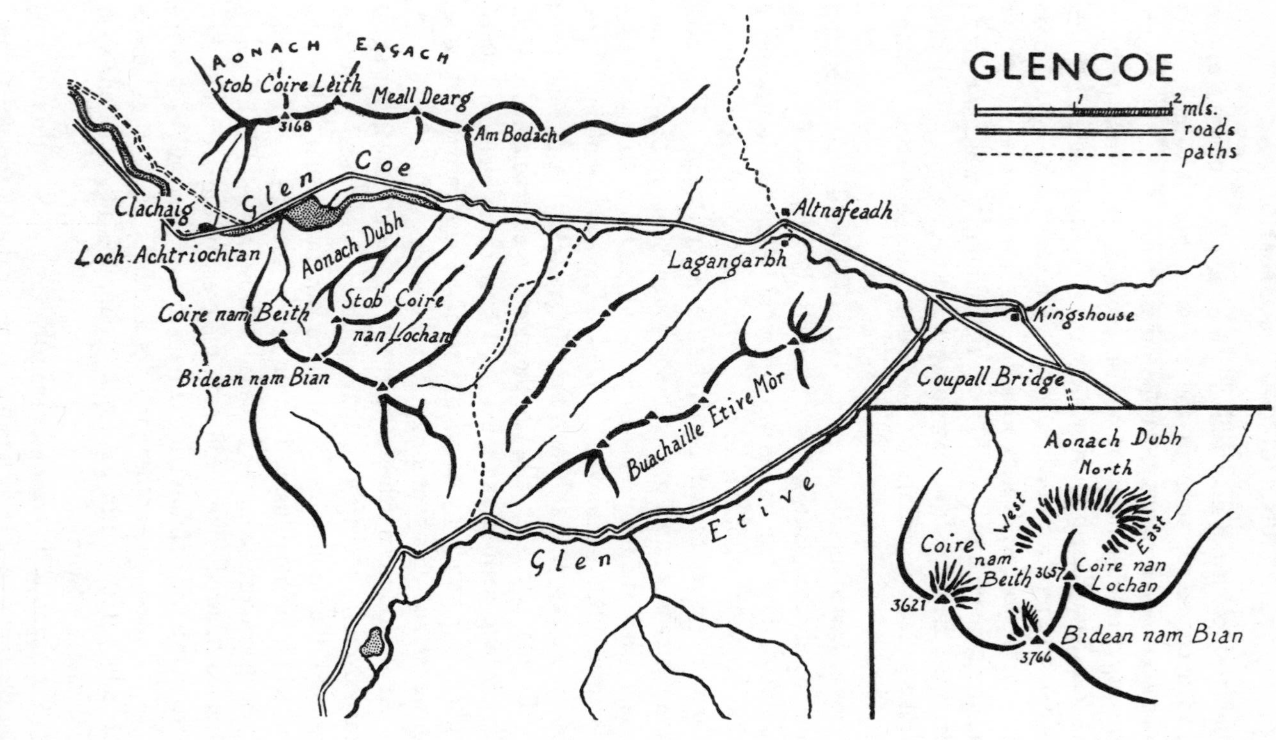

GLENCOE
1
2 mls.
roads
paths
AONACH EAGACH
Stob Coire Leith
3168
Meall Dearg
Am Bodach
Glen Coe
Clachaig
Loch Achtriochtan
Aonach Dubh
Stob Coire nan Lochan
Coire nam Beith
Bidean nam Bian
Altnafeadh
Lagangarbh
Kingshouse
Coupall Bridge
Buachaille Etive Mòr
Glen Etive
Aonach Dubh
North
West
East
Coire nam Beith
3621
3657
Coire nan Lochan
Bidean nam Bian
3766

first to look at the Buachaille Etive Mor, whose massive towers had a coarse-cut strength and crystal glint: they might have been hewn out of ice. At the other western end of the glen, hovering insubstantially in a crisp, clear sky, the snow-peaks of Bidean nam Bian burned whitely over the dark earth. At ten o'clock we repaired to Altnafeadh. The car's radiator was frozen so that we lost a priceless hour thawing it out. Then we drove to the base of Am Bodach, from the summit of which we might traverse the ridge from east to west and back again. A double traverse was essential, for we planned to be eastward bound at dawn.

We started uphill at 11.30 p.m. The cold was bitter and the wind keen, but we wore kapoc-filled flying-suits, which, although too warm on the way up, would allow us to spend more time to good profit on the crest of the ridge. We came to the summit at three thousand-odd feet about 1.30 a.m. Our eyes were drawn westward to the sharp and sinuous blade of our ridge, when suddenly a blaze of white light from the north made us turn. But we looked in vain. There was nothing there. Then we saw that although the sky was clear, stars were few; while the Lochaber hills to the north were remarkably dim. Everything seemed shrouded by a strange milkiness of atmosphere, for which no cause was seen. Southward of Glencoe, however, the hills were bright.

As we looked north the entire sky again lightened, but again turned dark so swiftly that we doubted our senses. Between us and the mountains of Mamore lay the Leven valley; its bottom invisible to us, its breadth nearly five miles. Across this great gap there suddenly travelled a broad wave of light, which seemed to break like a roller on the crest of our reef, and then stream in a wide, shimmering curtain across Glencoe. The wave was followed by another, and yet another. It was the aurora borealis. Henceforth its display continued all night, but with decreasing power.

We began to move west along the ridge. Slightly below us on the Glencoe side the craggy tower of the Chancellor seemed to be clothed in white light rather than frozen snow. It looked as savage as an Alpine *Aiguille*, and was linked to our ridge by a jagged snow-*arête*. Its final tower, which is the culminating point of a tall buttress, projects against the sky when seen from Glencoe, and the local people apply its name to the whole mountain, properly called Am Bodach.

We were now faced with a very sharp descent to the base of the next peak, Meall Dearg. We roped up, and cut steps in snow-ice down to the col. From the col to Meall Dearg, which is the highest point of the ridge, we had easy work in soft snow, and therefore more leisure to look at the mountains. Among snow-clad peaks under a good moon there is normally an icy shine and sparkle on the tops, most wonderful to behold. But to-night the moon's power and brilliancy were stolen by the light-waves from the north. They pulsed athwart the ridge with an almost mechanical rhythm, making our route as clear as in daylight. Our descent from Meall Dearg thus went easily until we came to a long steep slab encased in a double layer of brittle snow and ice. This passage, over which one scrambles thoughtlessly in summer, now caused us some anxiety.

When I tried axe-work on the slab I promptly found that if the snow and ice were completely removed the rock thus exposed was glazed and unsafe. If proper holds were cut, then the snow-ice was too brittle to endure any weight. An unpleasant compromise was our only course. I removed most of the snow and ice, but not all of it—I left a less doubtful substratum, by the use of which we disentangled ourselves from an unusual snare.

For a while we walked safely before one of the noblest sights in central Scotland—a direct view into the great north-east corrie of Bidean nam Bian. The icy triangle of Stob Coire nan Lochan, backed by the snow-dome of Bidean, threw outward to Glencoe two splendid ridges. Encircled by these rocky arms lay Coire nan Lochan, a broad snow-hollow, softly shining, gently shadowed, but austere. The closer one's approach to beauty the more pronounced grows that seeming austerity; on hills such true beauty would seem more evident in winter, just as it comes out in the character of men more in times of challenge than in days of ease.

We had arrived at the thinnest and most rocky section of the ridge. The glen below us lay deep in the grey shadow of frost, and a grey skin of ice covered Loch Achtriochtan. That men should choose to inhabit such frozen furrows of the earth's crust seemed mad and unnatural. But to balance on the silver wrinkles —ah! that was work for wise and enlightened men! When the ridge narrowed we expected trouble at two little pinnacles, which completely bar the crest and are frequently sheathed in thin ice. To our surprise we found them bare. We grasped them and swung round on the south side. We were even able to force a route directly up the vertical step in the ridge beyond. We were now on a long raised crest; one of the few places in Scotland where double cornices may torment the mountaineer. To-night there was no cornice but plenty of good snow. Its dry featheriness was searched out by the moonbeams, and its muted crunch underfoot was the only sound in the universe.

From this part of the ridge we were better able to see Bidean, to see it as a whole mountain—shaped by deep corries, thrusting its strong ridges outward to eight sparkling peaks, down-curving to lesser tops, emerging from the lowly blackness of Glencoe to a crescendo of light at the summit. That was the Bidean nam Bian of our physical world, by its mere presence there calling our hearts to the world inhabited by beauty.

The light-pulse of the aurora was beginning to lose a measure of its strength. We thought that dawn might come earlier up here than we reckoned, so we decided not to go on to the top of Stob Coire Leith, but to turn at once and start back along the ridge. At all costs we must reach Meall Dearg before sunrise. We faced up to an hour of toil and quick climbing; we drove our bodies relentlessly along the crest, dropped to the pinnacles, swung past and onwards, and so without pause or rest came again to the summit of Meall Dearg.

A cold, blue band lined the eastern horizon, with just a suspicion of light behind it. The hills below were snow-grey and night-bound, unlit by the moon, which was now thinly veiled by fast-travelling cloud. Dawn was a full hour away, so we hollowed seats in firm snow and sat with our backs against the cairn. At this point we enjoyed the qualities of our padded flying-suits. Despite quite exceptional frost we sat in comfort, observed the mountain scene, and were yet freed from the distraction of paralysing cold.

We were facing east. After a short desultory conversation we fell still—not a word was spoken for an hour. We drove from our heads every thought of self and simply observed the scene detachedly, allowing it, and nothing else, to flow into us. We were absorbed by the display that followed, which, although a continuous event and a unity, seemed to occur in three clear movements.

It was a simple enough scene: below us, in the near foreground, a short snow-ridge to Am Bodach; beyond, a wide expanse of moorland, swelling in white hills and pasturing flocks of ground mist. The horizon circled incredibly far away; throughout the length of its eastern arc was a faint flush of colour, turning to blue and deepening to black as the eye travelled to the zenith. The moon and stars were again bright. A simple scene, and not spectacular; for that very reason bearing in upon the mind more strongly its peculiar values.

On the land, silence; in the stars, calm. The more one listened to the earth's silence the more deep and intense did it grow: deeper still, and still more intense; one's mind was absorbed into it and pervaded by it. Thus there was conveyed into the mind by the hills and stars themselves and through part agency of the senses this knowledge that the night hush of earth is expectant: as though our universe were a live being, not a dead thing. Its silence is not the silence of sleep or death, but of life—intense—aware.

Towards the close of an hour the darkness lessened perceptibly. The horizon belt of pale cold pink developed deepening pastel shades of varied colour. No crude or startling effect was seen, but again this fell to advantage. We saw the more clearly how, at the touch of dawn light, the earth seemed to draw breath and stir to its shining.

The sunrise opened the final movement. At the first gleam of its rim great beams radiated across the earth's surface and middle air. Then the hills stood clear and the moors lay fresh, and the sky unfurled broad banners of blue. The act of adoration had begun, for this was the sun's hour of morning song. In that we shared; for we could say to ourselves: 'We had stood as the sure stars stand, and moved as the moon moves, loving the world.'

We came down in the forenoon to a point about a thousand feet above the Glencoe road. We now felt very sleepy, yet had all day before us; so we found a patch of sun-bathed turf, on which we curled up side by side and slept. There kept running through my head, between waking and sleeping, a recently read verse:

> Thou shouldst die as he dies,
> For whom none sheddeth tears;
> Filling thine eyes
> And fulfilling thine ears
> With the brilliance . . . the bloom
> and the beauty . . .

7 *Winter Days in Coire nan Lochan*

THE ICIEST WINTER that Scotland ever had in my own lifetime was the winter of 1947. For two whole months, mid-January to mid-March, the western highlands enjoyed continuous hard frost and clear sunny skies. There were only two bad days. Heretical mountaineers complained of too much ice in proportion to snow. On the other hand the gullies of Glencoe promised freak conditions and extreme severities. Early in January Donald McIntyre and I made a swift reconnaissance of Coire nan Lochan, and were startled to see that the South-Centre Gully, which is five hundred feet high, began with an unbroken ice-fall of two hundred and fifty feet. That lower half was all clear ice, not snow-ice. The upper half looked like hard-frozen snow with a cornice at the top. So far as we could discover only five ascents had ever been made, and not one in conditions so remarkable as the present. Indeed, was such a climb as this possible? At the end of January we returned to the corrie with Kenneth Dunn.

Success in Twisting Gully a month earlier had, I fear, given me optimistic notions of what we could attempt on our first ice-climb for the season. I had got up Twisting Gully despite a bad cold, but Twisting Gully had not been an ice-climb; rather was it a mixture of rock-snow-ice with the rock and snow predominating. One can get up very hard rocks when out of training if one strikes very good form. But good form is not enough on ice. The bodily strain is too high. First-class physical condition is essential. Our visit to the South-Centre Gully, therefore, was to be not so much a lesson in ice-climbing, as a discipline in humility.

There are mornings when it is ordained, no doubt for our benefit, that all things shall go wrong. And this was one. My car had starting trouble when we tried to leave Lagangarbh, so that we arrived late at the base of Bidean nam Bian. Our ascent to Coire nan Lochan had then to be made in soft snow, so that we spent three hours in reaching the corrie's bowl at three thousand feet. The time was a quarter to one. Otherwise conditions could not have been better. Nearly seven hundred feet above, our peak's white point stood against the sky. The lochans were invisible under a double sheet of snow and ice. A great stillness hung about the corrie, for the frost was hard. The cliffs facing us were no more than powdered with snow, but clad in drapings of ice, their most awesome feature being that deep split between the South and Centre Buttresses. We could detect no change in the lower half, except that a faint tinge of green had crept into the ice, like the green of a winter's sea, visible at a distance but not noticeable at close quarters.

We walked across the lochan and climbed snow-slopes to the foot of the gully. Its lower half held three ice-pitches of forty, thirty, and seventy feet respectively, linked by ice-slopes of lesser, but not much lesser, angle. The seventy-foot pitch, being high above us, seemed to be vertical, which we knew to be not true; while the lower one looked a more reasonable proposition, and that was equally untrue. The angle of an ice-pitch is always underestimated from close below. My own duty was to lead the long and exposed final pitch, and I accordingly asked McIntyre to deal with the first. We roped up.

He started cutting with his long axe, but the steepening angle at once forced him to carve handholds, and he then had recourse to a short ice-pick, which he could use one-handed with less effort. In twenty minutes' hard work he reached a bulge at the half-way mark, by which time he was so exhausted that he had to come down. On a second trial the bulge still over-taxed his strength. He then surrendered the lead. Watching him I had wrongly thought that he lacked only confidence, for he was a beginner on ice. But in this I was over-simplifying his troubles.

I soon discovered for myself what his primary trouble had been. The high angle imposed continuous strain on the arm and shoulder muscles—the left arm's strain of holding the body in, while the right took the still greater strain of cutting above the head—and our real handicap was a lack of training. The demands of severe ice-climbing are unrelenting. However, I cut over the bulge and neared the top of the pitch. But before going on we all consulted and faced facts. The ascent of forty feet had taken over an hour: a further two hundred feet of ice rose to the middle of the gully, and the time was 2 p.m. We abandoned the climb.

Here was one of the best ice-climbs in Scotland, and climbable —by a man fit enough to give it all that he had, plus hidden reserves if need were. We resolved to return next week. Meanwhile I trained by running hard each night for two miles and spending fifteen minutes every morning on exercises. At the end of a week I felt reinvigorated—at all levels the purgatorial process has its reward. We now wanted good weather and an early morning start. To be assured of the latter we planned to camp overnight in Coire nan Lochan. But the weather grew doubtful as the week drew to its close, for the frost slackened.

When McIntyre and I reached Glencoe by car on Saturday night, drizzle was falling. We halted at Altnafeadh, and looked out at the murk. It was a demoralizing sight. The night was surprisingly warm and convinced us that even at three thousand feet we should probably find thaw conditions with wet snow and ice. Glencoe offered us two dry roosts, the relative merits of which we now debated. One was Lagangarbh with a fire. The other was the summit of Bidean nam Bian. At three thousand seven hundred and sixty-six feet we could reckon on getting above the thaw-belt. With a swift resolution, which I have admired in him ever since that day, McIntyre urged that we pitch the tent on top of Bidean. Such was his enthusiasm that despite the dark and the drizzle I heard myself agreeing. Should the weather clear while we were on top we might descend into Coire nan Lochan in less than an hour. The summit was a good strategic position—barring storms.

At 9 p.m. we started uphill by way of Coire nam Beith.

Almost at once the skies began to clear. Stars twinkled. Unhappily there was no wind in the corrie; we opened our shirts and rolled up our sleeves—and were still warm. For two and a half hours we climbed by torchlight, then reached the snows of the upper corrie which gave us light enough to see clearly. As we neared the foot of the Church Door Buttress, which lies directly under the summit, the snow and air suddenly froze. We had climbed above the thaw-belt. Indeed we might have camped after all in Coire nan Lochan, but were now on the wrong side of the mountain. We cut our way to the summit by crusted snow-slopes.

At 12.30 a.m. we pitched our tent on the snow-cap beside the cairn. An icy wind from the south-east swept over the top. The exposure of the site was made extreme by the character of the mountain. Bidean is the highest peak of Argyll and dominates Glencoe and Appin. But how small a summit for so large a mountain! The flanks drop sharply to the corries, so that we felt pushed up at the sky on the tip of a finger. Despite freezing wind we made supper in comfort, for the tent had a sewn-in groundsheet and circular sleeve-doors. We could seal it hermetically, and relax in a warm fug. Winter camping need not be 'tough' when properly ordered. Two or three layers of newspaper insulated us from ground cold, and the continuous patter of snowdrift on the cambric, reminding us every moment of the airy and arctic world around, increased our sense of warmth in sleeping-bags.

After supper McIntyre went out to look at the weather. He at once called me to come, and the urgency in his voice made me hurry. At the moment of emerging I was conscious only of piercing cold.

'Look,' said McIntyre, 'above and below.'

A black sky, densely packed with electric-blue stars, winked and glittered frostily. The valleys likewise were black, but a grey sea-mist on Loch Linnhe thrust long tongues along the floors of Glencoe and the Leven valley, and licked around the base of Bidean. This tide of mist looked so much like cloud of the sky, yet flowed so distantly, that our peak by comparison pierced the firmament. We were poised in space at heights unlawful. After our first shock of wonder a wave of cold air broke over the peak and chilled us to the bone. We took a last quick look round and dived back to shelter.

It is idle to pretend that we slept well that night. We dozed. One sleeping-bag each was not enough. Early in the morning we peeped through a ventilator. Thick mist had fallen around us. Each time a gust of wind seized and shook the canvas we heard a sharp crackle from all over the roof, which sounded like the blatter of icy spiculae, travelling fast. In such conditions the gully would be impossible, and even ridge-walking an especial hell. We therefore lay back in our bags all the more happily and listened, between gusts, to that peculiarly soothing sound—the whisper of snow along the walls of a tent.

After a slothful morning and late breakfast we struggled outside to strike camp. Too late we discovered our mistake about the weather. A skin of ice, perhaps one-eighth of an inch thick, had formed over the tent fabric, and this it was that crackled to the wind-shake. The snow was not drifting. Moreover, the mist was only a cloud-cap on the summit—the other eight tops were clear! We walked the length of the north ridge over Stob Coire nan Lochan to Aonach Dubh. Dusky clouds billowed over the cols and rolled around the peaks and tumbled down to the corries, but spacious gaps were always left for the brown and red of the moorland heather to flame up from below. It showed how wrong is the common belief that the winter scene is without colour. The truth is that the colours are richer and warmer than those of summer.

The frost was hard in Glencoe that night, and continued for the rest of the week. Our hopes for a third attempt on the gully were high. Dunn and McIntyre joined me in Glencoe on Saturday night. We went up to Coire nan Lochan and pitched the tent in the middle of the loch. The night was windless and still, but the sky was veiled by a thin film of cloud, the presence of which we might not even have suspected had it not been illuminated from time to time by a flickering of the aurora. Stars were dim and sparse, but visibility was good and the corrie shone gently. There was nothing gentle, however, in the beauty of its west wall, where five cliffs towered stark and spiky, knifing the sky with a cold glitter like steel. The wild austerity of these frozen crags made a startling counter to the flowing lines of the corrie's bowl. Together they put forth a double aspect of beauty, each drawing out the power of its opposite, but both integrated in the beauty of the whole, named Coire nan Lochan.

That night we slept well. Profiting by our last experience we wore our kapoc-filled flying-suits inside our sleeping-bags. We woke at daybreak feeling warm, but shuddered when we heard the wind. It was blowing hard from the south-east, battering the tent. We looked out at sheets of drift driving across the corrie floor, and storming up the cliffs, which only occasionally loomed high and menacing through the spume. The weather looked like building up to a blizzard, so we hurriedly breakfasted, snatched a good snow-climb between the North and Central Buttresses, and withdrew, in moderating wind, to Glencoe.

Throughout the remainder of February Glencoe was blessed with unfailing sun and frost. Our final attack was now timed for 2nd March, when we should be reinforced by H. W. Tilman. He and McIntyre arrived in Glencoe on 29th February, and enjoyed an icy traverse of the Aonach Eagach ridge—despite delay in the glen with a frozen car engine. Boiling water, they said, had frozen while they were pouring it into the empty radiator. When I arrived at night and heard this tale I could not altogether suppress feelings of satisfaction. It seemed to me a tale of good omen. Our gully ought to be in perfect condition. This time I could think of nothing that could stop us getting on to our climb. The sky was clear and starry, and the moon so bright that we preferred to walk up and down outside rather than sit indoors. We stopped down at Lagangarbh that night, for the elapse of one month gave us daylight enough to dispense with a high camp.

Tilman is an early riser and works like a beaver on hut chores, so that we had time on hand to deal with our once more frozen car. At 9 a.m. we drove to the foot of Bidean and reached the upper corrie in two hours. The gully remained in the same general condition as before, the lower half being pure ice, but if anything thicker and more substantial.

Tilman urged that we try to by-pass the first ice-pitch by a rock-rib to its left. The rib projected seventy feet and bore a plating of snow and ice. None the less it might go more quickly if it *were* climbable. To allow us a choice of alternatives, yet not waste time, I asked McIntyre to begin work on the ice-pitch while I started on the rib. The crest of the rib went well to the midway point—good holds lay under the snow-plaster. On the upper twenty feet, however, the coating was thin ice with poor and scanty holds underneath. My technique was to balance on a boot-nail on these nicks and watch my holds take shape through the gouts of ice-spray that sprang from the axe-blows, then force every upward move. I reached a snowy platform on top, and brought up the others.

There followed a hundred-foot run-out on a thick, steep slope of clear ice set between straight walls. It gave joyous and satisfying climbing. I could take a full swing with my axe and hit the slope as hard as I liked. At each blow the pick drove in with a dull *click*, and the shaft vibrated on the palm of the hand. The chips came out clean at the third or fourth blows, and whirred down the gully. I reached a small spike projecting from the gully-bed. It could not have appeared more opportunely; for the slope steepened into an overhang about fifty feet above, and it seemed that my best course was to make a hard right traverse on to a raised chute, which now filled the right-hand half of the gully. The chute was seventy feet high and well iced. I brought up Tilman, who tied himself to the spike and brought up McIntyre. I fetched out my short ice-pick.

Since the chute was a raised one, my first move was to traverse rightward across its vertical wall, and so on to its upper face. The ice-work on the next fifty feet was all one-handed cutting, but from good foothold, for the ice must have been nearly a foot thick. The crux came just below the top, where I ran into a five-foot bulge. Ice overhangs can't be climbed. They have to be cut away. I spent a full forty minutes on these five feet. The excessive angle permitted no weight behind the axe-blows and the two-hundred-foot ice-fall beneath forbade jerky movement. Tilman and McIntyre could see nothing of me, their only means of gauging hope for the future being the volume of icy shrapnel raining through space and the fitful movement of rope. Writing later of his own view of this passage McIntyre said:

'The gully-walls rose steeply to imprison us. Ice-chips raced in a steady stream down the ribbon of ice and disappeared over the lip of the pitch below. They made a pleasant, tinkling, swishing sound as they went. The mist opened. The sun shone on the white crest of the Aonach Eagach, the lower slopes of which were rich brown. Cloud shadows moved leisurely. How pleasing was the blue of the sky above the white pitch and the black rock-walls! A fleecy cloud rushed over the top and, watching it, I nearly over-balanced. The mist closed in again, and we were conscious only of the pitch. For a long time the ice-chips still sped downwards; intermittently the rope ran out a few more inches.'

Fighting the out-pull of gravity I cautiously eased myself up the ladder of notches. Then the angle fell back and I was up.

I climbed firm snow for twenty feet and brought up Tilman. This was his first ascent of a Scottish ice-pitch and I was most curious to know what he thought of it. At last his head appeared over the top. He stopped on his last hold and looked up at me from under his eyebrows. 'This climb is an eye-opener,' he said, and climbed up. Tilman is not a talker.

He now took the lead and cut steps up two hundred and fifty feet of hard snow to the cornice. Its overhang looked flimsy and unsafe, and was unusual in being complete: no merely vertical passage offered a highway to the summit. To McIntyre, being relatively guileless, we gave the nasty job of swarming up first.

Tilman and I gave a double belay; I thought it more than likely that the cornice would collapse.

It held.

We finished our climb, and the sixth ascent of South-Centre Gully, at 4 p.m. The first sight that met our eyes when we crested the ridge was Loch Linnhe, and I can remember nothing else. All the colours of the encircling hills were in it, rich and subtle, the most potent of mountain bouquets. Under its influence, and a strong influence it must have been, I pitied Tilman. He had to hasten south this night and prepare to leave for the Himalaya.

Right before our eyes was the true country.

8 *The Leac Mhor*

THE SKY WAS DARKENING with thunder-cloud and a high wind was blowing up Loch Linnhe. I turned my car off the Fort William road and drove on board the Corran ferry. Then we got out and looked anxiously at the weather. With Robert Anderson, the artist, and Douglas Scott, the photographer, I was crossing to Ardgour to attempt an unknown rock-climb on Garbh Bheinn, and to make a record of it for a guide-book by the Scottish Mountaineering Club. One last problem had to be solved at all costs: what was the line of the direct route up the North-east Buttress? The buttress was twelve hundred feet high; an ascent of very hard standard had been made in 1943, but the record was scanty, the line of the route doubtful, the difficulties undescribed. Less than one month before, in May 1947, two very good climbers had been defeated before they got half-way up. Therefore good weather for ourselves was a matter of some urgency.

I turned to the ferryman. 'The sky looks bad,' I said, shaking my head.

'Yess, indeed, it iss a bad sky,' he replied. 'And you are the lucky man to be getting across. Thiss run will be our last run to-night.'

The boat began to lurch as the waves heaved under it. Alarm at the risk of the car's shifting position stirred up my memory. 'Did the ferry not sink once before the war?' I asked.

'Once!' exclaimed the ferryman joyfully. 'Och, man, it sank several times! But you will be all right now,' said he, 'for the new turn-table will float if the boat sinks under it. Och, yess, you will be all right.'

I began to wish that I was safely lodged on the face of some tall cliff. However, we relished the salt tang of the wind and the boisterous force of it. Although the sea ran high it did

Garbh Bheinn—North-east Buttress and Leac Mhor
lm, Leac Mhor

make us feel, by the time we grounded, that we had had value for money. Ardgour is notoriously hard of access, and when it adds high wind to the defence of its frontiers, one lands, if one lands at all, with a sense of privilege.

We drove south to Garbh Bheinn. There are no hotels near the mountain nor any other accommodation. Therefore we proposed to pitch a tent in Coire an Iubhair (the corrie of the yew-tree), which curves below the east face. We walked a quarter of a mile up the glen to a stretch of soft flat turf beside the river. Before we could unload our gear the skies split open. There was a blinding flash and a peal of thunder. The rain rushed down. Our tent seemed to go up with the speed of an opening umbrella. The guys and pegs were not nicely aligned, but luckily there was no wind in the corrie. We made supper.

We ate our meal to the loudest storm-music and our bedtime lullaby was the swish of rain on the tent-canvas. This had seemed daunting at first in view of our plans, but now cheered us the more the harder it came. Experience of west highland hills suggested that torrential downpours at night are often followed by a good morning. The weather truly to be dreaded is the windless drizzle.

We wakened next day to a blue sunny sky. At 9 a.m. we walked two miles up Coire an Iubhair to the foot of the North-east Buttress, where Anderson made an outline sketch and Scott took photographs. I endeavoured to trace out the line of the route. Although twelve hundred feet high, the cliff is crossed by three terraces, the middle one lying at a slant so that they form a reversed letter S, which divides the face into four tiers. The first tier looked of moderate difficulty; the second short and hard; but the third impossible. It is formed in one enormous slab, topped by an overhang. The last tier of all is a great tower.

It was obvious that the third tier was the point of supreme difficulty. The angle was excessively steep for a smooth slab, and I could hardly imagine how it might be possible to force a route through the overhang, which ran the full breadth of the slab and looked eighty feet high. There must surely be some breach invisible to us. Thus far the true size of the slab had not registered on my brain, for the scale of the buttress being so big, the slab fell into place as one normal-size tier among four. It was Anderson, the artist, with an eye trained to assess proportions, who first realized the import of what we saw.

'That slab,' said he, 'must be four hundred feet high at least and four hundred feet wide. One of the biggest in Scotland.'

I looked again. 'By heaven!' I exclaimed, 'you 're right. But there *is* no other single slab anything like the size in Scotland. The Cioch Slab in the Cuillin is barely ninety feet. We must get a name for this.'

'Let 's try and climb it first,' suggested Scott—'*if* we can.'

We had spent nearly an hour lying back in the heather; so we resolved to economize time by cutting out the first tier. This we did by means of an easy gully to its left, which led us on to the first terrace. The second tier was the shortest one, perhaps two hundred feet, and our route started near the left-hand side. We tied on the rope, and asked Scott to lead. He climbed only a few feet, hovered in indecision, and then came down to think again. The rock was a mixture of rough gneiss and polished quartzite, and slabby. The quartzite was hard as marble and Scott found his boot-nails very apt to glance off it. The rock was much more suitable for rubbers, but unfortunately was wet in patches despite the sunshine; and rubbers on wet rock are of more danger than help. However, Scott reckoned that the dry patches were big enough to allow us to use them almost exclusively. We should surely find some way of avoiding the wet quartzite.

Scott and I changed into rubbers and left our boots on the terrace. We climbed fifty feet on small, outward-sloping holds to a long grass ledge, where we stopped to bring on Anderson, who, not having rubbers, was determined to climb in boots and to rely on the rope for security. But these fifty feet convinced him of the worst. He found the struggle too severe a strain to be enjoyable. Scott and I, moreover, finding that projecting rock-spikes were barely adequate for belaying the rope, urged him to take off his boots. He did so, and threw them down to the terrace; henceforth stocking-soles and wet feet were his portion.

A further hundred feet of very difficult climbing led us to the base of a long overhang which ran along the tier like the eaves of a roof. We were forced to start edging to the right directly below it, taking our footholds on a slabby shelf. The drop below was a big one, foothold hard to find, and the way of escape hidden; thus the passage became most exciting. We began to feel, increasingly from now onwards, the sense of exposure on a great mountain-wall, where mistakes in climbing craft are barred, on pain of swift penalty. Treading delicately along the shelf for fifty feet we rounded the overhang, and saw before us an almost vertical wall, which was none the less so well weathered that we enjoyed good holds. Easy climbing led to the second terrace.

The principal obstacle of the day was now before us—the great slab, four hundred feet square with its overhung top. The bottom of the slab was either undercut or vertical to a height of twenty or thirty feet throughout its length. Thus our very access to the slab seemed to be a problem. Our eyes were drawn to a little bay below the left half, from which a wide crack or groove split the slab nearly to the great overhang, but exhibited another very short overhang at the half-way point. That groove was our only hopeful line; the slab to either side of it was uncompromising, destitute of belays for the rope. We therefore committed ourselves to the groove, but with a most uneasy awareness that should we get so far as the great overhang, and be stopped by it, we should be defeated very late in the day, and faced with an anxious descent.

We started from the bay. On the first vertical section we were aided by fissured rock and ledges. One had to summon up energy determinedly and expend it on strong arm-pulls; then the angle eased and the technical difficulties increased. Our delight in the climbing increased commensurately; for the situation grew ever more exhilarating as the wide sweep of the unclimbable slab on our right opened up to the thread of our route. We felt alive in every vein and tissue. We were poised in space, muscle and nerve tense, amid acres of arching rock, smooth rock in the sense of offering little lodgment for hand or foot, but coarse and crystalline, studded with quartzite that gleamed white on its grey setting. The beauty of it struck to the eye. Through the very uncertainties of our climb my mind became unusually observant, embracing many simple things that commonly pass unregarded. While searching for a handhold the eye would alight on a blade of grass peeping from a crack, and see the amazing grace of its fluting, the fresh brightness of its green against the rock; and although the joy was that of one second the memory lived on. We all know leagues of hill-side heather, but stand on the ledge of a tall cliff, look at a single shoot sprouting from a joint in the wall, its perfect leaf-design, the pureness of the bell, the harmony between the rich green and the purple, and there, in that one branch, you see a beauty matching the quality of a hill. Touch gently an uncurling frond of fern or the new shoot of a juniper bush—watch it closely, and the heart is suddenly filled with a love for all things young and growing. There is in these a tenderness most simple and exquisite, made doubly clear by contrast with the severity of rock-work.

We crept slowly up the great slab until we came to a huge boulder that straddled the groove. It looked most unstable. Scott tested it cautiously, while we watched with exceeding wariness. It was proved to be safe and the party gathered behind it for rest and lunch. Directly ahead of us loomed the short midway overhang. It looked much more fearsome at close quarters than it did from the terrace, and is, in fact, the crux of the climb. Conversation was desultory. Each of us felt much concerned to try conclusions without delay. Scott and I moved up to a small stance at the base of the overhang.

The groove was here broad and shallow, but abruptly narrowed to a ten-foot chimney which leaned gently outward. Since the groove continued above the chimney the obvious course was to try a direct attack. Scott tried several times, but failed. He tried again, standing on my shoulder, but in trying to make an awkward up-stretch wrenched a muscle in his back. He was now temporarily out of action, so I took over the lead.

I too failed on the overhang. One alternative remained. It was possible to climb on to the face of the great slab to our left. The angle was high, the rock exposed, the holds minute; but there was no other route. While climbing on to the slab I found it essential to use a wet, grassy foothold. This meant that relying on finger-tip holds I had to stand on the next sketchy foothold and dry my rubbers against the stocking of the opposite leg, an operation that placed a great strain on the fingers. After two more moves I was faced by a belt of quartzite. To my horror I found that this quartzite too was wet, and wet quartzite is like wet ice to rubbers. The holds were still tiny. I came down at once. Nothing more could be done. We were beaten—beaten not so much by the rock as by the thunderstorm of the preceding night. Any attempt to force the route in its present condition would be a courting of disaster.

We withdrew to the unstable boulder. Anderson, and then Scott, climbed down out of sight. I paid out rope and looked down into the distant corrie. Far below me a small white speck was travelling fast up the glen, bright as a snowflake against the brown hill opposite. The gull turned towards us and wheeled in a great arc over the corrie. Such superb mastery of space and depth made a defeated rock-climber feel positively dizzy. The liveliness of its white caused me to look with sudden interest at the brown hill which had been its background. That was a plain and humble hill if ever there was one. A shapely hump without the distinction of great cliffs or tower-like summit. I examined it in detail and detachedly, allowing it to make its own impression on me. The result was quite unexpected. The mountains had hit hard and defeated us—I confess we were just a little despondent. Now they came like some adversary of goodwill and smiled into our eyes. They won an unreserved devotion.

The slant of the sun across the hill picked out and burnished a multitude of scattered crags. They were light grey and clean-washed, and I felt refreshed in mind just by looking at them. The hill was dimpled by shadow where the hollows lay, but the broad sun-struck flank was a quilt of many colours; the quiet green of young uncurling bracken, the rust of massed heather, dark against old pale-yellow turf through which sparse new grass was pushing, the flash of torrents, and far up to the summit a cloud intolerably bright.

From each feature, all part of one mountain, there came its own glow of beauty, an arresting power. It evoked awe and reverence. These feelings stirred the thought that only a little earlier

I was warming myself at the flame of that same glow in a solitary blade of grass and fern-frond, in one shoot of heather and a stone of quartz. The sweep of hill in front of me contained these little material things by the million, not one of them visible in its own form or beauty, but uniting to clothe the mountain, building a new beauty of feature, in the glow of which the mountain shone, shone for miles across Argyll, a burning beacon of truth.

'My One Beauty is in all things.' By the light of the beacon read the word on the mountain-face. From the minutest body or the greatest concourse there shines out the one light of its underlying reality, plain for all men to love who will look—a light of innumerable rays, any one of which, if artificially separated by the mind, an aspect to be named material or spiritual or mental; but all in fact integrated, one light of truth. When glimpsed even most fleetingly its glory is too great to be given title. We separate a ray for study, and call our act the method of science or philosophy, but in the very act divorce it from reality. The light of truth is to be sought whole, or it will not be seen.

From somewhere below me there drifted up a call from Scott. I threw him the slack of the rope and climbed down, but have little recollection of that descent save a general one of steepness, difficulty, and a spacious void, until at last we reached the second terrace. An urgent time problem then pressed for an answer. If we were forced to descend the very difficult second tier we should arrive too late at Corran to catch the ferry. Therefore we followed the slanting terrace downward until we came to its end, where a rock-wall overlooked the gully on the flank of the buttress. We had no knowledge that a route could be found down that wall, but we tried. At one point we doubled a rope round a rock-spike and slid down for fifty feet; otherwise the rock was easy. We trundled down the scree-filled gully, made a detour to get our boots from the first terrace, and raced out to the middle of the corrie. We stopped there for a minute and looked back.

The buttress towered. The sun was now behind it, causing

it to look starker and more noble than ever. The great slab was vast and bare.

'That slab is the eighth wonder of the world,' said Anderson. 'We *must* find a name worthy of it.' Then after a while, and triumphantly: 'I 've got it—Leac Mhor. . . .'

'Lek Vore.' I sounded the words and strongly approved. 'What does it mean, and how do you spell it?'

'It means the Great Slab, and you spell it . . .'

We have not been back to climb the Leac Mhor since that day. In course of time we assuredly shall go back. But does it matter whether a man gets to the very top? If he penetrate to the heart of the Leac Mhor the mountain is his.

9 *The Forgotten Cliff of Aonach Dubh*

IN THE COURSE of our numerous visits to Bidean nam Bian during the winter of 1946–7, Donald McIntyre and I passed half a dozen times below an unclimbed cliff on the flank of Aonach Dubh, which walls the long lower part of Coire nan Lochan. Like scores of other climbers before us, we saw and admired—and passed thoughtlessly on. Between sight and reflection there seemed to come an occult barrier. Not until our sixth passing, in the company of Tilman, did we really *see* it, in the full sense. It was four hundred yards long and six hundred feet high on the south-east wall of Aonach Dubh—only one thousand feet above the Glencoe road, from which it is invisible. The angle looked remarkably high. And no one had climbed there! And this 1947! Truly it seemed incredible that in Glencoe—the most popular climbing-ground in Scotland—a virgin cliff of that size should pass unnoticed so long.

'What are we waiting for?' I asked McIntyre rhetorically.

'Spring—and the first good week-end.'

On one of these protracted May evenings, when the sun shines long and low up the fifteen miles of the glen, and the white foam on the River Coe takes an unaccustomed sparkle, McIntyre and I crossed the ford below Coire nan Lochan. This undertaking was no light one. We were heavily loaded, the river was high and twenty yards wide, and our route lay over the tops of spray-splashed boulders, irregularly dotting the water in a long, curved line down-stream. Of all boulder-hoppers McIntyre is *the* most expert. He learned the art in the Cairngorms at the age of sixteen. Accordingly, while I dallied on the brink, searching for my non-existent courage, McIntyre gave his amazing display of animal grace. From boulder to foam-washed boulder he leapt like an antelope, but with the speed of a gazelle, coming down always at the right angle to make his instantaneous spring for the staggered stone ahead. His rucksack seemed to serve all the better for its weight to steady and ballast him. The exhibition must have given him a tensely thrilling enjoyment, because on reaching the far side he strolled off with studied nonchalance, not looking back, to signify that all this was a mere nothing. I smiled delightedly at his high spirits. I was duly impressed. I was even inspired to follow, like the common goat.

An hour's climb up the corrie, which would be more accurately called a ravine, brought us to a black crag on the left side, directly facing the unclimbed cliff. A big overhang of the crag gave a sheltered bivouac, much improved by some person unknown, who had built a stone wall round the north end. We spread our groundsheets and sleeping-bags. We cooked a meal. Later, while we lay in our sleeping-bags, the sun set behind the cliff in front. The sun was thus invisible, but light reflected from a cloud stained the cliff's face dark oak.

The next morning was dry so we rose early. Our bivouac was on the shaded side of the glen, but the sun was already warming the uppermost rocks of the East Cliff, and every detail of its face was clear and precise in the hard morning light. We examined the rock intently.

The cliff was divided vertically by a bow-shaped chimney, shallow in its lower half. Beneath the face ran a wide grassy shelf, marked at its midway point under the Bow by a short crag, from the cracked top of which twin rowan-trees sprouted. The Bow and rowans made useful landmarks, for the cliffs to their right and left were of quite different aspect. The left-hand half was a blank face, unbroken by rake or terrace, but seamed by countless ledges. The right-hand half was divided horizontally by a broad terrace. Above the terrace a great basin scooped the cliff, topped by enormous overhangs. Below the terrace was a convex wall, slabby towards the right.

We were preoccupied over breakfast. We had not a notion where we should go first. Indeed, we had no clear idea as yet

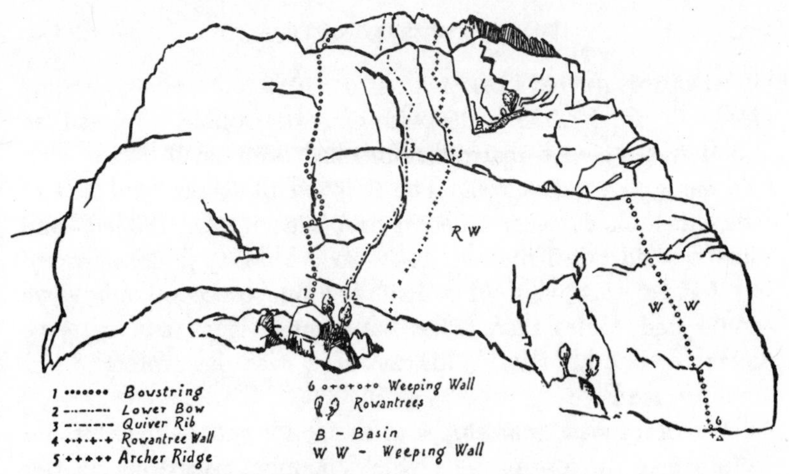

Aonach Dubh, east face from Bivouac

what the qualities of the rock might be. So that after breakfast we naturally gravitated towards the middle, thinking that were we able to make a route there, we might at the same time reconnoitre the cliffs on either side. Then, well to the left of the Bow, we saw the Bow-string—a long chimney starting about a hundred feet up the face. If we could reach it the route would go.

The leading of the Bow-string was to be McIntyre's work, his first essay on unclimbed rock, and so a great occasion. For the highest delight that rock-climbing offers is searching out one's own way on crags unknown to men—doubt of the issue, encounter with the unexpected, the sense of exploration. However, to economize our time, 'through leads' were desirable. The first pitch being easy I took that for myself. I climbed eighty feet to a tilting slab about the size of a hearthstone. The wall above being now vertical I surrendered the lead to McIntyre. He led through, crossing the slab rightwards to an awkward corner, up which he scrambled. I joined him later on a grass ledge. Thence we climbed into the chimney's foot. The interior presented no serious obstacle, and on either side the outer walls obviously offered the better route. By these we continued over clean and easy rocks to the top of the cliff.

That reconnaissance had been a quite remarkable climb. It

is taken for granted in Glencoe that a new route of six hundred feet will provide the leader with extreme trouble. Instead, so good was the rock that difficulties had been small. However, we dared not generalize. The rock on the right-hand half of the cliff looked a very different proposition. On the left-hand side we had noted the rock to be so indefinite, so criss-crossed by ledges, that no doubts disturbed our peace of mind—we could find routes there when we wanted them, and so leave them for another day. Our task now was the exploration of the Terrace Face.

We descended grass slopes at the south end of the cliff and returned to the foot of the Bow. The most fascinating quarter of the whole cliff was that above the Terrace, on either side of the great Basin. We should do well if we could open up the rocks there. We accordingly climbed at speed, unroped, up the lower Bow, and came out on the Terrace at its left-hand end. From here the cliff above looked alarmingly steep. But we were warmed up and at last on the warpath. The hardest-looking climb we could see was an almost vertical face of three hundred and fifty feet just to the right of the Bow. It was beautiful rock, of the shade of silver birch-bark, quite unlike the brown rock nearer the Basin. I did not seriously expect the sheer cliff to go, but felt the invitation of the lower part, where a hundred-foot rib projected like the Bow's quiver. Could we reach the top of it, who knows but some as yet invisible fracture might allow us to scale the unscalable.

McIntyre led the first half of the Quiver and I the second half. The rock had become exposed by the time we hauled ourselves on to the big platform on top. I looked up and confess to a twinge of conscience at encouraging McIntyre to face as leader the dire troubles in front. But I need not have worried. He is a geologist—the Ideal Geologist made flesh. Rock in any shape or form, at whatever angle, is the delight of his heart. He loves rock, in all circumstances. If he were ever about to fall off an overhang he would, just before parting company with the rock, draw his tongue over the surface to bring out the colour. I have observed him do this at other times and feel quite confident he would do it then.

'Your lead, Donald,' I commiserated. 'Bad luck.'

Looking all the while keenly up at the cliff, he swung his waist-knot to the rear, and his mouth tightened. He was in good training, I reflected, watching the spare face and clear eye. That would help him much when his situation became hopeless, and he had to come down; for such seemed the likely end to his efforts. Both to our right and directly above, the crag was impossibly smooth. On our left, however, a ledge ran diagonally up the wall for several feet, then appeared to peter out at the sheer edge. To this edge he slowly scrambled, and vanished beyond. My heart bled for him, especially when the rope continued to run out for another score of feet. His position must be getting more and more precarious, and return correspondingly hazardous. I began to look around for a still better belay. But still the rope ran out, and at no funereal pace. I stared in wonder as the whole hundred feet passed through my hands.

'Come on!' came the distant shout. I picked my way to the edge, passed cautiously round, and found myself on a smooth precipice. Running diagonally up and across, an unbroken thread of superb holds curved all the way to the top. The extreme airiness of the staircase made me tread warily, but the climbing could hardly be called difficult; perhaps moderate would be the better description. But exhilarating! The groove is unique in Glencoe. Agag's Groove on Buachaille, for example, is a wide groove, not a slender line like this. If we met no difficulties neither did we feel disappointment. We were charmed.

Down again to the foot. We had time for one more complete ascent, and this time had the good fortune to pick out, as our introductory passage to the Terrace, a route of high educational value, teaching us much about the rock peculiar to this East Cliff of Aonach Dubh, and so helping us later. The route chosen went up the great wall about twenty paces to the right of the rowan-tree block. Fifteen feet up was a grassy ledge, where we built a cairn. McIntyre started. On this occasion it was probably his very knowledge of rock that contributed to his defeat. For the rock was rhyolite—the same rock as on Buachaille Etive Mor. And at that angle rock on Buachaille is not normally climbable over long stretches. He went up ten feet and found the rock pushing him almost out of balance; he could see the pitch continuing at that angle for another eighty feet; he could not feel confident of getting holds to serve him throughout all that height: accordingly, and rightly, down he came.

I tried instead. The rock did require to be forced at ten feet, but I thought that I might be safe in pushing the fight as far as twenty. Holds were small but good. They *had* to be good; that was why it was so astonishing that they should still be of the same quality at twenty feet, at thirty, forty—right on until ninety feet of rope dragged heavily at my waist. I had a good stance then. McIntyre joined me and the rest was easy. At two hundred and fifty feet we emerged on the Terrace.

Directly above us, and just to the right of the Quiver, a ridge stood straight as an archer's back. It was obvious, at the first glance, that if this stiffly upright ridge could be made to go it would give us the best climb on Terrace Face. The upper third of the ridge looked impossible, but after our Quiver experience we were not to be intimidated. I started up.

Brown, tough rock. Coarse and clean. No trace of loose stone. We climbed two long pitches on the crest and swore that no better rock could be found in Glencoe. Then the edge sprang up fearsomely, little overhangs thrusting out against the clouds. I tried to climb through them, weaving a way among a tangle of slabs and walls, and failed. The descent taxed my ingenuity to the limit. We were obliged after that to traverse a thin ledge on to the right-hand flank of the ridge, which overlooked the Basin and its mammoth overhangs. Our only hope of ascent was then to go ninety feet straight up the vertical flank to a little corner under the crest. The wall was not broken: in other words, not climbable had the rock been normal. I might have been persuaded to turn away, for the place was exposed, had it not been for our recent experience down at the wall near the rowan-trees. My mind was becoming accustomed, at last, to the idea that we could expect all rock hereabouts to be *ab*normal. So I made an attempt.

Tiny well-made holds came readily to hand and foot. By the time I had travelled fifty feet and saw that I had still as far to go, the strain on my credulity was again only supportable as an after-effect of Rowan-tree Wall. Otherwise my lot would have been defeat by doubt. Were all the excellent holds required by the angle really there? They were too small to be visible more than a few feet ahead. Always, when I looked beyond, the cupboard was bare—hope could draw from it no nourishment. Yet at every step I took the next well-formed hold materialized out of the blank wall. I seized it, moved, and there was the next hold: I seized, moved, and there it was! Never failing. Such exercise in unflinching faith is common in rock-climbing; but certainly it is uncommon for our faith to be so fully justified. Not that each move was easy. The climbing was hard.

I was overjoyed when I reached the corner, and so was McIntyre, judged by the sparkle in his eye as he lifted himself up out of space. 'A severe!' he exclaimed. 'On the first ascent,' I agreed, '—less another time.' He took the lead and passed on to a second corner, fifteen feet up on the right, where he waited for me. His final move was an exit over the right wall, his body curved over thin air while he wrestled with awkward rock. I followed. Easy rocks led to the top.

We returned to our bivouac and supper. The cliffs across the ravine now wore a very different look to our appreciative eyes. The inscrutable visage of unknown crags in the morning had been transformed in a twinkling to a friendly and open face. 'Come back,' they said, 'often.' And there was need of return. Never before had any cliff presented to us four new routes in one day, and we could see for ourselves that another four awaited. We had still to penetrate the Basin, from which routes should go right and left. The huge wall to the left of the Bow should give a long route of no great difficulty. Below the right-hand end of the Terrace, splendidly arched slabs were marked, although dry, by the dark stain of a water-slide. This weeping wall seemed to promise the hardest climbing on the cliff. There were other possibilities.

So that we were very happy. Reason, being thus encouraged, suggested that our surest way of *not* enjoying the cliffs to the full was to keep them to ourselves until we had staked claims and worked them out. Before returning we must pass on the news to other climbers. The feast was spread.... A second reflection was that new climbs of extreme severity are not hard to find in Glencoe, but the discovery of simple and modestly difficult routes is so hard that something like an intervention of Divine Providence is required for their revelation. It was our remarkable feat this day to have made on Aonach Dubh no route of real severity. That East Cliff was a humble and generous cliff, giving freely the sound climbs that are the daily bread of the rock-climber; therefore of more value than many airy severities that I had happened on in the past.

On the East Cliff all men may climb.

Photo by A. D. S. Macpherson

MAMORE FOREST, LOCHABER
Sgor an Iubhair from the Devil's Ridge

Photo by Douglas

THE CROWBERRY TOWER

From the south

At the right-hand base is the snow-ledge by which escape can be made from the cre
Crowberry Ridge, which is hidden behind the Tower. At the bottom right-hand cor
the top of Curved Ridge, and the top of Easy Gully on its left

Photo by Douglas Scott

THE BUACHAILLE ETIVE MOR (North Face from Glencoe)

'he North Buttress falls direct from the summit, with the Crowberry Gully on its left. To left again is the Crowberry Ridge, its crest in the sunshine. The Crowberry Tower is ninent in the sun below and to the left of the summit.

'he Shelf route runs up the north flank of Crowberry Ridge midway between Crowberry .y and the crest. Its lower part may be seen as a dark score on the flank.

Photo by D. McKellar

GARBH BHEINN OF ARDGOUR (from Coire an Iubhair)
The Great Gully is seen directly under the summit

THE PLATEAU OF AONACH BEAG, LOCHABER

The Moor of Rannoch is in the distance

Photo by A. D. S. Macpherson

THE MOOR OF
RANNOCH
Winter

THE CARN DEARG CLIFFS, BEN NEVIS

Castle Buttress is the tongue-shaped buttress on the right, demarcated left and right by the South and North Castle Gullies. To its right is the broad Castle Ridge, and to its left the main mass of the Carn Dearg Buttress

Photo by W. S. Thomson

Photo by A. M. Sm

ON THE EASTERN BUTTRESS, SRON NA CICHE, SKYE

10 Rock-climbing in Rum

MY DAY OF RETURN to the Cuillin of Skye after six years of war was not, it seemed, to be a day of rejoicing. Yellow clouds were billowing over Sgurr Alasdair when I scrambled alone up the last rocks to the cairn. The rain sheeted down. The month was September 1945, and the wind wintry. Hardly a sign could be seen of the rock-peaks around me, save at moments when the clouds sank and resurged. I paused at the top for a few seconds only, but in these seconds a rift opened in the cloud and closed. Through the long shafts of that rift I caught a glimpse of a steel-like sheet of sea and one island. It lay ten miles out. There was a cluster of graceful peaks at the south end of it, but the north half was low. As I climbed down the south ridge the scene stayed vivid in mind: the Hebrides are enchanters of old, and I saw no other view.

A cluster of dark and secret peaks on a sheet of steel-grey sea. An unknown island—unknown at least to myself. It could be none other than Rum. I soon discovered that few of my mountaineering friends knew more of it than I. But throughout the following year I slowly gathered information.

'The whole trouble about Rum,' said a veteran mountaineer, 'is the trouble in landing. It 's a private deer-forest. There 's no pier and the owner discourages visitors—her ferry may refuse to lift you off the steamer. That means you 've got to raid the island by motor-boat from Mallaig, at a cost of £5 10*s*. And after that you 've got to get *off* the island again. You can buy no food on it, you can get no roof over you, and gales may stop you leaving just when you have to. In fact, is it worth it?'

I confess that my desire of Rum waxed stronger than ever. I then examined a young rock climber on his return from a recent raid. At once his eyes sparkled with enthusiasm. He was overflowing with praise.

'It 's the best of *all* the western isles! Six big tops strung on a long thin ridge. It gives a scramble like the Comb of Arran. But what views!—they 're the best on the Scottish seaboard—look at the map—just *look* at it!'

'What about the cliffs?'

'Gabbro.' A pause implied that no greater praise could be given. 'None of them big ones—nothing like so big as Skye. But there 's plenty of them, and no end to the new routes you could try. Go to the North-west Buttress of Askival—it may be the biggest on the island, and no one has ever climbed it. Then the whole coast-line is ringed with sea-cliffs. But they 're big—some a thousand feet high—and sheer. They 're not for us. Though they *are* good to look at.'

These dark peaks on a wide sea were still with me after two years. However, their magnetic power gradually overcame inertia, and in April 1948 drew me to action. My luck held at the outset, for I enlisted Michael Ward. He is a magnificent rock-snow-ice climber with a passion for exploring unknown hill country; one who has mastered the art of travelling light. He carries as little unnecessary baggage on his back as he does flesh on his body. Ward is young and lean, and the commander of great reserves of energy. Nor does he spare himself in action. This meant that a fortnight with him might be somewhat in the nature of a toughening course. He dispenses the medicine of strenuousness, of which I feel in need from time to time.

My second stroke of luck was in getting permission to land from Lady Bullough. She gave it most kindly and warned us only about the need for taking good food supplies and a tent. We were now free to travel by the Outer Hebrides steamer, which carries passengers twice weekly from Mallaig to Rum—an eight-mile sail for the modest fare of 5*s.* 6*d.*

At midday on 3rd May we arrived at Mallaig. Ward had excelled himself. He turned up wearing the torn and patched jacket of an old lounge suit. The patches were of black cloth, probably cut out of wartime curtains, and they had been clumsily sewn on by himself. However, the jacket served to cover a navy-blue rugger jersey, which was all that he wore underneath (the weather was cold). The trousers were peculiarly shapeless, even for navy-blue serge, and most wonderfully frayed. He might have passed for a tramp, utterly down and out, were it not for that upright bearing—and a food-filled rucksack. He had brought no change of clothing from London.

'After all,' he argued, 'we 're only away for a fortnight—and quite apart from the clothing our own skins are waterproof: we 're inside them and *can't* get wet!' He glanced at my fat and bulging rucksack, and looked swiftly away, as though embarrassed by an indecency, then allowed his deep-set brown eyes to wander over my face with a pained surprise. But he said nothing. I must admit that I had brought more spare clothing than was strictly necessary. Most of my food and fuel had to go into a second rucksack.

We sailed in the early afternoon. New snow had fallen that very morning on all Scottish hills. The skies were slate-grey, and the peaks of Rum white until noon, but the scene completely changed in the course of our three-hours' sail. The clouds evacuated the whole sea area in favour of the mainland, which blackened, leaving the seaward heavens a fresh and shining blue. The sun grew hot. Almost in the twinkling of an eye the snow-caps vanished. We steamed into Loch Scresort. The loch is a natural harbour on the east side of Rum and a motor-boat put out from Kinloch to meet us. We stepped on board to be warmly welcomed by Duncan McNaughton, head-stalker and uncrowned king of Rum. His welcome was my undoing. Out of the corner of my eye I could see that our gear was being unloaded along with the mail-bags. I assumed too hastily that no mistakes could be made. Not until we arrived at the jetty did we discover the loss of my rucksack, now bound for the outer isles with my sleeping-bag, change of clothing, cutlery, stove, and two cameras.

Ward was most kind and sympathetic. However, I can read his heart like an open book, and could see him reflect that my bad luck would do me good. Mercifully, my rucksack with the food was safe, so that from his point of view our situation had in no way worsened: he had a knife and matches. If the weather broke I should certainly have a bad time. Meantime it was good. Our immediate concern was a camp site, and Kinloch was attractive, too small to be called a village, despite a post office, and its situation sheltered. Indeed, the air was balmy and many kinds of blossom-bearing trees grew in the woods around Kinloch Castle. The castle is not a castle, but a rather beautiful palace of red sandstone, much too large for the barren isles of the west. We liked Kinloch, and we liked the people we met, and there is an excellent camp site on grass near the jetty. None the less we determined to carry our tent six miles south to Dibidil, a ruined cottage below Sgurr nan Gillean. There we should be close to the high tops and the rocks.

There is no road to Dibidil, but a track starts behind the woods fringing the castle. We wound slowly uphill for seven hundred feet. That is a rough track, sometimes barely perceptible, skirting along the top of great sea-cliffs. We were lured to the brink at one point and looked over the edge of an overhang. Several hundred feet below, Atlantic rollers crashed against the cliffs and roared white across reefs. They sucked back green and foaming from caves, and swirled black and smooth around blocks and pinnacles. On the south and west shores grey seals bask and bark, but not even seals could have lived near this fearsome cliff.

We continued our walk in high spirits. The sea was Mediterranean blue, and beyond was the long line of mainland hills, snow-capped and sparkling in a bright tumult down the full-length of the eastern horizon. Far to the north, at a great height above the mainland, were towering white clouds. These pleased us more than anything. 'They 're sure to mean good weather!' I exclaimed, and so fell headlong into error—a tempter of providence. . . .

Dibidil lies close to the shore, at the foot of a broad glen. We pitched our tent on short turf beside the burn. When we began to settle down inside, Ward, forgetful of his own comfort,

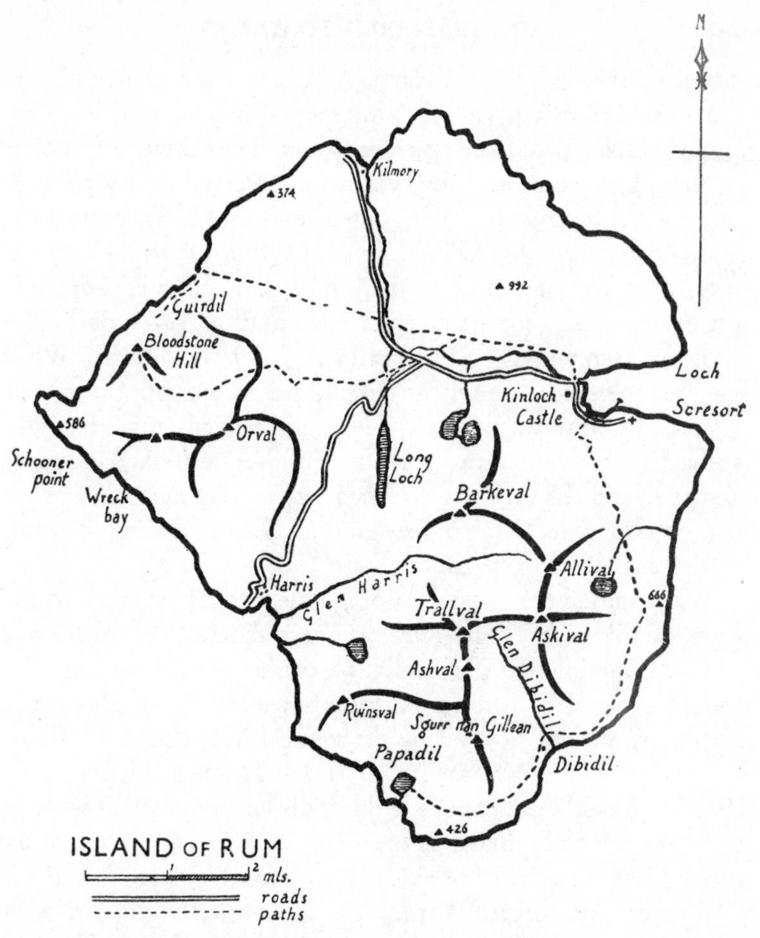

at once offered me his sleeping-bag, suggesting we share it night about. When I refused he gave me his only two sweaters. That first night was by no means so bad as I had expected. The soft and springy leather of climbing boots makes a not uncomfortable pillow, and although cold interfered with sleep I was able to doze.

We rose at five o'clock in the morning. If one lies hard there is no temptation to lie long. Moreover, we were eager to see the unclimbed North-west Buttress of Askival, and to make an attempt on it. Half-way through breakfast we heard a sudden patter of rain on the tent canvas. After such a clear night we were dumbfounded, yet when we looked out the tops were engulfed in mist, precipitating a steady, windless drizzle. It looked as though it would last for ever, so there could be no point in waiting for it to stop. We started immediately after breakfast and climbed up Glen Dibidil to the pass on the south ridge of Askival. We were now in thick mist, but traversed hopefully on to and along the north-west face, until at last a dark blur could be seen above. Our buttress. It looked broad. When we drew closer we could see definite ridges separated from one another by shallow gullies. The ridge second from the right seemed to be the steeper. Its left-hand edge looked sharp as shrapnel, and the top part vanished into woolly mist, so that we had no idea of its shape or feasibility. Greatly daring, we built a cairn at the foot to mark our start. We roped up.

Ward started the climb by going ninety feet up a crack to the right of the edge. The rock was crystalline: although it was wet and numbing to the hands, we could climb it without distress. I joined Ward on a platform bitten out of the edge itself. Direct ascent was stopped by the vertical nose above, so Ward suggested that I look round its left flank. I looked. I saw a long sheer drop below, and above, a thin right-angled crack of seventy feet, its walls smooth and at one point bulging. An attempt on it would be a hard test of skill on a warm, dry day. I said so.

'But do try,' urged Ward. He spoke pleadingly and with studied innocence, for he loves to see me in difficulties. He gave me an encouraging smile, full of simulated confidence, and in a moment of weakness I was persuaded. I traversed a narrow ledge to the foot of the crack, and after strenuous effort climbed three feet up. But every time I tried to move farther I felt my body pushed out by the rock, until at last I knew that one more move would unbalance me backwards. My only comforting reflection was that if I *did* fall off the angle was so high and the drop so long that I'd hit nothing—the rope would stop me. However, my fingers were numb and my heart was no longer in the battle, so I came down and had my revenge on Ward.

'I 'm sure you could do it, Michael,' I said. 'All it wants is a little forcing. Up you go!'

He tried hard. Again and again he reached the position where his body swayed out and his foot strained to the slipping point. The nervous strain of watching these efforts was much worse than that of making them, so my revenge was an unsatisfactory one. I began to urge him to wait for a dry day. He then gave up, and I turned my attention to the other side of the ridge.

A few yards to the right was a very steep wall of fifty feet. I climbed half-way up and the rock was so rough that I could balance on tiny holds without any sense of insecurity. But a mantelshelf at the half-way mark nearly defeated me. Every time I tried to raise myself on to that shelf, which was too narrow, an out-sway of the body was again evident. The wall behind it was bare of holds. A long pause ensued while I made tiny adjustments of body and feet. This was a fight fought out on millimetres of rock; to Ward below there was probably no sign of definite movement. When all was ready and the final attack took me over the top, I felt wild with delight—a much fuller and fiercer delight than in muscling up easy rock, however exhilarating its situation may be.

Ward joined me, and our route went directly up the crest of the ridge, which grew broader. The main difficulties were behind, for there was now a wide choice of route. We reckoned our climb to be three hundred and fifty feet when the buttress abruptly ended on the summit-ridge near the cairn. We were still in damp, dense mist, and invited each other with heavy irony to admire the finest view in the west highlands. We were not yet drenched quite to the skin, but the wind was cold and we hastened back to Dibidil.

A rainstorm blew up and continued all that afternoon and night. Our tent was not thoroughly waterproofed; it sprang several leaks and much of our time was spent bailing. I had to 'sleep' that night in my wet clothes, which is by no means so nasty as it sounds. It seemed to me that the very dampness of the cloth, perhaps by swelling the fabric, helped to exclude cold air and preserve body-heat. But in the early hours of the morning I had another tale to tell. The very worst kind of cold is a damp cold. I found that my best way to resist was to try to work up heat by regulated shivering. This was an art I had learned in central European prison camps in winter. One lies with a perfectly blank mind, midway between sleeping and waking, and lets the body shiver for five seconds in every half-minute. The process is reinforced at five-minute intervals by a few more strenuous wriggles. The result is a frequent boost to temperature, which helps to make the night a tolerable one. The process becomes automatic with practice.

What about risk? I wondered; and decided, very little. Only when health has been neglected is there cause to dread cold and wet. It is a good sign of a man's wholeness of mind and body if he can lie out and be numbed with cold, then thaw in the morning and be none the worse. He should be willing to run a risk now and then—health demands that sometimes he should forget his health, and expose his body to rain, wind, and extreme heat and cold.

The following morning was again wet, but cleared in the fore-noon. We decided that the quickest way of drying our clothes was not to hang them out, but to put them on and walk hard. We accordingly walked the coastal track south to the shooting lodge of Papadil. At the highest point of the track, which rises five hundred feet to the top of the sea-cliffs, we saw a herd of red deer, and one of these deer was white. We could hardly believe it was true. We had never thought a white deer possible. The herd was three hundred yards away, and I tried to convince myself that our white deer must in fact be a goat. For herds of black and white goats are common in Rum. They are not small and slender, like Alpine goats, but large, tough, and hairy. None the less our white deer when seen in outline was distinctly *not* a goat. It persisted in remaining a deer. We saved up this problem for McNaughton.

On our fourth day the weather cleared. We rose at 5 a.m. and decided that conditions were ideal for a traverse of the six main tops from Sgurr nan Gillean to Barkeval. That ridge-walk was the one thing I had looked forward to more than anything else. And at the end of it we could descend to Kinloch and collect my rucksack, which the steamer, we hoped, would this day return.

We started for Sgurr nan Gillean at 6.30 a.m. For the first time we felt the old-fashioned joy of an early morning in spring. An eagle was soaring between us and the summit. We climbed through cool air towards a blue sky, with sunlight washing over the wet ground. Sgurr nan Gillean is a shapely peak, but the ascent from Dibidil is a blank face of the steepest grass, the terrors of which were mitigated by banks of primroses on the lower half. On the hill-slopes around Dibidil primroses were thick on the ground, bare ground openly rejoicing in this bravery of woodland bloom. We gained the top in two hours, and started along the almost level ridge to Ashval. Cloud was forming round the Cuillin of Skye and the mainland hills, but the whole sea-view was clear to the west. The long low line of the Outer Hebrides ran from Barra Head to Lewis in the north, marking the edge of the world; beyond was a waste of seas like outer space made visible, apparently limitless. A great part of the fascination of the outer isles lies in that 'edge of the world' atmosphere: they are the last lands, the gateways—beyond them nothing is known (one feels). Thus they appear as the symbol of the frontier, those shores of the finite from which every man is one day launched upon the seas of the infinite, and makes voyage from life in time into life eternal.

We passed over the summit of Ashval, and began the steep descent to the bealach below Trallval. The ridge was very sharp half-way down, and not until we were past that point were we free to look round. It was then that we made a discovery of great interest to rock-climbers. We were looking into the south-west corrie of Trallval. Several hundred feet below the summit we saw a great gabbro cliff. There was certainly no record of a climb there, and the cliff would give the longest rock-climb in Rum if only a route could be found. We resolved to explore it next day.

At the top of Trallval the ridge turned sharply east to Askival. On the descent to our second bealach we were looking across the west corrie of Askival on to its North-west Buttress. We could see our ridge-climb of two days ago, now called the Atlantic Ridge, with a parallel and farther ridge that seemed equally good. It occurred to us then that we might fare better if we went up Askival by that parallel ridge instead of by the main ridge from the bealach. We traversed across the face to the buttress. At the foot of our proposed climb we came upon a cairn, and the lower rocks were nail-scarred. Like Robinson Crusoe on the sands, I stood like one thunderstruck. Someone had been up before us, and our own route farther to the right was not a first ascent of the buttress.

While uncoiling the rope we were puzzled to see several burrows in the turf ledges around us. There are no rabbits in Rum, and the holes were much too small for foxes. What other animal could have been responsible among cliffs two thousand feet up on a mountain-side? We could think of no answer until Ward put his ear to one of them and swore that he heard a noise like chirping. I listened. The chirping of a bird was unmistakable. But we knew of no bird that dug burrows; it seemed a fit companion for the white deer of Papadil.

We then repeated the slightly older climb and enjoyed it. The standard was very difficult and the rock good. We arrived on top of Askival just as the clouds began lifting off the Cuillin. They were already clear of the mainland, which probed much farther north than we had imagined possible. From its dim and distant tip hundreds of hills stretched south to the lands of Argyll, and we were quite unable to name even one of them. The angle was new to us, and we felt as though looking out to unexplored country, wrapped in thick mystery of the unfamiliar, but full of promise—each valley and mountain-barrier secreting its untold tale, calling us to the quest. I had never seen Scotland looking quite like that since my first climb.

We had now begun the best part of the main ridge traverse. The ridge between Askival and Allival is a scramble on rock, the narrow crest being blocked half-way down by a 'gendarme.' There is no tight-rope walking in thin air, but something of the same exhilaration without the nervous trial. From the top of Allival we had an unobstructed view of the Cuillin. They were less spiky than I had expected, but more gracefully proportioned. The peaks were well supported on broad rock-busts; they rose out of the sea in a blue-black cluster, massively. At their heart was the basin of Coir-uisg, of all solitary corners of Britain surely one of the least accessible. Ward and I were smitten with desire to go and live there for a week. It should be next week, we decided—if I recovered my rucksack; and if not, well—we should still go there.

From Allival to Barkeval was a level walk, after which we repaired to Kinloch, and sought out Duncan McNaughton. We found him at home at four o'clock. The steamer had called, and he had gone on board and taken off my rucksack. But that service had by no means exhausted his kindness. He asked us into his cottage, and his wife gave us a meal of two boiled eggs, tea, toast, hot scones, and lemon-curd. It made a joyful change from our porridge and pemmican. I asked him about our wonderland animals—the white deer and the burrowing birds.

'On this island,' he said, 'I 've got nine hundred deer, and one of them *is* white. From a distance it looks pure white, but when you get close up it is really pale fawn. I used to have a white stag too but a poacher killed it. I know of only one other white deer in Scotland—a stag in Ross-shire.'

'And the birds?' I asked.

'That 's the Manx shearwater,' said McNaughton, 'a mid-ocean bird, the size of a small gull, only black. It comes here in the spring, makes a burrow up on the mountains, and lays one egg. It comes out only at night—if you want to see it look for it with a torch. After the egg is hatched the mother fattens up the chick, then goes out to sea and leaves it. By September the young bird has worked through its fat, but it still can't fly, so one night it starts off in search of food and waddles right down the mountain-side to the shore, where it pushes off and feeds in shallow water. When it 's strong enough it flies off to mid-ocean.'

'Have you any eagles?' I asked.

'Three eyries all told. One of them on the low crags at Dibidil. And if you stay on another week you 'll see the sea-cliffs alive with puffins. They 're due to begin arriving any day now.'

After more tea and discussion Ward and I returned to Dibidil. That evening I took my first lesson in Atlantic bathing. An enormous weight of water thundered up the beach. I had to learn to run in quickly and take a powerful dive into each wave before it broke, otherwise it bowled me over and broke my skin on the shingle. It was all highly exciting, but enjoyable, if one was willing to accept some punishment.

The next day was cloudy but dry. In the early morning we crossed the main ridge and descended to the south-west corrie of Trallval, overlooking Glen Harris. We walked northward beneath our buttress. It looked much more intimidating at close quarters. In fact, on that first survey of its three hundred yards' length we saw no route at all. The rock was gabbro, distinguished by its great number of overhangs, most of them wet and streaked black and brown. The right-hand half of the buttress looked about four hundred feet high, the left-hand half about four hundred and fifty feet in two tiers.

Facing us across the corrie, on the north side, there was a smaller, triangular-shaped buttress. We thought that this too was unclimbed, and felt disposed to deal with it first. It gave us three good climbs on peridotite, an exceptionally rough and tough gabbro. By that time we were warmed up and more confident. We returned to the South-west Buttress.

At the very centre of the cliff was an ill-defined rib. We tried it, only to be turned back after fifty feet by holdless rock. The shallow gullies on either side of the rib were of no use to us, for both ended high up in great overhangs. We went forty feet to the right and looked again. The rock was there split by a crack of two hundred and fifty feet, vertical throughout. Again we moved forty feet rightwards, and then at last our blank eyes and long faces were enlivened by hope. A shallow gully ran up fifty feet to the base of a short pinnacle. Above and to the right of the pinnacle a broad ledge ran rightwards round a corner into a wide, right-angled groove. Thence it seemed just possible that a way could be found up one of the two opposing walls. They looked airy and remote, and led into an upper wall of slabs crossed by a line of overhangs, the difficulties of which were quite incalculable from below. In short, every passage was doubtful, but therefore hopeful.

We roped up and our troubles began. Ward climbed the initial gully, but found the base of the pinnacle to be dangerously shattered. He dared not touch the rocks lest they fell on him. He came down. I then led up the gully's outer left wall to a platform on the pinnacle's left side. Our task was now to cross the pinnacle to the main wall behind.

'Is the pinnacle safe from here?' asked Ward a bit nervously. Just in time I choked back that very question which I was about to put to him. Apparently Ward had a blind confidence that I would *know*. And I hated to shatter that innocent thought. I calculated quickly. If the pinnacle fell it would heel over slowly, Ward would be only six feet up, and ought to have time to jump back to the platform. In any event my stance was secure, and I could fully safeguard him with the rope. 'I think it will hold,' I said. 'We ought to go on.'

He scrambled to the top of the pinnacle. For a few seconds he hesitated, then spread wings of faith, and took a short bold flight across the top of the gully into a chimney on its right-hand side. Above this chimney was a vertical crack of twenty feet, but the holds were good, judging by the speed of Ward's ascent. He reached the wide ledge where I joined him. The next passage would determine our fate.

We walked rightwards along the ledge and climbed round the corner into a small bay. The huge right-angled groove springing up from the back of it looked impregnable, but the crest of its left wall was a sharp ridge. It thrust at the clouds, arrow-like. If its back were well notched we might get up; our chances were small otherwise. Ward started by going twenty feet up the groove, then struck straight up the left wall on to the crest. I joined him on a clean-cut ledge, and took the lead. The ridge was certainly very steep and felt exposed, but at every step the right holds came to hand and foot. We went up three rope-lengths, leading alternately, until the ridge merged in the final slab wall. The lead was now Ward's, for which I was duly grateful. Running across the top of the upper slabs was the long line of overhangs, which had looked even worse from below than they really were. To my surprise he went hard left, straight for the most exposed part, where a fine edge projected vertically against the sky. He worked his way slowly up a rough brown slab to the right of this edge, and then finally up the edge itself. All space seemed to ache beneath him, but Ward in good form is a joy to watch. Every move is sure and deliberate, and the foot placed with a kind of inevitable rightness.

When I followed him up I thought the pitch the best we had done in Rum, although not the most difficult. We had reached the top of our climb, and each feature of it had been one of character and interest. Our only remaining task was to name the buttress, for by tradition that was our privilege. The cliff faced Glen Harris, so we christened it Harris Buttress. The line of our climb I named the Archangel Route, for it is the prerogative of angels to balance on needles, and their leader is Michael.

We sat on flat stones and coiled up the rope. Our visit to Rum had come to an end—a good end despite the bad start. The bad hours already seemed unreal—wellnigh forgotten! 'It 's a trick of the mind,' said Ward. 'It always works. You can put up with extreme discomfort because you know that it won't last for ever and that you 're going to forget it anyhow. But what you don't forget is the sun-warmed rock on a good climb.' He looked down to the Atlantic. 'And things like that down there. . . .' he added. Travelling across the grey-green sea was a track of light, wrinkled and flashing, where a shaft stole quietly out from the clouded sun. In long, wavering lines, Atlantic combers creamed on the Harris shore. At our feet—brown crags and space.

11 *Coir-uisg*

AFTER FIVE DAYS ON RUM Michael Ward and I sailed for Skye, our destination Coir-uisg. It is the fate of all mountaineers to see their plans sometimes capsize, canoe-like in wild water. But on this occasion their end was to be more sharp and shocking than usual; perhaps because we planned for ourselves, greedily after our rough, first days in Rum, an immoderate share of sensuous and spiritual delight. Coir-uisg, ringed by its score of three-thousand-foot peaks, save for one narrow outlet to the Atlantic, appealed as the perfect camp site for lovers of solitude. Around the Black Cuillin and their great corrie, as we had seen them from Allival, hung an air of mystery as tangible as the blue haze of their atmosphere; for there is real mystery in all beautiful forms, and most especially in the quiet of remote mountains. In all the length and breadth of the kingdom where else could we find such seclusion, and on what other mountains such beauty? So we dreamed dreams about nicely balanced days of idleness and action, and planned to explore unclimbed cliffs from our haven.

At 7 p.m. we reached Sligachan. There was no chance of our reaching Coir-uisg that same night, but at least we might camp well down Glen Sligachan, and so cross the ridge to Coir-uisg next morning. Our week in Rum had disclosed how few of this world's goods are required on mountains, so we resolved to shed much gear and food. To this end we sought out Mr. Campbell, the hotel-keeper. He most kindly allowed us free storage space in an old attic room above a stable. Entrance was gained by a flight of outside stairs. The room was wood-lined, had one bed with a mattress, and a window facing Loch Sligachan. A day was at hand when this room would become our goal of all hope. We dumped our surplus stores, but took with us an extra tent, which we proposed to pitch and to leave in Glen Sligachan. From this second base we might later make a traverse of the main ridge.

At nine o'clock we set off down Glen Sligachan. It is a big, bare, and level glen, a mile wide, and running seven miles to the sea, dividing the east from the west Cuillin. Our route lay down the right bank of the river across moorland flats like marsh country. Even at the end of two miles, which was all we made that night, the hills had not begun to close round us. The twilight deepened; a grey-blue haze thickened over the flats. Long banks of mist appeared on the low and open ground around us, but the hill-tops were clear and stars twinkled. We camped on a little island of dry ground.

Next morning was dry and sunny. We went a further two miles down the glen, and pitched our second tent midway between Sgurr nan Gillean and Blaven—a good strategic position, but exposed to storm. Accordingly we pitched a high-altitude tent, which would stand in any weather, and crossed the Druim Hain Ridge to Coir-uisg with a light summer tent, which had no sewn-in groundsheet. Coir-uisg, we thought, was too sheltered to be troubled by storm.

We came down to the shore of Loch Coruisk near the sea-end, and had to walk a mile and a half north to Coir-uisg, which is the mountain corrie as distinct from the loch. Along the east bank there was just a vestige of a track, winding its way through shrubs and boulders, and dwarf trees and innumerable plants not yet in bloom. The smoke-blue peaks lay well back from the water, which stretched black and glistening like a seal's skin. At the north end was a shore-land of flat gabbro slabs, where we found a patch of turf for our tent.

Four days of fine weather ensued, yet our plans of action all went astray. The unclimbed cliffs of Sgurrs MhicCoinnich and Dearg still front Coir-uisg with a thousand feet of virgin rock—but they no longer tempt us. We crossed the main ridge to the Tairneilear corrie of Sgurr a Mhadaidh, and in Deep-Gash Gully, which too was virgin and fully five hundred feet high, were again routed on wet rock. Still, we enjoyed ourselves,

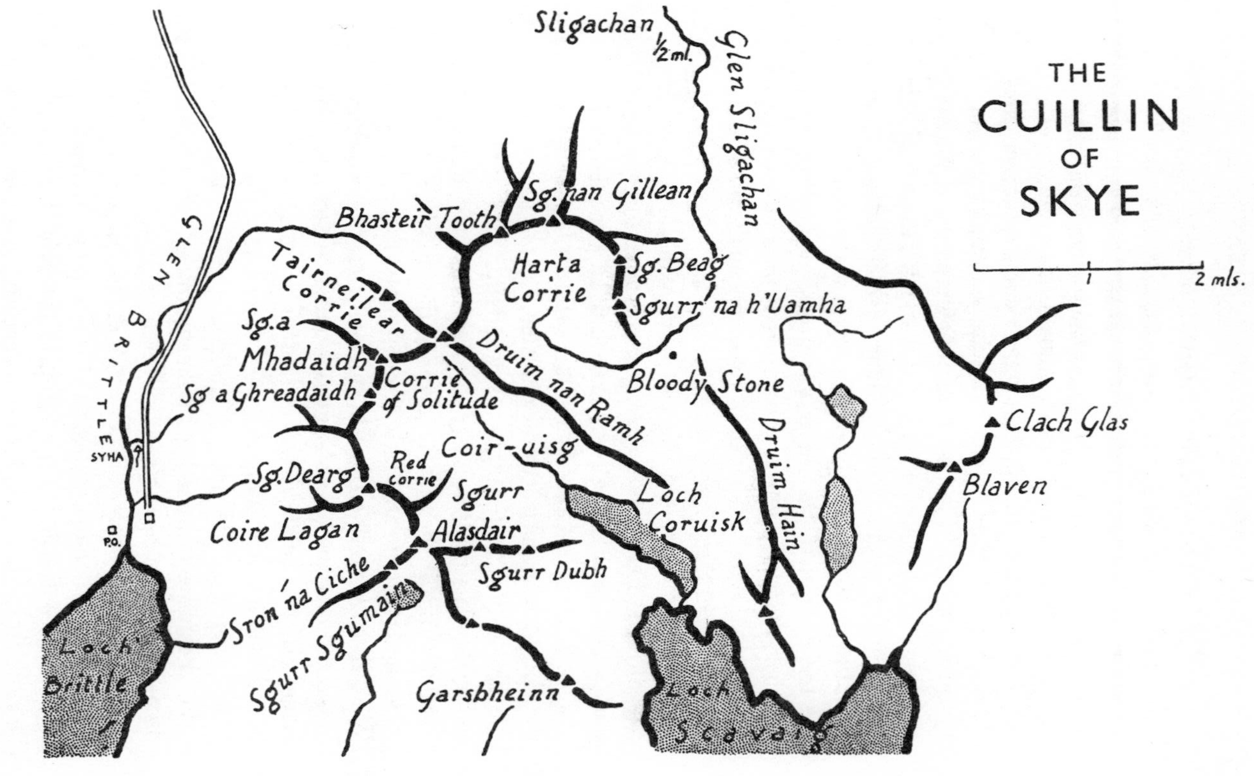
THE CUILLIN OF SKYE
1
2 mls.
Sligachan
½ml.
Glen Sligachan
Sg. nan Gillean
Bhasteir Tooth
Harta Corrie
Sg. Beag
Sgurr na h'Uamha
Bloody Stone
Tairneilear Corrie
Druim nan Ramh
Sg. a Mhadaidh
Corrie of Solitude
Sg a Ghreadaidh
Coir-uisg
Sg. Dearg
Red Corrie
Sgurr Alasdair
Coire Lagan
Sgurr Dubh
Sron na Ciche
Sgurr Sgumain
Garsbheinn
Loch Coruisk
Druim Hain
Clach Glas
Blaven
Loch Scavaig
Loch Brittle
GLEN BRITTLE
SYHA
P.O.

swimming in the ice-cold waters of Coruisk, sun-bathing on ridges, and exploring the Coireachan Ruadha and Corrie of Solitude. On our fourth day we transferred our headquarters to the tent in Glen Sligachan, planning to return to Coir-uisg by the traverse of the whole Cuillin Ridge.

Ward opened the final day by climbing Blaven and Clach Glas alone at three o'clock in the morning, starting from a bivouac on the ridge and rejoining me in the glen at 6.30 to climb Sgurr nan Gillean. We spent our next eleven hours on six miles of rock, scrambling in constant sunshine with a light breeze to fan our skins, and never a cloud in the sky. On the last quarter of the ridge we witnessed the brewing of a big weather change. The sky clouded from south-west to south-east, and the wind freshened. I speeded up the pace, and towards the end went very fast—severe work for Ward, who had now done fourteen thousand feet of rock-climbing. But the wind was blowing harder every hour, and at any moment we expected rain. On Garsbheinn, the last peak of all, the rain started.

Our descent to Coir-uisg took a full two hours. We reached the tent at 10 p.m. wet and exhausted. That hard cold wind on the last ridges had caught us when our bodily powers were reduced. We pulled on our sleeping-bags most thankfully, then looked round at the unholy chaos of tins, food, clothing, cutlery, rope, and gear of all kinds strewn about the floor of the tent. We wanted something to eat, but being more tired than hungry contented ourselves with a few spoonfuls of pea-flour and water. Even that simple meal was a trial of patience—every time we laid down a knife or spoon it disappeared. Long and industrious search is required to produce needles from haystacks. 'We'll have a good meal in the morning,' we reassured each other. 'Or perhaps in the late forenoon,' we added hastily.

We lay back to sleep. The rain drummed down on the roof. It drummed so hard that instead of sleeping we began to listen with some anxiety. If it continued like that the ground would be flooded. However, here we were and here we must stay, so we turned over to sleep again. Half an hour later great gusts of wind struck the tent. They must have struck very hard, for they wakened me. I piled all stores on the inside skirts to try to stop the wind blowing under the walls, but their weight was woefully insufficient. At 1 a.m. a gale sprang from the south-east—the only direction from which we had no protection. A guy-rope tore out on the windward side and flailed across the canvas, then another. I pulled off my bag and rushed outside to secure the tent. The wind nearly bowled me over when I stood up and carried blinding rain in my face. The night was so black that I could see nothing at all. I groped about for the guy-ropes, and found them, but the pegs had gone for ever. That our tent might ever be uprooted by storm at midnight had occurred to us only as a nightmare idea, which we never imagined could really happen to *us*. Such things happened only to other people. It was going to happen to us now. I could see no way out. For the wind was right under the tent, which was blowing out like a balloon. I felt the main end-guy tear away, seized it as it whipped in the air, and threw myself on the ground to hold the tent down.

'Michael!' I shouted. 'Pack up!'

'Try to hang on,' he answered.

It was like trying to hold down an open parachute. I needed all the strength I possessed to hold that tent, and the ropes were cutting into my hands. Ward was ramming all the stores and gear into the rucksacks, no doubt as fast as he could, but he took a long, long time. I made no allowance for the wild disorder inside, the weakness of his dying torch-battery, or the need to look out clothing for me. I heartily cursed him while my body went numb. I was soaked to the skin and the wind was bitter. After that ten thousand feet of climbing with neither a good meal nor sleep to follow, the twenty minutes' exposure to gale and rain was more than my body would endure. It mutinied and threw up the defence. I could feel the barriers go down and the cold sweep in. I knew then that there was going to be trouble. Meanwhile more urgent trouble pressed.

'Hurry up!' I shouted. 'I can't hang on!'

'One second!' cried Ward. Then: 'Let it go!'

I collapsed the tent. We groped about on the open groundsheet for wet stockings, sweaters, boots, and windproof jackets. Despite the fury of wind and rain lashing out of a total blackness, we somehow found them, or most of them, and pulled them on. We rolled up the tent and tied it to my rucksack.

'Sligachan?' asked Ward.

'Sligachan,' I said.

I tried to lift that rucksack and staggered under the weight. I could not swing it on to my back. I had to sit down to get it on, like a camel, and raise the weight on my legs. It seemed double the load I had carried to Coir-uisg five days ago. 'Michael,' I swore to myself, 'has stuffed the heavy things into *my* rucksack and all the light ones into his own.' That was the kind of thought that began creeping into my mind, which was closed to the obvious facts that saturated cloth accounted for one-half of the weight increase and fatigue for the other. Ward for the moment was something to be endured, like the storm. I could have eaten him up.

In the darkness we could find no trace of the path down the loch side and had to go at a snail's pace. I wondered whether we could make that seven miles to Sligachan over the Druim Hain Ridge. We were not willing to lie down and shelter beside a boulder, for the wind and cold were far too great. Our only hope was to keep moving: any other course would have meant our collapse through exposure. The first grey light of dawn filtered through thick layers of racing cloud, adding a new gloom to the storm-murk of the corrie. A full gale was still blowing up on the tops. Down at Coir-uisg the wind had dropped below gale strength, but raged on the white loch. The tempest showed an awful beauty, like a Flying Dutchman overture, but the beauty aroused in us neither awe nor any other emotion. We were too cold. That is why it is so important to note that we saw it.

When we turned east into the protection of the Druim Hain corrie our respite from wind was countered by the climb of a thousand feet to the ridge. We had to resort to the old device of making good each step as it came and refusing to think of the one ahead. After crossing the ridge we were exposed to the full wind-force, which swept up the funnel of Glen Sligachan with driving rain—driving straight, never flagging, obscuring the glen's farther wall in long bead-curtains of grey. Luckily our high-altitude tent had stood up to the storm. We opened the leeward door and crawled in, but rapidly decided not to linger. We had no dry clothing here, and the damp cold of that south-east wind would penetrate farther into us the longer we stopped. I felt very badly chilled. We ate an emergency ration of chocolate, then struck the tent, and packed up hurriedly. This extra load was Ward's. I remembered that he had now done fifteen thousand feet of climbing since the previous morning. In fact it occurred to me in this more benign mood that I was thrice blessed in having him as a companion: that he should ever crack up was unimaginable.

We started off on the last four miles with the wind at last battering us hard on the back. We had now a goal to draw us—the old attic room at Sligachan—wooden walls and a dry floor—even a spring bed and a mattress! It was too much! At the thought of it I felt a sentimental emotion flood through me, and at the same time a flush of heat spread over my body so that I felt able to speed along, floating airily over the stones and pot-holes of the path. But it was the head that floated and the rest of the body just hung on to it, as though flapping in the breeze. I had a high temperature and was light-headed. However, while the trouble was in the warm phase the body tingled and possessed a strange energy, but one mile from Sligachan the warm phase changed suddenly to the cold. My feet felt like lead, the rucksack like a hundredweight. The pace dropped to a crawl. A fit of shivering came over me, and I stopped several times to rest. Ward, as a man of medicine, was intrigued. I could see him turn a calculating eye on me and look puzzled, but through perverseness refused to give him the satisfaction of knowing what was wrong.

At 7.30 a.m. we arrived at Sligachan. There was a joint meet of the Scottish Mountaineering Club and the Alpine Club at the hotel, but we decided that such august company was not for us. We climbed to the old attic room and stripped off our dripping clothes. I had a dry change waiting for me, but Ward had none, and retired to his damp sleeping-bag. In a few minutes he was asleep.

Even with Shetland wool pullovers next to the skin I felt too shivery to lie down. Something drastic had to be done. It would be no remedy, I thought, to crouch over a fire or to put on innumerable wrappings. To avoid slavery to cold one must master oneself and the cold by action. I put that idea into practice. I swallowed two big spoonfuls of sugar, took Ward's clothes to the hotel kitchen to be dried, then went out again into the rain, and ran hard until I sweated. When I came back Ward awakened. We cooked a large meal of sausages and eggs, plum pudding, and hot sweet tea, and then we slept. By nightfall my high temperature had gone.

Next morning we returned to the mainland and arrived home in a heat-wave. When I sat down in my study a sweet fresh scent of apple-blossom and lilac poured through the open windows along with the sunshine. Azaleas and poppies flamed among greening trees. Rose-buds were bursting, the bees busy, and birds singing. The earth was quickening with life. I thought of the treeless isles and naked peaks of the west, yet could not find it in my heart to say: 'This is better than that'—least of all when I thought of Coruisk, raging white in the dawn. Discomfort of body is real enough at the time, but recollection shows it to have no standing power in reality; not even its sharpest pangs last. But remembered beauty is recognition of a power that *is* real. And it does last. Even when first seen in misery and labour it lasts. It returns to exact due tribute and to give out of itself all that a man can receive. Until he can receive, it waits for him.

12 *Tournament on Ice*

WHEN THE STATEMENT IS MADE by a mountaineer that he has done such and such a Scottish rock-climb in winter, the information he gives means next to nothing until one hears very precisely what the conditions were. If he talks of a gully it may mean that a route normally very difficult was found easy, or vice versa. If he talks of a long ridge or buttress under good snow, it means that however often that rock has been climbed before he has climbed a new route, engaged on difficulties the detail of which could not be foretold, and the exact likeness of which will not be seen again. One of the most sensationally radical of such changes known to me occurred on the Shelf of Crowberry Ridge. In December 1936 it was definitely a rock-climb, covered in loose snow, a long stepped trough running up the north wall of the ridge below and parallel to the crest. In March 1937 it was Scotland's biggest ice-climb—a ribbon of continuous ice five hundred and fifty feet long. Mackenzie and I had seen nothing like it before, nor have we since. It bulged seven times in distinctive pitches of blue, clear, and white ice, these being linked by runnels of snow-ice.

In the preceding December we had received on the Shelf the most resounding defeat of our lives. Loose snow and wind had caused unimaginable delays: *verglas* on the final slabs had forced us down after sunset: two hundred feet of rope had been left behind on the climb when we roped off the last pitches in a blizzard. We badly wanted to go and get that rope back. And we had wanted more ice on these upper slabs—ice that we could use—ice in which we could cut. Well, there was no question that now we should have it. The extraordinary conditions of March had been caused by three heavy snowfalls in January, February, and early March, each followed by heavy thaw and sudden frost, and latterly by days of blazing sun and by freezing nights. The Shelf had become a natural ice-trap.

Our decision to go on 28th March being made, I have never felt more nervous about consequences. We received great help from Miss Nancy Girvan of Inverarnan House, in Glen Falloch, where we stayed overnight on the 27th. She rose at 4.30 a.m., and made our breakfast. Years later I am still impressed by that act of generous toughness, which contributed more to the climb than a lead on one of its upper ice-pitches. The result was that we reached the head of Glen Etive in time to see the Buachaille, covered from peak to moor in thick snow, receive the first fire of the sunrise. For a few minutes only the tip crimsoned and faded. For a few minutes mellow sunshine flooded down the eastern face, creamily brilliant, turning to a dazzle of white as the light strengthened. The Buachaille, meanwhile, was giving birth to the day's first cloud. Around the base of the peak attenuated streamers of mist were forming. They joined and formed rolling banks, slowly drifting up the mountain's flank towards the blue sky.

The Crowberry Ridge was entirely snow-covered, even on its lower nose and on Rannoch Wall, where the angle is eighty degrees. Perhaps this 'snow' was mostly white ice. As a precautionary measure we called at Kingshouse Inn to warn other climbers not to send stones or ice over the Crowberry Tower. It was more than likely that we should have the seven hundred and fifty feet of Crowberry Ridge to ourselves this day, but were disinclined to leave the matter to luck. We then repaired to Coupall Bridge and at 8 a.m. set off.

There was not a breath of wind, and even at this early hour the strength of the sun was so great that we moved over the moor in our shirt-sleeves. The ground was snow-quilted but not embarrassingly so, and the heather-tops projected bushily. On the other hand, clear ice spreading thickly over outcrops of rock on the first steep slopes engaged us at too frequent intervals in axe-work. At the first opportunity we traversed into the lower reaches of the Crowberry Gully, and there found good hard snow all the way to the foot of Crowberry Ridge. Our proposed route was in full view. We looked at it—and could find nothing to say. All the usual adjectives used to extol a climb in superlative condition seemed too cheap or inadequate to find a way on to our tongues. Our admiration and eagerness were touched by dismay. Perhaps Mackenzie was immune from this unease, but certainly not I. Eventually he said 'Ice! Well, we *wanted* ice.' I answered: 'It 's more than I thought possible in Scotland.' And even at that we did not realize just how much ice there was. A great and craggy north face, topped by a tower of wilder outline than any other I knew in Scotland, divided by a narrow chasm from the thousand-foot cliff of North Buttress on its right, the whole face of which was plated in snow and ice from foot to crown: that was the bare framework for the line of our route. The Shelf on the north wall was badly foreshortened. We could see continuous ice for three hundred feet, which in itself was so far outwith our experience that we never imagined that to be only half the tale.

Running along the base of the north wall a steeply shelving snow-ledge allowed us to traverse rightwards to the first big step or butt of the Shelf. The first thing we saw there was the one-hundred-and-twenty-foot rope left by us last December. It hung free of ice, but its lower ends were embedded in deep snow-banks, frozen so hard that our most strenuous efforts failed to free them. The salvaging of the rope would have needed an hour's cutting, which we could not afford. The time was ten o'clock. We were now completely out of the sun, and could feel the sting of the frost in our lungs and around our necks. We pulled on all available sweaters, then roped up on a hundred feet of line, which we doubled.

Mackenzie dealt with the first pitch, which is a very wide rampart split by three chimneys. The best route to-day lay up the rib to the right of the centre chimney. To get on to it we had firstly to climb ten feet out of the chimney by its nearly vertical wall, which was larded with thin grey ice, and which at this early stage of the day we fondly imagined to be excessively awkward. We were soon to learn by contrast how meek and mild it really was; meantime we were glad enough to save a few minutes by making free use of the fixed rope for handhold. We thus emerged on the rib's back, which is slabby, and therefore, I thought, more likely to give us hard climbing than its lower wall. But the slabs were heavily iced in exactly the right places; if the cuttings of holds took time, the placing of hand and foot was easy.

Beyond the top a low rectangular crag gave a good rock-belay. The Shelf then rose in a straightforward slope of the type of white snow-ice common in the Alps, much more readily cuttable than the frozen water armour-plating the pitches, but not so deep as it might have been. Steps had to be slashed out too small to justify our moving together, and no axe-belays could be used. We arrived below pitch two, a chimney notable for the clarity of its great ice bulges. Another relic of our December rout—an eighty-foot fixed rope—was visible as the core of a huge pillar fully two feet thick. The very strands of the rope could be seen if one peered. It was not of very much use to us! Moreover, it lay to the left of the correct route, which went up the chimney—or rather up what I should say had once been the chimney. Now it was filled with ice of the first water, crystal pure. The cutting of holds in such ice was no easy work. Mackenzie took his short axe to it and struck hard. It was like trying to cut solid glass. The pick jarred. Splinters flew, but not in quantity. As he worked his way up I was at least able to give him some moral support. For I was tied on to the big ice-pillar, as safe as it was uncomfortable. The more normal stance is the cave under the pitch, but this was blocked with frozen snow. However, I barely had half an hour to wait before Mackenzie was up. On such very difficult ice this was fast work: of all things needed to-day speed and pace ranked foremost. Accordingly, to relieve and rest Mackenzie, we changed the lead.

A shallow tongue of snow-ice gave us technically, but not muscularly, easy work to our third obstacle, which was a wide chimney, mercifully short. The route lay ten feet up its vertical iced wall—an abnormal angle and brittle ice. Only the great thickness of the ice made the ascent possible. The exit required tricks of contortion reasonable, perhaps, on ten-foot walls. As we thus gained in height the Shelf grew steeper and more heavily frost-bound, and we became aware of it as a mere shelf in relation to the great scale of the rock-snow-ice scene: the chill and gloomy depths of Crowberry Gully close on our right, and the hoary north wall of the Ridge rising in overhangs on our left, and just across the gully the face of North Buttress, as vast in breadth as in height, blinding white in the upper sunshine but grey below. Everywhere was the glint of ice thrusting through flaky snow. As quickly as I could I cut up the trough to a third chimney, this one unusually wide and square-cut. All three walls were vertical and of height twelve feet.

Mackenzie resumed the lead. Technically this pitch was severe, but not being exposed put no strain on the nerves. There was exasperatingly little ice on it. All around us was ice in mass, green bosses, blue bulges, white boiler-plates; but here, on this twelve feet of rock, a black and skimpy smear. We had to go up by wedging back and foot on opposing walls, and had to be extremely careful how we did so; for slippery rocks and awkward angles of pressure made the positions enforced on us unusual. This was the very type of pitch that one feels to be climbable in the conditions only because it is short, and therefore fairly safe except at the top. For the third successive time I said to myself: 'If this had been long or exposed we should never have got up'—words that I should have to eat (twice over—and I do not joke when I say so) within the next two and a half hours.

The Shelf arched its back, and seventy feet higher ended against the upper and icy wall of the north face, on which we had still to climb two hundred feet or more to reach the crest of Crowberry Ridge. The crux of the whole route was the sixty feet of rock immediately in front. The ice there was again miserably thin. Remembering the trouble we had just had on twelve feet of thin ice, we did not relish the prospect of sixty. But an extraordinary climb is worth extraordinary effort: if only we could put this pitch behind us we should gain access to the final groove of a hundred and fifty feet which, in summer at least, presents no difficult way.

We stood in an up-curling corner in the angle between the flank of the ridge on our left and a broad wall on our right, the latter topped by a small pinnacle. In summer one climbs the initial corner by a crack in the angle, then may traverse left and upwards to the crest of the ridge—a route impossible now on account of *verglas* lying on slabs. Our alternative was to take the wall rightwards to a square recess thirty feet up, the back wall of which rose high above the other two in a square-cut pinnacle. The shape of the recess was thus like that of a high-backed throne with box-arms. The route would have to go on to the seat and then up over one of the arms, which were vertical walls of six or seven feet. We could see nothing beyond. Mackenzie started.

The first thin crack was filled with black, unusable ice, so instead he took to a steep corner more to the right which brought him on to very difficult and glazed rock. The delicacy of this passage can hardly be exaggerated, and I doubt if any man would have climbed it save in one of those fits of *élan* that come on occasion to all of us, as it came now to Mackenzie. Such rock could be climbed in no passive frame of mind; every move had to be forced, and took minutes to execute; for minute adjustments of body and balance had to be made and striven for before hand or foot could lift to its next hold. The axe was carried by wrist-sling, or between finger and thumb, ready for instant use in chipping at ice. He crept up until six feet below the right-hand corner of the recess. He could go no farther on that line, and I thought he was beaten, but he managed to make a turn and traverse hard left under the left-hand corner, there to make a second turn and shorter traverse up to the base line of the recess, into which he climbed over a low vertical wall. All this manœuvring on the iced rocks was made on holds too small to accommodate more than the edge-nails of his boots. He had spent one hour in climbing that thirty feet on to the seat of the throne, and the difficulties of the second thirty feet were to be still greater.

The seat was outward sloping, so he edged his way up to the pinnacled back. An escape out of the recess had now to be forced over the right-hand wall, and that proved the crux of the whole day's climb. After making one step up on this wall he discovered the angle to be too high and the face too holdless for a direct exit. He was obliged then to take the outside route by stepping on to a small and outward sloping hold on the wall's outer corner. For that he had no handhold of any kind. It was a pure balance-move above crusted slabs down-plunging several hundred feet to Crowberry Gully. By something very like a miracle there was no ice on the foothold. There he was, then, balanced by friction-grip on his right foot, with the urgent need of speeding rightwards round the corner, but with further move impossible unless he could change feet. When I saw that he was determined to try, without handhold, I felt almost sick with apprehension. It is better to lead a movement of that kind than to watch another.

Mackenzie lent slightly forward so that his solar plexus rested against the wall's sloping top, and so gave him a slight friction-hold, enough to help him for that fraction of a second in which the lightning change must be made. It was impossible for him to see the foothold, and if he should miss it nothing could then save him. He balanced, arms outstretched and finger-tips just touching the rock—then—one quick hop and the deed was done.

He rounded the corner and I saw no more of him for fifteen minutes. He would be in the long wide groove running up to the right-hand side of the pinnacle. At short intervals a bit of rope would scutter over the rocky arm and a few flakes float down through space. Later came a torrent of chips. Quite unexpectedly his head appeared from behind the top of the pinnacle. He looked not at all triumphant. The pitch had been too severe to allow indulgence in self-congratulations. He was just profoundly thankful. What had happened round the corner I could not know until twenty minutes later when I myself arrived there. After the feet-change my right foot came round into the groove and on to a very high and rounded hold, frost-hoared, but giving friction for an upward-propelling scrape of the boot-nails. Like the preceding move it was very severe, but brought good handhold within reach. Some ten feet of high-angle snow-ice led thereafter to a saddle at the rear of the pinnacle. The time was then 2 p.m.

Like Mackenzie I felt very thoughtful at the saddle. I was shaken. That was the hardest pitch I had ever climbed in my life, nor have I since been up another like it. I swore that I would never go back in similar conditions, which were too exacting for pleasure even in retrospect. Meanwhile we nibbled at food, looked about us, and with quite a start awakened to a bigger and wider world than the next two feet of ice-encrusted rock. In the foreground the walls of the North Buttress were dazzlingly sheeted, most emphatically crowned in glory, and in great contrast to the hills of the distant north, which were quietly beautiful. The sun spread evenly upon the broad flanks and penetrated the great snow-corries. Close at hand every crusted crag surged out dramatically white upon blue sky. But the background was wreathed in sun and sleep, and there the snows held fast the illusion of their everlastingness. Over all that land lay the sign of inner and hidden things, like the background to an old Italian painting, where no revelation is ever made but the promise of it always hinted.

Near and present realities pressed for attention. An ice-choked scoop on our right rushed up to the ridge, an unbroken ice-fall of a hundred and fifty feet, twice bulging in fifty-foot pitches. These latter were a great surprise to us. We had been prepared for an icy ribbon lining the groove, but not for the formation of big ice-walls.

It was my turn to lead. We had already climbed ten feet up the scoop before diverging left to our present saddle; so I began cutting nicks up the remaining twenty feet towards the first pitch. But I did not have very much cutting to do: the ribbon was only two inches thick; occasional patches of three inches were something to be welcomed. At the foot of the ice-wall I stopped to bring on Mackenzie, who took up position ten feet below me. I turned to examine the ice. It was the white and bubbly kind, as unreliably brittle as one could well find. Would it take my weight at *every* move on the fifty feet? The answer was certainly not known to me. Instinctively I looked down to see how Mackenzie was placed. He had been unable to find a rock-belay on either wall of the groove, so had belayed me instead to his axe-head, the pick of which had been stabbed two inches into the snow-ice. Well, it was a gesture—slightly better than absolutely nothing. Behind him the groove swept down a further twenty feet, to end at the edge of the wall dropping into the chasm of Crowberry Gully. The text-book answer to this predicament is simple: Unsafe ice, exposed position, no belay?—Turn back! But turn back with five pitches below us, one of which had taken two hours to ascend, and with neither rock-belay nor piton from which to rope off! The text-books have no answer to that, save to point a moral.

It seemed to me that we should have to go on and make the best of what the gods were giving us. I cut an experimental hold or two in the brittle ice and tried them. They held. Was the ice just 'leading me on'? I shall never forget that next five minutes' agony while I tried to make up my mind. If a hold collapsed I decided I should try to fall facing in, and brake with my pick the moment I landed on the ribbon. Mackenzie might then succeed in stopping me. I cut a few more holds, and eased myself on to each, trying to put as little weight as I could on my hands, and indeed attempting desperately not to put weight on anything, as though I were practising levitation. I began now to get the 'feel' of the ice and to judge its holding power. There was one harrowing patch near the half-way mark where the ice was replaced by frozen snow. The snow itself was good, but was it well frozen to the underlying ice? I cut at it above my head, using the gentlest of chip-strokes with the pick, not the blade, simply to minimize the jar of each blow. Thus I fashioned two handholds and two footholds. When I moved there was just the slightest subsidence of the handholds—an instant's alarm—but they held. On the last twenty feet the ice was so thick that security was ensured. At the top I had safe though shallow footing in frozen snow to bring on Mackenzie.

The second ice-pitch followed immediately. A narrow chimney of easy angle ended high up against a vertical face of white ice. The latter, we thought, could not be climbed direct, but trusted that some way of turning it might yet appear. I had trouble with the initial chimney despite the angle; for the too narrow walls prevented my cutting on the clear ice so thickly lining the interior. I had to go up by bridging. Near the vertical ice I managed to unravel a route over the left bounding wall, which gave me harder climbing than anything on the preceding pitch, but pleasanter. Sound rock and the sunny air of our near approach to the ridge gave me the first truly carefree moments of the day. Beyond the left wall I arrived in a short gully filled with firm snow. Mackenzie came on and a few minutes later the shining crest of the Crowberry Ridge was level with our eyes—a knife-edged *arête* crested by fins of translucent ice two feet high, through which we looked for a moment as through glass towards the Blackmount. Most regretfully we smashed the fins with an axe and stepped on to the edge.

After five hours of shade and frost we suddenly came out into a world of brilliant, warm sunshine, but with sharp, crisp air to preserve the snow and ice, which glistened everywhere, beneath our feet and on the rims of the distant hills. A sombre haze in the valleys picked out the succeeding and receding ridges of the vast southern panorama, where peaks soared like an Alpine chain, their shining crests heightened by the shade-girt flanks and hollows.

We turned again to our ridge. The Crowberry Tower was ponderous with snow and ice-plastered. Its ascent would take an hour at the very least. But running leftwards around the base was a snow-ledge overlooking Easy Gully. To save time we chose to follow it: an uneasy proceeding on unstable snow, tilting steeply to the Rannoch Wall. This traverse brought us into the upper part of Waterslide Gully, in which we kicked steps to the summit.

At the cairn we sat in sunshine for two hours, until the twin horns of Cruachan turned black in the orange sky, and blood-red clouds hung motionless behind Bidean. Then we walked west towards the col half a mile away along the summit-ridge. A bright flash of light marked the Firth of Lorne, and all the peaks of Lorne and Appin emitted that dull, hard glint, which can come from ice alone at the first approach of dusk. The snow of our ridge was already beginning to freeze again, and the new, thin crust crunched under us all the way down to the col. There we halted to put on gloves and balaclavas. Across Loch Linnhe the low line of the Ardgour mountains stretched dark behind long streaks of the sinking sun.

We turned south to Glen Etive.

13 *The Six Days' Challenge*

THERE IS A SOLEMN CANON published from time to time by the Scottish climbing clubs, in which (among other listed sins) the innocent walker is advised to avoid alcohol, but this wise declaration is immediately followed by the cheering counsel that 'a flask may be carried for emergencies.' Every April, after repeating the solemn canon, MacAlpine proclaims that a state of emergency exists: his birthday. This event is of variable date, always coinciding with a good week-end on a mountain, and celebrated by a noggin of rum on the summit.

There was one especially fine day when we celebrated the rite on the summit of Carn Mor Dearg, and promptly thereafter enjoyed a two-thousand-foot glissade right down to the Allt a Mhuilinn glen. I have never known a glissade like it. Two thousand feet of firm snow! At the summit I had been a happy mountaineer, receiving the spirit of the canon from the ministering hands of MacAlpine, but down below there were no bounds to my benevolence. So it came about that I accepted MacAlpine's challenge. For *he* arrived down in argumentative mood. He lit his pipe and looked at me. 'I can make one serious criticism,' said he, 'about men who write about mountains. You expurgate your diaries. You misrepresent your friends—make them out to be better men than they are. And does beauty move climbers as much as their later writings suggest?'

'It 's a question worth asking,' I acknowledged. 'On the whole I think diaries may often give *more* praise to men and mountains than later writing—diaries are written while enthusiasm is fresh.'

'I wonder! In fact, I doubt. Bring out your diaries—take three lucky dips—then publish the results if you dare!'

A few random recollections began to pass through my mind and the palms of my hands to sweat. 'A three-round contest might just be misleading,' I protested. 'But I'd take the challenge for six.'

'Done!' said MacAlpine quickly.

One evening after we returned home MacAlpine sat down in my chair as judge and I fetched out my diaries. 'Play fair,' he directed, 'no special selections—but ignore entries too short to give evidence.' I opened volume one.

ELEPHANT GULLY ON THE BRACK. *October 1938.*

Dr. J. H. B. Bell, Dunn, MacAlpine, Alan Garrick, and myself.

A foul and dismal day. Elephant Gully lies across Glen Croe from the Cobbler and splits a great crag six hundred feet below the summit. A gully three hundred feet high with vegetation enough to feed all the elephants that ever were. Yet there is no water in it. I myself climbed unroped. The others roped—I cannot imagine why, when any one of them could have led it. A poor climb. Standard difficult. After reaching the summit I was so wet and the wind was so numbing that I persuaded Bell to climb with me down the gully again, where at least we had some shelter.

We finally left Bell in Glen Croe in torrential rain, and the last we saw of him he was dancing about on the main road naked, preparatory to a bathe in the river.

I shut the book hastily. MacAlpine was beaming.

'My round,' said he. '*Now* we're getting down to hard facts. To foul and dismal mountains! Poor climbs! Doctors of Science—but do go on.'

'Don't exult too soon,' I growled. 'Wait till we see a few more.'

RECESS ROUTE ON THE COBBLER. *19th April 1939.*

R. G. Donaldson and myself.

To-day was the anniversary of my first ascent of a mountain—the Cobbler. So although it was a week-day Donaldson and I left Glasgow at 4.45 p.m., reached the foot of the Cobbler at six, and the upper corrie at eight. The best route on the mountain is Recess Route, right in the middle of the North Peak, so we went straight for it. We started up a high and difficult wall, then up a series of deep and difficult chimneys to a long grass ledge, which we followed rightwards to a smooth and somewhat exposed corner, which is the crux of the climb. The holds at this corner are small, and were getting difficult to see in the twilight, so that I had to spend a long time on the pitch—especially near the top where a great mass of turf had slipped down and formed an overhanging cornice. Donaldson used the rope to follow up.

On the last pitch, where a delightfully airy traverse from the shelter of an overhang gives on to an open wall, we could barely see the holds, and had to find them by feel. An excellent climb. We arrived out on the summit in a tearing wind. The sky was now clear and starry, and the out-thrusting crags of the North Peak projected over the corrie in great waves of frozen stone.

On returning to the corrie floor we looked back and saw the silhouette of the three peaks standing sharp and still in the starlit sky. Below their wild skyline all detail was engulfed in black. The perpendicular face of the South Peak seemed now as though it overhung the corrie—had actually begun to topple, and yet by a magic paradox was still. Time and space were swallowed up in eternity, and the stillness of rock in a still sky shed upon the world a perfect silence. I don't think I could ever have loved mountains more than I did then, nor fellow creatures. That silence was shed out of the infinite. The Cobbler was all mountains and Donaldson all men.

I was lucky having Donaldson with me. He says nothing.

We made our descent slowly in the pitch darkness. The strange and jagged outline of the summit gradually receded behind us—but weird and unforgettable to the last. Loch Long was streaked with shimmering pencils of light from the village windows. One by one they went out as we climbed down, until the loch was dark and silent as the hills above.

BEN VORLICH. *January 1939.*

Mackenzie, Dunn, and myself.

On Saturday Mackenzie came to me with a light of sudden and unusual virtue in his eye. Would I agree, he wondered, to a 4 a.m. start to-morrow, so that we could reach Glencoe at dawn and get a hard ice-climb on Bidean? I did not demur. Ice-climbs are ice-climbs. 'But how shall we ever fetch Dunn out in time?' I asked. From long and painful experience we knew that upon calling for Dunn at any agreed hour of the morning we must devote the better part of an hour to hounding him out of bed and to getting him dressed, fed, and properly turned out complete with climbing boots. The boots were important. They were sometimes apt to get left behind in the mad scramble of departure—irate friends clamouring in his bedroom.

Mackenzie was equal to this difficulty. 'We 'll tell him the starting hour 's three. He should just be ready when we call an hour later.' I approved this plan. It was most judicious. And so it was done.

On arriving at his rooms at 4 a.m. we found Dunn actually out of bed and half-way through breakfast. There was something truly great in the audacity with which he at once accused us of lateness. Secretly he must have thought us strangely tolerant that morning.

We had reached the head of Loch Lomond and were half-way to Glencoe when a terrific rainstorm broke.

The car's headlamp could hardly reveal the roadway through the spray of rebounding rain. In Glencoe there was probably a full blizzard blowing, so there seemed no point in going farther. At 5.30 a.m. I drew the car to a standstill before Inverarnan Hotel. The bleak eyes of its many windows glared through the driving storm. Inverarnan is our winter headquarters, but at such an hour in the morning we had no more hope of rousing any one than of raising the devil.

'Pity we can't get back to bed!' I sighed.

Dunn started. There was no doubt where *his* heart was. His face shone with new hope. 'An ice-axe,' he barked. 'Take an ice-axe and prise open a window. We 'll get an empty room and we *will* get back to bed!'

We carried out that job with a Sikes-like efficiency. Within ten minutes we had found a room with a bed big enough for three—the bridal suite, no doubt—and in no time our snores were a coronach to the death of our mountaineering hopes.

We remained undiscovered and slept happily until noon. It even began to seem likely that we should miss a week-end's climbing for the first time in eighteen months. This unendurable thought roused me to action, and I prodded my wrathful friends with an ice-axe. We threw on our clothes, walked boldly out by the front door, and climbed Vorlich in improving weather.

MacAlpine was again happy.

OBSERVATORY BUTTRESS OF BEN NEVIS. *August 1936.*

Variation of the Direct Route by Mackenzie, Dunn, MacAlpine, and myself.

We all foregathered at Fort William on Saturday evening and bought in stores. Not till 8 p.m. did we leave the distillery. The weather during the preceding week had been magnificent, but the day's forecast spoke of Atlantic depressions moving in on the west coast. They duly arrived. We climbed to the hut under a dark and lowering sky, arriving 10 p.m. At eleven the conventional Nevis drizzle had begun.

Next morning we delayed until 11 a.m. in hope of a clearance. Mackenzie was in one of his abstracted, maddening moods. He floated around the hut asking innumerable foolish questions. To MacAlpine, who was busy frying bacon and eggs, he said: 'Are you making breakfast?' He looked into a pot of porridge badly needing to be stirred, and asked: 'Are we having porridge?' Then he glanced at an old magazine which had lain around for a twelvemonth: 'Why did they bring this up?' And he wanted answers. MacAlpine lost patience first.

'For God's sake go and *do* something,' he ordered.

'Do what?' asked Mackenzie defensively.

'Go and fetch a bucket of water,' said MacAlpine briskly.

Mackenzie looked at the large, empty bucket. 'Is this the bucket?' he asked. That was the end. MacAlpine let fly a frightful oath. 'It looks damned like a bucket to me!' he thundered.

'All right, all right,' said Mackenzie hastily. 'I just wondered if there was another.'

He won. The hut exploded.

'Stop!' exclaimed MacAlpine. 'Is there any need to go on?'

'Well,' I laughed, 'you are doing well. But this entry is a long one. If ever we have a good climb I always write it up in full and not as a brief diary entry. I don't think you 've won this round yet.'

MacAlpine subsided. I continued reading.

At 11 a.m. we set off for Observatory Buttress. A long grind up the screes of Observatory Gully brought us to the start of the direct route—about the middle of the buttress and just to the left of a bulging rib. The weather was wet, the mist thick and penetratingly damp, and the rocks streaming.

Mackenzie led off on an easy upward traverse to the right, then back towards the left on moderate rock. After that the climbing changed, becoming distinctly harder and slabbier. We were all on one rope of two hundred feet, and had just begun to deal with the harder rock when a stone from far above hummed in among us. It cut the rope between MacAlpine and me. We thankfully tied the rope's ends and continued. Balance-climbing predominated, for the rock was slabby throughout and definite holds seemed few and far between. The further we thus advanced the more difficult the climbing became, until at last it was obvious to us that this could not possibly be the direct route, which is only very difficult. Our way was obscured by the grey, clinging mist, and of course by the high angle of the rock, which had no predominant feature to guide us. But these worries were Mackenzie's, and to him we confidently left them—save that we felt a sympathetic concern.

Progress suddenly became slower, and continued so. As third man on the rope I had to wait a while before I could see and understand the cause. The start of this long, new passage was a pitch of very great difficulty, topped by a short fierce chimney, which I am sure would be severe when dry and warm. The holds were minute. The rain was pelting down and flowing over the top edge of the chimney. Each time I took a high handhold a cupful of chill water poured up my sleeve and spread over my chest and stomach. The rock was cold, and each of us, I think, finished this exposed pitch with numbed fingers.

Our concern about the route was no longer just 'sympathetic.' It was real and immediate. Where were we? The rock *in itself* might have no terrors with Mackenzie in the lead, but we were soaked to the skin and chilled, and that plus demoralizing uncertainty could defeat us. I followed up for another fifty feet, gaining by a hand-balance movement a small platform set in an open corner. Above me a short chimney gave on to a blank face. I was dealing somewhat gloomily with this face when suddenly I heard a most joyful and infectious laugh from Mackenzie close above me. I had not even seen him for an hour. To hear that laugh come floating through wet mist on the face of a great cliff, on which the route is lost and the rock severe, was one of the most heartening experiences I had had in years. I forgot my chilled body, and eventually landed at a good stance to the left side of a long chimney.

Mackenzie and Dunn were there. But why the merriment? For the chimney was absolutely unclimbable. It was right-angled and well defined, but there was no route up it. None the less Mackenzie grinned at me from ear to ear. 'You 're doing a new route, Bill,' he said. 'Hope you like it.'

'But *where*?' I asked.

'It 's the belt of unclimbed slabs high up to the left of the direct route.'

'We just strayed on to it like browsing goats,' murmured Dunn.

'But we 're not going back,' added Mackenzie after a pause. 'We 're beyond the rocks that beat Hargreaves and Macphee. Main point is we know where we are.'

This comfortless knowledge seemed inexplicably to comfort Mackenzie; for he turned to the chimney, saw it to be hopeless, then without hesitation climbed up the open crest to its left, and so reached a poor stance. However, it had a belay, so he called up Dunn, who cursed but complied. All this manœuvring on little or no hold, in the midst of precipitating cloud, seemed at first sight a waste of time, because the wall they were on was no more climbable than the chimney. I reckoned they had nearly reached their limit, and I was right. However, Mackenzie had an ace up his sleeve.

He moved up a few feet farther to a slight overhang, and there indulged in what I still thought to be pointless gardening. 'Take cover!' he shouted once. I pressed myself as close as I could against the rock-face. A large stone came rocketing past, missing my right heel by six inches. His next move was to use the square hole thus created as a handhold, not to climb up as I thought he had intended, but to assist him in crossing the chimney from left to right. When I came to make this move myself I found it of great technical difficulty. The few holds are pressure holds awkwardly placed. When the crossing is made, however, one lands on a good ledge. While waiting there with my nose close to the cliff I suddenly saw the colours in the grain. Flecks of red, yellow, blue, crystal. Mouse-brown rock all flecked over. Beauty manifesting through the rock and as stirring as that of Mackenzie's lead. Each of its kind excellent.

Some way farther we reached a well-broken level area where we lunched. I imagined that our difficulties were over, but was disillusioned as soon as we reached the rocks beyond. They gave us good climbing for almost an hour.

More lunch in the Observatory ruins.

Thereafter we started down the North-east Buttress, and had trouble at first in hitting off the easy route. Dunn and MacAlpine, the rugged individualists, unroped and damned our eyes, then went back up the buttress to go down by the Carn Mor Dearg *arête*. Mackenzie and I persisted, almost at once found the easy slopes, and rattled down at breakneck speed to Coire Leis. We made the hut twenty minutes before the others, and thus honour was satisfied.

On our way back to Fort William the Herr Mackenzie sprained his ankle, and had to be supported all the rest of the way down by Dunn and MacAlpine.

A truly glorious night with a full moon. I travelled home in Dunn's open Morris, enjoying unobstructed views of Glencoe, the Blackmount, and Loch Tulla, all flooded with white light and backed by the starred sky.

The true kingdom, it seems to me, is not in some far-off and happier land. It 's here and now. (But how to learn how to get it?)

I sat back and waited. MacAlpine stared reflectively through his tobacco smoke for a minute, then said firmly: 'I give it to you, after all, on points.'

DIRECT ROUTE ON EASTERN BUTTRESS, SRON NA CICHE, SKYE. *June 1937.*

Dunn, Angus Smith, Marskell, and myself.

Showers in the early morning. We curled up in our sleeping-bags and listened with a good grace to the helter-skelter on the canvas. Then a northerly wind drove the cloud off the Cuillin. We left Glen Brittle in the afternoon and went up Coire Lagan. We surveyed the precipice of Sron na Ciche. Debate. Four different opinions about what should be done. To reintegrate the party I tried for agreement on first principles, which was easy enough—that our climb should be one that none of us had climbed before. The party sat on its hunkers among the boulders and smoked a pipe, choosing in the end the Eastern Buttress Direct.

We climbed on to the end of the Terrace, which we traversed a short way towards Eastern Gully. The route now went up the face of the buttress, but kept as much as possible to the edge overlooking the gully. Our delight was intense on finding ourselves launched upon the most charming route in Skye. None of us knows a better. The standard is difficult, but not by such standards should one judge the excellence of any rock-climb. The route goes on brown gabbro, in great clean-cut steps over steep and exposed rocks, round exhilarating corners, up an endless variety of slabs, cracks, chimneys, and edges.

We found belays to be sound and plentiful, the rock unimpeachable throughout, and open stances gave us wide views to Loch Brittle, where the sea was bursting on the beaches, brilliantly white in the new sun and the rain-cleansed air. The crux of the route came just where it should—at the penultimate pitch. The last two pitches were crack climbs on a steep wall. The first of them was very hard—decidedly harder than the route's official classification, although not exposed enough to be called severe. I cannot remember enjoying a Cuillin climb more than this one.

At the top of Sron na Ciche, Dunn retired by the Sgumain Stone Shoot, while the rest of us passed over Sgurr Sgumain and the *mauvais pas* to Sgurr Alasdair. Came down the Alasdair Stone Shoot in six minutes, *without hurrying*.

Every night just now is giving us wonderful skies of green, red, and dark orange, barred with long horizon clouds, such as only the Isles can show when the sun goes into the sea.

'A panegyric,' I said to MacAlpine. 'You must give me that one—written in the first burst of enthusiasm. What do you make the score now?'

'Call it three–two in your favour. Let 's have something more recent—skip ten years.'

I turned open volume two.

THE CENTRE GULLY OF BEINN LAOIGH. *February 1947.*

Norman Tennent, Trevor Ransley, and myself.

'It *may* be the best snow-climb in Central Scotland,' said my companion grudgingly, 'but the man who sets foot on snow at *that* angle must be mad! You 'll never get *me* there! Never!'

Such were the words of no less a person than MacAlpine, on Cruach Ardrain in October 1935, when he and I stared for the first time in our lives across the intervening miles of Strath Fillan to the Centre Gully of Laoigh. From here it seemed perpendicular, as do all snow-gullies seen *en face* even when quite free of rock- and ice-pitches—an elementary fact which we learned a month later when the intrepid MacAlpine took me to the Centre Gully of Beinn Laoigh.

I had the good fortune to meet Trevor Ransley in February 1947. I found him at just that stage occupied by MacAlpine and me twelve years earlier. He had not yet done a good snow-climb. So I dearly wanted to go with him to the Centre Gully; for I reckoned, judging him by myself, that that would be to him one of the classic climbs. And he showed me that I was right. We had now had a full month's frost and snow conditions this season were never likely to be better. We fixed a date and were joined by Norman Tennent.

The three of us arrived Tyndrum 9 a.m. and set off in a shrill and freezing east wind. The five-mile track running west to Laoigh was badly drifted. In one of the drifts we passed an abandoned car, obviously destined to remain there for another month—there were scores of drifts to either side. After three miles the great bend in the glen brought us to Coninish Farm, beyond which Laoigh raised that graceful peak for which it is famed, snow-draped and lustrous, deep into cloudless sky. Of its three thousand seven hundred feet the last seven hundred formed an icy wedge lifting up from the back of a great eastern corrie, which was flanked by sentinel spurs. The wedge had double summits placed close. Warning banners of drift flew from the twin tops, and between them the Centre Gully fell to the corrie.

Conditions, I could see, were going to be savage high

up, but could hardly have been more pleasant for our present purposes—the long grind to the floor of the corrie at three thousand feet. When the climber has plenty of windproof clothing, and can work up warmth by hard work, there is sheer elation in facing high, bitter winds, and joy in the hard play of the muscles. We made a speedy ascent to the corrie. On my last visit there in the late spring I had seen a lizard basking on a warm boulder. I like lizards and wondered what had become of it now. Not a rock was visible. Every boulder was buried in soft snow and each crag plastered with ice.

We waded across the floor and started up the long, lower slope to the gully. The snow had fallen as dry powder; now it was well packed and fairly firm. One kick made a step. At two hundred feet we had a short halt while Ransley practised falling, and stopping by braking with his ice-axe. It is a very easy thing to do, but at first needs resolution. Ransley was somewhat frightened about letting himself go, but quickly grew bolder. I think it doubled his self-confidence—as indeed by the nature of things it always must. Confidence ensured that he avoided a crouched position and stood erect in his steps, and so had surer footing. It was valuable practice for later events.

The slope steepened to the foot of the gully. We roped-up—Tennent leading, myself last. Although it is shallow—little more than a groove up the face—the gully was well filled with snow. The rocky flanks were plated with white ice, but in the gully itself no cutting was required. We made steady progress at an angle of forty-five degrees until within a hundred and fifty feet of the top. There the angle steepened; the gully's walls fell away so that we were out on the open face and at the mercy of the wind, which at three thousand six hundred feet was vicious. The snow was wind-packed and the crust hard as a board. At this point I took the lead from Tennent who had so far done all the work.

We had been moving all together on a short rope until now, so my first order was to lengthen rope and move singly from axe-belays. I was in no doubt about the discomforts of the climbing ahead. The wind was already hitting us hard. We had to be vigilant about balance. Every move had to be firm. The cutting of steps is a part of mountain-craft in which I personally revel, but on this occasion I soon found that neither rhythm nor revel was to be my lot. The short route lay straight up to the ridge between the two tops, but this ridge being corniced I went direct for the true summit on the left—a steeper route, rising to fifty degrees. At every step we gained we were more and more delayed by the wind, which bombarded face and eyes with icy spiculae. Sometimes I was unable to see the slope in front of me. It vanished in the flailing drift, and all I could do was drive in my axe-shaft to the head and hang on until the gusts slackened. But gradually, foot by foot, rope-length by rope-length, we fought our way on to the summit.

The wind at the cairn was so strong that we could not face into it. It fairly howled across the arctic world, heeled by hard sheets of drift that obscured the view and blinded us on impact. Directly overhead—no more than a few feet!—was the clear blue sky. That did madden us; for the mountain view that day must have been splendid beyond all telling—and there we stood in the main stream of the summit's plume. The cold was unendurable and we quickly agreed to make our descent by the north ridge.

Turning our backs to the wind we traversed the short ridge to the north top. Ransley belayed me with the rope while I crept—literally crept—to the edge of the north face and prospected. And there was the north ridge. It fell long and steeply. At a glance I could see it to be rocky and thoroughly glazed with snow-ice. Several hundred feet of downhill step-cutting was demanded, and that with speed. I let myself over the edge.

After cutting the first dozen steps I was overjoyed to find myself out of the wind. I was in perfect calm. The wind with its plume went streaming harmlessly over the north top. I rested for a minute, then thought of my companions freezing near to death just twenty-five feet above my head. I continued cutting until sixty feet of rope had run out, and waited for Ransley. When he joined me I had to move on, leaving Tennent still on top, for the footing was insufficiently good to support two of them during the delays of my own descent. At last I was ready. Tennent joined Ransley and Ransley came on. This was a moment that I awaited in mild anxiety. He could have no good belay from above, and the descent of hard-frozen snow on steep slopes is the beginner's most searching test. He amazed me. He stood up with his back as straight as an axe-shaft, his head poised, and every move a display of good balance. It was delightful to watch him—as it is to watch any man in complete control of himself, and working with skill and pace. The firm and easy sureness gratifies the eye: here is another fellow human fulfilling his powers! Probably he would not have moved one-half so well had the ground been easier and so less tonic to the nerves.

We were half-way down the ridge at sunset, and on the wrong side of our mountain, in the sense that our view was to the north-east. Yet if the sun were itself invisible the white-cowled community that filled the choir of Perthshire was growing every minute more glorious in reflected red, until the pure white by virtue of which they were able to receive the glow was transformed, utterly, into the full and holy fire of their sun. A vault of luminous blue arched them, and round their feet flowed the first dark tides of the night, the death that is the salt of the earth and life's brotherly shadow, flowing and rising, hazily and smokily blue along the glens.

Meanwhile I continued cutting. The air was very still

now, and the axe rang sharp. Chips scuttered on the glazed surface. The rope rasped on frozen gloves. Gradually the angle of the ridge eased and soon allowed us to stop cutting, and to creep down on edge-nails, and at last to face out and stride. The last colour had gone from the north-eastern tops, to be replaced by a cold grey, too much honoured by the name of light. On reaching the sentinel spur, Tennent and I enjoyed the long fierce swoop of a standing glissade to the corrie floor, where we waited for Ransley, whose swoops were shorter. Then we hastened down to Coninish, and set out upon the last of our nine hours over the snow-blocked miles to Tyndrum.

Under the arctic silence of a still, starless sky the only sound to be heard was the crunch of nails on the freezing track, sounding through the lifeless waste and the enveloping gloom.

14 *Gale Winds and Gabbro*

ONE MIDWINTER'S NIGHT I opened the Scottish Mountaineering Club's *Guide to Skye,* hoping to find ideas for a summer rock-climb—a climb, I calmly decided, considerably more than difficult. There was indeed no fearsome severity I might not enjoy; for I sat in my old arm-chair and the fire was red. Almost at once I came upon a challenging passage framed by an editor who understood winter nights and old arm-chairs and young climbers, and the surge of the coming spring: 'Sgurr na h'Uamha is the beautifully shaped peak situated a mile south of Sgurr nan Gillean. It rises steeply from the Harta Corrie, and forms the true northern termination of the main Cuillin Ridge. . . . There is no record of an ascent of the steep south-westerly buttress facing Sgurr Dubh.'

My exploratory instinct awakened with a start. I referred at once to maps and long-distance photographs, and saw from these that the South-west Buttress must be anything between five hundred and a thousand feet high. No other buttress of that size (as distinct from a face) remained unclimbed in the Cuillin; that no one had ever been there promised some exceptional technical difficulty. I wondered what the intimidating factor could be. Surely not the 'steepness' mentioned in the guide—steep gabbro is the delight of the rock-climber's heart.

In order to arrive at a rational explanation I began to take soundings in the treacherous waters of my Cuillin geology. The Cuillin form a seven-mile horse-shoe enclosing Coir-uisg, and the rock strata dip always to the centre. For example, on the northward-running section between Sgurrs Alasdair and Ghreadaidh the dip is eastward, giving on the west (or Glen Brittle) side a succession of good outcropping holds and ledges, which on the east (or Coir-uisg) side slope the wrong way for the climber. It is for this reason that no route has yet been found up the huge Coir-uisg faces of Sgurr MhicCoinnich and Sgurr Dearg. On the parallel, northward-running section between Sgurr na h'Uamha (pronounced *Hooa*) and Sgurr nan Gillean the dip should be southward. Accordingly the South-west Buttress should cut across the dip at an angle. The image that formed in my mind was that of a great tower whose outer walls were in a state of chaos: overhangs, slabs, and ledges mingled disorderly. The buttress bristled. Climbers would not have been attracted, if I were right, because there would not be an obvious route—no outstanding rib piercing the difficulties, nor continuous fault inviting attack.

The more I speculated about the buttress during the following six months the more clear and firm did the image become. Like all such images it evoked thought, and thought action. For the dream became a plan—that next June I should go to Sgurr na h'Uamha with Kenneth Dunn and one hundred feet of rope, and try to climb that bristling buttress.

Six months later I arrived in Skye with Dunn. We camped in Glen Brittle and climbed for a fortnight on the South Cuillin. I regarded all our time thus spent as so much training for *der Tag*. I had thought about Sgurr na h'Uamha until I was rather in awe of its imaginary difficulties. Usually I feel less nervous apprehension before a new climb than before an old that is highly classified; for not knowing what to expect on the new, I hope for the best instead of fearing the worst. When trial is made and the worst materializes, then, of course, it tests the nerves higher than a known route already ascended by mortal men. So new climbs are encouraging in advance. But *not* so Sgurr na h'Uamha. We reserved it to the last, waiting like innocents for the Perfect Day.

The consequence was that we came near to losing all chance of trying the climb. At first the weather was mixed, good days and bad alternating, but latterly the rain grew squallier, and we had to be thankful for heavy winds, which kept the clouds moving briskly. The risk we were running was eventually brought home to me on 25th June when we went to the Bhasteir Tooth and tried a face-climb, of which Dunn had made the first ascent some years before. The feature of the route is a 'stomach traverse' of sixty feet, where a long, narrow ledge slants up and leftwards across the south face. There is a big drop below and the rock immediately above the ledge projects like an eave, forcing one to lie on one's stomach and wriggle. After sixty feet the ledge thins out and, fortunately, so does the overhang, so that one may first kneel and then stand, being now on vertical rock with good holds. That was where the wind caught me. We had to abandon the continuation by the exposed upper rocks of Naismith's Route. We then withdrew and took refuge in the North Chimney of the north face—a corkscrew tunnel twisting this way and that through total darkness in the very heart of the Tooth, at last turning right-about so violently that we had to squirm along a horizontal funnel, from which we popped out on the Tooth's crown like rabbits out of a burrow. We had not realized that rock could be intrinsically funny until we found ourselves sprawling on the top helpless with laughter. In that respect, at least, the route seems to be unique.

The wind was now blowing hard from the south-west. If we had been forced by it to abandon a climb classed as *difficult* then what of our hopes of climbing a new buttress on Sgurr na h'Uamha? They were already imperilled. That is, if the wind were maintained. It was raining by the time we got back to Glen Brittle. Only one week remained of our holidays. It was a question whether to hold off our attempt for a few days longer or to strike at once. That evening the clouds rolled aside; for several minutes a strange warm light spread over the glen; the field around the tent glowed a rich and unnatural green. I suspected then that a big change for the worse was coming over the weather. That decided us. To-morrow's goal was Sgurr na h'Uamha.

Early next morning we drove the fourteen miles to Sligachan, and by 9 a.m. were walking down Glen Sligachan under layers of steel-grey clouds, hard at the edges and driving high, a dull, metallic glitter emanating from the under-layer. These were long-distance voyagers and carried no cargo for Skye. We had gone four miles south to the Bloody Stone at the entrance to Harta Corrie before we began to feel the kick of the wind, which was still blowing from the south-west; but so far we were protected from it in great measure by the long ridge of Druim nan Ramh. On the whole, conditions were good, provided that we were spared any increase in wind-force.

We walked a mile west up Harta Corrie, rounding the south face of Sgurr na h'Uamha. Its face was slabby, confirming my guess at the dip of the strata. But my intense curiosity about the South-west Buttress remained unsatisfied until the last moment. We struck uphill from the floor of the corrie and climbed several hundred feet up scree to the foot of the rocks, at a height of eighteen hundred feet. A short left traverse—and there was our buttress.

It was six hundred feet high. The lower half took the shape of a three-hundred-and-fifty-foot hump—and it bristled! It bristled with short overhangs and vertical walls, arranged in tiers, which were divided one from another by narrow, horizontal trap-ledges. I could hardly believe my eyes; for the rocks of imagination were realized in solid gabbro, correct in detail. Only one detail was incorrect. My imagination had created a tower for me, but the real rock was a broad-based pyramid. We built a cairn at the centre of its base-line, at the point where one may see into Lota Corrie on the left and Harta Corrie on the right. We roped up on a hundred feet of line.

Our problem was how to thread a route through that welter of wall and overhang. No line of weakness was visible—no continuous line to be picked out in advance and followed with hope. On the other hand, if the rock gave no promise, at least it made plain that only one tactical plan was possible: the overhangs of each tier must be turned on one flank or the other by means of traversing the horizontal ledges. Beyond that we could do nothing, save try; hope for nothing, save the best.

I climbed twenty feet up a wall of good rock to the first ledge below the first overhang. It was too narrow a ledge to accommodate Dunn also, at least not with advantage to either of us, so I traversed rightwards, blindly, with no idea what to expect. On the overhang's far side I found an inset corner. A steep groove in its back cut through the tier above, and up I went to the second ledge, where Dunn joined me. Like every true buttress ours was indefinite, and for that very reason we found the route selection of great interest. Every overhang we met henceforth we turned by a left or right traverse along ledges, until a corner, crack, or face gave a route to the next tier. Every unknown corner rounded was a doubt resolved, each overhang turned a tactical triumph. The pleasure of the exploration was cumulative. Our avoiding moves, however, were often exposed, and the wind, rising as we gained height, was beginning to buffet us nastily. Fortunately the gabbro was so coarse and tough that we felt fairly secure. Thus we climbed five tiers, the highest being eighty feet, and their total three hundred and fifty feet, to the top of the first hump.

The angle of the rock fell back for a hundred and fifty feet, then uprose in a further series of overhangs. This final rampart was obviously going to be the crux of the climb, for the wind had become ferocious. Lower down it had troubled us, but now it was rising to sudden long gusts of little less than gale-force. Every step we climbed over that next two hundred feet exposed us the more to its fury, which repeatedly staggered us. Perhaps it was strengthening at all levels.

High wind not accompanied by rain or wintry cold, and provided I can keep moving, intoxicates me. It goes to my head. I feel a redoubled energy. And so it was now. On top of that every muscle of my body was in wellnigh perfect training. So that instead of being tempted by a long slant of slabs to the right of the serried overhangs, I felt an urge to go for the overhangs themselves. I was spoiling for a fight. Accordingly

I climbed a great up-roll of slab to the foot of the first overhang, intending to repeat the tactics of the lower buttress. At the crease where this overhang rose out of the slab-wave a traverse had to be made right or left, but the crease was *only* a crease. Holds were small. Here it was not possible to climb, as I had hoped, relying simply on the effort of muscle and an overflowing energy to defeat the wind. The rock-holds were inadequate, and nothing less than big, well-cut holds would suffice, for the wind was beginning to wrench at my body, making suicidal any position that relied for security on balance rather than muscle. While I was descending the wind strengthened even further, and by the time I reached the foot of the slab-wave a full gale was blowing from the south-west.

It seemed to me probable that our retreat was now cut off, unless we could find natural spikes for roping down; the gale must now be playing on every part of the buttress. At all events we were still keen to go on rather than go down. A way of forcing the upper cliffs had to be found quickly, for I had forgotten my balaclava helmet and my body was beginning to lose heat more rapidly than I liked. Dunn, however, had all his winter climbing gear, barring an ice-axe, and already bulged like a brown bear in the autumn. I continued in the lead, none the less, because my hands were still preserved from numbness by fingerless woollen mittens.

We looked up and pondered the serried overhangs. It began to seem that our best route might be the one that at first sight, and in the particular conditions, had seemed uninviting. To the right-hand side of the overhangs were smoothly arching slabs one hundred feet high. Slabs have usually less definite holds than walls and cracks, and call more emphatically for the very kind of balance-climbing that we had now greatest cause to avoid. On the other hand, their angle was less high. It occurred to us that the gale, being south-west, would tend to blow us on to the slabs, to plaster us against them, rather than to blow us off. If the gabbro were the rougher kind, and technically simple, and were embellished by at least one midway stance, then we could go farther. For the moment we were sure of none of these things.

We made a right-hand traverse and I started up. At first I was scared to move, but quickly evolved the necessary technique. The first need was to have four good holds, then wait till the blow of the wind seemed steady, its jumpiness smoothed out, then make a quick, deliberate snatch of hand or foot at the next hold. The main consideration was always to have three points of attachment to the rock. The gabbro was luckily as coarse as only gabbro can be. I could feel the bite of my edge-nails right into the crystalline surface, the grasp of the whole palm on rounded ribs, or the tips of my fingers curl around square-cut edges. Never before had I felt such gratitude for the simple merits of weathered rock. I clung to it, not to wrestle as though with an enemy, but for succour against the real enemy—wind.

At fifty feet I found a stance. I turned to bring up Dunn. For one moment the wind threw my head back and stopped my breath. I could not exhale—my breath was forced back between my teeth. I had to tighten my neck muscles and bring my head down to my chest before I could breathe freely, and the pain of wind-blast on the eyes prevented my watching Dunn climbing. I took in the rope by feel.

As a result of confusion and trouble with the rope when Dunn arrived, I cannot recollect if he found a belay. I remember, however, dealing very slowly and cautiously with the upper passage. The slabs there were broad and splendidly arched, but the consequences of a fall would be worse for their greater height, and this thought was very much in my mind. I had a vivid recollection of a lesser gale on the Crowberry Ridge, at the September equinox, when I saw MacAlpine, on the rope below me, blown by one gust clean off the rock at the crux. He made an awe-inspiring sight—especially as I reflected, 'There, but for the grace of God, go I.' The way had thus to be forced in defiance of fear—the fear of treachery—a gust coming at an angle, or a violent whip of the rope. It was only the wind direction that justified us.

Consequently I continued to move in jerks—to hang on with all the strength of my body, every muscle of arm and leg continuously tensed—deliberately to pick out my next hold—to calculate the movement—to wait for the right moment, then—grab. I expended far more energy on this pitch than was strictly necessary, but the margin of safety had to be wide. Towards the end the climbing gave me sheer joy—the joy of free action over gale-swept rock.

The angle fell back. One hundred feet of scrambling followed on superb gabbro slabs. We were pushed in triumph and with great violence to the cairn. We paused there for one second, just to clap a thankful hand on top, and passed on. To the west and north the twenty black teeth of the Cuillin were sharp and clear in a sky fast changing in colour from steel to gun-metal. Everywhere was the heavy rush and thunder of wind. The terrific gusts, which had tormented us below the final slabs, had now merged into one continuously powerful blow, before which we fled to the col under Sgurr Beag, and thence down to Glen Sligachan.

Up on the tops the gale was mounting to a hurricane, which broke that night. Frcm between its teeth we had snatched our buttress in the nick of time. Down in Glen Brittle our frail canvas roof was drummed and punched for three days by storms of rain. We had opportunity then to assess the merits of our route impartially. In fine weather the buttress would present little difficulty, its features reveal no remarkable character: it would not be what in Wales is called an elegant route. The weather had *made* our climb—given us a better and tougher frolic than a classic route in fair weather. To all humble buttresses called Difficult I give belated homage. And to all winds called Gale——

But no, there is need of diplomacy. My days are not yet done.

15 *Rosa Pinnacle*

FOR A YEAR ON END, 1948 to 1949, my numerous efforts to reach Arran, in hope of climbing Cir Mhor by the Rosa Pinnacle, were foiled. Weather went bad, friends failed, work intervened. In a way these difficulties were right and proper, my ambition not being a humble one. By all reports—and these were few enough—the south ridge of Rosa Pinnacle was a tough climb, but almost unknown even to Scottish climbers. Its first direct ascent had been made during the war by J. F. Hamilton; thereafter, little had been heard of it. For some years following a first ascent, such is the fate of many a great climb.

I knew next to nothing about the route until 1948. One evening at Inverarnan House in Glen Falloch (a headquarters of mountaineering in west Scotland), I asked Hamilton over a plate of eggs and bacon: 'Is Rosa Pinnacle any good?' He looked startled, as well he might, and fixed me with a bright black eye. 'Well, well!' said he, very gently. 'I 'd say that climb was the best in Arran.' Then, with a sudden burst of enthusiasm: 'It 's terrific! There 's eight hundred feet of granite, but you 've never seen granite as rough—it 's as rough as gabbro. It 's terrific! It 's absolutely——'

'How hard?' I ventured.

'Severe in rubbers. Two bad pitches, one in the lower third and the other near the centre. The first 's a long crack like an S, and the second 's a lay-back crack with a delicate traverse above. A bit exposed. No one has done them in boots. Take rubbers and pray for a dry day.'

Dry days came and went (at infrequent intervals), but rarely did they coincide with my own leisure, and never with that of my climbing friends. In consequence, Cir Mhor by the Rosa Pinnacle grew ever more desirable in my eyes, until it quite ousted every other mountain route in Scotland. Penance having thus been done, atonement made, I was given a reward far greater than I ever deserved. When I stepped on board the Arran steamer at Ardrossan in June 1949 I was able to heave a great sigh of relief—three sighs all rolled into one. The first because I had thought I was going to miss the boat; the second in gratitude for a heat-wave, now in its seventh day and destined to last for a month; the third because I had a substantial part of my reward already on board with me: my companions were Norman Tennent and his wife Mona.

Arran lies west of Ardrossan some eleven miles. No trace of it could be seen through the heat-haze. When we landed at Brodick an hour later we were thankful to see the long hill-ridges stretched out upon blue sky. It was now the mainland's turn to be lost in pearly fog, while Arran lay bright as Paradise. Our plan was to camp in upper Glen Rosa, which runs from Brodick Bay four and a half miles north-west to the south face of Cir Mhor. We had brought neither tent nor change of clothing; for in such weather we might safely lie out on the heather in sleeping-bags. Should the weather miraculously break we need only call upon the boulder-lore of Norman Tennent. He knew the size and shape and relative merits of every stone in Arran big enough to shelter man or beast. He promised to find us a good cave near the foot of Cir Mhor if need were; or, if we preferred, individual boulders with overhangs. Tennent could stow away a whole mountaineering club on the bare slopes of an Arran hill, and have each man snug and happy. Our faith in him lightened our loads greatly. Fortunately the weather stayed dry.

When we had gone a little way into Glen Rosa I realized that I had never before been to Arran in June. The rich green of the trees and grass was astonishingly like that of the lower Alps. The path too was an Alpine path, a pleasure to tread (at least in daytime), for its rounded stones were firmly embedded in soil. The warm sweet scent of young plants mingled with the sharper tang of pine. We walked into the evening sun, which shone down the glen, not dazzlingly, for it was still well above the ridges, but slanting enough to flicker the air with the gleam of insects' wings.

In less than two miles the trees thinned and vanished. The path deteriorated. The glen broadened out to a moorland heath, where only thyme and bog-myrtle flourished, and sparse heather struggled through coarse grass. The glen turned sharply north. The rounding of that bend is a great moment among Arran hills. Deep pools of the Rosa Burn fill the hollowed foreground, from which the eye glances up long bare hill-sides, which guide it straight to the spikes of Cir Mhor and the Castles. They do not so much dominate the glen as consummate all its beauties. The long approach exacts its proper sacrifice of energy and sweat, but never yet have I heard of the mountaineer who turned the bend of Glen Rosa and then grudged his offering to Cir Mhor.

The Rosa Pinnacle, I knew, must be facing us. I searched eagerly for it, but the detail of the south face was not yet distinct. There was a faint haze in the upper corrie, washed blue by a slant of the sun's rays. We stopped about a mile from the summit, ate supper beside the burn, then slid into our sleeping-bags. Perhaps in contrast to the great heat of the day the night was cooler than we had expected. From time to time a sense of cold wakened us, when we gave a glance round at the hills and a swift wriggle, then dropped off to sleep again. Cloudless nights in the highlands at midsummer are no darker than twilight. Stars twinkled faintly, for though the sky was clear it retained in the north a pure and colourless light, which invaded the east and west, and permeated far southward. At any time through the night we might have climbed on rock.

Our full compensation for broken sleep came when the first sun-ray struck the highest crag of Cir Mhor, thus proving the summit. For the lighted rocks were not the summit as it appeared from Glen Rosa, but a seemingly lesser top to its right. A few minutes later the creamy fire touched the sharper tip of the mock summit, and flashed a short way down its east wall, which we clearly saw to be the Rosa Pinnacle. For a while I lay in

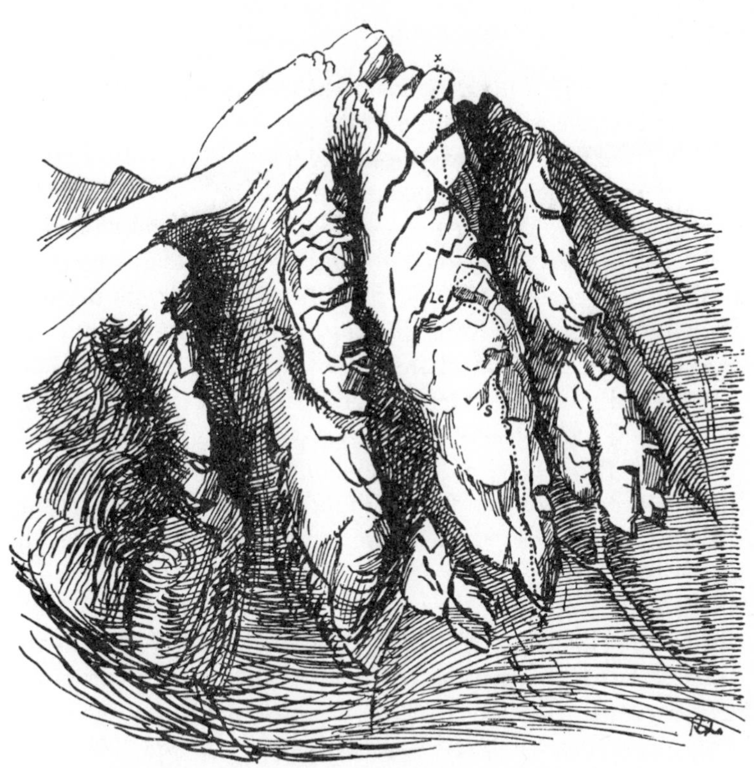

Rosa Pinnacle—south face of Cir Mhor, Isle of Arran
s, S crack. LC, Lay-back crack. ...., route

my bag and tried to imagine our party of three climbing up that sunlit shaft—tried to persuade myself that in a few hours we should be there. The idea was too good to be true: a vision of the kind that goes through the gate of ivory—not to be realized. Until men take action good ideas seem like that.

We took action by breakfasting. While we ate, the sunshine crept down the Rosa Pinnacle until its whole eight hundred feet had been won from shadow. The Pinnacle, we could see, was built in two parts—a lower buttress of five hundred feet and a final tower of three hundred feet. From a distance that tower looked by far the worst part of the climb, its great east wall close to the vertical, its crest a fierce *arête*, to be turned on the left only by vast sheets of slab, each dipping to the south-west and overlapping. However, we knew the real difficulties to be concentrated on the lower buttress.

When the sun spread over our bivouac site we set off to the upper corrie, which we reached in half an hour. Its floor offered remarkably good camping ground—no scree, plenty of short turf, and several big boulders with commodious overhangs awaiting Tennents. We could see from here all the detail of Rosa Pinnacle. The lower buttress, broad below and near the base quite gently inclined, steepened rapidly to a hundred-foot wall topped by an overhang. In the middle of that wall was an elongated S crack, sixty feet high, wide, shallow, holdless—obviously the real crux of the climb. Above the wall the buttress tapered to a ridge of rounded slabs, promptly rising again to a sheer nose, then sweeping back to a terrace under the final tower.

We moved uphill to the lowest rocks, where I took off boots and put on rubbers. We roped up with myself in the lead and Tennent second. As usual before a hard climb I felt nervous—very nervous. For my own protection on such occasions my imagination has to be consciously damped down. Again as usual, all nervousness vanished when I set foot on the rock. I began to enjoy myself. When that preliminary concern is absent my climbing suffers.

We scrambled over easy rocks to start the climb proper at the centre of the buttress. Between the main face and a protruding mass on the left was an open corner. I stepped on to a tilted slab under this corner, but its walls were too steep to be climbable, so I traversed several feet to the right and found tumbling down the face a narrow cascade of good holds. These brought me in fifty feet to a nest-like ledge, to which Tennent followed. All this while I had to be most careful what movements I made with my hands; the rock was so coarsely crystalline that a careless knock, however light, rasped the skin off the knuckles. Hamilton had modestly called it 'rough as gabbro,' but in truth it is rough as peridotite.

One more run-out of fifty feet landed me on a long, narrow

ledge directly under the S crack. While Tennent brought Mona to the stance below, I looked down and out to Glen Rosa's floor, where the speckles of bungalow boulders lay like clover on a lawn. Tennent joined me and anchored to a rock-spike. I turned to the crack. At my first glance I said: 'This *is* a different proposition.' It was a wide groove with a rounded crack inside. For the most part the crack was holdless, but extraordinarily rough. Yet the angle was so high that I had trouble persuading myself that rock-friction would avail me against gravity. At the very top the crack overhung. To Hamilton, who made the first ascent, I raised a figurative hat. After one tentative step up and return, I started.

All upward movement was made by the downpress of rubbers against the slabs of the groove. But while the feet were being raised, the body had to be held in balance and its weight supported. The only means of so doing was to thrust the right hand into the crack at chest-level and then try to jam it. The crack being a shallow one on the left side of the groove, only the right hand could be firmly wedged. I knew in advance that every wedge was going to lift off more skin, but never have I hesitated less over a sacrifice: I am not of the tigerish few, deaf and blind to the yawn of a drop. I gave all the energy and determination I had to each move up and jam—move up and jam—suffering no temptation to pause. I was surprised how soon I came to the half-way point. Sometimes a foot could be wedged, sometimes a handhold appeared; then I came under the 'overhang,' which was, after all, vertical. It would be impossible without a handhold or two, and I hardly dared believe that *now* they would appear after being denied to me so long. I edged up as high as I could, and stretched up the blank left wall with my left hand. The fingers gripped a perfect, cup-like hold. The whole S crack is made remarkable by the gratitude that fills the mind at that moment. A noggin of rum would not have made me happier. I now enjoyed the exposure of the face for its own sake; enjoyed it again when more good holds came to hand beyond and above the crack. I swarmed over the top edge.

I arrived on a wide, out-dipping shelf slanting left. A detached pinnacle stood on it, ten feet high and triangular. It offered the only belay for the rope, which saddened me. No doubt it is really as safe and solid as all good pinnacles are in a happier, far-off land, but I have seen a bigger, better, and safer-looking crag collapse over a sheer precipice under one man's weight. The incident has conditioned my reflexes. I viewed the pinnacle with suspicion, pronounced it safe, and not without misgiving threw a loop of rope over the apex. Tennent began to take in Mona's rope.

The rock scene at the pinnacle-shelf is as bold as any I know in Scotland. On this granite there is no blemish of vegetation. To each side, walls, corners, edges, thrust cleanly up. The rock is an ashen grey, almost cream, its every face showing a sparkle of crystal-grain. The sweep and lift of the crags give to the very air an added airiness, and this it is that from start to finish of the day has impressed my memory.

Tennent began to climb. Like me, he moved quickly. I could see nothing, but could feel the pause when he came under the overhang, and hear his delight when his hand entered the cup. Perversely, I smiled to myself when his right hand floated over the edge bearing blood on its back. Mona in turn showed the same joy at the overhang, the same rasped hand above. Every party aspiring to Rosa Pinnacle must be prepared for that sacrifice of the flesh. They will give gladly enough when the call comes.

We had no idea how the route continued. At the low left end of the shelf there was no inviting way. Directly above us, by climbing over the detached pinnacle, we might reach an overhanging wall of thirty feet which girdled the buttress. It was split by a straight-edged chimney, possibly climbable. Hard to our right was a high and exposed corner. We could not see what lay beyond. One of the delights of rock-climbing is traversing round exposed and unknown corners. After an awkward descent of three feet from the pinnacle-shelf I balanced round the corner on a sloping slab. At first there seemed to be few handholds and these too far apart, but the traverse is simple when the drop below is ignored. Once round the corner I came on to a wide rectangular ledge, cut clean as a *route aux bicyclettes*. The others followed. On our right the ledge abruptly ended at another mysterious corner.

Standing at the end's lip we looked down a sheer face, and round the corner at an open chimney which split the face from top to bottom. I traversed into it, three feet across a perpendicular wall. The ascent of seventy feet, coming after the S crack, seemed not at all difficult. The party foregathered on easy slabs at the crest.

The buttress had narrowed, and might henceforth be more aptly called a ridge. Sixty feet above, it whipped up again. The edge overhung and looked unclimbable. Reconnaissance showed that we might turn it to the right or left by long traverses, although it was not clear by what means we should arrive back at the crest. If we went left I guessed that we might now arrive at the Lay-back Crack, which was, Hamilton had sworn, an experience not to be missed. Therefore we made the left traverse—a walk on rolling slabs for a hundred feet or more—while the ridge continued to rise on our right. Our soothing slabs at length upcurled in a great wave against a greater vertical wall, which barred the ridge. In the angle between this wall and the flank of the ridge we saw a long crack. It was the only breach, and lay on a tilt from left to right. Underneath the crack a similarly tilting slab gave Tennent and me footing. I would not call it a good stance. None the less it gave a flake-belay at knee-level. Tennent could tie on, lean back on the tight rope, and say honestly that he was safe, perjuriously that he *felt* safe.

Our climb back to the crest looked about sixty feet. I was alarmed at the prospect of having to make all that height by the lay-back technique: it is most exhausting. When a thin crack divides right-angled walls, which are holdless, one may grasp the edge of the crack (which must be sharp), place the flat of the feet against the opposing wall, then lean back on the hands and walk up. The pull of the hands against the push of the feet masters gravity. This difficult technique is made easier for a man short in the leg, but for a long-legged animal like me few things are more tiring. He is doubled up and straining all the time.

What the top part of the pitch was like I could not properly see on account of a sun-shaft streaming across the ridge straight into my eyes. So blinding was the stream that I was doubtful of seeing the holds even when I got to them. Although usually leader, Tennent is also the complete second. He produced a white sun-hat and clapped it on my head. I pulled down the brim and started. By lay-back technique I made no more height than two feet. I stepped down and looked again. It seemed that one did not start with a lay-back. I tried instead a rounded foothold on the left wall, and then took the lay-back position a foot higher than before. I moved up successfully, shifting the hands a few inches, then the feet a few inches, then the hands, until at ten feet I saw an excellent blunt spike ahead of me which I just managed to grasp with a quick movement. One heave up pulled me on to its top. That was the perfectly sited resting-place. I stopped for a while and panted. I was in good training, but lay-backs are not my forte. Whatever happened I swore that I would not continue up the crack, for its edge had become rounded. I looked rightwards. Across a wide expanse of wall and slab ran a chain of irregular knobs. I crept out on them for six feet to a point where the chain broke, but continued four feet higher, swinging sharply up. Obviously I had to use the knobs now as handholds instead of footholds. The point of real difficulty was that first step at the break. The right foot had to be planted on a steep slab, and trusted for friction-grip, while the body swung over and up to use the higher hand-rail.

I was still unaware whether all would now be well. At each move of the circling traverse I feared another break in the chain, feared it especially in the absence of definite foothold. However, the uncertainty was soon over, because there could be no loitering on that rock. I kept going at fair speed, and emerged once more on the sharp crest of the ridge. Just over its edge was a grassy hollow big enough for three bodies to stretch out in comfort—a sun-trap—the perfect, archetypal stance.

I fetched up Tennent. I expected Mona to have difficulty, for women are not muscularly so strong as men. The traverse being delicate, any leg-tremble or arm-shake due to muscular exhaustion at the crux would be fatal. But she arrived at the top more speedily than either of us, and by skill distinctly fresher than me. We resolved that this was lunch-time, less because we wanted lunch than because the hollow was made to be lunched on—it appealed to our hearts rather than our stomachs. The ridge above us overhung in a high nose. On all other sides we saw nothing but empty space, into which the crest of our ridge projected like the keel of an upturned boat. It was sunlit space, and sun-washed granite, and the sun's heat smote full upon us. A cool breeze made all that sun endurable. Looking back upon the scene I wonder that we ever prevailed upon ourselves to stir. There we should have lain, I think, until the hills crumbled into dust, satisfied in one part of our nature by sloth and ease, in another by the liveliness of beauty, had it not been for that third part, which brews energy and would always be stirring up trouble. In a quarter of an hour I was on my feet again.

The route goes to the left of the great overhang by triple chimneys spaced in vertical tiers. The total height may be a hundred feet. The first two gave plenty of muscular work and asked for little skill. The last was the type and epitome of all three. Under Chimney III Tennent belayed me in a right-angled corner between the ridge and an open wall to its left. On this left wall was the chimney. It was only ten feet high, exposed, and overhanging at the top where a big stone was jammed. The ascent was crude work at the top—a pull up on the stone—none the less giving unadulterated joy: it is so safe, yet the body swings free over thin air; the muscles tighten exhilaratingly; the climber within revels in what Tennent derisively reminded me was 'a glorious out-of-balance movement.'

Beyond the barrier the angle eased. We climbed together up gentle slabs to the Terrace below the final tower. The Terrace is a grassy scoop inclining obliquely right to left, by which one may walk off the buttress. Such a dismal detour would be taken by no man in his right senses. Straight ahead soars the rock of the pinnacle. From its sharp *arête* enormous slabs slope down to the left, overlapping each other in tiers. At each overlap is a vertical wall of ten to thirty feet.

We started our first slab at its lower left-hand edge. By a long ladder of tiny cobbles we came in a hundred feet to a vertical chimney splitting the first overlap. The holds were big. So, at each tier, the slabs yielded in the same way—a slender line, usually a crack, giving passage to the next wall. Towards the top we kept to the right-hand *arête*, where our way poised us on the edge of the great eastern cliff. The granite was rough as ever, and having been exposed to the sun since dawn, was hot to the hand. We climbed on ideal rock, on an ideal mountain, in ideal weather—the kind of mountain-day we dream about on raw nights in November—or at midsummer dawns in Glen Rosa. Our dream, after all, had passed not through the gate of ivory but through the gate of horn.

We came out on the topmost point of Rosa Pinnacle aware that something unique had happened to us: we had had the best summer rock-climb of our lives.

We descended into the Pinnacle Gap and climbed the last slope of Cir Mhor. Mona and I sat down on the west side of the cairn, but Tennent, thank heaven, corrected us. He hailed us on to the very tip. Only when we stepped on to that short thin ridge did we discover that a fresh wind was blowing on to the north-east wall, and striking vertically up: we had to stand on the brink to get the air-stream on face and chest. There was no distant view, and little colour from the sea and nearer hills filtered through the haze. But a good wine needs no bush and Cir Mhor no view. All height and depth, endless space, and the slender tips of all mountains—they were ours. We took deep breaths of the air shooting cool and fast out of the deeps of Glen Sannox and found it heady.

We also found it sobering. Rosa Pinnacle is a buttress. We had climbed Cir Mhor.

16 *The Traverse of Liathach*

ON THE AFTERNOON of 7th January Edward Mortimer and I walked down Glen Torridon in Wester Ross towards the west end of Liathach. New snow blocked the road. The going was heavy, but our way lightened by Mortimer's enthusiasm. He had never seen a Torridon mountain before, and that first view of Liathach from the Kinlochewe side certainly does fire the heart of a man too long accustomed to rounded shapes and long slopes of grass. Here, gaunt sharp peaks soar heavenward. Barely distinguishable at early dusk against the palest of blue skies, the white cone of Liathach floated like a cut feather —hovered in a cold remote region, a stratosphere far removed from earth, or concern of man, or the toil of a drifted highway in Torridon. It looked a mountain to be watched from afar, I thought, but not one inviting so slight a thing as flesh and blood to the summit.

'It's beautiful!' exclaimed Mortimer. 'To-morrow we'll climb it.'

'In this north-east wind,' I reminded him, 'it's going to be the very devil getting up the Northern Pinnacles, and after that a tough battle along the ridge.'

'And I'm dying to explore that northern corrie,' added Mortimer inattentively. 'The scent of the unknown creeps right down to the roadway.'

At the shores of Loch Torridon we overtook an old stalker going to Inver Alligin.

'Good evening,' I said as we drew level. 'It's been a bitter wind to-day.'

'A good day to you,' said he. 'Yess, indeed, it hass been a cold north wind. It will not be good for the hills,' he added,

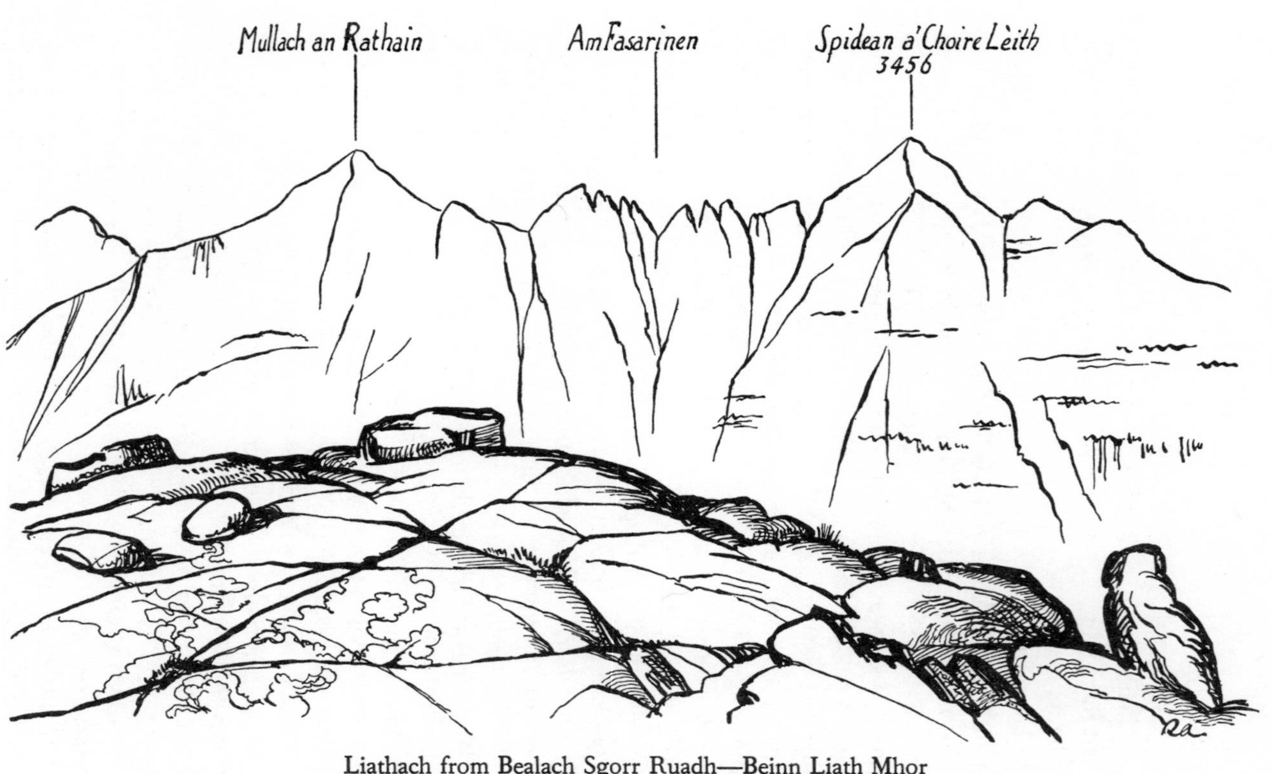

Liathach from Bealach Sgorr Ruadh—Beinn Liath Mhor

eyeing our boots and axes, 'unless it iss that you are chust the hikers?'

'We like the look of Liathach,' I replied.

'Liathach!' exclaimed the old stalker enthusiastically. 'Man, but there iss no other mountain like her in the whole of Scotland! She iss machestic!'

He turned to us sharply. 'But you will not be thinking of climbing her? Not in the snowy weather?'

'We thought of climbing it to-morrow,' said Mortimer.

The old man was outraged. He shook his head. 'She iss not to be tampered with!' he warned. 'No indeed, she iss not.'

We said good-bye to him at Torridon House, where Glen Mhic Nobuil sweeps round from the back of Liathach to meet the loch. A camp there would place us favourably for a west to east traverse next day. We pitched the tent on a bleak snow-field. In the near background a black semicircle of pines gave us some protection from a biting wind, which rushed down Glen Mhic Nobuil and swept furiously through the branches. Long, grey skirts of hail trailed across Loch Torridon, which gloomed flatly. Inside the tent we were comfortable enough, and candle-light seems cheerful at night. Surrounded by the usual wild confusion of gear and food, we lay on our stomachs inside warm sleeping-bags with a one-inch map between us.

Our problem was a calculation of time. The Northern Pinnacles Route, which was unknown ground to us, followed by the main ridge traverse, would give us the best winter ridge in Scotland, but might take us every bit of eight hours to the summit. In such heavy snow conditions we dared not reckon less. It was accordingly debatable whether we should get off the mountain in daylight. The ridge of Liathach is four miles long with six tops, running due east and west. The south flank drops in craggy slopes to Glen Torridon, but the north wall is a precipice, enclosing with its cirque of four great peaks the sanctuary of the Torridon Forest—the Coire na Caime. The summit lies at the far end of the cirque. At the near end is the second highest peak, Mullach an Rathain. Its north-easterly ridge, set at right-angles to the backbone, is a down-sweep of five pinnacles, known collectively as the Northern Pinnacles. Since their first discovery by Hinxman in 1891 they have not often been climbed—least of all in winter. Having no clue to their difficulties we felt unsure of our time allowance.

'Let 's rise at five,' urged Mortimer.

I was horrified. 'Five 's all right in a monastery,' I argued, 'where you enjoy the reward at once. But on a cold and squally mountain seven is the limit.'

We compromised at six, each gloating over the hour wrung from the other. At six o'clock next morning it was still night and sleeting. We breakfasted by candlelight on oatmeal, kippers, and brown bread. Big gobs of sleet sploshed and spurted on the canvas. Altogether I remember no other morning quite so discouraging. However, this was Mortimer's last day, so we rolled up our sleeping-bags, lest we should fail to endure the temptation. By eight o'clock, when we set out, the sky had cleared.

Grey light helped us through the woods, where the line of an excellent path could still be traced under shallow snow. In the open valley beyond, the snow lay deep and the path vanished. The Mhic Nobuil glen swings in a great arc round Liathach from west to north. To reach the base of the Northern Pinnacles we had to walk four miles to two thousand feet. We were both in first-class training, and not inclined to spare ourselves, yet reckoned that we should need three hours to that four miles. At the half-way region thick cloud blew up and a wall of driving snow advanced down the glen. It hit us with heavy gusts, slowing us down still further, beating our eyes with snow-particles, forcing us to move crabwise, and to shield our faces with gloved hands. In half an hour it was all over. Broad fields of blue opened across the sky, and over them sunlit clouds galloped like white stallions, purposefully, as though 'going places.' The wind remained north-east. It was clear that our day's weather was to be alternate sunshine and squalls. But—which would predominate?

After going two and three-quarter miles up the broad and desolate glen, we could see the cliffs of the Northern Pinnacles a mile away on our right and a thousand feet above. We struck uphill but were still several hundred feet under the ridge when our second squall came over. It could not have chosen a worse time; hiding our objective in mist, it left us to guess where the best start might be. However, we soon came upon steep, rocky slopes, which could be nothing else, we thought, than the start of our ridge. At this higher angle the snow lay less thickly. The ground was free of technical difficulty and allowed us to climb unroped. We had made considerable height before the clouds began to thin out and lift. Then the whitened towers above slowly emerged, as though crystallizing out of the fog. They seemed rather too far to our left. With a moment's pang of dismay we realized that our ridge was not the pinnacle-ridge but a subsidiary one, separated from the other by a deep gully. However, we soon saw that a descent could be made into the top of this gully, whence we might climb a chimney to the lowest col or notch of the true ridge, thus arriving beneath its better half. For the lower ridge is a buttress, swelling gracefully in wall-and-terrace form to the first col, where a fundamental change occurs in its character. It becomes a rocky spur, pinnacled on its narrow crest and walled by red sandstone slabs.

We crossed the gully, kicked steps up the steep snow-chimney to the notch, and looked for the first time into Coire na Caime. Our straight-down glimpse to its floor showed a frozen lochan, pale green around the edges, lying below a ring of black cliffs. The cliffs rose high above us to buttress the main ridge. Their ebony was probably a contrast effect caused by the pure whiteness of new snow lining countless cracks and ledges, which ran up and down and across the face, dead straight as though drawn by ruler. Depths of blue space, and a chill, refreshing air, filled the corrie as spring-water fills a well, offering new vigour to men.

We were most grateful for the accident of this particular approach. It had brought us suddenly to the very essence of the mountainous scene, a true sanctuary at the inmost fastness, to which no man penetrates save the mountaineer. Our approach was also the quickest to the pinnacles. On the lower half of the ridge we might still have been wrestling up short walls—harder climbing no doubt, but disadvantageous. Time was our enemy. We moved up the crest to the first pinnacle. It faced us with thirty feet of vertical rock, which looked rotten and doubtfully cemented by frost. I traversed rightwards and climbed by a chimney to the top.

The second pinnacle was much longer and is no doubt easy in summer. On this occasion the rock-rib on which we started and then the long slope of high-angle scree above were filmed with thin ice. The rock was manageable but not so the scree. A dusting of powder on top made it worse. One put the foot down, allowed it to slither in all directions until at long last something seemed to hold it, then, calling loudly on one's Maker, one stepped up. The wearing of a rope would have given us no kind of protection. We took a leftward trend to avoid more iced rock ahead and entered a gully, which dropped down to the lochan. The snow was iron-hard. The blade of my axe stuck at every blow, forcing me to use the pick. From the top the third pinnacle, rising on the far side of a three-foot gap, looked most straight and formidable. Abrupt chutes flanked the gap, on each side of which was a short knife-edge of snow. At a first glance the gap excited the imagination, but its passage was easy. One kick flattened the knife-edge.

We had now a choice of ledges running left and right around the pinnacle. We tried to follow the right-hand ledge but soon thought better of it, for it girdled a crag to a cul-de-sac over all space. We turned and tried leftwards. This ledge wound upwards above the cliff overlooking the east gully—again an easy ledge in summer, but to-day piled to a high angle with floury snow lying on ice. The ice was the clear glossy kind, thin except at the lower edge, where icicles two yards long overhung the corrie. We cleared the powder and cut the ice, our picks ringing metallically on the rock below. Many of the steps had to be scratched out rather than cut. We edged up cautiously, until at last good rock on our right gave us a sense of real security. At the top we came out on a most graceful snow-saddle, an aerial perch between low corries and blue sky.

Our luck in getting so high between squalls had saved us much time and pain. Technically easy as it is, the ridge is undeniably narrow and in places steep; these plus treacherous ice and loose snow might have dealt hard with us in high wind. Meantime we gambolled in calm air—while our third squall was speeding up Glen Grudie from Loch Maree, and already breaking on Coire Mhic Fhearchair of Beinn Eighe. Our urgent task was to race it to the top of the fourth pinnacle. To get all possible speed out of ourselves we stripped off the rope and crammed it uncoiled into a rucksack, then climbed fast up a deep snow-slope to the pinnacle. All went well at first. One or two corners required careful footwork. Then we came to a sloping slab on the west face. Our next move had to be a horizontal traverse straight across the slab. A sheet of brittle white ice covered the rock—not frozen water, but melted and refrozen snow. Its stability being uncertain, we hesitated. The first cloud was around us and the wind was rushing among the crags. Plates of ice torn off the east wall went soaring high over the pinnacle. An occasional pellet of snow stung the cheek. Tentatively I cut a hold or two, decided that the first man across would be safe, and the second not, and proceeded alone. Mortimer fetched out the rope, coiled an end, threw it across. We tied on. Mortimer was half-way over when the skies opened and cascaded hail. It fairly bounced off the rocks. Unhappily he stopped for a minute to let the shower slacken, then, just as he reached the near side, one terrific gust knocked him off. His whole weight came on the rope, but I held him without trouble. After moving a few yards we continued unroped.

The fifth pinnacle was deeply snowed up but easy. With the wind behind us we went in leisurely manner to the top of Mullach an Rathain. There we turned east along the main ridge, and received the full blast on our left cheek. The time was shortly after two o'clock—seven hours since breakfast. We felt much in need of food, but the idea of stopping was not tolerable. For nearly three-quarters of a mile we had straightforward walking, rather slow walking because of low visibility and our intermittent fear of cornices, but rarely in deep snow, long stretches of which had been stripped off the crest. Rock and scree were exposed naked to the wind, and to a continuous stream of drift, speeding close to the ground and breaking over each stone in white spurt and gout.

The squall passed its climax. The wind slackened. Coire na Caime grew visible as a darker gulf. The mist above us became dry and shining, and from time to time windows opened through it to show bright clouds riding high. Below on our right a cloud-bank was surging and swaying, tunnelled by widening shafts, through which we glimpsed the pale gleam of the River Torridon, with a dark belt of trees by its shore. Broad grey flats at the head of the loch held a wet orange glow. On the blue-black loch itself were multitudes of white speckles, growing thicker and ever more like the silver scale on salmon the farther the eye travelled west, until they merged in a haze of gold air. Over the Atlantic hardly a trace could be seen of the storm-clouds, which only half an hour earlier had overwhelmed the mountain world. Some had been whisked away into nothingness, others raised to lordly heights, where they puffed out white breasts, like fantailed pigeons, and strutted.

We lunched. A cloud was trapped in Coire na Caime and tried in vain to pour itself over the ridge. Great wisps boiled up out of the corrie. On to one of these wisps, when we rose to go, the sun threw our shadows tall as trees. Our Brocken Spectres paced us through the gossamer air. Bright halos crowned them. The symbols were flattering, too flattering to humbug mountaineers whose near future was stormy. We had reached the midway point, where the ridge changes direction north-east, when our fourth squall began darkening the hills around Loch Maree. At the same time a weak sunset flush spread over all the snow-peaks to the north and south, becoming wonderfully bright on the underside of high clouds. Above the sunset belt the sky paled, became green, was unsullied by one breath of vapour. The glow deepened on the mountains. The Sail Mhor of Beinn Eighe, pointing a leviathan fin out of the mist-sea beyond Coire na Caime, was touched by a fire like live coal.

We reached an eminence where the ridge fell away to the col below Am Fasarinen, whose triple pinnacles are Liathach's chief defence. The clouds approaching from Loch Maree were being held by the five-mile barrier of Beinn Eighe, but an outflanking attack had swept down Glen Torridon from Kinlochewe, and the first gauzy mists were flitting past the Fasarinen. The pinnacles are big and blunt. They had been well wind-swept, but grey hoar and a dull skin of ice encrusted the rocks, which, thrusting stonily through delicate mists, looked stark and stern, much larger than life as it were, more real than reality.

We dropped to the col, and moved unroped up the first pinnacle. Before we reached the top the clouds swept over and the wind struck. Throughout the day neither cloud nor wind ever arrived in advance of the other, but always together, with force and paralysing cold. We had to fight for our holds, luckily big enough to give us footing even when icy. The *ascent* of each pinnacle was relatively easy, for we climbed on the lee-side, but the descent to windward was a thrice-repeated nightmare. We climbed down blind. No route-selection was possible. Except for the six feet of frosted quartzite directly under our boots nothing could be seen through the veils of snow and hail, which throughout the passage of the pinnacles drove vertically upwards. On the ascent the sight of snow 'falling up,' and of whirlwinds at the top lifting the snow in tall, spinning columns, gave us great interest, but the actual passage of the tops and subsequent descents gave us hell. On the second or third descent we were astonished to find ourselves above a sheer drop. Mortimer went first. He lowered himself by the hands from a tiny ledge on one side of an overhang, and just managed to drop delicately on to a foothold, arms outstretched to preserve balance. Whether he was now some ten feet from the pinnacle's base or else poised on a north wall falling a thousand feet to Coire na Caime he could hardly tell short of jumping off. Yet he was seriously trying to get down farther. I leaned over my safe ledge and said mockingly: 'And the angels will bear thee up, lest at any time thou dash thy foot against a stone.' To Mortimer the hint was so broad that he turned at once. He had a struggle to get back. It is easy to drop down without an intermediate foothold but not to climb up. To save fetching out the rope I dropped him the end of my scarf. He took a twist round the forearm, we both pulled hard, and up he came.

We climbed right back, groping our way through the swirl of snow on top, and descended a gully on the pinnacle's south flank. It plunged into a seething white nothingness. 'This *must* be the route,' we said to each other reassuringly. We had to say it once or twice. But there could be no other. We kicked and cut our way down for fifty feet, then made an exploratory left traverse through hurtling fog.

Great was our delight when this move brought us to the ridge near the foot of Spidean a' Choire Leith, the shapely summit peak of four hundred feet. Unhappily it is also a stupendous scree-dump—loose, sharp, quartzite scree. We had rejoiced too soon. The ascent is purgatory on a good summer day, but when every stone is glazed and each hole masked by powder, cloud driving, and a north-easter shrilling across the face, it magnifies the name of Lucifer. At almost every step we had to stop and regain balance. It was half-past four and dusk when we passed over the summit.

We steered by compass for the north-west ridge. All our hopes of getting off the mountain before dark had gone. Our most pressing objective was to win clear of the northerly summit-crags before light wholly failed, for we could not contrive such a clearance by torchlight in dirty weather. This last 'squall' had become a sore disappointment by proving itself to be no squall. It was on for the night, and worsening. There was no increase in wind-force, but snow came thicker. Having nothing to sight on, we took a dozen bearings on the first five hundred feet, ran into crags on the right and left, disengaged, and pressed on over broken ground. The lower we went, the deeper the snow—with this advantage, that we could see the way without torchlight; and this disadvantage, that sharp drops over low crags were invisible—all merged in apparently continuous grey slopes. I had two very narrow escapes from a crash. It became plain that a man could kill himself this way, on technically easy ground. We fetched out our torches.

The first misfortune of the day at last overtook us. Our intention had been to follow the north-west ridge right down to the Mhic Nobuil glen, but we must have borne too far left, for we fetched up in Coire na Caime. For a while we felt uncertain of our whereabouts. We seemed to be in a sunken bowl, and only discovered the lochan when snow and ice collapsed at the edge. We went in up to the knees and came out blaspheming. The summit had only been 'like' hell, but this *was* the ninth and inner circle. Three feet of the softest snow lay in this Nameless Pit, so that we could not distinguish the lochan's margin. We had to contour round, ploughing a furrow thigh-deep in search of an exit, while we repeatedly broke through into icy water. At last we came upon an issuing stream. 'No matter where we are,' I remarked, 'this stream will lead us down to Loch Torridon.' But I was reckoning without that three feet of snow. Although the stream was flowing level the banks rose and fell craggily. Some of the drifts exceeded three feet by far. The leg had to be raised so high for each step, and then sank so deep, that after we had gone a couple of hundred yards the muscles at the front of my thighs were red hot. One touch of cramp would have finished us completely: we were thankful now for the recent discipline of bad-weather training. We rested for ten minutes.

Upon starting again we both felt so utterly worn out that we toyed with the idea of a bivouac, and made tentative efforts to scoop out a snow-cave in a drift. But the snow seemed too soft, and I suspect that our efforts were not whole-hearted—we were wet from the waist down. Moreover, although we had each, secretly, given up hope of reaching camp that night, neither would openly admit the thought. Our exhaustion was just muscular. So 'Go slow,' urged Mortimer. 'Halt often,' said I. This counsel of conservation saved us. Mortimer, whom I admire as a man of spirit and untold energy, would never, I said to myself, admit failure. So neither would I, as yet. I had got to the clenched-jaw stage, consciously forcing each step, when at last our stream ran out on open, undulating hill-slopes. They were exposed to wind and the snow lay lighter—a mere twelve inches. Our uncertainty of the route cleared away when the River Mhic Nobuil appeared black and foaming in the torch-beam. As we followed the three-mile course down the glen the falling snow gave place to sleet, and sleet to pelting rain. We made camp at 9 p.m.

Our sopping clothes would have flooded the floor of the tent had we gone in. So we stripped to the skin in the wind and darkness, then dived inside to pull on dry sweaters and sleeping-bags. We heard the music of a purring primus, watched pure snow change in the pot to grey slush, then to bubbling clarity . . . we brewed up.

We were silent over our mugs, each preoccupied for a while with his own thoughts about that tough, thirteen-hour job on Liathach. Our thoughts, it appeared, were short and simple.

'She iss machestic!' exclaimed Mortimer at last.

'But she iss not to be tampered with,' I added.

17 *The Moor of Rannoch*

THE FAMOUS HEAT-WAVE of June 1949 persisted into July. The drought afflicting the whole country became chronic. West highland villages had to get water brought in by carrier, and that was something I had not heard of before. Conditions for rock-climbing had never been better: I could think of some new routes that I wanted to try. And yet—I thought also of the Moor of Rannoch. It is the greatest moor in Scotland, one of the most accessible too, yet curiously enough the least explored. It is vast and trackless. Perhaps that intimidates walkers? While mountaineers, who like deserts if they like anything, notoriously prefer their deserts vertical.

Too long had I been counted among the latter. At first, while my ignorance was darkest and heaviest, Rannoch Moor was damned just because it was flat—that was enough! Later, when cold reason was admitted to my counsels, it was damned because it was bleak, bare, featureless, and quite excessively extensive, therefore no fit place for a hill-lover, to whom a peak is paradise; and no whit short of hell in foul weather, when damp mists sink on to it, prospectless, and the bogs are full, or when snow-winds scourge it. So that in the end Rannoch Moor had to conquer me through my heart, and reason had to *follow* perception, not lead. Which is just. It was that eastern view from the Glencoe summits that won me—the sparkle of the numberless tarns at noon—the phosphorescent gleam of their night-eyes—the spike of Schichallion pushing up beyond blue haze at the farther rim, thirty miles away. I had been fascinated, too, by the distant sight of wild swans and great flights of smaller birds coming on to Loch Ba and Loch Laidon, which stretch in a linked waterway ten miles across the moor.

The scene from my watch-tower on the Buachaille showed

me that the most interesting way of crossing the moor would be to keep close to the main chain of waterways, which rise in the Blackmount at Coire Ba of Stob Ghabhar, and run east through Lochan na Stainge, Loch Ba, and the five miles of Loch Laidon to Loch Rannoch—a distance of fifteen miles. Loch Rannoch continues beyond the moor fifteen miles to Schichallion, thence by the Tummel and Tay to the North Sea. The moor's northern boundary is the group of low hills called the Black Corries, the south boundary the high group of Achallader. Its entire area is said to be fifty-six square miles. My reason, now stripped of its old prejudice, informed me that from the centre of this unvisited moorland all the mountains circling round its rims would be seen anew, and charms not as yet known to me revealed. And of the moor's own secrets what did I really know? Not a thing.

On an evening of mid-July I arrived by road at the south-west side of the moor and camped between Lochan na Stainge and Loch Ba. I came alone. Let me confess at once that I prefer being alone among hills, provided that I am not climbing in the technical sense; prefer it also on moors, unless in dirty weather. But on this occasion I was not quite alone. I had as company a Golden Labrador bitch called Heather. She is a fine mountaineer with sufficient tops to her credit and ability enough on rock and snow to satisfy the Scrutinising Committee of the Scottish Mountaineering Club, from membership of which club she is disqualified only by sex. Her big black pads give her a grip on slabs and a quick, confident technique superior to that of her envious owner. Like me she is twice as much alive among hills as at sea level. And she doesn't talk. She just looks; which is quite enough.

We pitched the tent well to the east of Loch Ba because damp grey mist was rising off all the lochans. The day had been very hot. The fog, however, in appearance if not in temperature, was much like a mid-winter's ground mist. It cohered in banks, gently rolling sometimes this way and sometimes that, for no apparent reason—the night being windless. The sinuous sway

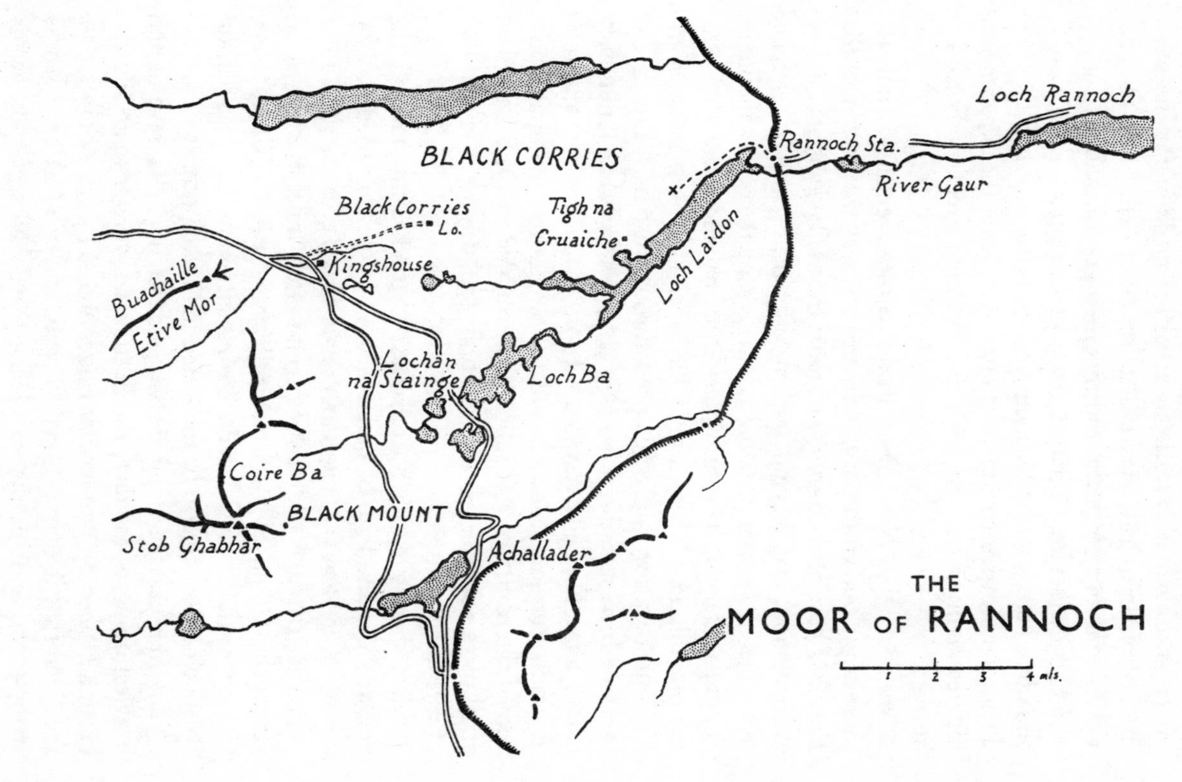

Loch Rannoch
Rannoch Sta.
River Gaur
BLACK CORRIES
Black Corries Lo.
Tigh na Cruaiche
Loch Laidon
Kingshouse
Buachaille Etive Mor
Lochan na Stainge
Loch Ba
Coire Ba
BLACK MOUNT
Stob Ghabhar
Achallader
THE MOOR OF RANNOCH
1 2 3 4 mls.

of its forms would have been a perfect medium for the weird display of light had only the moon been full. But the stars were strong in a black sky and the mists greyly chill.

I had deliberately pitched the tent on top of thick heather and thus had a springy couch under me for my night's sleep. The other Heather curled up at my feet. After the experimental nibbles at my toes were over she made an excellent hot-water bottle.

We rose at sunrise. Not a trace of mist remained; nor was there any cloud in the sky. So striking was the latter fact that I realized how often in the past I must have talked about cloudless skies without ever having spoken strict truth, save in reference to a narrow view from close country. In the wider mountain skyscape, always, in some quarter of that mountain sky there has been cloud, perhaps a long bar of cumulus low down at the horizon, or a few puffs glimpsed through a pass. But to-day east, north, west, and south—clear sky, peculiarly and luminously empty like a heavenly vacuum. From behind the blue a colourless radiance shone, more than usually suggestive of infinite space and of the reality of that infinity. Provided that this were seen at all there could be engendered only one attitude of mind, that of a reverential awe.

After sharing the dog's breakfast I struck camp and left the tent at the roadside to be collected later by passing friends. By six we were away. The early start was necessary because I intended to make a double traverse—ten miles north-east to Rannoch station, then thirteen miles west back to Kingshouse, Glencoe—and because I had a strong suspicion that distances on Rannoch Moor were to be measured in time, not miles.

The first passage along the east side of Loch Ba gave us the heaviest going of the day; the heather was longer there and the ground broken by hummocky ridges and old water-courses. A short and twisting river linked Loch Ba to Loch Laidon. It was at these two ends of the two lochs that I had seen wild swans fly in and duck come down among the heather. In the breeding season black- and red-throated divers visit the lochs and behave like submarines when alarmed, slowly submerging until only the head and neck remain above water, like a periscope. The wide mosses farther away from the lochs harbour greenshanks. And that is the limit of my knowledge about Rannoch bird life, which is certain to be very much more extensive than I ever dream. These lochs would repay the bird-watcher. I should be most interested to know, for example, what birds find food or shelter on the wooded islands. They are small islands, well wooded with birch, yew, and pine—indicating that Rannoch Moor might yet revert to its Old Wood of Caledon days were it not for the hungry deer. I should like to be spared the wolves, the brown bear, the boar, and the outlawed brigands, but the natural forest that sheltered them I would have back if I could. New growth seems to flourish on the water-protected isles, which are inaccessible except to a man prepared to swim a hundred yards—and, if he wants to botanize or bird-watch, to push a raft with his clothing in front of him.

On reaching Loch Laidon I thought that the ground improved, although a certain amount of leaping from tuft to tuft was still part of the day's work. On the other hand there were surprisingly few peat-hags. I remember no more than one or two, still exposing the bare bones of the Old Wood, but I imagine that in other parts of the moor they must be abundant. On the line I chose, always close to the loch, the moor was well drained, and over its whole area I judge it to be equally well drained by the countless tarns. I met no bogs. One gets across in dry weather with dry feet.

Admittedly we had the moor in perfect condition. A west wind was blowing, of the kind we may truly call a zephyr, but the heat was semi-tropical, and away from the waterways must have been as consumingly fierce as the south Syrian desert. Unlike Loch Ba, Loch Laidon had a fairly straight margin: we could travel close to the shore, which we found indented by innumerable tiny bays. These were filled with a clean and gravelly sand, most tempting on a hot day. We had one bathe near the start, and ten minutes later, feeling as hot as ever, we had another. There were going to be more. Faced with the personal example of Heather's ever-readiness, I began to see my own repeated dressing and undressing as a pointless waste of time. There was little or no chance of meeting any one during the day. So I stripped once and for all and stuffed my clothes into my rucksack. The zephyr could now get at my skin, and the need for frequent dips became less urgent.

But for the bays our day would fast have become a sheer trial of endurance—worse by far for Heather than for me, her great handicap being fur and a lack of sweat-glands. During the first few hours' enthusiasm she covered three times as much ground as I, ranging out eastwards in wide circles. I let her do this to see what game she might start up. It astonished me that she drew a blank. Not one hare, not a rabbit or grouse, did she raise—absolutely nothing. The moor at this time of day seems to be bare of all animal life. Throughout our traverse I never once set eyes on a deer, although every winter great herds congregate by the roadside. I assumed that they would all be up in the corries of the Blackmount. The lack of other life is stranger.

We came to the north-east end of Loch Laidon where the River Gaur flowed out sharply right towards Loch Rannoch. The river must have been fifty yards wide. I hoped that it might be all the shallower on that account, and tried to get across by wading, my rucksack balanced on my head. Before I was a third of the way over the water had crept up to my chin, and by natural buoyancy my body was tending to float and capsize. Since the water looked much deeper and swifter in front, I came back and moved on a few hundred yards, then tried again with no more success. In the end we had to make a half-mile detour downstream to a ford, where a line of great boulders offered a dry route. After all my vain efforts to wade I was determined to wade at the last, and did so through chest-deep water. On the other hand Heather, who had already swum the river twice, and been forced each time to return in high dudgeon because I had failed to follow, was determined that since the ford was now found she would use it. She bounded clumsily on the polished boulders, not being able to get a good purchase on them with her wet paws, and landing each time in a splashing sprawl. But she was over long before I was.

We had now been going four hours. Cutting out the last few hundred yards to Rannoch station we rounded the head of Loch Laidon. There we struck an excellent track going half a mile back along the farther shore, *en route* to Kingshouse, then suddenly degenerating into a mere sheep-track. This northern shore was decidedly pleasanter than the southern shore. The sun was shining in front instead of behind, and there were wild flowers by the path. One little bay was full of water-lilies, and another, about a mile down the loch, had the best of all the sandy beaches. We turned aside on to the latter. It was backed by short granite crags, and covered deeply in coarse clean sand, on to which the sun had been beating several hours daily for a month. It was hot to lie on. There I lay, my back upon the warm granite, and lunched with Heather. On this side of the loch the shore shelved more steeply; one could dive in after a knee-deep wade. From time to time one or the other of us would rise and go down to the water for a plunge, then come back and sprawl. An hour passed away. We just luxuriated. Sometimes I would wonder whether to have one more swim in those blue waters or to go on towards the wide, sunlit corries of the Blackmount, or to the glens of Glencoe where the peaks were darkening against the sun. The walk to Kingshouse would certainly be the shorter, and even so was consuming time in a way that I had not believed possible. Twelve more miles, said the map? I had better allow six hours for it.

In due course we continued three miles up the loch-side, until at the ruined cottage called Tigh na Cruaiche the track swung away to the west, aiming straight for Glencoe. The so-called 'track' had long since become a purely imaginary line on the map, having no basis in a present reality. At the south wall of the ruin a barn still provides roof and shelter in foul weather. I could think of no better headquarters for a natural historian bent on adventure, or for bird-watchers or fishermen; for only a hundred feet below, a great bay of the loch contains seven islands, two of which are well wooded. No one will find comfort at Tigh na Cruaiche; only bare shelter and perfect solitude.

We had still to cover four and a half miles to reach the Black Corries Lodge. This part of the day we both found most exhausting. Heather was now following close to heel of her own free will. For my part I found the ground badly folded and the heather too thick. Only now was the day-long breeze strengthening and beginning to feel rather too cool on my unprotected skin, so that when the lodge came into sight I was glad enough to put on clothing. The average height of the moor is a thousand feet; the lodge around twelve hundred: it thus commands a wondrously wide prospect across Loch Ba to the Blackmount. Had the tarns all been tiny the moor might have resembled a cratered battlefield; but the waters were broad and long enough to add beauty to desolation, both of their kind matchless. The circling hills of the east and west Blackmount, and the deep ranks of Glencoe, were in proper perspective, full in stature, clean-carved by corrie and glen, a deep and dusky blue in the hollows. I realized that not until this day had I ever seen the Glencoe hills as they really are. From the glen itself the mountains are sadly foreshortened, but this fact is never guessed, never realized, until one goes miles out on to Rannoch Moor.

I have no especial love for road-walking—a road is a tyrant, directing a man in ways planned for him, and most wearing on climbing-nails, which are costly. But I have a good word to say for the road from Black Corries Lodge to Kingshouse: it is only four miles and downhill all the way. I could appreciate that, in the circumstances. I was very tired. And a good dinner being only one hour away, I found myself still full of enthusiasm for the moor of Rannoch; for its own sake as well as for its new revelation of old hills. At last I knew it—and at that checked myself. Moors, like mountains, are not known so easily as first visits tempt one to think. However, I had seen something of it in summer. What of winter? In winter I knew only the moor's western fringes. I had watched the sun shine low over wind-rippled snow-fields, and glance across frozen lochs, make of an ice-bound tree a flashing chandelier and strike fire from the frozen tower of Buachaille. A winter traverse of the whole moor would give a man these and other things, and an adventure into the bargain for which he would have to be as fit and as well clothed as for a mountain expedition. I had had enough experience of Rannoch blizzards to know that they rival Cairngorm blizzards in everything save wind velocity. In new, deep snow a crossing in one day would hardly be possible, but on old snow, in hard frost and fine weather, all should be more than well.

It may be that I exaggerate the worth of the day? It does seem to ask strenuous work and a sacrifice of either comfort or convenience. However, greater worth has always in my own experience asked greater effort, and the reward has borne proportion to effort, on one plane or another. Summer and winter there is a day for Rannoch.

18 *Ben Nevis by the North-east Buttress*

NO MAN WILL EVER KNOW Ben Nevis. No man ever *has* known Ben Nevis—not even the famous Clement Wragge, who made a daily ascent for eight months; nor yet Dr. Graham Macphee, who wrote the Nevis guide; certainly not I, who have climbed on it only thirty-seven times.

In winter the level of perpetual snow sinks below the summit, which lies right in the storm-track of the North Atlantic hurricanes, so that massive accumulations of snow and ice can build up on the northern cliffs in a few days' time. Routes like the North-east Buttress and Tower Ridge then give totally different climbs in successive weeks. The mood, temper, climate, and conditions of Nevis are inexhaustibly various; their changes swifter and more radical than on any other hill, and not predictable even one day in advance. No other mountain has been more roundly cursed by the disappointed climber, or so lavishly praised by the fortunate: because nothing he ever gets is expected.

The clearest insight I ever had into the wayward character of this best and worst of mountains was granted me one March. Douglas Laidlaw and I knew the North-east Buttress in summer as the biggest cliff on the mainland, eighteen hundred feet in height, presenting a ridge to the north-east and a vast face to the west. On the ridge we hoped to have one of the best winter climbs in Scotland—given good weather. I need hardly say that when we arrived below the mountain on Saturday night the weather was foul.

Our starting-point was the distillery under the north-west flank, which is a notable rendezvous on two counts. By its grounds access is gained to the track up the Allt a Mhuilinn glen; within its walls a whisky called Dew of Ben Nevis is distilled. It is thus an important crossroads where the Devil takes his opportunities. He whispered to me now so loudly that I was sure Laidlaw must overhear: 'Outside, torrential sleet and thick darkness. Indoors the golden dew of bliss! What joy of the Nevis cliffs may not be found doubled in the Nevis bar?—and with what less effort! and what more ease!' I translated aloud into English. But my words were a mere casting of pearls—the far-away look that came instantly to Laidlaw's eyes showed that his heart had already climbed two thousand feet to the S.M.C. hut in the upper corrie. He trampled the pearliest of wisdom underfoot.

'In the Nevis bar,' said he, 'you get the uplift first and the headache after. On the Nevis cliffs the pains first and the joys after. If it were the other way round a blind drunk would be the good life and pubs temples. That,' he added after a moment's reflection, 'is morals summed up.'

I was astonished at his doctrine. I laughed. I even assented. And thus it came about that Laidlaw and I climbed Nevis. Our first move was to reach the hut. Before we were half-way up the night was pitch-black, blowing, and snowing hard. The rather faint track, which is never easy to find and follow at night, was drifted over. More than once we were forced into the frozen bed of the river, which gave us the only sure line to the hut. Time and again we stopped, swore that a hurricane raged on top, that to go on was madness, and to climb next day impossible. But I could never resist adding: 'And pubs is temples.' So that we always laughed and always went on. We reached the hut at midnight.

Our ascent of three and a half miles had taken four hours—double the normal time. We made a good fire and supper. At 1 a.m. I went out for my last look round. The hurricane had torn away the cloud in a rent as big as Nevis itself, and the moon shone full upon the two-mile range of cliffs close above me. Thinning mists still clung along its arctic wall and picked out great ridges and buttresses and many a spectral tower, all whitened with new snow. Within half a minute a cloud-mass broke over the summit, and with one mighty roll engulfed the cliffs. A second billow, charging over the col between Nevis and Carn Mor Dearg, choked Coire Leis and spilled down into the Allt a Mhuilinn glen. It began to snow hard.

I scrambled into my bunk. I lay back gratefully, watched the stove glow red hot through the darkness, and listened to the wind thunder on the walls and roof. 'We 'll get a long lie to-morrow,' I thought, and sighed happily. 'Not a hope of any climbing.'

Imagine our astonishment, therefore, when we woke up in the morning to blue skies! The cold was extreme. After a hurried breakfast we walked up the corrie to the North-east Buttress. The wind was still blowing from the south-east. Puffs of powder raced down the corrie and stung our faces with flying spiculae. The spume hid the lower part of the cliffs, but the uppermost drift, twisting through crisp air, caught a sparkle of the sun. Beyond this battle-fog of ice we could see blue sky, and that greatly encouraged us to go on—to suffer our measure of pain now in hope of the bliss to come. In a wind so violent and snow so heavy our prospects, none the less, remained poor. I knew of two parties forced to spend a night out near the top, one just below a famous rock-nose of ten feet called the Man Trap, the other slightly above it where an icy traverse had to be made round a corner and over slabs. We might suffer that fate if we failed to arrive at the crux before dark, but in truth our real concern was not that, but whether we should even get quarter-way up.

The noblest feature of Nevis that morning was undoubtedly the North-east Buttress. We looked straight on to its vast white face, which by an optical illusion seems always to be toppling over. Our day's route lay up the sharp left-hand ridge, which was silhouetted against the sky and from this angle looked unclimbable. It seemed far too sharp, steep, and icy. Worse still was the lower part, where a pyramid rises seven hundred feet to the First Platform. It loomed monstrously through the smoke and turmoil of drift.

We contoured below the base of the buttress to its east side and climbed laboriously a broad and broken runnel of powder-snow up to the crest at the First Platform. This so-called platform is a short, level part of the ridge, which steepens sharply again to a wide barrier-wall. Even from a hundred feet below the appearance of this wall gave a sure sign of the conditions we might meet higher. Its face was plastered, not with new snow, which is always bright, but with snow of a grey tinge, suspiciously like frost-hoarings, laid on in layers and basted by wind, which had ripped off the new snow as it fell. The entire ascent would thus take longer than we had bargained for: a great deal of cutting might have to be done. Had we not known something of the habits of Nevis we should probably have given up the climb and tried a more sheltered route elsewhere. Instead we said to ourselves: 'The day is too young to be judged—our proper course is to continue the climb meantime, and be prepared to smack it hard *or* to return.'

The wind was certainly blowing strong, but only in gusts. Moving slowly in soft deep snow we began to kick steps up a long scoop running obliquely right to left up to the base of the barrier-wall. We were nearing the top of this scoop when Nevis performed two of its lightning changes. The snow froze and the wind died. Every rock and slope had a hard crust. But for that drop in the wind we should not have gone farther.

Our own mood changed as quickly as the mountain's. At once excitement mounted and our hearts rejoiced. We were going to get a climb—a hard climb! We set to work on the frost-bound wall with real enjoyment. It lies close to the vertical for sixty feet, but the holds are so big that our task of climbing with axes held ready to scrape snow-ice off each ledge as we came to it was fairly simple. When the angle eased above this wall the hard work of the day began. On every ledge and groove was hard-frozen snow, so that every step had to be cut. For this reason we kept as close as possible to the right or true crest of the buttress, where steeper rock meant lighter snow and quicker progress. Upon making this discovery we stuck to our straight and narrow path too religiously. Several hundred feet above the first barrier-wall we struck a second one. This, if anything, is steeper than the first, shorter but more difficult. Half-way up, a traverse must be made on rock that pushes out one's body awkwardly. Knowing that in summer the foothold is excellent I had no hesitation in going straight up until that midway traverse stopped me. It looked precarious. I brought up Laidlaw to give me a belay at close quarters, but did so with an uneasy feeling that we should not be there at all. When all was ready I edged out leftwards. The handholds I needed at the critical step were glazed, like the foothold. I had now no real intention of making that risky move, but for obscure reasons spent a few minutes as though trying to do so. Laidlaw broke the spell by telling me the time. We returned to the base of the pitch. 'And *that* is just a moderate wall in summer!' we reflected. Truly a Nevis ridge under heavy snow is transformed out of all recognition.

We traversed leftwards and turned the impasse by snow-scoops, then cut our way back to the crest, which had become much narrower than before—a true ridge rather than a buttress. The angle had slightly steepened, giving us delightful climbing free from all anxiety about route selection—but time consuming, for the snow was everywhere like iron. The ridge ran straight and true towards the plateau; its frosted edge, turned to a blazing cloud near the summit, gave a star-like glitter. On this crest we plied our axes for an hour or two until late in the afternoon it narrowed, again steepened, and confronted us with that ten-foot nose, called the Man Trap.

Although the ridge was so narrow at this point we had good footing below the crux—a little platform on which we could stand or sit in comfort, but not lie. We inspected the Man Trap apprehensively. Nevis had performed yet another quick change. We were only two or three hundred feet from the summit-plateau, and this whole upper part of the mountain was clad in a thick deposit of fog-crystals—even vertical and overhanging crags were covered. Some of the crystals grew out like fir-cones, two feet long, others were massed in overlapping banks, shaped like huge fig-leaves. They made our further ascent look a fearsome task, but in hard fact their presence was not in itself a serious matter. The trouble was that these crystals were only a top-dressing. I scraped them off the Man Trap with the blade of my axe and underneath disclosed thin, clear ice.

This ice was true *verglas*: it could not be chipped off the rock. We tried. However, the pitch was short. I climbed on to Laidlaw's shoulders, steadied myself, and reached to the top. But the ledge above bulged with ice—a boss of pale green ice, like candle-wax. In this ice I cut a few handholds but found them of no use to me—between Laidlaw's head and the green bulge I still needed one foothold, and that I could not get. I came down again.

We looked round the flanks in search of some avoiding move. On the left flank the rock was quite clear of fog-crystals, which at this particular point had been wind-blasted. The rock fell away in smooth convex slabs, which rose to near verticality at the wall beside the Man Trap. The only semblance of weakness there was a shallow chimney, filled from side to side with a twist of thick black ice. Its ascent was not possible. For the first time we began to feel alarmed. The sun had long since dropped behind Nevis: the metal of my axe had become sticky to the touch of a bare hand, and the evening stillness noticeable.

We examined the right flank. There was here a much greater and more open expanse of rock, tumbling one thousand two hundred feet or more to the chasm between North-east Buttress and Observatory Ridge. Close under us the slabs were seamed by ledges, supporting much grey-green ice and snow which fell away at a high angle. On this face it might be possible to cut out a traverse and regain the ridge higher up—it *might* be possible.

Laidlaw gave me a very tight rope while I lowered myself from the platform and cut holds down a steep groove leading on to the face. I began to hew out a traverse. The falling chips scuttered on the crusted rocks with a hollow sound, took to the air in whirring hops, and then in long bounds as they vanished into the depths. Their noise seemed loud in the still air. With every step I took the more unpleasant my prospects grew. The rocks were slabby and offered no belays. However, it looked just possible to regain the crest by a forty-foot chimney choked with white ice—but again, no rock-belay, a twelve-hundred-foot cliff below, at least an hour of cutting—the mountain was asking too much of my nervous system. I turned and went back.

If we had reached the crux earlier in the day it is probable that we should not have pressed the attack further. But the horizon skies were green in the south, and the upper snows of Carn Mor Dearg red. There could be no thought now of climbing all the way down that rocky and frozen crest. We *had* to get up. I made one more attempt on the Man Trap, and although it failed I thought I saw a solution. I held my axe above my head, its point resting on a thick pad of scarf on my hip, its head against the glazed wall, while Laidlaw, the lighter man, climbed on to my shoulders and head, then stepped on the axe-head, and pulled himself up. I was not too happy about the soundness of the manœuvre, but those extra few inches made all the difference. He disappeared above in search of a stance.

I looked rightwards across the cliffs on to vast accumulations of snow upon Observatory Ridge. It seemed incredible that only a few months before I had been climbing the buttress on its far side in sun so hot that we had stripped to the waist. Or there was that other day when we strayed in thick mist and rain on to unclimbed rocks. We had some long halts *that* day with rain streaming down the slabs and down our own skins. I remembered how the film of water drew out the most varied colour from the rocks—rocks that are just dull brown when dry—little flecks of red and yellow, and blue and crystal, gleaming with so unexpected a beauty that I remembered them now after all the discomfort had been forgotten.

I brought my mind back to the Man Trap. Laidlaw was still cutting. The red glow had vanished from the snow-peaks, which now were grey. The cliffs were as bleak as some long-deserted city. The stillness gripped the mountain-world, strongly persisting behind the occasional ring of Laidlaw's axe when the steel struck rock. The first faint stars emerged, brightening as the sky darkened to navy blue.

Laidlaw called me. I joined him with the aid of a strong pull on the rope. Immediately above us the ridge rose in another high step, and this one, I think, is unclimbable in summer. The only way of turning it is to traverse left round a corner and climb up a slab. We had just enough light left to us to make the traverse to the corner, which bristled with spears of fog-crystal, and to see the slab, which was sleeky with ice. The cutting of nicks up that slab looked like giving us most delicate climbing, for the coating was only half an inch thick. The situation looked most forbidding. The rocks beneath our feet were indistinct in thickening dusk, and swept away into a bottomless pit of dark. The possibility of taking a fall in such an exposed situation made my skin creep. Since the previous pitch, normally climbable in a few minutes, had taken more than one hour, I began to fear that this last obstacle of the ridge might have to wait until morning.

Balancing with my chest against the corner I swung off my rucksack and fetched out an electric torch. The moment I switched it on how different everything looked! The slab gleamed like a mirror, its numberless frost-cressets sparkled, the snow shone. They reflected light from so many different angles and textures that something of the beauty of a musical score in terms of light was presented whole to us—gay music: the music of the Dance. It enlivened my weary muscles. Moreover, the gloomy abyss had vanished away in the outer dark. For us it no longer existed. This short and beautiful slab was all that we need think about, and all that we need climb. I cut the nicks, and climbed, and cut again, lifting myself only on my edge-nails, but blissfully unconscious of anything precarious in our position, so that in ten minutes I had reached easy ground with a straightforward route opening ahead among huge and broken crags. Laidlaw followed. The way was clear to the plateau.

At first we had to climb little pitches, and cut an occasional step, but very quickly the snow became softer. We both remarked on the relative mildness of the air, and suddenly realized that Nevis was about to give us yet another and characteristic change—a temperature inversion. As soon as we stepped on to the plateau we saw that our guess was right. All southward valleys brimmed with cloud, from which the tips of high peaks projected like skerries. Eastwards the clouds were low down, spilling along the valley floors. From one of these cloud-lakes the moon was just swimming clear. Its upper half was yellow, like honey; its lower half blurred red. When it swam clear a mellow glow suddenly bloomed on the cloud surfaces; in a few minutes they flickered, as though with wild-fire, then changed to an even silver. On the broad snow-fields beneath our boots each crystal crumb threw its own shadow on to the gleaming crust. The whole frozen world was alive with the shining of light.

No man will ever know Ben Nevis.

On the other hand Nevis will always help him to know himself. There is no end to such knowledge. Likewise there is no end to the joy of getting it.

19 *Benalder Forest*

IT IS ONE OF THE unlisted privileges of belonging to a mountaineering club that one may meet men of the most adventurous instinct. They together possess a remarkable store of information about strange crannies in the high or remote parts of this earth's surface. This storehouse does not lie open, like a reference library, for all to draw upon at will. Rather it is like an orchard, where one waits for the fruits to ripen, until they may be plucked, or more likely fall from above and hit one on the head. In other words one must like one's fellows sufficiently well to learn by listening: truly it is wonderful what may be picked up from scraps of conversation. Many of the good days I've had on new climbs or in exploring new hill-country have been due less to my own initiative than to bright ideas given to me by unwitting mountaineers. For example, they gave me Benalder Forest.

Of all remote unget-at-able mountains in Scotland, Ben Alder ranks among the first. It lies in the heart of that roadless area of two hundred and fifty square miles between Loch Rannoch in the south, Loch Laggan in the north, Loch Garry in the east, and Loch Treig in the west. In the middle are the mountain ranges of Benalder and Corrour Forests, and hard on their east flank, under the east slopes of Ben Alder itself, is the fifteen-mile length of Loch Ericht, running south-west to north-east, its top end close to Dalwhinnie. A climber coming by road, say from Glasgow, must cover a hundred and twenty miles to get at Ben Alder, ten of which are on foot by the short hill-route from Loch Rannoch. Being thus too far for week-end climbing, and in summer holidays not far enough, the Benalder Forest is unknown country to all save a very few mountaineers. And it *is* troublesome to reach: the idea of investigating it never came to me until, little by little, scraps of information accumulated.

An alert interest was first roused in me when I was told that Ben Alder's north corrie was buttressed by crags which had not been explored; then that good pony tracks wound scores of miles among the hills and rivers between Lochs Laggan and Ericht; that these tracks could be followed forty-four miles from Dalwhinnie to Fort William by way of Loch Pattock, the bealach Dubh of Ben Alder, Loch Ossian, Lochtreighead, and at last by the Amhain Rath to Glen Nevis, with only one short break in the track from the bealach Dubh down to Loch Ossian. That drove me to the map, and by the map I was wholly fascinated. Even on coloured paper, all that country around Ben Alder bore the unmistakable stamp of the wild and the wilderness, recessed by corries great enough to have at their backs still wilder fastnesses, where secret things awaited inquiry. What *kind* of things? you might ask. But, of course, I did not know.

Finally I heard of an unoccupied and open cottage at Alder Bay, on the south shore of the mountain. This was said to give comfortable shelter, but not necessarily a good night's sleep. The cottage was haunted. At first I did not take the tale of the haunting seriously. Its theory, however, was said to be backed by the fact that a previous tenant, a stalker named ——, had hanged himself on the back of the front door. It seemed to be a sound enough proposition that some undissipated energies thrown off from his dying body might persist for a while as poltergeists, and undirected by intelligence cause aimless dramatic effects and loud noises. What I did not credit was that such effects had in fact been observed. It is the usual weakness of these tales that one never meets the first-hand witness. So that I was drawn to Ben Alder not by poltergeists but by those unexplored cliffs of the north-east corrie and the hinted mysteries of a one-inch ordnance survey map.

My first attempt to reach the mountain was made in March from Loch Ossian. I stayed four days at the empty youth hostel on the edge of the frozen loch, listening to the hollow report and crackle of ice under the weight of wind rushing on to it from the hills, and to the endless drumming of drift on the

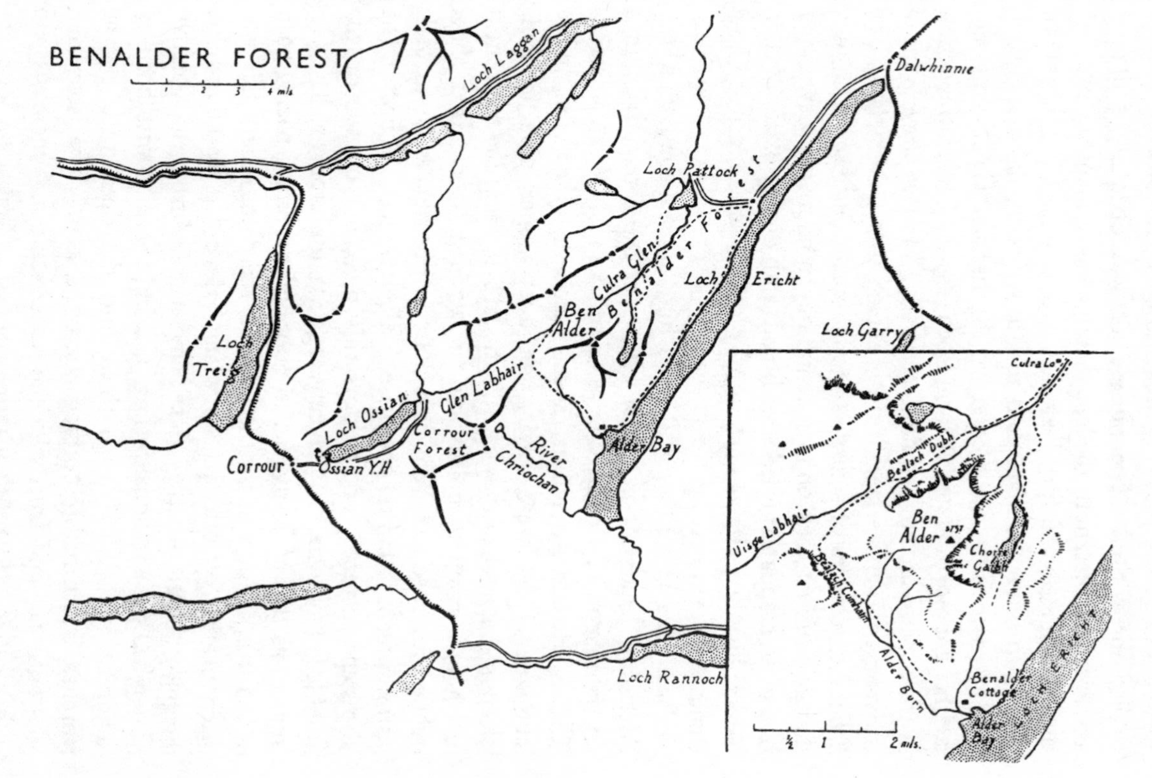
BENALDER FOREST
1
2
3
4 mls
Loch Laggan
Dalwhinnie
Loch Pattock
Benalder Forest
Culra Glen
Loch Ericht
Loch Garry
Ben Alder
Loch Treig
Glen Labhair
Loch Ossian
Corrour Forest
River Chriochan
Alder Bay
Corrour
Ossian Y.H
Loch Rannoch
Culra Lo.
Bealach Dubh
Ben Alder
Choire Gaibh
Uisge Labhair
Bealach Cumhann
Alder Burn
Benalder Cottage
Alder Bay
LOCH ERICHT
½
1
2 mls.

wooden walls. On the rare occasions when I opened the door —to get fuel for my blazing fires inside—swirls of white powder eddied far within. The outside air was opaquely white. I could see my feet, none the less, therefore movement was possible and no excuse valid for idleness. Accordingly I did make two efforts to cross the watershed to Loch Ericht: the first by the bealach nan Sgor, the second by the bealach Cumhann. On neither attempt did I get far from Loch Ossian. It is intimidating to face a hill-blizzard without company. It has powers and a striking edge and a stark reality denied to a poltergeist. The labour it requires of a man is prodigious. Once or twice, just before I turned back on my second day, a momentary sweeping away of clouds revealed the broad and distant back of Ben Alder, luridly white against an inky pall of sky, hunched like a chalk Atlas supporting the heavens.

Ever after that glimpse I had a high respect for Ben Alder. Meantime I met my first-hand witness of the cottage hauntings in the person of Robert Grieve of the Scottish Mountaineering Club. He and a friend had spent a most disturbed night in the cottage. They were having an after-supper pipe in their sleeping-bags when they heard footsteps entering the room next door and tramping noisily on the wooden floor. In a short while they rose and went next door to investigate but to their astonishment found no one there. They returned to bed. The footsteps recurred, not indoors this time, but outside on the cobbled causeway, which runs against the front wall. The noise was that of heavy, nailed boots on the stone, pacing back and forth, up and down the front of the cottage, and this was accompanied by brief pauses when Grieve and his companion strongly sensed that they were being watched from the window. They had the additional feeling of being regarded with hostility as intruders. That drove them into the open with electric torches, but as before nothing was to be seen. They inspected the outhouse and barn with the same result, and there was no other cover. Again they retired to bed. And again footsteps entered the room next door. After some aimless tramping there came a moment's pause, then the quite distinctive sound of heavy furniture being dragged over the floor, the kind of noise that would be made by the legs of a heavy table. Grieve and his friend were well aware that there was *no* furniture next door, so they once more went through to look, and found—a bare and empty room. They gave up then and retired for the night. Grieve freely affirms that he now felt frightened. But apart from continued noises no untoward event occurred.

That, of course, is by no means the only report of the hauntings, but is the only report I can trust. Grieve is a level-headed and practical man. He does not go around telling this story, for he feels that normally other men discredit abnormal experiences in which they themselves had no share, and their disbelief confounds the man who knows his experience to be true, yet not so important to the world as to be worth exposing to ridicule. Grieve, in short, convinced me as a reliable witness.

I made plans to go to Benalder cottage at the autumn holiday week-end in September 1949. Norman Tennent was the ideal type of youthful unbeliever to accompany me on this trip. He and his wife Mona and I agreed to spend two nights at the cottage, our main purpose being the exploration of the northern cliffs.

We arrived on a perfect evening at the west end of Loch Rannoch. The world was putting on its strongest colour—red and yellow on the open hills, smoke-blue on the loch; the air was still as in hard frost yet mild as the mellowing sun. That nine-mile walk to Loch Ericht was for once a delightful prospect. Our first four miles went by a surprisingly good track, which ended at the dam in the south bay of Loch Ericht. The dusk thickened. The way now went north-west over trackless moors in order to round the head of the loch and gain the woods of its west shore. Of this crossing I had been warned with many a blasphemous oath—rainstorm and low, dense mist, heavy going, boggy and featureless ground, endless compass bearings—my counsellor had not been lucky. But to-night our guiding marks were the bright Pole Star and the black arc of a bealach cutting the sky seven miles away. I think it says much for the ground that we could go with our heads often raised to that high sky-line yet stumble rarely enough to keep in good temper.

Flowing into the head of the loch is the River Chriochan, to the crossing of which I had looked forward with misgiving; it looked on the map a bad obstacle if full. To-night it proved to be harmless, and an easy ford near the junction let us across to a well-made pony track heading north towards Alder Bay. The barren moorland soon gave place to richer ground, our way leading among fir-trees, between the wide gap of whose branches could be seen a great shining of stars, and through broad avenues among the trunks a dim glimmer from the velvety loch; leading through that most charming of all country, a natural wood, where each individual tree has living space, where there is no regimented crowding, but light and life and a healthful air, most gracious to the human soul lucky enough to be brought thither. The naturai and unaffected response of the mind is to meditate—to receive the trees' symbol of life perfectly at one with Reality: then not just to dream or desire, but of free choice to *live* that life.

We had one more mile to go when our track petered out. Half a mile farther a thickly wooded hill persuaded us down to the water's edge for passage. We rounded a blunt point and arrived on the shore of Alder Bay. At the toe of the hill across the bay a bright light shone. Benalder cottage! I wondered if by some mischance it were filled with estate stalkers, for it was the height of the season. If so we should be refused entrance, indeed chased away in wrath. But I knew the cottage to be normally deserted in the stalking season—to be at all times one of the most desolate in Scotland. We sat down to think things over.

While we rested among the firs by the water's edge a light suddenly flashed at the far shore. That was fully a quarter of a mile away. Shooting stars were dropping frequently out of the crowded sky, but the flash was not that, nor yet the light from the cottage. The loch was black, the farther shore jet black. From the beach a light twinkled over the water and went out. A hundred yards to its left a second light flashed and went out—flashed again more openly at the loch, and went out. These flashings mystified us, for they were unaccompanied by movement in any particular direction; they seemed aimless. Something strange was happening around Benalder cottage. The time was now ten o'clock. Stalkers do not wander around like that on a cold September's night. They yarn round a good fire or else get to bed.

Another surprise was in store for us when we began to walk round the bay. Where the firs thinned out nearer the Alder Burn we saw an enormous fire like some coronation beacon, fed by a ring of four or five men who moved like demons among the towering columns of smoke and flame. We moved closer. They were young men, tough, but not more evil than we. We stepped into the firelight.

'Heading for the cottage?' they asked, and smiled doubtfully when we said 'Yes.' '*We*'re sleeping out here,' they added. Their voices showed that they had no doubts about which was the better 'howff' for the night. Otherwise they were not communicative. We pressed on to see for ourselves this source of all mystery. We had still to cross the Alder Burn which is notoriously fast and unfordable in spate, but the low water gave us an easy passage on boulders.

The cottage was then right before us—a two-room stone building with a porch in the middle, a sound slated roof, unbroken windows, and a big corrugated iron shed attached to its west gable. The rooms were candle-lit. We opened the front door. To either side of us then were two other doors, and straight in front a small, dark store-room. From behind the right-hand door came a noise like all the devils of hell let loose. Not *one* poltergeist—a whole legion of them—was in full occupation and hard at work. I turned the handle and swung the door quickly. There was sudden, dead silence. Ranged round the walls, fifteen pairs of eyes stared at mine. However, I held my ground and took a steady look at them. These fifteen poltergeists were, for the moment at least, clad in the flesh of male humans between the ages of eighteen and twenty-five. The eyes were bright and laughing, mouths still grinning through the sudden check of breath. On one side of a roaring fire sat a cross-legged youth, his lips still round a mouth-organ; while at the other side sat another, head tilted, fingers still hovering at the stops of a penny whistle.

At a quick glance I knew that these men were not climbers. 'Fishing?' I asked. 'No,' said someone. Then with a roar the whole chorus, whistle and mouth-organ, resumed the song at the very note on which they had halted four seconds before.

I stepped out laughing, and closed the door. Questions, it seemed, were not welcomed in this part of the world. I had never seen anything more like a band of robbers, and all in the tradition of Robin Hood, as indeed we were soon to find they were.

Next door were six humble fishermen. Theirs were the lights that had flashed along the shore, and the catch, we could see, had been good. They offered to make room for us on the floor. In both rooms the walls were wood-lined and the floors dry, but three more bodies would make for excessive heat and congestion. So we decided to look at the shed, and were thus introduced to the all too real ghost in the cupboard.

We went out and round to the shed door, gave it a push, and flashed on a torch. The first thing we saw was a bloody corpse hanging from a beam in the roof. This time we were startled in real earnest. A closer scrutiny revealed the victim to be less a corpse than a carcase. This was a gralloched stag. We began to understand the aims and objects of the Brotherhood indoors. Fortunately the shed was big and spared us the need to sleep under the dripping meat. There was room for a score of us and the floor was of dry wood-chips. We had no complaints.

Next morning we were up and away by nine o'clock, for there was a long day ahead: first of all a five-mile walk to the north corrie, then the exploration of the unclimbed cliffs, and finally a four-mile return over the summit. For three miles the path kept below the south flank of Ben Alder by the line of the

Alder Burn. Like all the tracks in the neighbourhood this one was a relic of the golden age of stalking—broad, straight, and well drained. The sun fell bright on the loch behind us. Away to our left, moorland five miles wide swept up and westwards to the high corries under the peaks of Corrour and Rannoch. All of that country was far more spacious than the Middle East deserts as I remember them. Hill-distances make no less an impression of majesty on the mind than the most noble cliff scenery. It is well said of a Tchaikovsky symphony that it leads men to the edge of the Infinite and leaves them for minutes gazing into that. Something of the same could be experienced that morning in watching the swell of the far-away moors lifting into the grey screen of an autumn haze that lay thick in the distance, and beyond it lifting again to the clear mountains, up to the last hard curve of one peak, and there vanishing, at the edge of the Infinite. Too little of that beauty can ever break through the distractions of a path and company.

After climbing to two thousand two hundred feet the track swung north into the head of Glen Labhair, which fell four miles leftwards to Loch Ossian and rose rightwards to the bealach Dubh of Ben Alder. The glen below us was full of roaring stags and the shout of the hills' echo and re-echo. We took the uphill track and made the bealach. Culra Glen fell away five miles north to Loch Pattock. Mist banks forming at the lower end had risen to obscure the entire north flank of Ben Alder on which our cliffs lay. Until that mist cleared no profitable move could be made and we accordingly settled down for lunch. The time was shortly after midday.

A few minutes sufficed to establish that the cliffs *were* there, intermittently looming through rolling veils on a mile-long front. At the middle of the face a great ridge repeatedly appeared and vanished. Occasionally the mists would clear on its near side. It was directed away from us obliquely, so that all its upper half was silhouetted against the cloud as a knife-edge, set at no mean angle. Lower down the glen we could see the bottom quarters of three other ridges; these were slower in clearing. An hour's waiting brought the reward. They emerged, rock-crests picked out to great advantage by woolly wisps lingering in the gullies between. Tennent liked these farther ridges best and I the central ridge. However, the distance was too great for their real merits to be assessed. We walked half a mile down Coire Dubh.

We stopped directly under the Central Ridge and climbed a few hundred feet up grass to its base. It then seemed that the best name for it would be the Mythical Ridge. It had vanished. In its stead was a broad buttress of mingled grass and crag. There was no continuous rock-climb. Yet that ridge *had* looked imposing from a distance. However, there was a little corrie just to the left of the buttress and projecting over its lip were rock-columns, looking more attractive than the triple ridges lower down the glen. These latter, we were almost sure, were as broken up and as grassy as Mythical Ridge.

After struggling up scree to the corrie's lip our confusion was complete. The promising columns, the Mythical Ridge, the triple ridges farther north—not one was a full-bodied crag—all were mouldy, mica-schist skeletons, richly apparelled in blaeberries and a voluminous plant life. Had we only been botanists, with what unaffected pleasure might we not have flushed! Being rock-climbers we scowled ferociously. The day was lost—our so suddenly valuable time wasted. We cursed our luck.

And this was where our education began. For we scrambled up to the plateau by a zigzag line on the left flank of Mythical Ridge, and at last came out on to the top enjoying ourselves. And this was not simply due to the fact that our mouths were full of blaeberries. The plateau is a mile and a half wide. How very much like a Cairngorm, I thought; how open and lofty were the hill moors, all red and yellow and caverned by corries with lochs. In all the waters were as many shades of blue as there were lochans—a score of them—more no doubt than I ever saw—a country as bright as Spain. The root of its fascination was that all of it was unknown. We had never set eyes on it before. Here it was, in the middle of Scotland, and we, in our ignorance, might well have spent our energies searching out the corners of some far-off and less excellent land—had we not been lucky.

The maps had been encouraging enough. They had shown us that maze of right-angled valleys and high hill passes and tortuous waterways between Loch Ericht and Glen Nevis. They had enticed us with the emerald splash of woods, and crag-ringed hollows where unexplored corries lay, and lonely bays in blue lochs, great blanks of undetailed moor, ravines, peaks sharp and sweeping. The maps had promised us much. But the reality spread before our eyes was more moving still; for the scale was so much greater than we had appreciated, the land so much more colourful, and by Nature so very much better furnished. Exploring a tract of country like that was a worthy task for a man, besides which a short, severe climb up a small crag in one of those hundreds of corries was a triviality—something to engage a spare couple of hours before proceeding with the more enthralling pleasures of discovering the undiscovered country.

Our visit to Ben Alder had therefore turned out to be a reconnaissance. We arrived at the cairn, and each contemplated the scene in a manner suiting his own temperament. Mona sat on a boulder facing the northern panorama and pretended not to look at it in between bites at raw carrot. Tennent went a few yards to the edge of the eastern corrie and made a careful study of the depths. As for me, I lay on some flat stones and slept in the sunshine. I should have to come back soon, I decided, and make that walk from Dalwhinnie to Fort William. How long should be spent on it? Three days at least; preferably a week. I blessed the day that had introduced me to the Scottish highlands—a much better country than I had thought possible up to so late a date as the hour before. I felt an intolerable urge to know more of it; meantime there was nothing like enjoying what was at hand. I pillowed my shoulders on more comfortable boulders and let the sun soak in, and the wind brace, and the scentless air invigorate.

The wind became somewhat more than bracing after half an hour. We moved off southwards round the head of Choire Garbh. This is the eastern corrie, a mile long and a mile wide, its floor filled by a loch that is said to be alive with trout. Much rock was exposed on the corrie's walls—our hearts missed a beat, hopes jumped—but too short and discontinuous to interest a mountaineer. We descended south to Benalder cottage.

The sun was low but still shining over the tops of Corrour and Rannoch Forests when we got down, so we fetched out our food from the shed and dined in the open air. We were hugely interested to see the robber band set off, with a most business-like bearing, up the line of the Alder Burn. 'Where?' we asked ourselves, 'and why?' Dusk was falling as we finished our meal, by which time the band reappeared in parties of four, dragging three stags, which they carried out of sight round the back of the cottage. These must have been shot during the day. Within an incredibly short time the leader of the band came to us with a stag's liver 'for to-morrow morning's breakfast.' The liver weighed pounds, but my real delight was in the man who delivered it. The full description he deserves is barred by our acceptance of the 'hush-money.' Like the rest of his brotherhood he was young, in hard and lean condition, simply overflowing with high spirits and enterprise. He had already spent two months hitch-hiking round Europe. I could not but feel an admiration for all of them. They had no money, but according to their lights made full use of their inheritance, hills and freedom. Stalking in Scotland is the privilege of the landowner; but the deer, in the end, are proving tougher than the dying lairds: they pay no death duties. None the less, I hope that the semi-feudal system of the highlands will never die. Hunting another man's ground is one of the deep, dark joys of which we must never be deprived. The chance of it, at least, must always be there; life not made duller than it is. I wondered whether our poachers' energy, directed to such purpose in Benalder Forest, would have been directed at all in Glasgow—or just dissipated? If they are no better men than myself, then I fear the worst. For my own part I am no poacher because I love creating and loathe killing.

Next morning's weather was better than ever, with less haze and a hotter sun. After breakfast we sunned ourselves on the grass before the cottage. The robber band dispersed, some crossing the moors to Rannoch, a few making for the high passes to Corrour, each man carrying a rucksack weighted with a hundred pounds of venison.

When every one had gone the peace and quiet seemed so wonderful that we postponed our own departure. We lay in the quiet as one lies in an eiderdown quilt, luxuriating. I was sufficiently refreshed in half an hour to want a swim in the loch, whose waters were blurred with trembling autumn stains, stretching far out from the slopes of the far shore, but blue, *icy* blue at the near margin—as Mona and I found when we swam. Life and warmth in the body seemed doubled when we came out. Tennent painted, scoffed, and was lied to about the water's heat. At midday we set out for Loch Rannoch.

Although so much of our time had been spent on Ben Alder it was not till we were well down the loch that we saw it whole for the first time. An Alpinist, I suspect, would call it a shapeless lump—but what will astound and baffle him about those central highland lumps is how they contrive to be shapeless so gracefully. I watched Ben Alder now, an Empty Quarter of the skies, ash-pale in Arabian haze, wound around by the mirage of an everlasting river, and by the long blue flicker of the loch. From our feet to the desert's edge a green mile or more of broadly scattered firs stretched cool and erect in short single-files, or at ease in clumps, up to the ever-winding river. As it now was, so is the scene fixed for ever in reality, changeless. I watched the lift of the trees' heads and the free sweep of a bird scouting high to Ben Alder. And I confess that I watched all this with a mind completely blank. I absorbed the beauty along with the sunshine, untroubled by desire to act or think. However, stray thoughts stepped forward from time to time and presented themselves for inspection. In the mountain scene around me the fittingness of everything most impressed me—the way in which so great a wealth of detail—diverse detail too—was integrated with the whole, a unity of order in which the good was manifested and beauty revealed. Man cannot live in that harmony with the good, as do the trees and birds and animals, blindly through the grace of nature: he has to do it of free will. And that seemed to be the purpose of man's life, as seen from Benalder Forest.

20 *Castle Buttress*

TO GIVE SAFE CONDUCT to a mountaineer on the Scottish rocks in winter, all the wisdom of the owl, the cunning of the fox, and the guile of the serpent would seem to be of themselves insufficient. Desirable as they are as attributes, to them something else must be added.

I had long known that Castle Buttress of Nevis was a winter climb of which to be wary. Its upper slabs are smooth, and loose snow lying on them in quantity is notoriously apt to avalanche. Presumably it was for this reason that I could find no contemporaries of my own who had climbed the buttress in winter. Its history had been too discouraging. None the less I felt confident that by exercising a little foresight one should be able to outwit the elements. All that was asked of a visitor to the Castle was that prior to climbing he should acquire a knowledge of the snow conditions; then, if there were dry powder on the cliffs, or bulky snows in thaw condition, he could leave it for a day when the snow was firm. Theorizing in an arm-chair I believed that it might be as easy as that to judge a Nevis climb so inscrutable as the Castle. Not that I underrated the Castle: I underrated the difficulties of getting an exact and detailed knowledge of the snow.

During our day on North-east Buttress I told Laidlaw of the Castle problem. Would he go with me when the right weather came? I had climbed with him only two or three times so far, but had found him a born mountaineer, remarkably speedy and safe for a man of just less than eighteen years. Rather too promptly and unreflectingly he said sure, he'd love to come. He had still a blind faith in my infallible judgment only to be cured by repeated shatterings. So next January we carried a light tent up to the Allt a Mhuilinn glen and camped at the deer fence, about half-way to the hut. The hut was alleged to be full. We met a party of climbers descending and obtained from them a full report about weather conditions during the preceding week. Seven days ago there had been a snowfall of several inches—normal type snow, neither wet nor powdery, which had consolidated well. This had been followed by incessant south-easterly wind, perhaps more south than east. In other words the wind had been blowing along the line of the cliffs. There had been no further precipitation and no drift had been seen blowing about the plateau.

Had they climbed on the Castle area, I asked, or on the Carn Dearg half of the mountain? No, they had kept to the high half, left of Number Three Gully. My opinion after hearing them out was that Castle Buttress would be safe. Although the wind had been southerly the touch of east had put an edge to it, and there had been no trace of thaw. And no powder had fallen. It seemed to me that conditions must be very nearly ideal for our purpose. One clue to the contrary had been given to me, but so subtle a clue that I overlooked it.

Some fortunate premonition, however, made me declare for a 6 a.m. start, and Laidlaw's presence held me to it. He had been brought up in a stern school. His elder mountaineering brother (whom I now blessed) had trained him to rise in the early hours of a cold morning to waken his party and get the stoves going. He did this willingly, or at least uncomplainingly, being wild with enthusiasm for life in general and mountains in particular. He would keep waking up at every hour from midnight onwards to take a look at his watch and make sure that he was not sleeping in. The result was that at eight o'clock next morning we were plodding up towards the preliminary snow-slopes directly under the Castle.

The sky was cloudy grey but fairly clear as yet to eastwards. The first and last sun of the day was shining on to the Castle. Its wide upper turrets were heavy laden with snow, sparkling, almost dancing, against the leaden grey of the west and the massive, darker battlements just under them. All these top-most crags were ringed below and walled on their right-hand side by snow-sheeted slabs, and they projected heavily above the remaining four-fifths of the buttress, which depended from them like a down-thrust tongue. I guessed the total height to be eight hundred feet. The tongue tapered to a blunt and overhanging tip, and from top to bottom was encased in frozen snow. There were two bare patches where ice showed: the first of thirty feet, low down near the tip, probably caused by thinner snow melting by day and refreezing at night; the second an icy groove near the centre, probably scooped and scored by a snow slide from the upper slabs. The latter thought gave me pause for a minute. Then I rationalized, saying that if too much snow *had* come on to the slabs and so avalanched off, that very fact was our best guarantee of safety now, for I knew that no more snow had fallen since. We continued.

The shape of the Castle was determined on right and left by the clean deep clefts of the North and South Castle Gullies. They were snow-filled, so much so that no pitches showed, which surprised me at this early month of the season. They swept down either flank, dividing the Castle cliffs from the long pinnacle of Raeburn's Buttress on the left and the Castle Ridge on the right, and converging under the tip of the tongue. The whole form was a noble one. We approached the tip, for access to the buttress must be gained by a direct ascent of the overhang. In summer this overhang is twelve feet high, now shortened to six feet by a cone of snow, which had formed underneath. We stood on the cone's top and roped up on a hundred feet of line. Laidlaw had still to lead a big winter climb. I was determined that he should lead this one, at least as far as the slabs. After his initial modesty had subsided he agreed and started.

That first overhang is very difficult in summer, when good holds allow it to be climbed without a shoulder, and in winter I imagine it will often disappear altogether under the cone of avalanche debris. To-day, with six feet projecting, it might have been a simple obstacle had the rocks not been so icy. After a few tentative efforts Laidlaw had failed to get over the upper

Castle Buttress of Ben Nevis
s, Slabs. IS, Ice-scoop. x, Turning Point

lip. I could see perfectly well that he was self-conscious about style and not 'warmed up.' He stepped down and invited me to go ahead. Had I done anything of the sort his confidence in his own power to lead would have been spoiled for the rest of the day. My refusal on the grounds that it looked too hard for me bore much fruit a few hours later. Meantime I urged him to use my shoulder. He did so and began cutting foothold in the bulge at the lip. After a couple of blows his pick suddenly pierced the ice with a hollow *plop* and out flashed a spout of water. It came straight on to my face when I was least expecting it. The splash of the icy jet made me swing back involuntarily, and Laidlaw on top lost balance and capsized. We both rolled down to the foot of the cone. That was the most inglorious start I have ever made to a rock-climb.

We picked ourselves up and dusted ourselves down and tried again. To avoid the stream between the rock and the ice Laidlaw cut holds higher up to the left, but to get purchase to raise himself he had to step from my shoulders on to my head—his nails were tricounis, with sharp points. The rock above the overhang continued steeply and still thinly iced for twenty feet. Every hold cut filled immediately with water but the ice itself was surprisingly sound. Although it cut easily it held weight firmly. With thirty feet of rope out, Laidlaw reached a belt of rotten snow, a lower apron to the main mass of good snow, which he reached at fifty feet where the angle eased, and which became firmer and tougher at every step he took. We shortened rope after I joined him.

For a hundred feet at most we were able to kick steps in the snow, which thereafter gave Laidlaw constant cutting with the blade of his axe. The underlying rock is well broken up, with plentiful steps and ledges on which one may scramble in summer for a few hundred feet. For that same reason the rock is capable of holding snow in depth and piled at high angles. The whole back of the buttress was raised, polished, hard frozen, and felt distinctly exposed with its two gullies racing down to each side: an inspiriting position when things are going well as they were now. On this lower part of the buttress we climbed together without belays.

Three hundred feet of such climbing brought us at last to the icy scoop that we had seen in the centre, which at close quarters proved to be a short gully, a natural drainage line filled from side to side with pale green ice. A belay was needed here. For Laidlaw would have a long run-out. And who knows what may come down a drain-pipe? The snow-fan under the gully was so hard that an axe-shaft could not be driven in. I had to descend twenty feet and go left to get suitable snow. Looking up I wondered whether the rope would now be long enough to let the leader reach good snow above. I suspected too that he would take more time than we bargained for, so I put on spare sweaters and settled down for a long wait. The precaution was fortunate. He must have spent forty minutes cutting up the first fifty feet, losing time first on viscous snow-ice in which the pick stuck firmly at each blow, and then on the bare ice which had to be hit very hard. I enjoyed my leisure. The north face of Carn Dearg Buttress is worth studying in winter. On its near flank the long upper spire of Raeburn's Buttress, snow-covered on the slender crest, looked like the mast of a tall clipper iced up as it rounds the Cape. I had clambered up it in summer, but never yet had I risked it in winter—and I wondered. . . . It would be a most spectacular climb. But the Castle was enough for the present. It was interesting to note how alarming the downward vista could look just because the surface had a glazed crust. Had the snow been soft it would have appeared much milder in angle.

Laidlaw took me up to a snow-patch at fifty feet and continued again on ice, which quickly gave place to snow. I was now right in his line of fire. As time wore on and his rope was running out he was *still* not getting snow to please him for a halt. He was beyond the gully but the snow was so hard frozen that he could not cut it with the blade of his axe—he had to use the pick. That is unusual on Scottish snow. The chips were beginning to shoot past with a horrid *whirr*, and when they hit they hurt. A larger fragment struck my head so violently that I was nearly stunned. I stopped him then and went up without a belay. The slope above the gully was at no great angle, and we moved together for a hundred feet to softer snow at the foot of the slabs.

Our first difficulty lay in dealing with a short corner caked with a kind of snow called *névé*—tough and tight-packed. It gave most reliable holds, but all movement was exposed and belayless. We then followed a line of least resistance leftwards to the foot of a long chimney, the first fifteen feet of which was choked with white snow-ice and the upper section with a light, almost feathery snow. As reward for previous sacrifice I now took the lead. I intended to enjoy myself, and to add to my comfort at the take-off cut a small platform and chipped out holds for seven feet up the chimney. I had moved up on these and was just clearing out some loose snow above with swipes of a gloved hand, when a minor avalanche of powder poured off the crags above and burst over the top of the chimney in successive waves, which apparently all found their way down my neck. When all was quiet again and the laughter from below stilled, I climbed another few feet, laboriously dusting the fresh snow off the rock. The difficulties were not inconsiderable, but whether I might eventually have overcome them was unfortunately never proved. For at this moment another torrent of powder-snow swept over my head and shoulders, and that was followed by a third. My whole face felt painfully iced. I was having no more for the moment and modestly resigned the lead. During all this time the tail-end of the rope had been convulsed with hysterical merriment. He then stepped forward, to confound my malicious expectations by climbing the chimney without further bombardment. He had trouble in plenty. Everything went well for fifty feet, but he had then to leave the chimney and cross a corner to snow-bound slabs on the right. The move greatly perplexed him. It was not skill he lacked but experience of unusual moves. At last it was done. The slabs were coated with an inch or two of *névé*. He cut rapidly and

I soon followed in his tortuous tracks up the chimney and round a corner, and over twenty-five feet of slabs in two hairpin bends, this to avoid thin ice, and so to a snow-filled scoop. He had me belayed there, after a fashion, so I carried on past him, fifty feet up the scoop to a big and snow-piled ledge.

The route now lay to my right, over and up slanting slabs. These were bolstered with enormous snow-puffs, snow having a convex curve to its surface, and quite remarkably sleek. It was unlike any other snow we had seen this day, and much bulkier. The silken sleekness worried me. Against the wall to my left I saw a large detached stone and prised it loose with my spike. I pitched it on to the slabs. An instant after the strike I heard a rip, and a crack opened across the snow-sheet. Nothing more happened. The silken sheet was a wind-slab crust, which would avalanche off if disturbed further. I fetched up Laidlaw then and said that I should not like to risk going on. The wind-slab crust was not in itself particularly thick. Assuming that it would slide off when we stepped on to it I did not envisage the weight of the breaking slabs carrying us away—not if we had good footing below. But experimental soundings with an axe showed at once that under the wind-slab loose dry powder lay upon smooth, glazed rock-slabs. The powder seemed to be held together mainly by its wind-slab shell. We were astonished that it should ever have collected there, on such slabs in such bulk. If the shell went the underlying snow would go too, and it would be not the shell but the powder that would carry us off. We should then fall over the cliff on the right-hand half of the buttress.

'Not another yard!' said I. 'We have other climbs to do besides this.'

Laidlaw looked aghast at the prospect of descent. Our balcony did seem exposed when one looked out and down. I thought he was thinking of the icy slabs and the traverse into the chimney. 'I'll go down last,' I reassured him. 'Even if it does take hours we'll manage it.'

'Oh, I wasn't thinking of that,' he said. 'There's just one

thing you 've forgotten.' He pointed his axe at the split wind-slab.

For one moment I looked blank, then realized what he meant. From now onwards the split wind-slab was liable to come away and the powder with it, and gather to itself any snow of a similar kind that might lie on the cliff below, and any loose boulders lying on ledges. This avalanche, if it ever occurred, would sweep the line of our descent. Our first stage of retreat by the chimney would be protected, for that lay to the right (looking down) of the avalanche track, but all the rest would be exposed. The extraordinary speed with which all the circumstances attending our climb had changed appalled us, and made us feel peculiarly helpless. We had climbed for four and a half hours in apparent safety, and now, in a few seconds, objective dangers threatened no matter how we might turn. No rats, confidently sprucing their whiskers, had ever walked more briskly into a trap than we.

'Let 's have lunch,' I growled. 'It 's past one o'clock.' Lunch, I thought, always remedies depression. But to-day our squashed jam sandwiches seemed even more squashed and dismally jamless than usual. We munched in silence and looked aimlessly around. A cloud, which had lain all day on the summit of Nevis as far north as Number Three Gully, had now spread still farther north to cover the top of Carn Dearg, and its first long tongues were licking around the crest of the Castle, close above our heads. The air was gloomy. 'It will be dark soon to-day,' I said. 'We had better not wait too long.' Silence. I could remember getting caught in only one other trap as nasty as the present one—the day when Mackenzie and I encountered brittle ice above the crux of Shelf Route. We had climbed out of *that* one in half an hour, but in this one half an hour would just see us farther into it, and every hour after that our position would get worse, with no hope of relief until the last low overhang was above us.

'Where *could* all that powder and wind-slab have come from?' asked Laidlaw. 'There wasn't any lower down.' We held a five-minute *post mortem.* I could think of only one answer: the south-east wind blowing across the plateau must have been a cold and humid wind and therefore an erosive wind. In that event drift eroded from the crust of the plateau would be swept along the surface by that south-south-east wind and a day-long trickle deposited gently over the northerly edge of the Castle. No drifting had been seen by climbers—but that only confirmed the theory of erosion. A mere trickle of drift continuing hour after hour for days on end would soon amount to the bulk we now saw on the slabs, and any surplus spilling off would be carried into North Castle Gully by eddies of south-easterly wind, which in turn would account for the absence of loose powder on the middle and lower buttress and for the well-packed gullies.

We were pleased with this theory. 'If anything happens to us,' said Laidlaw with a suddenly cheerful grin, 'it 's good to know *why.*'

The cloud had thickened over the Castle, completely obscuring the upper turrets, and in a few more minutes sank right over us. That was a remarkably cold cloud; it drove us to quick action. Snow began to fall while we were climbing down the scoop—only a few, floating flakes soon verging towards sleet. At the bottom of the scoop I had a long wait while Laidlaw edge-nailed down the slabs, then worried his way round the traverse and eased himself into the chimney. He must have spent half an hour on them, but encouraged me by never coming on the rope. None the less, he was sufficiently agitated when he reached the bottom to shout up, urging me to drive in a piton, and come down on a doubled rope. It is true that I had in my rucksack one piton and a spare hundred feet of line, but I wanted to keep that piton for later emergencies. It had occurred to me that if the slabs avalanched while we were down on the lower third of the buttress, who knows but there might be some little crag beside us into which we might just have time to drive the piton—clip on the rope—and pray briefly. Such was the pass to which we had come. Perhaps my idea was a mad one. Meantime I preferred to climb down.

The long wait in sleet-chilled mist had numbed my hands, and I felt sluggish with cold when I came to the awkward traverse. While in trouble there I remembered that Laidlaw had almost certainly no belay. I called down to him: 'Take off the rope. You couldn't hold me anyhow.'

'I 'm *on* your rope,' he called back. 'I 'm going to stay on.'

The only thing I could do was just not to fall off. A difficult end to achieve. The greatest difficulty, after I reached the chimney, was trying to see the footholds below; everything was whitened with the powder cascade of midday and the lower part of my body blocked the view. However, I managed it somehow, and over the last five feet revenged myself on Laidlaw by stepping heavily on to his shoulder.

The whole upper crag of the Castle had now vanished into purpureal gloom. The mist clung more thickly around us, although the lower vista was clear all the way down to the desolation of the Allt a Mhuilinn, save for a scattering of wisps in the middle air. Suddenly there came a smart shower of hail, immediately followed by a hissing noise from our axe-heads. The cloud was charged with electricity. We could feel the tingle of it on our eyebrows and the fringe of the hair above the forehead. I had clipped my piton on to my waist-loop with a karabiner (a steel clip-ring), and these too began to sing complainingly. We scrambled hastily down thirty feet of easy rock and the caked corner at the foot. There was all the while a very strong antiseptic smell in the air, probably caused by ozone.

We began descending the very hard snow leading to the centre ice-scoop. *En route* we reaped an advantage from the too big steps Laidlaw had cut on the way up, more than cancelled out by the too big space between. Intermediate steps had now to be cut to preserve our balance; a slip on this frozen sheet would have been hard to stop, and sometimes impossible. Yet speed was a prime necessity. We were now right in line of fire from the upper slabs. There was one thing of which I was becoming more scared than of anything else—a lightning flash and thunder on the crest of the Castle, because the tremendous vibrations there would almost certainly start the avalanche. While a thunder-cloud is actually resting on a Scottish summit, I remembered (from Observatory records) that discharge rarely occurs. The dangerous moments are while the cloud approaches, lifts, and moves off—especially the latter. At the moment of departure a violent flash is probable. Accordingly, our immediate objective should be to try to get as far down as we could before the cloud moved.

I asked Laidlaw to take the position of honour as last man down, and went to the front to do the cutting. One hard slash with the corner of the blade made a scrape sufficient to take at least our edge-nails safely; that was good enough for an intermediate step. We went down facing sideways, and made fair speed to the ice-scoop. Here we had to go down facing in. The holds had been well spaced, so Laidlaw went first while I paid out rope and kept a wary eye aloft. To my dismay I saw that the danger area was exposed to view. This meant that the cloud *was* lifting. It could not possibly have begun to happen at a worse time; our position was the one spot on the whole buttress to which everything that fell would most naturally converge.

I shrugged my shoulders and turned away. There was no point in worrying any further. We had taken in advance all right precautions, gained reliable reports on the snow, risen early, and climbed as well and as fast as we could. Our own share had been done and the rest was not for us to decide. This was only the last of many occasions when events had impressed on me, both on mountains and off them, that skill, energy, foresight, and the strenuous prosecution of plans, are by themselves quite insufficient for success. One's own best efforts must always be made, but having been made they have still to be seconded by Providence: therefore let us make them, always hopefully, and resign the rest without self-concern to God's will. His energies alone must bring *all* human actions, trivial or of great moment, to their best end. That was how I felt while I waited at the scoop for the cloud to lift. There is no such thing as luck.

I told Laidlaw not to stop half-way, but to carry on to the foot. Before the hundred feet ran out I gave him a final shout of warning and began descending at the same time as himself. For the first time for several hours I felt in high spirits. I enjoyed the green ice, and wished we had had a little sun to draw out the colour. At the bottom I found myself smiling at Laidlaw instead of growling as before, and he, always an extraordinarily responsive youth, grinned delightedly at being smiled at. 'Things are going well after all,' he said. 'Even that cloud 's lifting off the top.'

I hesitated—but what would be the use? So I said nothing. I turned and looked up. The cloud was right on top of the Castle, but the main body of it was leaning in a vast bulge to northwards. 'Let 's get going,' I urged. 'It will be dark in no time—four o'clock already.'

Speed was of far more consequence than any security the rope might give us, so from now onwards we moved together and dispensed altogether with belays. I went first as before, at as hard a pace as I dared, cutting only when I had to as fast as inspired muscles would move. It was a most glorious sensation to feel on top of the world, and to have every and urgent need so to feel. Dusk was gathering when we reached the steep iced rocks thirty feet above the last overhang. We were so near—and yet this last part was going to take, indeed to devour, time. I looked again at the turrets. I could not see them properly in the darkness, but could distinguish the mass of the cloud towering aslant and obviously near to pulling away. The flash would be any moment now.

I did not see how we could get down that next thirty feet in less than thirty minutes if we *climbed* down. This was the very place for my long-treasured piton: we fetched out electric torches and looked for a suitable crack into which to drive it. After a few minutes' search we had failed to find one and grew impatient. So I let Laidlaw try to climb down on the end of a tight rope. However, the acute difficulties of finding small ice-holds by torchlight from above were beyond him. I lacked a good enough stance to lower him all the way, so back he came. We searched anew and at last uncovered a suitably thin crack. I drove the piton—tied a spare loop to it—doubled the rope through. Then we roped off. I have never gone down a rope faster. I burned my hands. As my feet struck the top of the snow-cone all the nervous apprehension I had felt above the ice-scoop returned for a space.

'Don't stop to coil the rope,' I barked, as I jerked it down through the loop. 'We 've to get clear while we can.'

We took to the lower snow-slopes at a run, and were several hundred feet down, and stumbling with weariness, before I would consent to halt. We coiled the rope. All remained quiet above. We walked leisurely towards the Allt a Mhuilinn and crossed to the path on the right bank. We had gone maybe a hundred yards on this path when a flash and thunder peal came from the Castle, echoing in stupendous volume from the cliffs. Before the echoes had died there was a second and much greater flash, lighting the white walls of the Castle corrie from top to bottom and side to side. The simultaneous and reverberating roar, and the long-drawn echoes, completely drowned all other noises. It was not possible to tell whether the slabs had avalanched. Latterly we heard a rattle of stones, quickly muffled. But no man could have said whence they fell.

21 An Teallach and Dundonnell Forest

BY 1950 it had become one of the anomalies of my mountaineering life, a trick of fate one might say, that An Teallach, which started me climbing (a few words describing its summit-ridge having had power to flush me from my roost in the plains, and send me winging over the mountain world), should be one mountain that I had never climbed. It lurked always in the back of my mind—lurked not phantom-like, but dynamically, the ideal mountain.

Time and distance cut me off from it at first; opportunities for going to Wester Ross and the Dundonnell Forest never arose of their own accord. Nor did I make such opportunities at a later date: I feared that An Teallach in the flesh must disappoint me. I dared not expect it to live up to the original vision, which had been so powerful as to overcome an inertia as great as mine, and start body and soul into exploratory action. But in February 1950 I was forced to dismiss these fears. Three friends and I planned an expedition to the Himalaya, starting in April, and it seemed to me unthinkable that I should venture there never having known An Teallach—whose name means 'The Forge'—upon which I had been hammered these fifteen years.

On 21st February, at 5 p.m., MacAlpine, Richard Meyer, and I arrived at Dundonnell. We stopped on the roadway two and a half miles short of Little Loch Broom, at the point where a hill track runs five miles southwards to the lonely Strath na Sheallag. We had heard of a deserted cottage there called Shenavall, on the south flank of An Teallach itself. Judged by the map it would make an excellent base, if weather-proof; it stood right in among the hills at the meeting place of three deer forests, and looked across the breadth of the Strath into the east corrie of Beinn Dearg Mor, where cliffs of untouched sandstone awaited explorers. From Dundonnell these cliffs were hopelessly inaccessible but from Shenavall almost convenient.

At 6 p.m., loaded with four days' food, we started over the seven miles' track to Shenavall. The track rose eleven hundred feet to a moorland pass, yet was neither steep nor stony, so that in little more than an hour we were crossing the watershed. Dusk had fallen. Two miles to northwards the white and crowded towers of An Teallach encircled their east corrie. The great length of the ridge augured a long day. Would it be next day? I wondered. I thought not. The sky showed starred patches, but the west wind was fetching too heavy masses of cloud up the sea-lanes from the coast. My day on An Teallach must be graced with perfect weather—or I would not go: upon that I was determined; which meant that we might have to spend some days skirmishing for position.

A long descent in wellnigh total darkness brought us at last to the flats of Strath na Sheallag and to the solitary house of Achneigie. We were surprised to hear cattle in the byre and see a bright light in the house. For I would not have believed that in winter people could have been found to live here. The only links with civilization are the hill track to Dundonnell or a ten-mile track west to Gruinard Bay. There is no other occupied house in the glen.

We knocked at the door and met Mr. Urquhart and his wife, their three children—and a schoolmistress; for it is the law of Scotland that all children shall be educated, and where they cannot go to school the school comes to them. They all welcomed us. Later they gave us milk and food. But they had no accommodation so on we went to Shenavall.

Shenavall at the first glance looked a very small cottage, but proved to be surprisingly commodious within. There were four rooms downstairs and three above. There were tables and chairs, spring-beds and mattresses. Even firewood. The house had been unoccupied for ten years, yet was dry inside. A heavy deposit of mice dirt lay spread over the floors, but that was a trifle. Within the hour we had a good fire in the hearth and hot soup inside us. We had settled in.

I awakened in the morning to the patter of sleet upon the sky-light window. It swirled thinly from grey cloud. This was no day for An Teallach. I turned over, rejoicing in sloth; until suddenly I remembered Beinn Dearg Mor. That north-east corrie had to be reconnoitred. All a human's difficulties about getting up in the morning are his not having sufficient incentive. Now I could rise at once and hardly notice the morning's raw-ness. At 10 a.m. we were off.

The approach to Beinn Dearg Mor from Shenavall is short on the map, but the flat and marshy ground presents two temper-testing hurdles in the shape of rivers feeding Loch na Sheallag—broad rivers unbridged, fast-flowing after rain, and deep. They have to be waded. One's feet are to be stung and frozen four times in one day. Beyond the second river the ground rose steeply for a thousand feet or more to the east corrie. The floor was the mountain's snow-line. I have never seen a corrie more shapely. A double summit pointed up from the centre, pillared by broad walls of sandstone. These were the central buttresses of a circle of seven, perfectly disposed in size and situation to contribute the utmost possible distinction to the main peak above them. The corrie's beauty inspires one to think big and look for a climb hard enough to honour the hill. But such aspirations had to be sternly curbed to-day. Grey and lowering clouds, the occasional drizzle of sleet, the raw damp wind, and the loose snow massed upon crags unsuitably weathered for winter climbing, would have made any long hard route a misery. Such a climb could have been done, but with several days in hand we were in no mood for it. Instead we climbed a gully to the left of the summit. It gave a snow-climb much like the Centre Gully of Beinn Laoigh.

In summer the buttresses would all give rock-climbs, perhaps of every order of difficulty.

We sped home by the north ridge and corrie and prepared for better things on the morrow. That night the wind got up from the north-west. It came sweeping over the shoulders of An Teallach and struck the corrugated-iron roof with a *boom*, like a hammer hitting a gong. Our second day was thus worse than the first and I began to fear that An Teallach was to be denied us. The sleet fell as thinly as before, but continuously, and not just in swirls. Late in the forenoon we wandered up to the east corrie of An Teallach, but could see nothing, save grey veils. The outing was a mere taking of exercise from which we returned dismally to a cold squalor at Shenavall and tried, with indifferent success, to warm ourselves up with great fires and meals. The weather was most decidedly growing colder and colder. As the night wore on it hardened to frost—even robbing us of sleep in the small hours. But this time our reward was a clear sky at dawn.

We were up at 7 a.m., unregretful of bed and eager to be off. Air and sky sparkled, and ground too, for the turf was frosted and each furred blade raised its individual spearhead. When we moved off at 9 a.m. the grass slopes above Shenavall felt like rock under the boot. We climbed leisurely, idling up with an exaggerated slowness, just waiting for the springs of energy to flow, as they would suddenly, and carry us easily up to the south-east top, Sail Liath. For our plan was to traverse the summit-ridge from south-east to north, and then descend to the east corrie. After we had climbed an hour from Shenavall the moment of flow came. We struck rhythm. The pace of ascent grew swift and painless. Until then we had climbed in a stupor: now the world came alive. Dry crisp snow lay on the frozen ground, but the sun shone with the full, refreshing warmth of an early spring morning. We were out on the rounded back of the ridge where it could reach us. Consciously we lived and moved in it and were no longer blind to the liveliness of the mountains. Boulders thrust red heads out of the snow, the slant of the sunlight fetching a glow from them, dotting the flash of the slope with colour, unexpectedly. As we gained height our speed increased; for we felt stimulated and even excited by the sharp air and sun, and our movement towards the sky, and the near approach of our great ridge.

The last slope of Sail Liath was a wind-packed snow-field, arching up to a huge silver dome. The edge of the dome had a curve like good china, a vast and flawless curve starting out against the blue behind. The blue was lucid: that early morning blue, which one associates with South Sea lagoons; and the snow-dome's edge flowed upon it. I had seen nothing on mountains more simple than this edge, and nothing more beautiful. It is a beauty that every natural thing manifested through the universe seems to exhibit by reason of its very being.

Sometimes I find it distressing on mountains to see beauty alone. I want others to see and share it too, otherwise I have a sense of vicarious frustration; beauty is meant for all men. I hovered to let Meyer catch up. He was beaming with enthusiasm.

'What a day!' he exclaimed. 'What a country!' The words convey nothing but the tone of voice satisfied even me. I grinned, and we followed our own ways to the cairn, where MacAlpine soon joined us. We rested no more than a minute, for a breeze was blowing from the north-west. A quick glimpse over the northern edge showed us where the great corrie lay, fourteen hundred feet below, its Loch Toll an Lochain hidden from us by the bulge of the precipice. Far beyond, a screen of grey-blue haze covered the full length of the Atlantic; but the mainland side stayed clear, from the distant ripple of the Cairngorms to the nearby spikes of Torridon, and between, a white innumerable mob of no outstanding character. A more individual ruggedness lay close at hand. The towers of our ridge curled like a whip-lash through the sky—flicked two miles around the corrie. An Teallach waited.

At midday we set off north-west round the ridge, which at first was broad, going easily down to a col and over a second rounded dome. Then the ridge narrowed. It was buried deep in the soft snow of the recent fall. This proved little hindrance while our course lay downwards, and our subsequent ascent to the third peak was at first aided by rock out-crops. These, we could see, were topped by a high summit-buttress, destined to give trouble. The prelude to the ridge was over. At once the crest narrowed again. We scrambled over massive blocks until halted by a fifteen-foot wall. Although steep it was snow-covered, for the weathered fracture-lines in sandstone can support a thick skin.

This last thought encouraged me. When high-angle rock is able to support much soft dry snow there must be excellent holds underneath. And so it proved. Their excavation cost time, but they were good enough to let us climb unroped to a higher crest of now Alpine narrowness. The buttress jerked out of the ridge close above. I moved to its foot and we roped up. As I turned to watch the others a golden eagle swept round the corner of the buttress immediately behind them, so close to their backs, indeed, and so fast, that collision seemed certain. But the astounded bird stood on its tail just in time, and swept back the way it had come, over the corrie.

I appropriated the lead. This, I felt, was an occasion: An Teallach ought to get the best I could give. But for quite other reasons my decision to lead was to prove doubly fortunate. The route again lay up a short wall, just to the left side of the crest. Under its thinner snow-coating I could see long wrinkles, small and dipping out. From a snow-ledge on top the buttress sprang with a renewed steepness. Meanwhile MacAlpine belayed me. I brushed over the wall with gloved hands. I scraped the wrinkles with my axe. This revealed one hold in the middle, giving a move that none of my party will forget in a hurry—a balance move on a crease. I could just get the edge-nail of my boot on to it, but it sloped out and bore a thin lichen. Being frozen, the lichen was slippery, and the question was whether my nail would hold. The upward lift from the hands had to be made with the aid of press-holds only. Thrice I half made the move—raised myself just a few inches from the holds below, and each time returned to think again. MacAlpine, watching from directly below, swore that my one-nail hold looked excessively alarming. No doubt he was thinking, as a good second should, of the best way to stop me if I fell; but I was now reasonably well satisfied that my tricouni nail (serrated cast-iron) would bite on the sandstone. So I made one quick lift, and the nail held, on the extreme outer curve of the crease. I pulled myself up.

The ledge above was good—mercifully good, for MacAlpine and Meyer were wearing Vibram rubber soles. These are excellent on Scottish snow and ice, and on clean rock, wet or dry, but on wet or frozen lichen hopelessly bad. Torridon sandstone being rough and tough, like gritstone, Vibram soles would at first sight appear to be eminently suitable; but close inspection shows much of this sandstone to be patched with lichen of delicate brand. MacAlpine's foot slipped badly on the crease and he had to come up on a tight rope. By the time that Meyer reached the fatal spot the polish had become fatally perfect. He is one of the best Alpinists in England but he had to be pulled up.

The whole passage of the third peak was a new revelation of the astonishing transformations that overtake a Scottish ridge in winter, when snow is thick and the frost hard. I have heard no one report any difficulty on the ridge of An Teallach in summer—not in the technical sense.

We had now a choice of routes: either by the right flank, up a cleft cutting the vertical face, or by a long traverse leftwards across the equally steep west face. Above that cleft or beyond this traverse we could not guess what happened. The right-hand or east face lay in shadowed frost, so we went left into sunshine. We edged carefully along a shattered ledge, then climbed a hundred feet up the flank by snow-choked scoops. On these we moved together until halted by a final chimney of fifty feet. One at a time we wormed up its snow and pressed up its iced walls, until we came out on open snows among great blocks of poised stone, and over them to the top of our third peak.

The ridge down its far side went like an aerial rail on a free flight through space. There were delightful walls, snow-crusted, down which we dropped on to narrow landings of highly inclined snow. Going down first I enjoyed these walls; while

Meyer, coming last on the rope, enjoyed the ledges. The descent eased to the col. There we saw the tracks of a fox cross the ridge from west to east and traverse the face of an incipient cornice banked at sixty-five degrees above the eastern cliffs. None of us would have dared to move on such snow without a rope, but the fox had scampered quite gaily, for there was no trace of hesitation where it crossed the *arête*. I put my nose to the paw-prints and the musty stink made me rise in a hurry. They reeked. The fox must have crossed this forenoon. But why—and to what end?

We continued along the ridge rising towards our fourth peak, a cluster of four towers called Corrag Bhuidhe. The name means 'The Yellow Finger,' for which no reason was apparent from this angle, the ridge being barred near the top by crags standing markedly red against their background of white and blue. Intense weathering had given the sandstone the piled-block formation for which the granite of Arran is so well known. We climbed direct to the first tower of Corrag Bhuidhe, then crossed a gap to the second tower.

A new surprise met us there—the titbit of the day: a stretch of ridge like a high, dry-stone dyke running a hundred feet to the third tower. Crested with a sharp snow-edge, the flanks fell sheer, notably on the right-hand side, where a cliff dropped one thousand seven hundred feet to the loch. I had seen no comparable *arête* outside the Alps, although I have no doubt that in similar conditions its counterpart will be found in the Cuillin of Skye. We dealt easily with the soft snow; none the less we had to balance along step by step, arms half outstretched, and defy a natural inclination to sit astride. The third tower was only a knob at the end of the ridge, but cut off from the fourth by a vertical cleft, which could not be taken direct. So I returned a few feet, doubled a rope round a spike on the ridge, then roped off on the left flank. This brought me on to a slope just above the col. The others followed and flicked the rope down after them. We climbed easy crags to the fourth tower.

From this viewpoint the knife-edged dyke behind us looked

extraordinarily sensational, nicked along its crest by our footsteps. The whole mountain scene around—plum-coloured isles and bays, bared teeth of the Cuillin fifty miles south-west, the clean dazzle of the highland ranges—this whole, rich panorama fell into place as a mere backcloth to the drama of An Teallach's crest. Towers and edges hung in space without visible means of support, hung over the frozen void of the east corrie, but turned to the sunny south a gay lining of snow. The edge ran stark between: it alone seemed fully real, and really true, the essential An Teallach—The Forge, which bore us.

We continued down the blade of our ridge, and up to the sharp point of the fifth peak, which bears the inappropriate name of Lord Berkeley's Seat. The Leaning Tower of Dundonnell would be more truly descriptive, for it overhangs its base—leans right out over the corrie. Our descent by the north edge went on a wafer of rock curling out over the east face like a huge cornice. Dry snow was massed loosely on rock twice pierced by holes, through which we prospected a thousand feet of hoared cliff. This north ridge is unique in Scotland.

We lunched down on the col, then climbed the south ridge of Sgurr Fiona, 'The Peak of Wine.' It reminded me of the Second Pyramid of Gizeh, being not only shaped as such, but having its top section seemingly enclosed by an outer rock-casing. The snow at least lay smoothly in a pyramidal cap over the summit. Our ascent was a treadmill labour in dry snow—praise be to God—for it might have been wet. However long the sun may shine at this time of year in Scotland it has no melting effect on snow, for its declination is too low. Melting has to wait on warm winds. The quality of morning snow changes not at all in the afternoon. Snow conditions are thus less Alpine than arctic. We reached the top of Sgurr Fiona, point 3,474, with dry feet.

The pinnacled ridge had now ended. There followed a pure snow-ridge, falling to a col at three thousand feet, thence rising to point 3,483, called Bidein a Ghlas Thuill, 'The Peak of the Grey Hollow.' It is the summit of An Teallach. Under a heavy plaster of snow it is a great mountain. In ideal weather with few halts, but without hurry, that two miles of ridge had taken nearly six hours of our time.

The sun was sinking, but would not set, I wrongly thought, for another hour. Every horizon was in haze: smoky to the west; southward blue, with glens receding into it in successive planes; to the north-east, silver grey. Over Gruinard Bay a streak of white smoke issued from an invisible steamer. Not even the Summer Isles, close in to Loch Broom, were clear. The Hebrides loomed indistinctly as humps. I wanted to wait up on the ridge for sunset, which would be unusually spectacular, but the northerly air-stream spoke an icy NO.

We turned east along the north arm of the horse-shoe. Upon leaving the cairn we observed great claw-marks in the snow-bonnet of a boulder and a still deeper imprint five yards below on the corrie-flank of the ridge, where an eagle had taken one heavy hop before launching itself over the cliff. After traversing a quarter of a mile we felt free to follow its example, and so launched ourselves down a twelve-hundred-foot snow-slope to Loch Toll an Lochain. We glissaded fast, and were half-way down when the south-eastern peaks stopped us. Creamy-coloured for the last hour or so, now they reddened, while the once blue sky above turned sea-green.

The full display to be seen only from a summit had been lost to us, but as we came to the shore of Loch Toll an Lochain constantly changing lights began to play along the full length of the easterly haze-bank. It might have been a skin, inhabited by some celestial chameleon, so rapidly did the colours react to the altering west, and blend: all shaded subtleties of red, green, blue, and yellow, bloomed and faded, renewed themselves and died, coming and going with a stealth quite imperceptible, so that always one saw them there, yet never caught the flicker of the change.

The floor of the corrie flattened at the entrance to form a mountain belvedere, from which we looked far out across the valley of Dundonnell to half-hidden and mysterious ranges.

I stopped to let the others go on. It is not the sort of place that I ever feel inclined to leave. A last pallor had taken the hills; the tops were shrouds, the skies just so much empty space, the haze-banks fog. Within five minutes of this sudden death the re-awakening started. Pale blue colour flowed back into the north-east sky and the peaks whitened. Before I had realized what was happening all the haze had gone. For a while I had thought that it was simply whitening, but instead, the white solidified, stepped forward, as it were, in form of mountains, revealed to their feet for the first time this day. As the blue of the east deepened the air sharpened, grew clean, and the night's frost swept the land. A star twinkled above the corrie.

I turned to look up at An Teallach. The first of the moon-light was filtering between the pinnacles. The vast circle of their frozen walls stared down at a frozen loch—a sombre circle, but lifting high in the centre to that five-pointed crown rimmed by light.

Corrie and mountain are the natural altars of the earth to be used as such before one goes.

22 *Effects of Mountaineering on Men*

THE EFFECT THAT MEN have had upon mountaineering, and the record of their climbs in the club journals, constitute mountaineering history, about which much has been written. It is a safe subject: there the records are, and no man may gainsay them. But very little has been written of the effects of mountaineering on men. For *that* subject is downright dangerous, snags and snares abounding. Yet a report true to fact may be made if a man records detachedly, and does not exceed, his own observations and experience; accordingly I make no effort to treat the subject comprehensively; for, of course, I cannot know what all the effects of mountaineering are. Nor do I set down all the effects I have seen or experienced. I choose only those that I judge to be particularly worth noting.

The men to be met on mountains are not better than other men, and I should not be greatly troubled if they were shown to be worse. The important point is that on mountains they are known in the heat of action: it is there and then that men, more frequently than in other sports, are forced back upon their real selves. I am assured by historians that man in his usual habit is an ignoble, crawling organism; but contrary to what one might infer from such a premise, it is my experience that men's behaviour is most inspired, displays a self-forgetful spirit and nobility of soul, when circumstance is most adverse. Some of the greatest changes in men occur when storm and danger and difficulty appear together on rock, snow, and ice. I have seen quite ordinary men behave then with a fearless resolution, move with unprecedented certainty and precision, as though some *deus ex machina* had descended out of the clouds to take charge of them, and so save the situation in defiance of probability. Just to have watched that performance at close quarters has been a permanent gain to me. It has filled me with a respect and admiration for man's spirit, as then giving expression to fundamental qualities far more moving than any expression of an artist's brush or a composer's music: in this sense, that these latter have aroused my enthusiasm, but have never moved me to try to alter my own character; whereas the former has inspired me with that very desire—to be firm in adversity and bold in emergency and fearless to the end. The personal virtue is the more powerful in effect, and the more lasting. The emergencies that call out such an example are, or ought to be, of rare occurrence.

The trials of mountaineering, small or great, awaken elements of character left dormant by professional life. This fact is especially obvious at the start of a man's climbing career. Some of his latent powers of personality have been given no adequate field of action in the concentrated book-work of school and office or university, or in the routine of the factory, and may be in danger of perversion if not atrophy. He has become a jail-bird temporarily. Then perhaps for the first time he is given on mountains the field of free action he sorely needs to give growth and expansion to those unused elements of his character. A gradual self-fulfilment is the purpose of the individual life, and mountaineering does help in it. The beginning is modest enough.

Here I quote my own experience. For a year I hill-walked by myself. Simple work you would say? Its effect on me was considerable. I discovered that when a man has to find his own way for the first time across wide moors, and long narrow summit ridges, and over the high plateaux, the work gives him a sense of achievement which lasts all his life. Should he meet foul weather as well—as he certainly will—and have to steer through it by map and compass, he develops a confidence that grows at each repetition. Confidence in his own manhood and powers of action is one of the most valuable possessions that a man can have; it clears the way to his getting the two keys to success in more than mountaineering: knowledge of his goal and singleness of purpose.

In every branch of the craft one gets a training in self-reliance without ever looking for it. Routes have to be selected, obstacles mastered, decisions made, hard work and weather faced. The training is naturally more intense in winter. On big winter routes the climber repeatedly encounters rock and ice that cannot be climbed in the unimpassioned frame of mind sufficient unto the days of summer. They more often have to be forced. He may have to climb to his limit, and having done so, then grip the mind and stir up energy—and go still farther. His battle is fought out on small holds and icy corners, on bare slabs and frozen rock, often in discomfort, for the frequent reward of joy. The intense effort by which every step is won, and all skill employed, and the way through the difficulty resolutely engineered, brings together all the joys of the triune craft, rock-snow-ice. The mind has mastery of the body and knows it. In such moments all a man's diffidence about his own capacities is cast off; all his lack of push, due to uncertainty of his powers, is replaced by a singleness of purpose, from which springs strenuousness and real powers of initiative.

When a man is a very young man he is of necessity unsure of himself. He cannot have true confidence because he does not know what his capacities are. They are, of course, far greater than he ever dreams. But he has got to find that out. Mountains make a good testing ground—a better ground than war, which is a perversion. It is of untold benefit to him, and to us all, to be brought face to face with realities in their harshest aspect. The occasional experience of it has an educative power from which we can learn much at merciful speed—learn in a few minutes what would otherwise take years. These sharp experiences can always be turned to our good, although rarely reckoned as blessings.

In August 1949 Fred Baker and I went to the Montenvers above Chamonix, and at 4 a.m. on our first morning set out to climb the Grands Charmoz. At 6 a.m. we were moving up the Nantillons Glacier, just where the ice steepens under the Rognon. We stopped to put on crampons. Suddenly we heard a roar and looked up to see an ice-cliff collapse at the left side of the glacier and spill towards the centre. There was no time to run —apparently no way of escape—and I had just said 'By God, we 've had it!'—when the first ice-block went whizzing past. At the same instant I saw a long crevasse ten feet above me. I leapt into its near end, which was only eight feet deep—in marked contrast to the far end. No sooner was I under the protection of the upper lip than the main weight of the avalanche went thundering over the top. I presumed Baker to be lost. When all was still I looked out to try to see where his body was, but could see not a sign. Then to my right-hand side a quiet voice said: 'It 's all right!' And there was Baker, crouching in a mere depression, an incipient crevasse with a vertical upper wall of only three feet. The avalanche had gone shooting over his head as it had shot over mine. His was the more remarkable escape.

We continued our climb, and had an excellent day on the Grands Charmoz. But for a long time after that, if any bearer of ill-tidings had come to me reporting the total loss of everything I possessed in this world I should not have thought the news too serious. I had health and life and the ability to support myself by work. I should not, like the bankrupted financiers of Wall Street or the City, have cast myself from the top window of a skyscraper or more modestly blown out my brains. Life was seen very much in its proper perspective.

In the ordinary course of climbing similar lessons are learned, less spectacularly and more enjoyably. When a rock-climber is nearing the middle of Rosa Pinnacle on a warm day of summer, employing much skill and energy to lift himself up those next twelve inches of granite, all the other worries of life vanish, and although they most certainly do return afterwards, they return permanently shrunken: no longer do they augur the end of the world. Minor disasters are seen to be minor. In other words, the man has grown a little in stature.

Life on earth gives to a man the chance for a full development of his powers and potentialities. Their need of fulfilment arouses the spirit of exploratory adventure in all planes of his life, according to the degree of his soul's unfolding. The mountaineer, as such, is distinguished from other men only in finding some of the help that *he* needs more readily among mountains. The expression of his need is his love of them; their offering is beauty and adventure, which he accepts. The adventurous spirit is in every man. Deny him outlet for it—and there is hell to pay. Repression is evil. By that let us not mean that any lust at all should get expression; rather that all of a man's energies get a sanely directed outlet, on the human plane, not the animal.

In 1946 I assisted Kenneth Dunn in taking some youthful Glasgow gangsters on to the Glencoe and Arrochar hills. They came from the district between Anderston and the Gorbals, where street gangs abound, and were selected as giving at least some promise of an interest in climbing. We found them likeable men, aged sixteen to eighteen, with a keen sense of humour and no especial love of the gangs, of which they were members, they said, for the sake of their own protection. The larger gangs, like the San Toy with a hundred or two members and a motor-car, had armouries. A member with a feud on his hands could draw from the armoury his necessary weapon, called 'The Message,' which might be a revolver and a round or two of ammunition, a razor, or else some blunt and heavy instrument, or a motor-bicycle chain. He would wrap the chain in adhesive tape if his modest ambition was to stun the victim, but would use it bare if he desired to rip off the flesh as well.

One of our youths had a recent razor-slash on his shoulder, received on no greater provocation than his walking through a public thoroughfare, the territory of a rival gang. But a more common cause of feud, he told us, arose at a dance-hall in the Gallowgate. Men and women pay their own way in. A man may then select a partner and be getting on well with her, when someone taps him on the shoulder and says: 'Hey! Leave off. This is my moll.' If he turns a deaf ear he is waylaid in the gents' lavatory, knocked down and kicked in the face and stomach, and perhaps gets a parting razor-slash on his way home.

Well, these men had been denied an outlet for their adventurous energies. And there was hell to pay. Those whom I met I liked. Of the six whom we introduced to mountains I should guess that two would continue of their own accord—given the means and the opportunity.

The provision of a field of action is thus essential, and the beneficial use that can be made of mountains is demonstrated by one of my friends. His father died, leaving him at the age of sixteen to support his mother and sisters in London. He achieved this duty by hard work and, being untrained for any profession, by taking what he felt to be menial jobs. In the course of a year or two these gave him a sense of social inferiority and frustration, which continued after he came to Scotland. There he found mountains. *They* gave him the common rewards —beauty of scene, joy of the craft, sport and its comradeship, the health of free action through all weathers—and in addition the opportunity of working off his sense of inferiority. He took this latter opportunity in his rock-climbing, which he prosecuted with an unexampled rashness and vigour. His reputation for audacity became legendary. For example, when he went to the Right-angled Gully of the Cobbler in winter and found the wall at the direct exit too icy, it was said that he drove the pick of his axe into the frozen turf on top and climbed up the shaft. I have no idea whether that particular tale was true, but it was typical. Upon accomplishing difficult feats he would feel that after all he was not inferior to other men of his age; that indeed he was the equal of any of them. The upshot was that in a few years his sense of inferiority had been killed stone dead. My friend went on to complete his triumph by becoming one of the soundest and most skilled mountaineers in Scotland without going to the other extreme of feeling superiority on that account. To any man who is able to use mountains thus we wish good fortune. They restore him to more perfect health. And to all young men abounding in high spirits and somewhat over-bold we should not only be tolerant but give the occasional word of praise they need and deserve. The fool who sneers is in need of some dire misfortune for the cure of his soul.

Although the phrase 'working off inferiorities' has become a common idiom, containing as it does a grain of truth, none the less it is still far too shallow an interpretation. When we are dealing with man in relation to his kind any talk of his inferiority is a negative, wholly inadequate way of stating the positive truth: which is, that a man's goal in life is his self-fulfilment. To that end he acts both on mountains and off them. It is not *primarily* by belief in a creed that he is moved to act. He is in reality acting all the time. He never stops acting from birth to death. He is unable not to act. He acts daily, yearly, and all his life long in search of his self's *best* interest. His one source of all trouble is ignorance—ignorance of what his best interest is and what his 'self' is. He has to learn by experience—his own and not someone else's. At one stage he may feel well satisfied with wealth, or with a blind drunk at hogmanay, with the dictatorship of all the Russians or the first ascent of a rock climb in Glencoe, with scholarship or gipsydom. But when these in the end are found not to give lasting satisfactions, on he must go, until at the last the archetypal man is realized. To that end all men move—move now, always have moved, and always will: while they have life they will seek that which they lack, on mountains or elsewhere. In that process mountains do play a part because on them men do grow and unfold.

It is encouraging to reflect that we do that best of all when we climb mountains just to enjoy them.

But we must not be so innocent as to think that the effects of mountaineering are necessarily good. Mountaineering is like every other human activity without exception, from prayer to party politics, in this respect: that the quality of its effects upon us is determined by our purpose. We have power to choose. And the effects will shortly be very evident to our fellows and our purpose revealed. During the year that I write I have seen mountaineering used to display bounce, boast, brag, lying, vanity and deceit, and a greed for severe climbs to give a boost to a man's reputation. I have seen it bring on an unholy pomposity and the contempt for men who are beyond some predetermined pale. In all the history of mountaineering perhaps the ugliest phase was its use by the Nazis and Fascists during the late nineteen-thirties as an instrument of nationalist propaganda, breeding ill will among Alpinists on a scale not hitherto attempted. In mountaineering we have a choice. Is our best interest to be served by a self-regard or by a selfless love of the hills and men? Some men choose one and some the other. The two results of such opposite decisions were demonstrated before me in one day in July 1947, in the Dauphiné Alps.

The scene was set as follows. John Barford and Michael Ward had been climbing with me on the north-west side of the Ailefroide. We decided after a few days that next morning we should change our centre and cross the northward-running ridge from west to east by the Col de la Coste Rouge, descending thence to the Glacier Noir. We arrived at the col at 9 a.m. Our descent on the far side went by a couloir of four hundred feet, normally easy and free from stonefall. To-day soft snow lay on ice, and there was a bergschrund below, so we roped up. We were half-way down the couloir when half a dozen stones fell from the wall of the Ailefroide. They came straight at us. We were all struck and fell together. I did not lose consciousness, and felt myself stopped by a wrench on the shoulders, the lower three-quarters of my body swinging in space. I realized then that my shoulders and heavy Bergan rucksack had jammed in the mouth of the bergschrund, but I was blinded by concussion and by blood running into my eyes so that I could do nothing at first. After several minutes' labour I dragged myself out. Barford and Ward were still in the bergschrund and still roped to me. I climbed back in and found Barford on a ledge. He was dead. Ten feet below, Ward was jammed by his shoulders and rucksack at a narrowing of the walls just as I had been. A deep chasm opened below him. His head was badly gashed, but he had regained consciousness and was beginning to struggle. Standing on the ledge I used all the strength I had to pull on the rope, and after long and desperate efforts he managed to clutch his way up. That is where the story begins.

Like myself, Ward had a fractured skull; in addition, the top of his ear was half off and his memory had gone. He did not know my name, or Barford's, or what mountain he was on, or where he was going. As quickly as I told him he repeated the questions. However, after he had taken stock of me he agreed to go with me downhill. With an unreasoning obstinacy I decided to carry my heavy rucksack, but Ward wisely left his behind. We slowly descended on to the upper glacier basin where the heat was intense. The Glacier Noir now stretched below us seven kilometres to the Ailefroide valley. We halted and looked at it somewhat hopelessly. Just then I saw a Frenchman on the far side of the glacier making for the Col de la Temple. I sounded an S O S on my whistle and he came over to us.

He was a man of forty. Judging by his equipment, confident bearing, and good training, I have no doubt that he was a competent mountaineer. I told him what had happened—that Barford was dead in the bergschrund, and that Ward and I were doubtful of having enough strength to get down the glacier to the valley. Would he go with us, to make sure we arrived there? He surveyed us carefully. We must have made an ugly and bloody sight. He reflected. Then he explained that he had been making for the Col de la Temple in order to descend to La Bérarde, where he had an engagement. If he were to go down the Glacier Noir with us that would take him in the opposite direction. Therefore, with our permission, he would continue on his own way. Meantime was there anything he could do for us? A mouthful of wine perhaps? He was most courteous. He could not possibly have cared less.

I would not argue. I felt too sick with disappointment in him. Ward and I continued alone down the glacier. There were numerous crevasses to be crossed, all narrow, of the kind one may readily jump. These delayed us greatly. We would hover on the brink, trying to summon up enough energy to *make* those easy jumps. In a short while I began to feel dreadfully hampered by the weight of my rucksack, and no doubt I looked troubled. Ward, following behind, offered to carry it for me.

A trivial service? But consider the position. Ward had fractured his skull, lost much blood, did not know who I was, and had been unable to lift his own rucksack off the ground. But he was now proposing to help me with mine. Selflessness is often thought of by the more grossly ignorant as a negative virtue; it is in fact so positively inspiring that on this occasion it relieved Ward of the need to call common-sense to his rescue and refuse at the last to implement an offer divinely mad, because it gave me all the energy I required to shoulder my own burden. A curious situation then arose: in consequence of his injuries Ward was in some small measure dependent on myself for getting him down the glacier, but the energy by which I was enabled to do so was derived from him.

In seven hours we reached the valley. As soon as we saw other humans our sustaining vitality vanished, leaving us in a state of collapse. We were removed by ambulance. All the French people we met thereafter treated us with unfailing kindness, and a month or two later we were none the worse.

When we reflect upon the actions of these two men, the Frenchman and Ward, compare the choice before each and contrast the differing results, we are brought to a conclusion of importance: that when we go among mountains, although they will always produce effects on our personalities, yet whether they are good effects or bad is determined entirely by ourselves. It is our own attitude of mind that determines effects. Always the choice is ours. Like the jungle, mountains are neutral.

It would seem to be an office of mountains to present to us the two extreme aspects of reality: the tough, harsh aspect entailing battle with the elements and the ideal aspect manifesting beauty. There are those amongst us who would have us turn away from the one, or turn from the other, but any man who would have his mountains whole—and his own life whole—should turn from neither (undue risk of accident excepted); but to the contrary receive all that he may of both. From the schooling and discipline of the first we may learn much, and from its recreation renew our health. But what of the second aspect?

Beauty gets a very different reception from different men. Its manifestation through the mountain scene may be refused acceptance in one century and not another according as prejudice veils men's eyes or detachment clears them. A particular acceptance or rejection of that kind is in the long run of no great consequence; for beauty is manifest in the whole natural creation, and men will find it where they feel disposed to look. At the present more men than ever before are disposed to accept it from mountains. But how different is the degree in which they do so! I remember that when one of our young gangsters reached the top of the Cobbler on a fine day he did not proceed to enjoy the view, the like of which he had never set eyes on before. Squatting on the cairn he buried himself in a Sunday paper, the sports column of which wholly absorbed him until the time came to go down.

Assuming, however, that we have recognized beauty, then as with the other aspect of mountains it is for ourselves to choose what effect it has upon us. It is the good habit of men to draw occasional refreshment of their spirits from beauty, and a temporary pleasure; their bad habit to dismiss thought of it thereafter as being of no further use. On the other hand, there may be a sound core to the instinct that holds as ineffective and of little true value to man the perception of a beauty in art or nature that does not bring in its train right action. Ideals that are not practical are profitless. But—every true ideal may be *given* practical application in our active living. In brief, our response to beauty is inadequate if we passively receive and there stop short. Something more than that is expected of us. We can receive true values only if we are willing to give, to the raising up of our consciousness and way of life, that strenuousness (and also toughness) which on the physical plane men devote so willingly to mountaineering. The effect of beauty upon us may then be no less powerful than that of battle and no less profound.

Let us see how this may be so.

If we make a survey of mountaineering literature we can hardly fail to observe the frequency with which writers express perceptions of a beauty that baffles their powers of description. 'Beauty unutterable,' 'Beyond comprehension,' are favoured terms of reference. These perceptions are sometimes accompanied by a certainty of the universal unity or by the premonition of an ultimate reality, the spiritual ground of things seen. Even a hard-headed nineteenth-century scientist, Professor John Tyndall, an agnostic of the Victorian school, and therefore usually sure of himself, writes of the view from the Weisshorn: 'I opened my notebook to make a few observations but soon relinquished the attempt. There was something incongruous, if not profane, in allowing the scientific faculty to interfere where silent worship was the reasonable service.'

He writes here of that same beauty that we take so very much for granted while we climb through good, photographic scenery; not of something different, nor of greater power. The eye of his soul has been more clear, that is all. Every sensitive and intelligent man has similar experiences during his life, maybe at long intervals; but most assuredly, if he is an active mountaineer, his opportunities are many. For mountains throw into high relief a beauty that fairly takes the eye by storm. But the bodily eye is not the mind, and the mind not always receptive. Opportunities are more often lost than seized.

May it not be possible by some practical method to help one's mind to grow in awareness of beauty, to develop that faculty of perception, which lack of exercise frustrates and stunts? In truth, growth may be given to the spiritual consciousness as simply as growth and health are given to the body—by awakening it from slumber, by providing nourishment, and then by giving hard exercise. Effort must be expended, sacrifice must be faced; without *these* only imaginary mountains are climbed.

The awakening is a free decision to use the spiritual faculty and to seek a target. Its awakening is widest and consciousness most keenly alert when it is briefed for the highest of peaks—to bring union with ultimate reality. A lower goal will induce a correspondingly lower efficiency. The nourishment provided is that of feeling. It is a matter of experience that all feelings of disparagement, underestimation, contempt and carping criticism, anger and lust, are poisons that starve, stunt, and wither the spiritual faculty; and that feelings of compassion, reverence, and devotion are foods that nourish it and bestow energy. The exercise to be given makes use at first both of material forms and simple discursive thought or reflection. It is necessary to be very practical in arranging for this exercise. Time must be allotted and the habit made regular. Five minutes daily is not too little nor an hour too much.

Our search for beauty being conscious, our best policy is to begin with simple things, infinite in number and commonly disregarded: the touch of wind on the cheek, rocks, the smell of pines and bog-myrtle, morning dew and the song of water, snow-ridges in sun, tall trees and corries. Let us see their beauty and remember, and then take a wider sweep to embrace the greater things: a sea-loch winding among hills, cloudscape and sky, a mountain entire in its shape and setting of moorland, cloud, and atmosphere. Seeking always the underlying beauty, and proceeding from lesser forms to greater, we end with the form that displays to us greatest beauty, and dwell upon that: we allow it to evoke in our hearts devotion and reverence.

Encourage these feelings of love for the ideas of beauty. Let them grow and fill and reverberate through the consciousness. For within the soul they nourish a power that gradually opens the spiritual eye. Then truly our minds are in a state of growth, for where perception penetrates and love aspires, understanding follows, and reason may assume its role of guide.

The full action of meditation is usually made difficult or impossible on mountains by wind and weather, time and company. But our observations can be made for later and more effective use in privacy. We should then recall the forms of beauty, visualizing each until our love for its beauty is aroused, and end with the greatest beauty known to us—it may be a sunrising or sunsetting, or a night sky or mountain, the beauty for which no words can be found. Encourage unreservedly the awe and wonder to which this last gives rise. These feelings of the heart give nourishment and life to the will and mind, which all acting in unison raise consciousness to a new state of awareness.

At the beginning of such an expansion of soul a man's powers of perceiving beauty are doubled, and one danger of the ascent may become noticeable. He may fall into the habit of stopping at the pleasure received and exhausting it, continuing the work primarily for the pleasure rather than for love of the beauty. As soon as that element of self-seeking is introduced growth will automatically cease, and the immature spiritual faculty dwindle. With most surprising promptitude the mind reverts to its old lop-sided state. In this work there is no static position: one goes on or one drops back. We need, above all, to persist.

Our remedy is not to deny the enjoyment, but likewise not to stop there. We must persist in working inwardly towards the widening of consciousness, reflecting upon beauty and the inherent principles of truth and good, its universal presence and inward significance for the individual self and mankind, and the ways and means by which we may realize its living presence within us, so that we, in turn, may manifest them in serving our fellow men. We must be very practical, and not allow either reason or the heart wholly to dominate us. When our work has continued a while, we become aware that infinitely various as the forms of beauty are, it is changeless and eternal. This beauty is increasingly known by the mind; for the more the will turns the mind as a mirror to the sun of beauty the more clear and revealing does its light become. We are fired by desire to be made one with beauty, in knowledge and love. By a natural law the mind grows like that which it loves, and knowledge grows as love grows.

The way in which beauty, the infinite One, reveals in the symbols of nature the infinite diversity of its life, allows us to glimpse the universe as the outer expression of an inner and spiritual unity: the one as the many and the all as one. Analogies invariably break down when pushed too far; remembering this, let us take one from music, where a single idea of beauty in the mind of a composer creates a complex symphony. That creative beauty orders the ideas and emotions that must be expressed, the balance and structure of each requiring a movement with themes and melodies, which in turn determine the phrases, the harmonies of which order the relation of the notes, each note determining the number of air vibrations required to produce its sound. We have finally a complex of air vibrations arrayed through time and moving in space. They impinge on our eardrums, combine to give sounds in sequence, and lead us back step by step through phrases, melodies, themes, and emotions to the full symphony and its root idea of beauty, which we at last know in its true ground beyond time and space. The creation of the world, and our upward ascent in meditation from the many to the One, would appear to follow a course singularly like that of our analogy. Our own part is to cast out every inner distraction and impurity so that our minds may be clear, unfretted —and receptive.

This casting out of distractions is a process of purification—a tough and exacting trial of our earnestness besides which the trials of mountaineering sometimes seem like play for children. It is again a most practical matter and not one to be by-passed, for only through it may the mind have hope of illumination and the soul of union. Beauty has been found at first in natural forms as an impersonal reality, but now it is found within ourselves and men and all creatures as the Being, Life, and Intelligence through which and in which we have our own being, the Light that lighteth all and our true End.

To that End men move, move now and always, for the most part blindly, not recognizing at first their true self and best interest, yet, while they have life, seeking what they lack, their power of choice free. . . . It is most fortunate for man that beauty, unlike mountains, is not neutral.

INDEX